Multi-level Finance and the Euro Crisis

STUDIES IN FISCAL FEDERALISM AND STATE–LOCAL FINANCE

Series Editor: Wallace E. Oates, *Professor of Economics, University of Maryland, College Park and University Fellow, Resources for the Future, USA*

This important series is designed to make a significant contribution to the development of the principles and practices of state–local finance. It includes both theoretical and empirical work. International in scope, it addresses issues of current and future concern in both East and West and in developed and developing countries.

The main purpose of the series is to create a forum for the publication of high quality work and to show how economic analysis can make a contribution to understanding the role of local finance in fiscal federalism in the twenty-first century.

Titles in the series include:

The Political Economy of Financing Scottish Government
Considering a New Constitutional Settlement for Scotland
C. Paul Hallwood and Ronald MacDonald

Does Decentralization Enhance Service Delivery and Poverty Reduction?
Edited by Ehtisham Ahmad and Giorgio Brosio

State and Local Fiscal Policy
Thinking Outside the Box?
Edited by Sally Wallace

The Political Economy of Inter-Regional Fiscal Flows
Measurement, Determinants and Effects on Country Stability
Edited by Núria Bosch, Marta Espasa and Albert Solé-Ollé

Decentralization in Developing Countries
Global Perspectives on the Obstacles to Fiscal Devolution
Edited by Jorge Martinez-Vazquez and François Vaillancourt

The Challenge of Local Government Sizes
Theoretical Perspectives, International Experience and Policy Reform
Edited by Santiago Lago-Peñas and Jorge Martinez-Vazquez

State and Local Financial Instruments
Policy Changes and Management
Craig L. Johnson, Martin J. Luby and Tima T. Moldogaziev

Taxation and Development: The Weakest Link?
Essays in Honor of Roy Bahl
Edited by Richard M. Bird and Jorge Martinez-Vazquez

Multi-level Finance and the Euro Crisis
Causes and Effects
Edited by Ehtisham Ahmad, Massimo Bordignon and Giorgio Brosio

Multi-level Finance and the Euro Crisis

Causes and Effects

Edited by

Ehtisham Ahmad

Center for Development Research, University of Bonn, Germany and Asia Research Centre, London School of Economics, UK

Massimo Bordignon

Department of Economics and Finance, Catholic University of the Sacred Heart, Milan, Italy

Giorgio Brosio

Department of Economics and Statistics, University of Turin, Italy

STUDIES IN FISCAL FEDERALISM AND STATE–LOCAL FINANCE

Cheltenham, UK • Northampton, MA, USA

© Ehtisham Ahmad, Massimo Bordignon and Giorgio Brosio 2016

All rights reserved. No part of this publication may be reproduced, stored in a retrieval system or transmitted in any form or by any means, electronic, mechanical or photocopying, recording, or otherwise without the prior permission of the publisher.

Published by
Edward Elgar Publishing Limited
The Lypiatts
15 Lansdown Road
Cheltenham
Glos GL50 2JA
UK

Edward Elgar Publishing, Inc.
William Pratt House
9 Dewey Court
Northampton
Massachusetts 01060
USA

A catalogue record for this book
is available from the British Library

Library of Congress Control Number: 2015950502

This book is available electronically in the Elgaronline
Economics subject collection
DOI 10.4337/9781784715113

ISBN 978 1 78471 510 6 (cased)
ISBN 978 1 78471 511 3 (eBook)

Typeset by Servis Filmsetting Ltd, Stockport, Cheshire

Printed and bound in Great Britain by
TJ International Ltd, Padstow, Cornwall

Contents

List of contributors	vii
Introduction: how multi-level finance has contributed to the crisis and is affected by it *Ehtisham Ahmad, Massimo Bordignon and Giorgio Brosio*	1

PART I MANAGING SUB-NATIONAL LIABILITIES IN EUROPE

1	Promoting stabilizing and sustainable sub-national fiscal policies in the Euro area *Teresa Ter-Minassian*	21
2	Political economy of information generation and financial management for sub-national governments: some lessons from international experience *Ehtisham Ahmad*	49
3	History of the constitutional debt limits in Germany and the new 'debt brake': experiences and critique *Georg Milbradt*	66

PART II INCIPIENT PROBLEMS IN THE BIGGEST COUNTRIES IN EUROPE

4	Multi-level finance and the Euro crisis: the German experience *Paul Bernd Spahn*	83
5	French sub-national public finances: on the difficulty of being a decentralized unitary state *Pierre Garello*	103

PART III THE TROUBLED COUNTRIES OF SOUTHERN EUROPE

6 Economics and politics of local Greek government 133
   Georgios Chortareas and Vassileios E. Logothetis

7 Portugal's multi-level finance adjustments within the sovereign debt and Euro crises 148
   Mário Fortuna

8 Multi-level finance and governance in Spain: the impact of the Euro crisis 175
   Santiago Lago-Peñas and Albert Solé-Ollé

9 Economic crisis and fiscal federalism in Italy 212
   Maria Flavia Ambrosanio, Paolo Balduzzi and Massimo Bordignon

PART IV CITIES, THE OLYMPICS AND GROWTH

10 A tale of two cities: the Olympics in Barcelona and Turin 249
    Giorgio Brosio, Stefano Piperno and Javier Suarez Pandiello

PART V ACCESSION STATES

11 The impact of the global crisis on Macedonian local governments 277
    Marjan Nikolov

PART VI SOME GENERAL LESSONS

12 Clientelistic politics and multi-level finance: some implications for regional inequality and growth 299
    Alex Mourmouras and Peter Rangazas

13 Incentives facing local governments in the absence of credible enforcement 326
    Leo Fulvio Minervini and Annalisa Vinella

Index 359

Contributors

Ehtisham Ahmad, London School of Economics, UK and University of Bonn, Germany, and former Senior Advisor, International Monetary Fund, Washington, DC, USA

Maria Flavia Ambrosanio, Professor, Catholic University of the Sacred Heart, Milan, Italy

Paolo Balduzzi, Assistant Professor, Catholic University of the Sacred Heart, Milan, Italy

Massimo Bordignon, Professor, Catholic University of the Sacred Heart, Milan and President of the Italian Public Finance Society, Italy

Giorgio Brosio, Emeritus Professor, University of Turin and former President of the Italian Public Finance Society, Italy

Georgios Chortareas, Professor, University of Athens and Kings College London, UK

Mário Fortuna, Professor, University of the Azores, Portugal

Pierre Garello, Professor, University of Aix–Marseille, France

Santiago Lago-Peñas, Professor, University of Vigo, Spain

Vassileios E. Logothetis, Professor, University of Athens, Greece

Georg Milbradt, President, Forum of Federations, Vice Chair of the German Fiscal Council and Professor, University of Dresden, and former Prime Minister of the State of Saxony, Germany

Leo Fulvio Minervini, University of Macerata, Italy

Alex Mourmouras, Division Chief, International Monetary Fund, Washington, DC, USA

Marjan Nikolov, Director, Center for Economic Analyses, Skopje, Macedonia

Javier Suarez Pandiello, University of Oviedo, Spain

Stefano Piperno, former Deputy Director, IRES, Turin, Italy

Peter Rangazas, Professor, Indiana University–Purdue University Indianapolis, Indiana, USA

Albert Solé-Ollé, Professor, University of Barcelona, Spain

Paul Bernd Spahn, Emeritus Professor, University of Frankfurt and former President, House of Finance, University of Frankfurt, Germany

Teresa Ter-Minassian, former Director, Fiscal Affairs Department, Washington, DC, USA

Annalisa Vinella, University of Bari, Italy

Introduction: how multi-level finance has contributed to the crisis and is affected by it

Ehtisham Ahmad, Massimo Bordignon and Giorgio Brosio

1. EUROPE AND THE CRISIS

The financial crisis that swept the world economy in 2008 has produced some paradoxical results that would have been impossible to predict, and indeed were not predicted, at the time. The European Union compact was based on principles of economic and political integration. However, sustainability entailed adherence to fiscal rules at national and sub-national levels together with the assumption that national governments would have the incentive and ability to implement them. It also assumed that sub-national entities would have an incentive to comply with the broad directions of the European compact, and how they managed their affairs was largely their business. The financial crisis exposed several limitations inherent in those assumptions, particularly the futility of fiscal rules in the face of poor information flows on liabilities at the sub-national level as well as state-owned enterprises. These have permitted the effective buildup of risks to the overall macroeconomic framework that in many cases had become unsustainable.

The 2008 crisis originated in the US as a result – with the benefit of hindsight – of overly generous monetary policy and poor regulation of the financial markets and of the banking sector. Many scholars at the time thought that the crisis meant the end of the market-style, financially ruled, deregulated Anglo-Saxon capitalism. Indeed, at the outset of the crisis, most continental European leaders dismissed it as essentially a problem for the US, and presented it as a clear proof of the superiority of the more socially oriented European market system. Yet, almost a decade later, it appears clear that the adjustment in Europe is far from complete, and there is increasing resistance to the cuts in employment, public services and living standards that the adjustment may require. The needed adjustments threaten the European compact. However, the US appears to have weathered the crisis and has seen a resumption of growth and employment generation.

Interestingly, the European country that performed best after the crisis was the UK, which had opted out of several EU regulations. Although the UK had not joined the common currency, it maintained its position as one of the largest financial markets in the world. There are also clear winners and losers within the Euro area. Germany and, to a lesser extent, some of the smaller Northern European countries quickly recovered from the crisis and resumed a growth path, albeit historically quite limited. In the periphery, the recovery in the Southern European countries has been much slower.

At the time of writing, real GDP in Italy is still 10 percentage points lower than in 2007 and 25 percentage points lower in Greece. Other countries, such as France or Belgium, have stagnated, with output levels that have only now reached the 2007 levels. Green shoots are appearing in Portugal and Spain, but with accentuated separatist tendencies in the latter. But more generally, all of the Euro area seems to be caught in a vicious circle of deflation, sluggish demand, low investment, high unemployment, and increasing social conflict and centrifugal tendencies. Indeed, the needed adjustments, including at sub-national level, concerning basic public services and employment, have added to the stresses on the Euro compact.

The crisis presented a picture that is a far cry from the promises of harmony and prosperity that were at the basis of the European Union and even more of the Euro area. This dismal situation is reflected in an amazing loss of consensus for the European project and the European institutions. The European Parliament increasingly includes parties that are explicitly anti-Euro and anti-EU; the UK is facing a referendum about continued membership amid a backlash against European migrants; and, at the time of writing, while the threat of a 'Grexit' has receded, the country's position remains precarious.

2. INTERGOVERNMENTAL FISCAL RELATIONSHIPS IN EUROPE AND THE CRISIS

The weakness of institutional arrangements in Europe is often ascribed to the limited effective political sovereignty – i.e., the absence of a federal or con-federal structure of government (Eichengreen 2015). Despite Eurostat standards, the effective generation and coordination of information flows was largely left to governments at different levels. It had been assumed that coordination would result from broad Maastricht rules regarding levels of debt, and that deficit constraints would suffice to ensure the necessary macroeconomic coordination needed to underpin a common currency area. The importance of uniform standards of information on public finances across and within countries was not fully appreciated. The pervasive lack of standardized information flows across and within countries, especially at different levels of government, enhances both the incentives and ability to engage in game-play. Consequently, a degree of game-play resulted, with varying concealment of liabilities in and across the Eurozone, and open disregard of the rules including by the strongest members – Germany and France.

The game-play has both exacerbated the underlying fissures that led to the crisis, and the effect of adjustments to the crisis. The open disregard by Germany and France of the need to respect the Maastricht Treaty rules on public deficit in 2004 led to a decision by the Council to revise the Stability and Growth Pact to avoid imposing sanctions on the two most influential countries in the EU. This represented a turning point in economic relationships inside the Euro area. It signaled to markets the lack of credibility of the European fiscal rules. It also signaled to other countries that it was fine to evade the fiscal rules and to accumulate fiscal and external imbalances. These proved to be disastrous as the contagion from the crisis spread from the US to the Eurozone.

The problems in Germany in 2004 reflect the financial and political relationships and imbalances between the Bund and the Länder that lay in the post-World War II Constitution of West Germany. These were exacerbated by the absorption of the Eastern Länder following the collapse of the Berlin Wall. The imbalances in intergovernmental fiscal relations were clearly recognized, and there were attempts to address all the aspects sequentially during the period of the coalition governments, 2005–09 (Föderalismus I and II). The Commissions largely failed to reach agreement on any of the substantive (16 issues) under discussion, but adopted the Swiss 'debt brake rule' (see below) to come into operation in 2020. As argued by Milbradt (Chapter 3 in this volume) and Spahn (Chapter 4 in this volume), the underlying characteristics in Switzerland were quite different to those obtaining in Germany. The adoption of the debt brake rule, as part of a Constitutional Reform to take effect in 2020, amounted to one of several measures that 'kicked the can down the road'. As pointed out by both Milbradt and Spahn, the consequences of the debt brake rule without reforms to intergovernmental structures are likely to be dire. Yet, the same rule has become the basis for revisions to the Fiscal Compact across the Eurozone and none of the underlying fissures has been addressed. In particular, the incentives for 'game-play' remain, especially without a standard recognition of liabilities, e.g., with respect to public–private partnerships (PPPs), or adoption of a common reporting standard that also governs the coverage of the budget.

Another example of 'game-play' lies in the accumulation of bubbles in the real estate market crisis in Spain. Again this reflects the specific political and fiscal relationships between Madrid and the regional governments, particularly the powerful Autonomous Communities (see Lago-Peñas and Solé-Ollé, Chapter 8 in this volume). And even the fiscal problems of the weakest economy, Greece, would be hard to understand without considering the lack of financial control that the Greek central government historically had over its municipalities (see Chortoreas and Logothetis, Chapter 6 in this volume). While the Troika has focused on rationalizing the number of municipalities and their functions, a 'safety valve' has emerged in the privatization of local functions with the establishment of enterprises that provide local services, largely financed by the center, and that help evade strictures on local employment and budgets. The political costs of the reform agenda, and the consequent attempts by the Greek government to contain them, were not well understood by the Troika and the problems remained, leading to a backlash by voters.

The European experience represents a good opportunity for the analysis of the impact of a macroeconomic crisis on intergovernmental relationships. A deep and prolonged recession is bound to induce severe strains on the internal organization and operation of governments. It is interesting to analyze how the different intergovernmental systems in individual countries, involving own-source revenues, responsibilities and information flows, affected incentives for different levels of government. We also examine how financing, transfers, fiscal rules and political relationships managed to cope with the crisis and how they were reformed as a consequence. This volume attempts to disentangle these strands in the individual countries and their consequences for the Euro compact.

3. MANAGING SUB-NATIONAL LIABILITIES IN EUROPE

3.1 One or More Crises?

Teresa Ter-Minassian sets the stage for the volume in Chapter 1, providing trends on the fiscal stance of national and sub-national levels of government in the Euro area since the inception of the crisis in 2008. She shows that fiscal policy in Europe went through two separate and different stages. In the first period, all countries attempted to run an anti-cyclical fiscal policy to support aggregate demand. This varied across countries, depending on their respective fiscal space available and on the extent of adjustment that had been carried out before the crisis broke. Sub-national governments were doubly affected. Most were responsible for a significant proportion of spending, including social protection measures that increased significantly as a result of the crisis. In addition, sub-national tax revenues were also adversely affected. The response was to increase central transfers to the regional and local levels. In addition, there was an easing of the regulations that forbid local governments access to the credit market or to run deficits. This, in turn, had the effect of increasing both national and sub-national debt levels. The poor information flows helped to 'kick the can down the road', and the crisis continued.

Many of the accommodative counter-cyclical measures, especially in Southern Europe, were rolled back in the second period from 2010, as debt sustainability became a concern and large capital outflows led to a crisis of market confidence. In 2010–11, the Greek crisis, and the poor management of the response by European and international authorities, introduced serious fears of a breakup of the Euro area. This forced the countries affected (including Ireland and, out of the Euro area, the UK) to implement strong and rapid macro-fiscal adjustments in order to improve market confidence. As a result, transfers were cut, taxes increased and expenditures curbed, with restrictions that were usually tighter on municipalities and regional governments than national ones. There was no time or inclination to address the deeper structural problems that largely remain. The contractionary fiscal stance, occurring simultaneously in countries with strong interdependencies among them, had a negative effect on growth and output levels. This perversely resulted in increasing debt relative to GDP in these countries. On the whole, the debt–GDP ratio in the Euro area increased by over 30 points during this period.

Ter-Minassian also provides a taxonomy of the different fiscal rules on local levels used in Europe, discusses their ability to function during the period, and illustrates the characteristics of the new European pact. The amended Fiscal Compact arose as a result of the crisis, and most European countries (all the Euro countries plus some Eastern European countries) adopted it in 2012. The new pact focuses on structural budget balances (i.e., netting the effects of the macroeconomic cycle on budgets). It also gives larger executive powers to the European commission on the monitoring of the pact and imposing sanctions. The requirements of the pact were also directly inscribed in the constitutions of the member countries, affecting sub-national entities as well. Ter-Minassian discusses the difficulty of effectively implementing the pact at sub-national levels, and raises the issue of the pro-cyclicality of fiscal rules and the difficulty of maintaining an adequate level of financing for local investments, already severely reduced during the crisis. Finally, she also raises issues of implementation, such as lack of proper accounting standards and information. This lacuna has allowed local governments in Europe to avoid national and supranational rules, moving part of their liabilities out of their budget, for instance, to 'publicly controlled' private firms.

3.2 Governance and Institutions

Chapter 2 by Ehtisham Ahmad takes up the issue of sub-national institutions and incentives. He argues that appropriate institutional measures affecting management of expenditure and tax assignments, as well as policy design, are needed to provide proper incentives to sub-national governments, e.g., by expanding own-source taxation at lower levels, and by adopting more flexible but also more effective budget management requirements. These must be accompanied by uniform budget standards, such as the IPSAS accounting rules, particularly for PPPs, and the IMF's GFSM2014 standards, to limit the problems with asymmetric information and consequent game-play between enterprises and the public sector in general and between the center and lower levels of administration. The chapter offers several examples, from both Europe and other regions, of sub-national governments reacting to controls on indebtedness by parking liabilities in activities or vehicles that are difficult to monitor. Political gaming operates even in Germany, when local governments resisted the adoption of IPSAS Standard 32 that required disclosure of the liabilities of PPPs in the balance sheets of the relevant levels of government – with appropriate provisioning. This resistance would have taken the deficit of general government further above already high levels (e.g., in 2004), and would also have limited the flexibility of local governments to carry out needed infrastructure investments. Thus, a weakening of standards by the most 'responsible country' in Europe was to have a demonstrably bad effect on the weaker countries, reducing incentives for responsible behavior. This ability to continue kicking the can down the road also limited the incentive to carry out meaningful structural reforms of intergovernmental fiscal relations, and reduced the effectiveness of those proposed or imposed, e.g., by the Troika on Greece.

3.3 Intergovernmental Structure and Fiscal Rules – What About the German/EU Debt Brake?

Georg Milbradt (Chapter 3) offers a fascinating story of the evolution of budget rules and national and sub-national debt in the German context after World War II, emphasizing the absence of effective reforms on the key structural issues. He focuses on the difficulties of controlling general government finances in a federation, where both the federal and state governments cannot be linked by a hierarchical relationship. The lack of accountability is reflected in the absence of own-source tax powers at the Länder level, lack of a tax administration at the federal level, and complicated and overlapping competencies. He describes in detail the two constitutional reforms (Föderalismus I and II) that were attempted in the 2000s by a national coalition government of the two main parties. These reforms were intended to enforce, first, a stricter separation of competencies and the reduction of co-financing between the Länder and the Bund. None of the structural measures was passed, and as a compromise, the parties agreed to introduce the Swiss model of a 'debt brake rule'[1] for both federal government and the Länder. However, without the structural reforms intended under Föderalismus I and II, the characteristics of the German and Swiss federations differ significantly, and this will lead to problems with the implementation of the 'debt brake' in the future. He focuses in particular on the lack of own-source revenues at the state level that will make it difficult for them to adjust to downturns. However, German municipalities remain de facto free from fiscal rules. There will, thus, be a tendency to push deficits down to municipalities, made easier by the lax rules on PPPs. He also questions the extension of the 'debt brake' to the other European countries (the 'Fiscal Compact'). This discussion illustrates the tendencies of politicians to make commitments that do not disturb existing allocations of resources and competences – in effect protecting existing power bases – and leave it to future governments to face the consequences. The absence of much-needed structural intergovernmental reforms remains a challenge in individual countries and for the European experiment. As a result, centrifugal forces are becoming more apparent in the EU as well as in individual countries, as the levels of popular dissatisfaction increase with the cuts imposed on pensioners and in local public services.

4. INCIPIENT PROBLEMS IN THE BIGGEST EUROPEAN COUNTRIES

It is generally believed that the Northern European countries behave in a more responsible manner than other EU members, and have thus managed to escape the worst effects of the crisis. As we see below, the intergovernmental structures are critical in explaining schisms and weaknesses, and the Northern European countries continue to face serious challenges ahead, whereas some countries in Southern Europe have taken serious measures to address imbalances and hence may have improved their long-term prospects.

4.1 Germany

Paul Bernd Spahn (Chapter 4) discusses in more detail the case of Germany during the crisis. He shows that the adjustments of the German public sector, forced by Unification, left public finances in a better condition in comparison to the overall fiscal position of the other European governments. This allowed for a quick anti-cyclical response by the federal government that supported, with increased transfers, state and municipal expenditure, in particular on social assistance. The policies implemented not only followed the usual Keynesian guidelines, but were also combined with gradual adjustments that had enhanced the competitiveness of German companies. However, these measures could not prevent a sharp increase in total debt and a fall in local investments. The intergovernmental reform agenda did not make much progress, however, and Spahn raises concerns similar to those of Milbradt regarding introduction of the constitutional 'debt brake'.

Spahn's conclusion is that Germany will be propelled toward crisis by the debt brake – or by the incomplete measures taken to avert the crisis. This strengthens the conclusions of Milbradt that the structural intergovernmental schisms need to be addressed as a matter of priority in the little time left to make adjustments.

4.2 France

Pierre Garello (Chapter 5) discusses the case of France, which, like Germany, was able to defy the European Commission (EC) in 2004 and get away with it. There is a very complex network of sub-national governments in the country (an ever-changing *millefeuille*) and recent, and often contradictory, reforms. These begin with the Constitutional reform of 2003 and the further proposed reforms, affecting the ability of this system to cope with the crisis.

The basic conclusion is that the existence of four levels of sub-national government (municipalities, associations of municipality, *départements* and regions) and the overlapping of functions and tax bases between all these governments (for instance, the residential property tax is shared by three local governments out of the four) reduces accountability and transparency. Most worryingly, in 2010 a sub-national tax (the *tax professionelle*) was eliminated and substituted by a very complex system of intergovernmental transfers. This further reduced transparency in intergovernmental fiscal flows.

The fact remains that, in spite of the multiplicity of governments and several attempts to move toward decentralization, France remains a strongly unitary country. With a combination of law, fiscal rules and administration, as explained in the chapter, the central government maintains a strict control on local public finances. This explains why French local governments fared relatively well during the crisis (for instance, local public investments did not fall as much as in the other EU countries). But the costs were borne by the central government and this led to a breach of EC limits on general government debt. In a situation of overall deteriorating general government public finances, France might eventually be sanctioned by the European Commission. It is not clear how the intergovernmental institutions will respond if that happens. As it is, unemployment pressures and rising xenophobia are contributing to a backlash against immigrants – especially of non-European descent – leading to a real prospect that the anti-EU National Front might be voted into power.

5. THE TROUBLED COUNTRIES OF SOUTHERN EUROPE

5.1 Greece

Georgios Chortareas and Vassileios E. Logothetis (Chapter 6) address the fascinating (and clearly tragic) case of Greece. The country has been characterized by weak political institutions and widespread rent-seeking and clientelistic practices that affect central and local governments alike. Management of local public finance was weak and hiring at the municipal level has often been used to buy political influence, a practice made easier by the fact that part of the labor costs at local level were, and still are, actually borne by the central government and did not appear as local spending, even though local service delivery was the object of that spending. As a consequence of the crisis and the Memorandum of Understanding (MoU) signed by the country with the European institutions in exchange for financial help, a rationalization policy for local governments was also implemented. The number of municipalities has been largely reduced, eliminating the smallest units (communes) and merging others, so that there are now only 325 local governments (reduced from more than a thousand at the beginning of the crisis). This has been accompanied by a disentangling of functions, with municipalities formally assuming more power in fields such as public health, social welfare, urban development, environmental supervision and public education. Furthermore, fiscal rules constraining debt at local levels, as well as imposing layoffs of thousands of local employees, have also been implemented.

A political game has been played with the Troika that focused on formal local budgets. Many local functions were privatized, and thereby taken off the books of local governments, but continued to be supported by central subsidies. This remained the main safety valve in the face of crumbling safety nets, cushioning the worst effects of the crisis on the living standards of the poor and vulnerable, particularly the unemployed. Consequently, opacity in intergovernmental fiscal relationships remains, and the authors are skeptical about the long-term results of the reforms, incomplete institutions and information flows.

The Syriza government faced the difficult choice of either having to impose further pain on an exhausted population that they were elected to protect, or face the economic chaos and the political risks (from the coming to power of hard-line nationalist or proto-fascist parties) of an exit from the Eurozone. The austerity choice has taken new strength after the very recent national election when the Syriza party secured a large share of the vote, but political pressures against it remain.

5.2 Portugal

Mário Fortuna (Chapter 7) discusses the case of Portugal. He provides a historical discussion of the structure of the country, made up of Continental Portugal and the two autonomous regions of Madeira and Azores since the establishment of democracy in 1974. He provides a detailed discussion of the evolution of both regional and municipal financing, including the evolution of rules for the transfer mechanism. The general picture is of one of poorly designed accounting rules; structural problems concerning the sustainability of local finance, particularly in the autonomous region of Madeira; and poorly managed equalization transfers, leading to an effective soft budget constraint at the sub-national level. When faced with stricter fiscal rules, municipalities and regions made extensive use of PPPs, hiding liabilities in publicly owned enterprises, and other off-budget practices, to circumvent the rules.

The chapter also details the changes in intergovernmental relationships induced by the crisis and by the MoU with European institutions following Portugal's access to ESM financing. This included the reform of the budget framework law, reduction in transfers and wage cuts at the local level, more encompassing budget rules to eliminate off-budget practices, and more detailed information on fiscal flows and local taxes. There is also a provision for the future reduction in the number of municipalities.

The problems in Madeira were addressed with a tight IMF-style program administered by the Central Government in Lisbon. However, proposals to introduce significant structural changes in the intergovernmental design made by the Fiscal Council were not adopted by Parliament.

Although the tighter fiscal management by the Central Government has helped to smooth over the worst effects of the crisis, the absence of meaningful structural reforms remains a cause for concern.

5.3 Spain

Santiago Lago-Peñas and Albert Solé-Ollé take up the case of Spain (Chapter 8). They argue that the current crisis in public finances has both external and domestic origins. The real estate bubble at the beginning of the 2000s was induced by the flows of international capital after the accession of Spain to the Eurozone. They also carefully analyze some of the main domestic causes, due to the design of the decentralization process in the regions and municipalities, in particular concerning tax design and equalization transfers.

With the decentralization of the 1990s, Autonomous Regions have been given significant responsibilities in the management of important social policies, such as health and education. However, they were assigned resources that were strongly pro-cyclical, and had limited tax autonomy. The exceptional buoyancy of revenues induced by the real estate boom (paradoxically, with the exception of the property tax, whose base was adjusted only partially and with lags following the appreciation in house prices) induced overspending by all levels of government. There was a strong increase in corruption cases among local and regional politicians, mostly again linked to the real estate sector (e.g., money in exchange for an increased number of building permits). Tellingly, the level of overspending appears to be higher where the quality of political accountability (as measured by reported corruption cases) is lower.

Incidentally, the crisis was not foreseen, as Spain continued to be complemented by the IMF in 2008 for meeting Maastricht limits on stock of debt and deficits. With the bursting of the real estate bubble, all levels of government experienced a severe financial crisis, with rapidly increasing deficits and debt levels. Consequently, general government debt and deficits quickly exceeded the Maastricht limits.

According to Lago-Peñas and Solé-Ollé, the central government, led by a center right party, seized this opportunity to recentralize the system, exchanging financial support to regions for severe cuts in local and regional expenditure and letting regions take the blame for the reduced level of services. However, this strategy might well not succeed, as shown by the rise of populist parties opposed to remaining in the EU (Podemos) and the resurgence of a strong secessionist movement in Catalunya (Catalonia). The results of the October 2015 elections led to the separatist parties obtaining the majority of seats in the Regional Council. This threatens the unity of the country, if not its continued membership in the Eurozone.

5.4 Italy

The case of Italy, discussed by Maria Flavia Ambrosanio, Paolo Balduzzi and Massimo Bordignon in Chapter 9, has some similarities with Spain, given the inadequate intergovernmental structure. Unlike in Spain, the dire situation of public finances did not allow the country to operate a counter-cyclical policy when the crisis first hit it in 2008. This led to massive output and employment losses, which were only partially recovered by 2010. But the Euro crisis in 2011 led to massive capital flight and raised doubts as to the sustainability of the huge national public debt. This forced the country to embark on a severe fiscal adjustment program that plunged the country into an even more serious recession.

Some signs of easing of the crisis appeared only at the beginning of 2015. Taxes were sharply increased, capital expenditures more than halved, and current expenditures frozen in nominal terms, with an impact more or less equally distributed between the center and sub-national governments. However, the latter were not just simply 'squeezed' by the central government, but were also forced to raise money, through enforced savings, to finance the general government budget.

The crisis effectively changed the de facto balance of power between levels of government leading to recentralization. It appears increasingly likely that this new equilibrium will also be consolidated de jure by a further constitutional reform, currently under review in parliament. This is expected to further reduce functions and resources of regions. Yet, not all the proposed interventions have negative implications. As a consequence of the increased financial effort imposed on local governments, the central government was forced to increase tax autonomy at the local level, improve accounting procedures, and rationalize the number of governments, with the elimination of an intermediate level of government (Provinces) and the forced aggregation of small municipalities in political 'unions' for the provision of basic services. The silver lining is that these beneficial structural reforms have finally been forced as a result of the crisis, and this may eventually lead to a return to sustainable growth in the medium-term if there is no further external turbulence.

6. CITIES, THE OLYMPICS AND GROWTH

Cities have a major impact on decentralization prospects, and the needed investments are critical in ensuring sustainable growth and revitalization of depressed regions. It is useful to juxtapose the country case studies with the effects of significant investments in cities in order to host the Olympics. The choice of Italy and Spain for the case studies also permits us to juxtapose the experience of the Olympics in Barcelona and in Turin with the overall trends in each country.

Giorgio Brosio, Stefano Piperno and Javier Suarez Pandiello (Chapter 10) look at the ways in which Barcelona and Turin managed the problems of organizing and financing the Olympics (Summer Games in the first case, and the Winter Olympics in the second). They address the long-lasting effects of the two events, both financially and economically. Interestingly, Barcelona provides support for the Peacock and Wiseman theory of a displacement effect due to an exceptional event (such as a war), with citizens that, even after the event is concluded, still accept the need to pay (partially) the higher taxes required to finance the event. However, Turin does not fit that model. The long-term economic consequences also seem to have been different.

The concentration of investment in the depressed areas of Barcelona helped to regenerate the city, and subsequently led to sustained growth. This may also explain the willingness of citizens to continue to pay higher taxes for the benefit of better public services, which in turn attracts further investments and growth. In Turin, perhaps due to the dissipated nature of the events for the Winter Games, the investments did not have the same regenerative impact, and the city was unable to regain its role as the regional hub as the main automotive and textile industries continued to decline.

7. ACCESSION STATES

Would the crisis in Europe have an impact on the accession countries? What measures should they take in relation to structural issues that are not formally part of the accession criteria but which might be to their benefit in the longer run?

Marjan Nikolov (Chapter 11) looks at the case of Macedonia, which is not yet a member of the Euro area (it is still an EU Candidate country). Interestingly, many policies affecting local governments during and after the international crisis do not look that different from the policies followed by the Eurozone countries. Thus, the higher autonomy offered to local governments in connection with property tax allowed them to better cope with the crisis, in spite of falling transfers from the center. A similar measure may help in cushioning the effects of a possible exit of a country from the Eurozone.

On the other hand, it would make for a more robust entry into the EU if the structural intergovernmental reforms in Macedonia were well established. This is not normally a formal criterion for accession, but we argue that it is quite important.

8. SOME GENERAL LESSONS

8.1 Political Economy

The political economy underpinnings of successful intergovernmental transformations are clearly important, as we see from the country case studies and the difficulties faced in countries from Germany to Greece. These are also relevant in multi-level countries around the world – including in China and Indonesia, or federations such as India, Brazil, Mexico or Nigeria.

Alex Mourmouras and Peter Rangazas (Chapter 12) analyze some of the incentive effects underlying the changes, and provide thought experiments as to the critical elements involved. These issues will come into play not just in Greece, as it struggles to stabilize within the Eurozone or out of it, but they are also relevant for Germany as it seeks to avoid the negative impact of the 'debt brake' that is likely to put the federal structure under severe stress in a relatively short period of time.

Mourmouras and Rangazas look at the interactions between central and local governments in the allocation of grants with special emphasis on the poorest regions. They use a political economy framework, in which the relations between levels of governments are framed by clientelistic politics. More specifically, politicians operating at different levels collude by exchanging transfers for electoral support. The political setting is also characterized by corruption, particularly at the local level and in the backward regions. The combination of clientelistic politics and corruption allows the authors to reach interesting results. These also reflect the experience in the EU with the allocation and the use of structural funds and other transfers. For example, while the allocation of transfers is also determined by political influence, i.e., the capacity of local politicians to provide electoral support to those operating at upper levels, the corruption at the local level undermines their capacity to produce results required by the center (or Brussels), as resources are channeled to the private benefit of local politicians. This kind of clientelistic politics also undermines the working of fiscal institutions, weakening, e.g., the budget constraint and other fiscal rules. The chapter also advances some policy suggestions, such as greater use of co-financing schemes instead of pure transfers, although these schemes disadvantage the poorest regions, whose resource constraints were the motivation for the transfers in the first place. This issue remains a promising area for further research.

8.2 Asymmetric Information and Soft Budget Constraints

Following on from the themes in the country studies concerning incentives and circumventing budget constraints, Leo Fulvio Minervini and Annalisa Vinella (Chapter 13) explore and build on some of the recent literature on the political economy of soft budget constraints. They show that in some limited cases, there is a welfare gain for the central government to guarantee critical investments, even if this results in a softening of the budget constraint at the sub-national level. However, the general prescription against generating soft budget constraints remains a good guide to policy making, as Ter-Minassian reminds us, and we see from the case studies.

Building on the general theme, Minervini and Vinella also examine issues related to asymmetric information in relation to PPPs that might lead to game-play and evading hard budget constraints. This has major consequences not just in Europe but also in other parts of the world, where there is an increasing focus on the need for sustainable investment, and PPPs are seen as an easy solution to an increasingly difficult problem. The game-play needs to be addressed in contract design and the role of incentives that are governed by full information, non-distorting transfer systems and availability of own-source revenues at the margin, without which sanctions and strictures from higher levels of government are simply not credible.

8.3 Common Themes

The experiences of the different European countries during and after the crisis have clearly differed, depending on institutional and historic heritage. Much depended on how severely the 2008 international crisis struck them, and on the fiscal space that different countries had in facing this crisis. Moreover, contrary to the international financial crisis of 2008, which was a global phenomenon affecting all EU countries simultaneously, the Euro crisis of 2011–12 severely affected some countries in the Eurozone more than others. It might actually have benefited a few, like Germany, e.g., which as a safe haven attracted much of the capital escaping from the troubled countries of the Euro area during the crisis. Yet, in spite of all these differences, we derive some common trends and themes that contributed to the crisis or were aggravated as a result of it.

First, there is a constitutional issue. The difficulties of managing sub-national finances properly have their roots firmly in ill-defined constitutional assignments of functions, resources and powers. Germany had to change its constitution twice in order to impose fiscal rules on the Länder. However, the basic schisms remain unaddressed – despite repeated attempts to reform – and the lack of a hierarchical relationship between the Bund and the Länder remains the main threat to the fulfillment of the new debt regulations, and to Germany's continued growth potential.

Similarly, Italy is attempting to revise its 2001 Constitution, which created too many overlapping competencies between the center and the regions. This, in effect, further reduced the already low level of efficiency of public administration. Similarly, the recentralization of intergovernmental relationships in Spain finds its roots in a constitution that does not sufficiently 'protect' the autonomous regions, allowing the central government to impose expenditure mandates without guaranteeing adequate levels of finance and own-sources of revenue. Re-centralization, or the introduction of more severe controls on sub-national governments, has been a common theme of all countries during the crisis, and might have long-lasting consequences in terms of stability of existing political orders. Separatist tendencies have appeared in the UK, with a narrow decision in the Scottish Referendum to remain as part of the UK. The sweeping victory of the Scottish National Party in the General Election in 2015 suggests a difficult period of adjustment in intergovernmental fiscal relations ahead in the UK. A similar situation arose in Spain, with the 2015 elections in Catalonia.

A second theme concerns the number of levels of local government as well as the number of governments at each level. Too many levels of government lead to overlapping of competencies, loss of information, and to a reduction in accountability. Having too many small and fractured local governments does not allow individual governments to reach a scale sufficient for an efficient provision of services. Not surprisingly, a common trend during the crisis has been the attempt to reduce both levels and numbers of sub-national governments. France is again trying to come to terms with its extremely complex structure of local governments, reforming and streamlining their functions and reducing their number; Italy abolished a level of government, and forced small municipalities to offer their services jointly; the number of municipalities has been dramatically reduced in Greece; and similar provisions are likely in Portugal. In many unitary states, there is an attempt to create an effective regional tier to anchor convergence of investment and growth – this is apparent in England and Portugal, but also in Latin America from Colombia to Chile.

A third element that emerges from the analysis is the importance of sub-national taxes and own-source revenues – at both regional and local levels – for a proper functioning of intergovernmental relationships. Again, it is not obvious how the German Länder will cope with the debt brake regulations and also control the fiscal behavior of their municipalities, lacking any flexibility in their resources. Insufficient access to own sources of revenues for local governments is also a problem in Spain, Portugal, France, and part of Italy. The problem is exacerbated by an inadequate design of transfers that vitiate incentives to use any tax handles, even if they were available.

A related issue concerns the proper source of taxation for effective local government. It is commonly argued in the literature that taxation of immobile property is a good local tax; because it is easy to administer, the tax base reflects the local services offered and can thus fulfill the benefit principle, and it is less subject to tax competition problems. Still, the experience of Spain shows that local governments whose revenues are strongly indexed to the values of real estate (through the stamp duty, taxes on the transaction of real assets, permits, etc.) were likely to be adversely affected once the bubble in asset prices burst. Paradoxically, the property tax behaved better, but only because the tax base was not revised fast enough to follow the appreciating values of the assets, and was less affected by the downturn. On the other hand, it was precisely because the property tax base did not reflect the increasing value of assets that cities such as Turin ended up in financial difficulties, as they were unable to fully recover the costs of investments involved.

A fourth common element is the difficulty in imposing binding fiscal rules on local governments. In virtually all countries, sub-national governments appear to be engaged in game-play, trying to escape from regulations on expenditures, hiring, or deficits. This is typically done by parking liabilities in activities or vehicles that are difficult to monitor, or by using publicly owned private enterprises to act on their behalf. Publicly owned private enterprises, PPP agreements, arrears and window-dressing, financial derivatives, etc. have been extensively used to this purpose everywhere. Not surprisingly, the central governments have tried to react by improving accounting rules and information requirements and by forcing the local governments to adopt more encompassing budget rules. This has happened in Greece, Portugal and Italy for instance, where the use of derivatives by sub-national governments has been prohibited or strongly regulated.

But the issue seems to be largely unsolved, as the rules have to be standardized across the Eurozone for yardstick competition to work effectively.

This begs the question as to whether the EC can persuade countries and local governments to adopt internationally accepted norms such as the IMF's GFSM 2014 framework or IPSAS rules on PPPs. This may be easier in federal countries than in currency unions, although it is not impossible to envisage rules such as the Sixth Directive regarding VAT across the EU.

A final issue concerns the fiscal rules themselves, and in particular the new European Fiscal Compact. These affect the general government finances of the Euro countries, and thus also need to be implemented at regional and local levels. The new rule does not forbid borrowing, but allows it only for addressing a downturn in economic activity, as shown by the structural balances of each government. But structural balances are controversial and difficult to build even at the national level, and are basically impossible to compute and enforce at sub-national levels.

The risk therefore remains that the new pact might end up by prohibiting borrowing even for useful public investment purposes. This is worrying from the perspective of the future growth of the Euro area, as public capital expenditure has already fallen dramatically everywhere in Europe during the crisis, endangering the future prosperity of the continent.

NOTE

1. This is a rule introduced in Switzerland. It aims at a structurally balanced budget in the short run by annually setting a cyclically adjusted expenditure ceiling. It also puts a brake on the accumulation of public debt via corrections of future expenditure targets for past deviations from projected fiscal balances.

PART I

Managing Sub-national Liabilities in Europe

1. Promoting stabilizing and sustainable sub-national fiscal policies in the Euro area

Teresa Ter-Minassian

1. INTRODUCTION

The Euro area (henceforth EA) has been buffeted by major shocks in the last five years or so, first the global financial crisis and subsequently its own crisis, which affected most acutely the so-called 'periphery' (Cyprus, Greece, Ireland, Italy, Portugal and Spain), but also impacted adversely, because of its economic and financial integration, the rest of the area. There are, as of mid-2014, incipient signs of recovery of confidence and demand in most of the EA, but growth in output remains subdued, and too low to make a significant dent in the area's historically high unemployment rates. The stresses associated with needed adjustments continue to have political reverberations, especially in Greece.

The public finances of the EA member countries have been sharply impacted by the two crises, through the operation of the automatic stabilizers, discretionary stimulus packages in 2008–09, and in some countries the realization of contingent liabilities, particularly from rescue operations for domestic banks. The average overall general government (GG) deficit in the EA jumped from under 1 percent of GDP in 2007 to over 6 percent of GDP in 2009–10, and remains slightly above 3 percent of GDP, despite substantial fiscal consolidation efforts in a number of the area's countries (Figure 1.1).[1] All but three of the EA countries still recorded structural fiscal deficits in 2013. The average gross public debt rose by nearly 30 percentage points of GDP between 2007 and 2013, to over 95 percent of GDP (Figure 1.2).

Against this background, it is clear that significant further fiscal adjustment efforts are going to be needed by most EA countries in the years ahead, although views can legitimately differ on the appropriate pace of such adjustment.[2] Given the substantial, and in some countries still growing, role of the sub-national (state/regional and local) governments

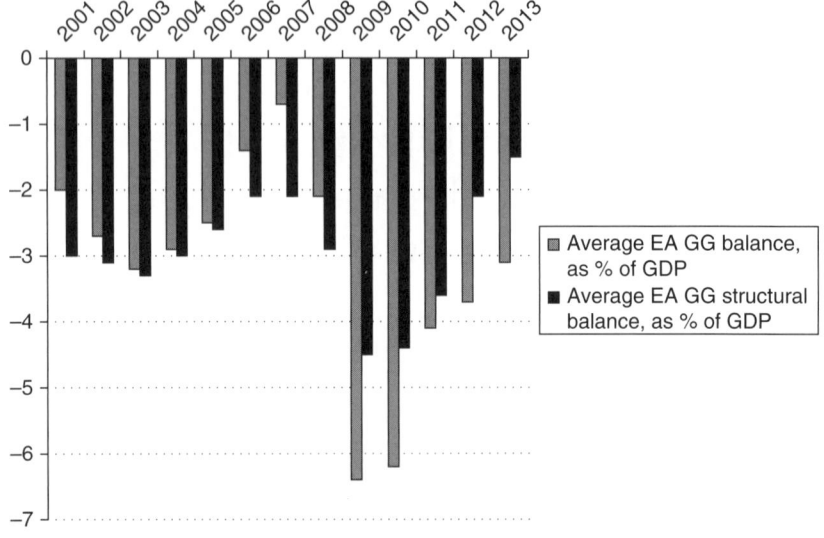

Source: IMF database.

Figure 1.1   Average actual and structural fiscal balances in the EA

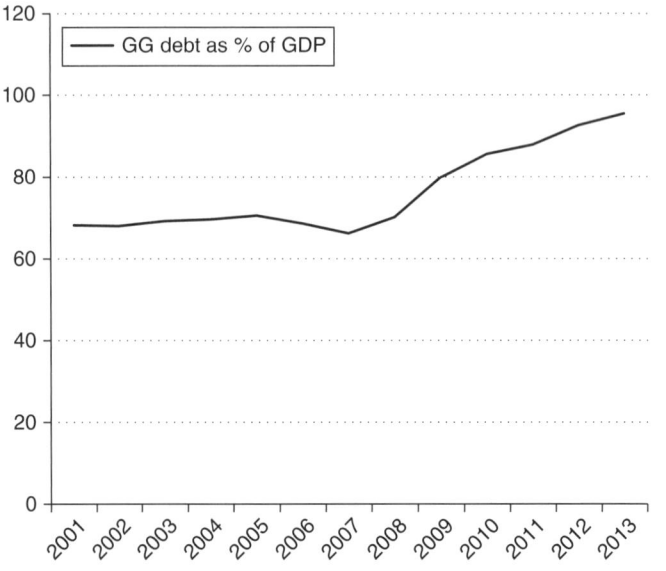

Source: IMF database.

Figure 1.2   Average gross public debt in the EA

(SNGs) in the delivery of essential public goods and services (as well as investments?) in the EA, SNGs will need to contribute to such adjustments, and in as efficient and equitable a manner as possible.

The impact of the global and Euro crises on the public finances of the EA, and the policy responses to them at both the national and the European Union (EU) levels, have been amply analyzed in the literature in recent years. There has been more limited focus on the effects of the crises on the area's SNGs, and on their policy responses.[3] This chapter analyzes developments in the EA's sub-national finances during the crisis period 2008–12, drawing lessons from this analysis for future sub-national fiscal policies and management.

Section 2 provides a brief review of the impact of the crises on sub-national finances in the EA as a whole and, in particular, in the 'periphery' countries. Some of these experiences are analyzed in much greater detail in the case studies included in the book. Section 3 discusses the main types of institutional arrangements used by EA countries in recent years to promote sub-national fiscal discipline and sustainability, as well as broad consistency with the nation-wide requirements of the evolving EU fiscal framework. The section also reviews the limited empirical evidence available to date on the effectiveness of these arrangements. Section 4 looks at the challenges that the recent reforms of the EU fiscal framework (in particular under the so-called Six-Pack and Fiscal Compact) pose for intergovernmental fiscal relations in the EA. Section 5 presents some conclusions.

2. A BRIEF REVIEW OF THE IMPACT OF THE RECENT CRISES ON THE SUB-NATIONAL FINANCES IN THE EA

The EA's member countries present a wide array of intergovernmental fiscal arrangements, differing in the degree of revenue and expenditure decentralization,[4] statutory and de facto autonomy of their SNGs, and systems of borrowing controls. Four of the countries (Austria, Belgium, Germany and Spain) are federations, the other fourteen are unitary states. However, there is no clear correlation between the federal or unitary structure and the degree of decentralization. Therefore, area-wide averages mask significant variance across the EA, and may not be representative of developments in individual countries. With this caveat, Figures 1.3–1.6 present a broad picture of developments in the EA's sub-national finances in the run-up to and the aftermath of the global financial and the Euro crises.

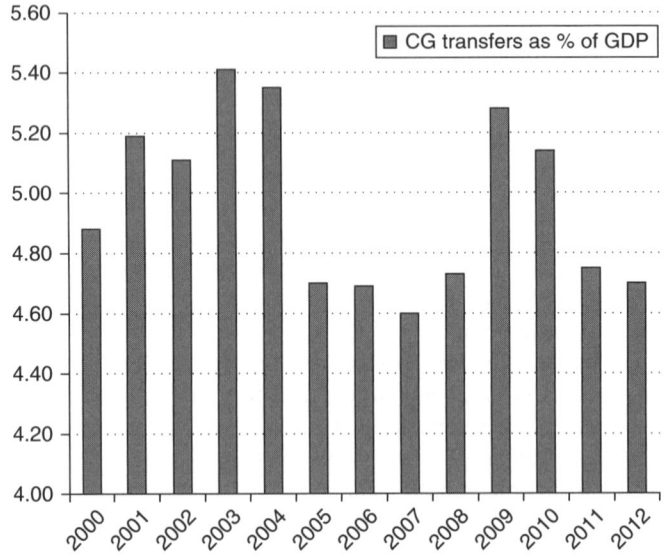

Source: OECD Fiscal Federalism Network database.

Figure 1.3 Average transfers from the CG to SNGs in the EA

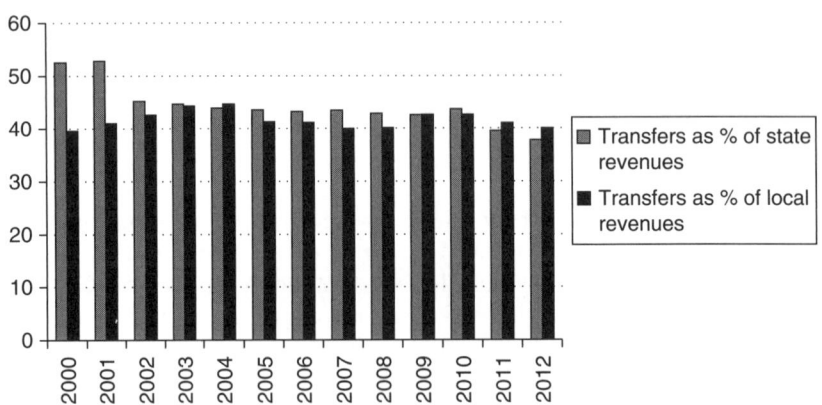

Source: OECD Fiscal Federalism Network database.

Figure 1.4 Average composition of sub-national revenues in the EA

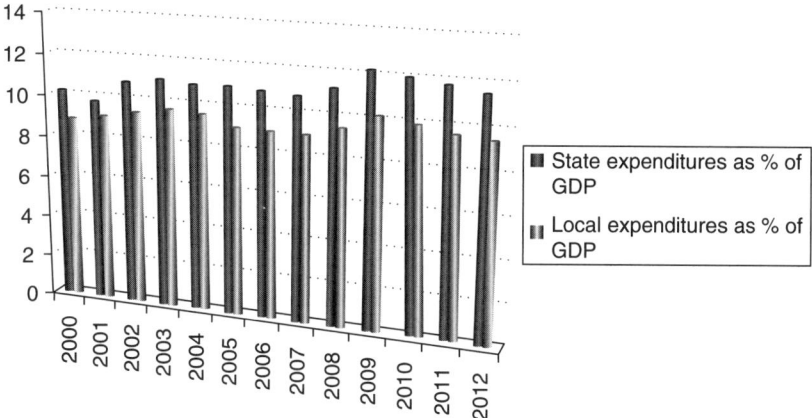

Source: OECD Fiscal Federalism Network database.

Figure 1.5   Average state and local expenditures in the EA

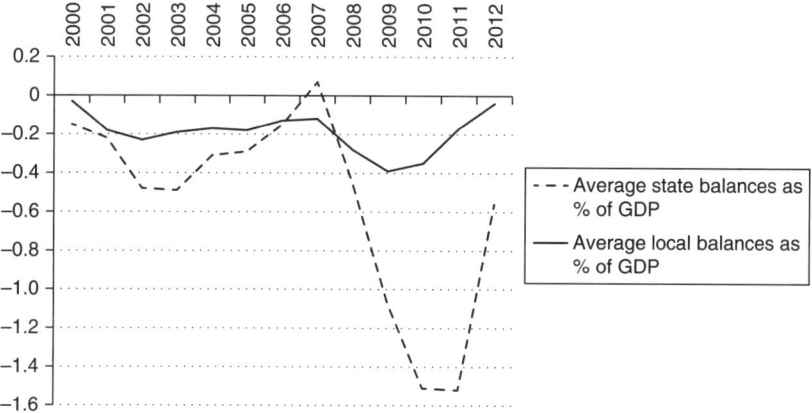

Source: OECD Fiscal Federalism Network database.

Figure 1.6   Average state and local balances in the EA

As is well known, the initial reaction of most EA central governments (CGs) to the global financial crisis in 2008 was not only to accommodate the effect of the automatic fiscal stabilizers on revenues and cyclically sensitive expenditures, but also to adopt (more or less significant) stimulus packages to support the rapidly falling domestic demand.[5] These packages included a variety of tax cuts, increases in transfers to households and firms, and cuts in public investments. In many of the countries, national governments channeled a substantial share of the increased spending through their SNGs, boosting transfers to the latter, to compensate for falling sub-national own or shared revenues, support social assistance programs, and carry out additional public investments (Figure 1.3). As a result, both the share of intergovernmental transfers in total sub-national revenues and the share of sub-national spending in GDP increased appreciably during 2008–09 (Figures 1.4 and 1.5).

Moreover, a number of the EA countries suspended or eased existing legal or administrative limits on sub-national borrowing, allowing increases in sub-national deficits, especially marked at the state level, in 2008–09 (Figure 1.6). As a result, sub-national debt, which had been broadly stable as percent of GDP during the first half of the 2000s, began a steady upward trend (Figure 1.7). On the whole, the fiscal response of SNGs to the global crisis was clearly counter-cyclical during 2008–09 in most of the EA countries.

Concern with mounting national and sub-national debts, as well as signs of a fledgling recovery from the global crisis, led many countries in the EA to embark on a fiscal consolidation path in 2011–12, which included cutbacks in central government (CG) transfers to SNGs (Figure 1.3). Sub-national spending was, however, cut back even more, leading to some improvement in the average state and local balances in the EA. Sub-national debt continued to rise, albeit at a moderating pace. As output gaps

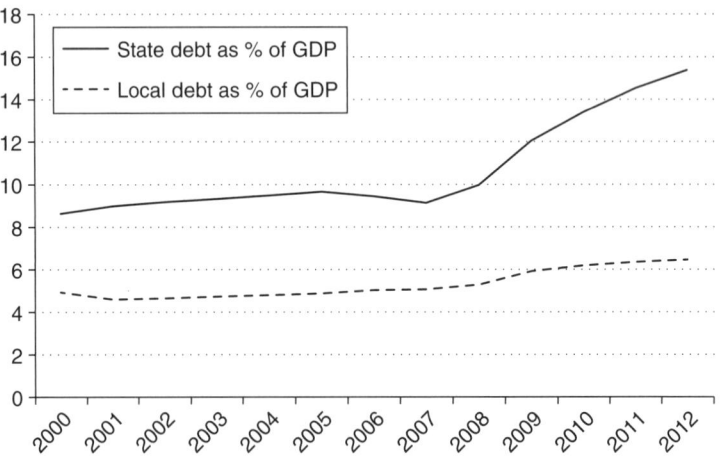

Source: OECD Fiscal Federalism Network database.

Figure 1.7 Average state and local debt in the EA

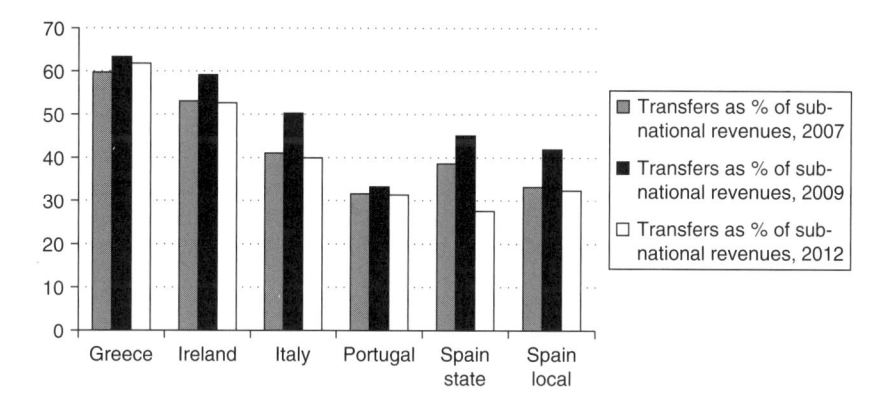

Promoting stabilizing and sustainable sub-national fiscal policies 27

Source: OECD Fiscal Federalism Network database.

Figure 1.8 Impact of the crises on intergovernmental transfers in the EA 'periphery'

remained significantly negative in most of the EA during 2010–12, the withdrawal of fiscal stimulus at the sub-national, as well as the national, level implied a shift to a pro-cyclical fiscal stance.

The average EA trends were magnified in the 'periphery' countries, where the initial fiscal easing at the outset of the global financial crisis was more than rolled back, as financing constraints associated with markets' loss of confidence forced abrupt and strong fiscal adjustment at both the national and the sub-national levels. CG transfers to SNGs were reduced (more or less sharply) in all the 'periphery' countries between 2009 and 2012 (Figure 1.8). Sub-national spending was further constrained by financing difficulties (Figure 1.9), leading to significant improvements in sub-national fiscal balances in most of the periphery countries (Figure 1.10). Sub-national debt broadly stabilized as percent of GDP in Greece, Ireland and Italy, but continued to rise in Portugal and Spain (Figure 1.11), partly reflecting the recognition of previously accumulated liabilities.

The composition of the sub-national fiscal consolidation has varied across the 'periphery' countries, with some (e.g., Italy) relying significantly on tax increases, and others more on expenditure cuts. In all countries, however, public investment bore the brunt of the adjustment. Moreover, in some of the countries, the crisis altered the political balance of powers among the different levels of government, providing the respective CGs an opportunity to tighten financial controls over their SNGs. A detailed account of developments in the sub-national finances of several 'periphery' countries is provided in the respective case studies.

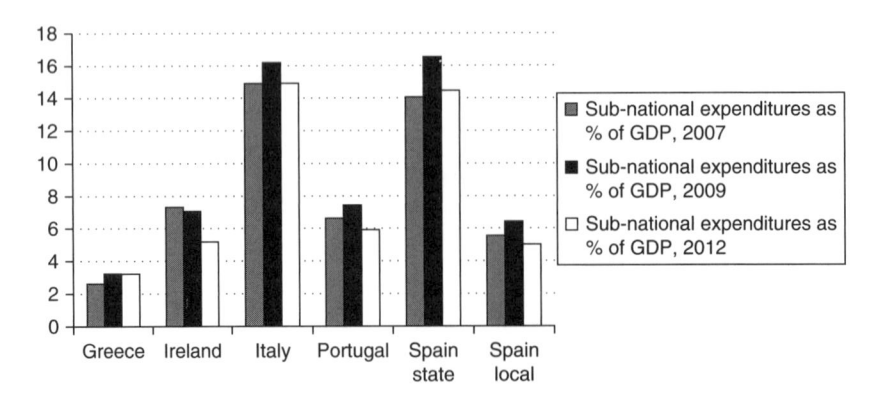

Source: OECD Fiscal Federalism Network database.

Figure 1.9 Impact of the crises on sub-national spending in the EA 'periphery'

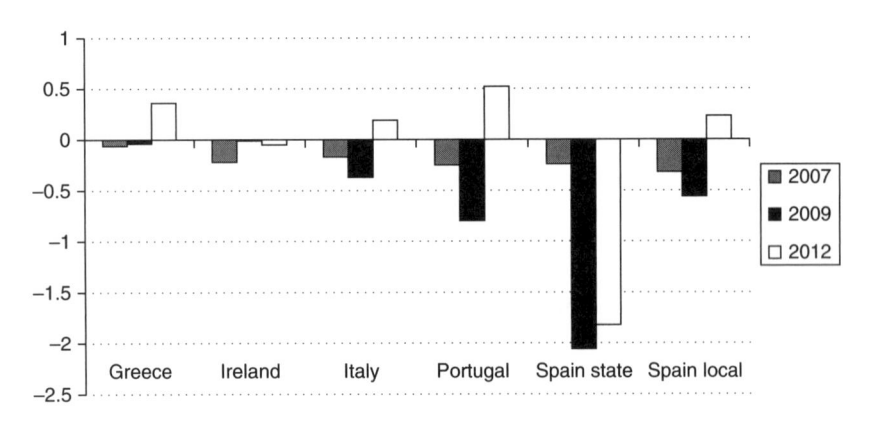

Source: OECD Fiscal Federalism Network database.

Figure 1.10 Sub-national budget balances in the EA 'periphery'

3. ARRANGEMENTS TO PROMOTE SUB-NATIONAL FISCAL DISCIPLINE IN THE EA

3.1 Overview

CGs around the world are concerned with ensuring sub-national fiscal responsibility and longer-term debt sustainability, and use a range of

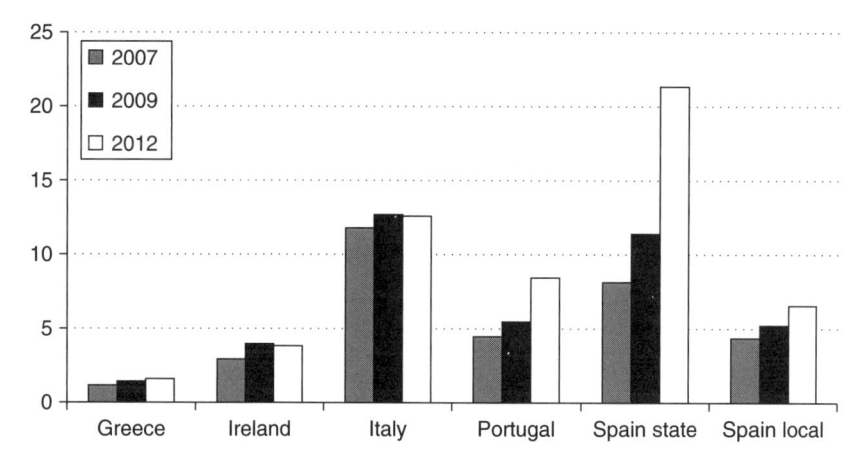

Source: OECD Fiscal Federalism Network database.

Figure 1.11 Sub-national debt in the EA 'periphery'

different types of borrowing controls to promote these objectives, with varying degrees of effectiveness. Some are also concerned with minimizing pro-cyclicality and avoiding substantial fluctuations in the delivery of essential public services of sub-national responsibility, and pursue these objectives through a variety of tools, such as counter-cyclical intergovernmental transfers, requiring SNGs to create rainy day funds, etc.

For EA countries, there is an additional challenge: ensuring that fiscal developments at the sub-national levels are consistent with the fiscal balance and public debt requirements of the EU, which refer to the general government, but hold the CG responsible for compliance. This section presents an overview[6] of the arrangements that EA countries have used in recent years to promote sub-national fiscal discipline (Table 1.1), and briefly discusses the limited available empirical evidence on their effectiveness.

The following section discusses the increasing challenges in this respect that recent reforms in the EU fiscal framework are posing for EA members.

Table 1.1 suggests that arrangements to promote sub-national fiscal discipline and debt sustainability have varied significantly across the EA in recent decades. Of the four main types of such arrangements, standing fiscal rules have been by far the most common. Although most countries have various institutional mechanisms for intergovernmental coordination, only a few (mainly federal or quasi-federal) have relied on (more or less) negotiated arrangements (the so-called Internal Stability Pacts) as the main instrument to secure sub-national fiscal discipline. Primary reliance

Table 1.1 Different arrangements to promote sub-national fiscal discipline in the EA

Country	Reliance on market discipline	Internal Stability Pacts	Fiscal rules	Administrative controls
Austria state		X		
Austria local		X		
Belgium state		X		
Belgium local		X		
Estonia			Debt rule	
Finland	Municipal Finance Corporation		Budget balance over 4 years	
France	X		Current balance/Current revenues	*Ex post*
Germany state	X		Golden rule. Structural balance rule from 2020	
Germany local			Golden rule, with borrowing limits set by states	
Greece			Debt service rule	Limits on debt
Ireland			Limit on total local debt	CG apportions total debt limit among municipalities

Italy		Golden rule
Netherlands	X	Debt and debt service rules
Portugal	X	Golden rule and debt rule
Slovakia		Golden rule and debt service rule
Slovenia		Limits on structural deficit and debt, and expenditure rule
Spain regions		Same as for regions
Spain local		

Source: Author's compilation.

on market discipline or on administrative *ex ante* CG controls on subnational borrowing has been rare in the EA.

3.2 Fiscal Rules

Sub-national fiscal rules used in EA countries have typically focused on ensuring debt sustainability, while preserving some room for borrowing to finance public investments. Accordingly, the most common combination has been that of a golden rule (requiring that SNGs' current budgets be at least balanced) with limits on sub-national debt stocks or debt service, relative to the SNGs' current revenues. Some countries have used rules on the composition of sub-national borrowing, e.g., by prohibiting their SNGs from issuing bonds, but not from borrowing from banks.

Few countries have utilized standing rules targeting the overall (as opposed to the current) balance, although targets for the latter have been frequently included in the Internal Stability Pacts (see next sub-section). None has yet targeted sub-national structural or cyclically adjusted balances (although Finland has used a rule requiring balance over a four-year period). A growing, but still small, number of countries have used expenditure-based rules.

In most countries, the debt or balance limits have been applied to individual SNGs. In Ireland, the debt limit is instead specified for the local government level as a whole, and the CG is empowered to distribute it among the individual localities.

The coverage of the rules has been typically restricted to public administration, excluding enterprises owned or controlled by individual SNGs, thus creating a potential loophole that has been utilized by many SNGs to circumvent the limits. Another vehicle to escape the constraints imposed by the rules has been the recourse by SNGs to PPPs, since contingent or actual future liabilities incurred under such arrangements are typically not covered by the debt limits. Significant examples in this respect have been the region of Madeira in Portugal (see Ahmad, Chapter 2 in this volume) and some of the regional governments in Spain. Some countries have sought to limit sub-national exposure to contingent liabilities by setting ceilings on the guarantees provided by their SNGs.

The monitoring of compliance with sub-national fiscal rules remains fraught with weaknesses, despite recent improvements in some of the countries, especially those under adjustment programs supported by the EU and the IMF. The main weaknesses in monitoring arrangements stem from the fact that controls typically focus on end-of-year accounts, which are available only with significant lags; and that sub-national accounts are often cash-based, and therefore do not allow a monitoring of arrears. Also, responsibility for the monitoring has frequently been shared among different agencies (e.g., the Ministries of Finance and of the Interior, and Audit Institutions), leading to duplication of tasks and reporting requirements, and ultimately to a dilution of accountabilities.

Experiences have varied regarding the rules' enforcement mechanisms. Legal provisions have included various types of financial sanctions for non-compliance, and the possibility of administrative interventions by upper levels of government (CG or state) in local administrations in serious financial distress.[7] Some of the rules have also included provisions requiring non-complying SNGs to pursue a pre-specified correction path for their fiscal aggregates. There is, however, little evidence of actual application of such enforcement mechanisms so far.

In view of the above-mentioned weaknesses of monitoring and enforcement of sub-national fiscal rules, it is not surprising that the empirical evidence available to date points to a limited effectiveness of the rules in influencing sub-national fiscal outcomes. An IMF study (Escolano et al., 2012) found little or no evidence of effectiveness of fiscal rules on SNGs' fiscal performance in EU countries. Similar results were found by Blöchliger (2013) for OECD countries, based on simple correlation analysis. A 2012 analysis by the EC found limited effectiveness of sub-national rules targeting the budget balance, but a more significant one for rules targeting the debt. These rather disappointing results probably also reflect the fact that the studies did not control for other features of intergovernmental fiscal arrangements that affect the degree of 'softness' of the sub-national budget constraint (e.g., the degree of revenue autonomy of the SNGs, and the degree of discretionality of CG transfers to SNGs[8]).

3.3 The Internal Stability Pacts

Some of the EA countries have relied during the past decades on agreements between the CG and the SNGs regarding fiscal balances and debt (the so-called Internal Stability Pacts), rather than on standing fiscal rules. The main examples of such pacts can be found in federal countries (Austria, Belgium during 1992–2001), Spain[9] and Italy.

The pacts have varied across countries in a number of dimensions, such as their duration; the nature, coverage, and level of their targets; the role played by the CG in their negotiations; and their monitoring and enforcement mechanisms. Such differences reflect the significant diversity of intergovernmental fiscal systems in the four countries, as well as the respective political power balances among government levels. The pacts have evolved over time, as steps have been taken to strengthen their effectiveness, mainly in response to the Euro crisis and to changes in the EU fiscal framework.

Austria has had a series of Internal Stability Pacts, stipulating targets for sub-national fiscal balances, since 1996. The compliance record, initially strong, weakened after 2002, partly reflecting lack of enforcement, and was marred by sub-national resort to various accounting stratagems, such as reclassification of public entities. Deviations from the Pact's targets were especially pronounced during the crisis years, leading to a downward revision of the targets in 2011.

The 2012 Pact (which covers a transition period to the full implementation of the Fiscal Compact in 2017) sets nominal budget targets for all levels of government until 2016. From 2017 on, the CG will be required to limit its structural budget deficit to 0.35 percent of GDP, and the states theirs to 0.08 percent of their respective GDPs. Local governments' deficits should not exceed in aggregate 0.02 percent of GDP. The distribution of the latter total among individual localities is to be decided by a state-level coordination council. Limits are also envisaged for the total public debt in accordance with the Six-Pack directives (see Section 4 below), with their distribution among government levels to be guided by their respective shares in the current stock of debt.[10] The Pact also includes a rule limiting the growth of expenditures to that of potential national GDP. Various escape clauses and a debt-brake-type correction mechanism are envisaged in this latest Pact. Monitoring is entrusted to the federal Court of Auditors, and an intergovernmental Conciliation Body is given enforcement powers (including fines) in case of breach of the rules.

The initial results of the 2012 Pact have been encouraging, with sub-national deficits declining to below the targets. However, little progress has been made to date on broader intergovernmental fiscal reforms (including increasing sub-national own revenue responsibilities and eliminating expenditure overlaps) that would help harden the sub-national budget constraint and ensure continued compliance with the EU objectives in the future.

The internal stability pact framework in Belgium has involved until recently an annual determination of budgetary targets for the federal and the regional governments, based on the recommendations of the multi-partisan High Finance Council (HFC). The latter typically has recommended a distribution of fiscal adjustment efforts between the two levels of government in line with their respective expenditure shares. *Ex post*, however, the CG has ended up contributing more.

The national legislation enacting the Fiscal Compact, only approved in late 2013, links more explicitly the fiscal targets to the EU requirements, but still envisages that their distribution between the levels of government will be determined annually through cooperation agreements based on the HFC's recommendations. The latter are supposed to refer henceforth to structural budget targets, estimated on the basis of the evolving EC methodology on the subject. The legislation refers to EU rules for the correction of deviations from the targets.

Italy has had a series of Domestic Stability Pacts (DSPs) since 1999, complemented by pacts setting targets for health spending (which is largely a regional responsibility).[11] Until 2009, the DSPs' balance or expenditure targets were largely determined by the CG. A 2009 framework law to implement the 2001 Constitutional Amendment on intergovernmental fiscal relations – which envisaged a strengthened role for existing fora for intergovernmental dialogue, including on fiscal targets – has remained largely unimplemented. In fact, the Euro crisis and related fiscal consolidation efforts have led to rationalization of levels of government (see Ambrosanio, Balduzzi and Bordignon, Chapter 9 in this volume), with the consolidation of some municipalities, a proposed reduction of the role of the regional tier of government, and a planned elimination of the provincial tier.

The DSPs' targets have been changed frequently, undermining the SNGs' ability to plan. Their increased focus on curbing sub-national spending has contributed to a compression of public investments in infrastructure. Monitoring has been carried out on an *ex post* basis by the General Accounting Office (*Ragioneria Generale*) of the Ministry of Economy and Finance, and by the Supreme Audit Court, with significant lags. Further progress is needed in improving the quality and timeliness of sub-national fiscal statistics. The enforcement of the Pacts has been progressively tightened, including through automatic increases in some own taxes for non-complying SNGs.

A recent Constitutional Amendment to implement the Fiscal Compact mandates sub-national contributions to the EU objectives for the structural budget balance and the public debt.[12] However, the translation of these principles into a detailed legal framework is still in process.

In Spain, fiscal targets for the different levels of government have been set on a multi-annual basis by two successive Budgetary Stability Acts (2001 and 2008). Annual targets *ex ante* consistent with the requirements of the Acts have been set by the CG, reflecting negotiations with the regional governments in the Council on Fiscal and Financial Policies, which includes the respective Ministers of Finance.[13] Compliance with the Acts was weakened by significant resort of the regional governments to PPPs and accounting stratagems, and was practically abandoned during the global financial crisis.

Since 2012, negotiations on sub-national targets are carried out within the framework of a new Organic Law on Budgetary Stability, which mandates convergence of the public debt of central, regional and local levels of government to 44 percent, 13 percent, and 3 percent of GDP, respectively; limits structural deficits of the general government to no more than 0.4 percent of GDP, and expenditure growth for all governments to that of potential output; and strengthens enforcement mechanisms.

4. CHALLENGES AHEAD

4.1 The EU Fiscal Framework after Recent Reforms

Recent reforms in the EU fiscal framework (Six-Pack, Fiscal Compact, and Two-Pack, summarized briefly in the Appendix), which are aimed at remedying some of the excessive rigidities of the SGP while strengthening its enforcement, have further complicated the framework and its practical implementation, including with respect to the EA's SNGs. In particular, the reformed framework involves a plethora of targets for, and related constraints on, general government aggregates (Table 1.2).

These multiple targets and constraints may not always be fully consistent. For example, actual deficits below 3 percent of GDP may not ensure a convergence of the public debt to the 60 percent ceiling in a number of countries within the area, if their real GDP growth remains sluggish over the foreseeable future. In contrast, sustained observance of the Medium Term Objective (MTO) could imply a decline of the debt to well under 60 percent of GDP over the longer term in most of the EA members. In addition to potential inconsistencies among themselves, the EU-mandated targets and limits may not always be fully consistent with the national fiscal responsibility legislations, most of which are of a constitutional level and therefore hard to change.

A further concern with the EU framework is that it can unduly constrain the room for public investments, since the MTO target implies that the bulk of the investments should be financed through public savings, irrespective of a country's levels of debt and debt-servicing capacity. This requirement can adversely affect the EU members' longer-term growth potential, as well as inter-generational equity.

Finally, the use of the SBB as a hard numerical target (as opposed to one of a range of indicators of the fiscal policy stance) creates substantial operational challenges. A number of papers have highlighted the difficulties of estimating SBBs in real time – given the substantial revisions that measures of potential output typically undergo over the span of two to three years[14] – as well as the uncertainties affecting the estimation of the elasticities of revenues to the cycle. Moreover, the identification and

Table 1.2   Multiplicity of fiscal constraints under the reformed SGP

Target	Constraint on
Under SGP's preventive arm	
Medium-term objective (MTO)	Structural budget balance (SBB)
Adjustment path to MTO (at least 0.5 percent of GDP reduction in SBB a year)	Change in SBB
Expenditure rule	Rate of growth of expenditures
Under SGP's corrective arm	
3 percent of GDP deficit limit	Actual budget balance (ABB)
60 percent of GDP debt limit	Gross public debt
1/20th minimum reduction of excess of debt over 60 percent limit	Change in gross public debt
Country-specific annual budget deficit limit for countries under EDP	ABB
Annual fiscal effort for countries under EDP	Change in SFB

Source: Author's compilation.

quantification of one-off factors to be purged from the SBB measure is also challenging, and can open scope for manipulations of the data.

The risk of manipulations can be reduced by subjecting estimates of the SBB to the scrutiny of independent fiscal 'watchdogs' (the EC and/or national independent fiscal councils, which are in the process of being set up throughout the EU), but the technical challenge of obtaining robust estimates of the SBB is still far from being resolved.[15] Moreover, the super-imposition of different national and supra-national layers of fiscal monitoring and assessment can give rise to differences and even conflicts, requiring better coordination arrangements than those currently in place in the EU.

4.2 Implications of the Reformed Framework for the EA's Sub-National Finances

The fact that the EU-mandated targets and limits for the general government are now backed up by stricter enforcement mechanisms (see the Appendix) makes it more compelling than before for the EA's CGs to put in place effective arrangements to ensure an adequate contribution of their SNGs to the achievement of the targets. This objective poses a number of significant challenges in both the design and the implementation of these arrangements.

The main design challenges are:

- To define appropriate criteria and mechanisms for both the vertical and horizontal apportionments of the EU-mandated general government budget targets and debt ceilings;
- To minimize risks of sub-national pro-cyclicality;
- To preserve adequate room for public investments (increasingly a sub-national responsibility); and
- To identify and carry out any structural reforms in the system of intergovernmental fiscal relations needed to promote an effective compliance by SNGs with their respective budget and debt targets.

The main implementation challenges are:

- To ensure a robust legal basis for sub-national fiscal rules/targets;
- To estimate sub-national SBBs;
- To put in place more timely and reliable monitoring arrangements; and
- To strengthen the effectiveness of enforcement and correction mechanisms.

While some of these issues have already been addressed by most EA countries in the national legislations implementing the Fiscal Compact, others remain unresolved so far. The following sub-sections present some reflections on the pending agenda in this area.

4.2.1 Design issues

A first question to be addressed refers to the institutional arrangements to be used by the CG in seeking to ensure consistency of sub-national fiscal policies and developments with the EU targets. Specifically, are standing rules preferable to coordination mechanisms of the type of the Internal Stability Pacts?

Rules have the significant advantage of reducing the scope for periodic bargaining, thereby hardening the sub-national budget constraint. They also provide a more stable framework for sub-national planning and budgeting than frequently renegotiated targets and limits. Coordination arrangements, on the other hand, provide more flexibility to adjust sub-national fiscal targets to changing economic and fiscal circumstances, including changes in the estimates of the national output gap. They are also likely to increase sub-national ownership for the targets, thereby promoting improved compliance.

The appropriate balance of these considerations is likely to vary across the EA countries, reflecting a number of factors, including:

- The legal power of the CG to legislate standing rules for its SNGs;
- The degree of its political leverage on SNGs (standing rules may help relatively weaker governments 'hold the line' against pressures by SNGs to minimize their share of any needed fiscal adjustment); and
- The degree of vulnerability of the country to unforeseeable exogenous shocks (including regionally asymmetric ones) that require adjustments in fiscal policies (coordination arrangements may allow faster and more flexible responses to such shocks than standing rules).

National legislations enacted so far tend to present a mixture of arrangements, with most privileging rules regarding the (vertical) apportionment of the targets among the different levels of government, and negotiations regarding the (horizontal) apportionment within each sub-national level of government.

The appropriate criteria to guide the vertical apportionment of EU targets and limits are difficult to define on a generalized basis. In principle, the criteria should take into account the following main factors:

- Initial conditions (e.g., the respective aggregate budget disequilibria and levels of debt of the different levels of government);
- The degree of dependence of the state and local levels of government on transfers from higher levels (the case for balanced budgets is more compelling for SNGs that are very dependent on CG transfers); and
- The relative rigidities and socio/political sensitivities of the expenditures assigned to the different levels of government.

In practice, however, the relative contributions of different government levels are also likely to be significantly influenced by political economy factors, especially the balance of respective political powers.

The appropriate criteria for the horizontal distribution of targets and limits are also difficult to generalize. Distribution formulas should take into account initial conditions (i.e., the relative balance and debt levels of individual SNGs, requiring more adjustment from SNGs with larger initial imbalances), as well as relative debt-servicing capacities. SNGs with higher own-revenue efforts, and thus greater debt-servicing capacity, should be allowed greater borrowing room than those with lower ones. On the other hand, differences in revenue-raising capacities, as well as in expenditure needs or costs, should be dealt with through equalization transfers, not through differentiation in rules/targets. Of course, a reliable measurement of revenue capacities and efforts as well as expenditure needs is a challenging task (although a number of EU countries, including Spain and the Scandinavian countries, have made considerable progress in this regard), and both the criteria for target apportionment and the design of equalization transfers may have to be based on second-best proxies of those variables. It is however important to avoid using actual levels, as this changes the incentive structures underlying the formulations and may lead to increasing deficits.

Given the substantial (and often growing) weight of sub-national investments in total public investments in most EA countries, preserving some room for such investments within the constraints imposed by the EU framework constitutes a significant challenge for the area countries. It is clear that an unfettered resort to borrowing by SNGs to finance their investments is inconsistent with the EU framework. However, CGs can create limited room for debt-financed sub-national investments by increasing their own savings. If compatible with the statutory sub-national autonomy in the country, the CG could define an aggregate limit (a kind of pool) for permits to borrow to finance sub-national investments, and set up a bidding mechanism for SNGs to access such a pool.[16] The project bids should be supported by well-articulated business cases, including cost-benefit analyses based on standardized methodologies.

An additional important challenge for governments of the EA is to reduce the risk of sub-national fiscal pro-cyclicality. In principle, specifying sub-national budget targets in structural terms could minimize such risks. This approach would be consistent with the increasing focus on the SBB in the EU fiscal framework. However, the already substantial difficulties in estimating SBBs in a timely and robust way at the CG level are magnified at the sub-national level, in particular by:

- The fact that regional and local economies are subject to idiosyncratic, and typically asymmetric, shocks that make estimates of sub-national SBBs based on national output gaps quite problematic; and
- The longer lags in availability of sub-national GDP data.

Therefore, other approaches to mitigating sub-national pro-cyclicality risks may be preferable in practice, namely:

- The use of structural or moving averages of actual CG revenues as a basis for revenue sharing;

- The use of trend revenues to calculate proxies of structural balances; and
- A requirement for SNGs to save revenue windfalls into 'rainy day' funds, with clearly specified rules for withdrawals.

4.2.2 Implementation issues

It is essential to ensure a robust legal basis for any framework to promote sub-national fiscal discipline. Countries' approaches to this task have to reflect their specific institutional context. In federal-type countries, the statutory treatment of sub-national autonomy may require higher-level legislation as the basis for sub-national rules. This has been largely achieved in the EA with the legislation implementing the Fiscal Compact. However, the issues mentioned above that are not covered by this legislation are likely to have to be resolved mainly through negotiated arrangements (preferably multi-year ones). This may require the creation of new intergovernmental coordination fora, or the strengthening of existing ones.[17]

As regards monitoring arrangements, a first issue to be addressed is who should monitor sub-national compliance with the rules or agreed targets? Possible candidates are: the CG's Ministry of Finance; a Secretariat of the intergovernmental coordination forum; the country's Supreme Audit Court; or the national Fiscal Council. There are advantages and disadvantages to each option. Assigning the responsibility to the national Ministry of Finance would maximize the chances of prompt responses to sub-national fiscal slippages. On the other hand, SNGs are likely to favor the other options that they are likely to view as more 'neutral'; and they may carry sufficient political weight to have their preferences prevail.

Improving the timeliness and reliability of sub-national fiscal data is crucial for strengthening the effectiveness of any sub-national monitoring arrangement. Appropriate steps in this direction would include:

- Enacting legislation requiring all SNGs to follow standardized accounting and reporting requirements, consistent with those used for fiscal surveillance by the EU;
- Requiring improved reporting of fiscal risks from PPPs, guarantees, and other explicit contingent liabilities;
- Increasing frequency and reducing lags in sub-national fiscal reporting (in particular for states/regions and large localities); and
- Introducing and consistently applying penalties for failures to report as required.

As concerns enforcement mechanisms, an effective design of sanctions needs to take into account a number of country-specific factors:

- The degree of statutory and de facto autonomy of the SNGs;
- Their degree of financial dependence on transfers from CG; and the compulsory or discretionary nature of such transfers (cuts in discretionary CG transfers can constitute effective sanctions for non-compliant SNGs);
- The possible role of intergovernmental coordination fora in enforcement;
- The legal scope for administrative intervention in case of serious violations that raise the risk of a financial crisis; and
- The legal scope for holding sub-national government officials accountable for serious failures in compliance.

It is also important to introduce or strengthen correction mechanisms for sub-national deviations from the targets. Such correction arrangements could be modeled (in a simplified manner) on the example of the Swiss 'debt brake' system[18] (although see Milbradt, Chapter 3 in this volume; and Spahn, Chapter 4 in this volume for some limitations).

5. CONCLUSIONS

The crises that have buffeted the EA in recent years have taken a substantial toll on the public finances of most countries in the area at both the national and the sub-national levels. With the average general government deficit still slightly above 3 percent of GDP, the average structural deficit still above 1 percent of GDP, and the public debt above 95 percent of GDP, it is clear that further sustained fiscal adjustment will be needed in the years ahead, although its pace should vary appropriately both across the countries in the area and over time.

The recent reforms in the EU fiscal framework have aimed at strengthening the likelihood of such adjustment, not only by introducing some elements of flexibility (increased focus on the SBB, and differentiated paths of adjustment depending on initial conditions), but also by strengthening enforcement. In the process, however, the framework has been significantly complicated, creating further challenges, especially as regards its application to the sub-national levels of government.

This chapter has provided an initial exploratory discussion of these challenges, as well as in the light of EA members' experiences with the application of the previous versions of the framework. A lesson that emerges clearly from those experiences is that there is no one-size-fits-all prescription for ensuring an appropriate contribution of SNGs to fiscal convergence under the EU framework. Some countries have privileged more or less permanent sub-national fiscal rules (on balances, debt or spending); others more negotiated arrangements, reflecting different institutional settings and political power balances. There is no firm evidence that one approach has been consistently more effective than the others. It is also clear that weaknesses in monitoring and enforcement mechanisms have significantly undermined the effectiveness of both rules and negotiated arrangements, especially in the run-up to the global crisis when market discipline was conspicuously absent (including at the sub-national level) in the EA.

Looking forward, while the national legislations implementing the Fiscal Compact have addressed some of the complex design and implementation issues that the revised EU framework poses for inter-governmental fiscal relations in the EA, more reflection is clearly needed on a number of these issues. This chapter has put forward some initial thoughts on such issues, while recognizing the preponderant role that political economy factors are likely to play in this area.

In particular the chapter has discussed some of the criteria that should guide the vertical and horizontal apportionment of the EU-mandated deficit and debt targets. It has also advanced suggestions on safeguarding some room for sub-national investments within the (probably too strict) constraints posed by the EU framework.

Reducing pro-cyclicality in sub-national policies remains a challenging task, in the EA as elsewhere. Given the state of technology in estimating output gaps and the still relatively long lags in the availability of sub-national data, the, in principle, best approach of specifying sub-national budget targets in structural terms does not appear very practical at the present time. The chapter has suggested some second-best, but probably more feasible, approaches in this area.

Finally, improving monitoring, enforcement and correction mechanisms for sub-national rules or negotiated targets is crucial to improve their effectiveness. The chapter has indicated a number of steps that could and should be taken as soon as possible toward these objectives.

NOTES

1. A recent paper by the EC, 2014, estimates the overall structural consolidation effort in the EA (excluding Cyprus, Greece and Latvia) in 2013 to have amounted to about 0.7 percent of GDP, albeit with significant variance across the area members.
2. The EA members' Stability and Convergence programs for 2014 target a slower pace of structural fiscal adjustment, equivalent on average to about 0.3 percent of GDP. The average debt-to-GDP ratio in the area is projected to peak in 2014, but to remain well above the 60 percent target for many years to come.

3. For analyses of the effects of the global financial crisis on SNG finances in the OECD, see Ter-Minassian and Fedelino (2010); Blochliger et al. (2010); Foremny and von Hagen, 2012; and Wolman (2014).
4. The central government's share of overall general government expenditures ranged from 60 percent in Finland to 94 percent in Greece in 2012. The corresponding share in revenues ranged from 57 percent in Spain to nearly 97 percent in Greece. Accordingly, SNGs' dependence on transfers from the CG varies significantly across the EA, albeit remaining well above 50 percent on average.
5. Among the large EU (and more broadly OECD) countries, Italy was the only one that did not introduce discretionary stimulus measures, and indeed did not fully accommodate the automatic stabilizers, a fact that resulted in some fiscal pro-cyclicality (Ambrosanio et al., Chapter 9 in this volume). This reflected concerns with fiscal sustainability, given the already high level of the country's public debt at the outset of the crisis.
6. This stylized overview is intended to capture the key features of individual countries' arrangements, rather than to provide a detailed description of each of the latter (a task beyond the scope of this chapter). More details can be found in EC (2012).
7. Most EA countries, however, have not put in place legislation envisaging formal bankruptcy procedures for distressed localities, such as, e.g., Chapter 9 of the US Bankruptcy Code (see Canuto and Liu, 2013, for details).
8. For a discussion of empirical evidence on the importance of such factors in determining the softness of the sub-national budget constraint, see Ter-Minassian (2015).
9. Since 2002, Spain has shifted to a more rules-based framework.
10. Specifically, 88 percent for the CG; 8 percent for the states; 2 percent for Vienna; and 2 percent for the other municipalities.
11. See Piperno (2013) for a comprehensive analysis of the Italian DSPs.
12. Specifically, regions are required to ensure not only equilibrium in their own budgets, but also in the aggregate budget of the local governments within their territory (albeit not of each individual locality).
13. See Tournemire (2014).
14. See, e.g., Kempkes (2012).
15. In its annual Reports on the Public Finance in the EU, the EC discusses ongoing work and advances in this area.
16. A similar mechanism (*fondo concursable*) is used at the CG level in Chile to determine which new investments should be included in the budget each year.
17. Tournemire (2014) provides a comprehensive review of current intergovernmental coordination forums in the EU.
18. For a description of this system see Danninger (2002).

REFERENCES

Blochliger, H. (2013), 'Fiscal Consolidation across Government Levels – Part 1. How Much, What Policies?', OECD Economics Department Working Papers, No. 1070, Paris.

Blochliger, H., Charbit, C., Pinero Campos, J.M. and Vammalle, C. (2010), 'Sub-Central Governments and the Economic Crisis', OECD Economics Department Working Papers No. 752, Paris.

Canuto, O. and Liu, L. (2013), 'Until Debt Do Us Part: Subnational Debt, Insolvency, and Markets', World Bank, Washington, DC.

Danninger, S. (2002), 'A New Rule: The Swiss Debt Brake', IMF Working Paper 02/18.

Escolano, J., Eyraud, L., Moreno Badia, M., Sarnes, J. and Tuladhar, A. (2012), 'Fiscal Performance, Institutional Design and Decentralization in EU Countries', IMF Working Paper 12/45.

European Commission (EC) (2012), 'Report on Public Finances in the EU', Brussels.

European Commission (EC) (2013), 'Report on Public Finances in the EU', Brussels.

Foremny, D. and von Hagen, J. (2012), 'Fiscal Federalism in Times of Crisis', Centre for Economic Policy Research, Discussion Paper No. 9154, London.

Kempkes, G. (2012), 'Cyclical Adjustment in Fiscal Rules: Some Evidence on Real-Time Bias for EU-15 Countries', Discussion Paper, Deutsche Bundesbank No. 15/2012.

OECD, Fiscal Decentralisation Database, http://www.oecd.org/tax/federalism/oecdfiscaldecentralisationdatabase.

Piperno, S. (2013), *La finanza decentrata in Italia*, Bologna: Il Mulino.

Schaechter, A., Kinda, T., Budina, N. and Weber, A. (2012), 'Fiscal Rules in Response to the Crisis – Toward the "Next-Generation" Rules. A New Dataset', IMF Working Paper 12/187.

Ter-Minassian, T. and Fedelino, A. (2010), 'Impact of the Global Crisis on Sub-National Governments' Finances', Bank of Italy's Proceedings of Public Finance Workshop.

Ter-Minassian, T. (2015), 'Promoting Responsible and Sustainable Fiscal Decentralization', in Ahmad, E. and Brosio, G. (eds), *Handbook of Multilevel Finance*, Cheltenham, UK and Northampton, MA, USA: Edward Elgar, pp. 437–58.

Tournemire, G. (2014), 'Coordination Arrangements across Government Sub-Sectors in EU Member States', European Economy Economic Papers 517, Brussels.

Truger, A. and Will, H. (2012), 'The German "Debt Brake" – A Shining Example for European Fiscal Policy?', Institute for International Political Economy Working Paper No. 15, Berlin.

Wolman, H. (2014), 'National Fiscal Policy and Local Government during the Economic Crisis', German Marshall Fund, Urban Papers Series.

APPENDIX THE NEW EU FISCAL GOVERNANCE FRAMEWORK[1]

The economic and fiscal governance of the EA and of the rest of the EU has been significantly strengthened in the wake of the Euro crisis, which exposed fundamental weaknesses in its previous design, and especially in its enforcement. The main building blocks of the reformed framework are: a set of five Regulations and one Directive, effective from December 2011 (the so-called Six-Pack); the Treaty on Stability, Coordination and Governance (the so-called Fiscal Compact) signed in 2012 and now ratified by all signatories; and two additional Regulations approved in 2013 (the so-called Two-Pack). They are briefly summarized in what follows.

1. The Six-Pack

The Six-Pack applies to the 27 EU members, with some specific rules for EA members, especially regarding financial sanctions. It covers not only fiscal surveillance, but also macroeconomic surveillance under the new Macroeconomic Imbalance Procedure.

In the fiscal area, the Six-Pack strengthens the Stability and Growth Pact (SGP). It reinforces both the preventive and the corrective arm of the Pact, i.e. the Excessive Deficit Procedure (EDP), which applies to Member States that have breached the 3 percent of GDP deficit debt limit. The Six-Pack ensures stricter application of the SGP's fiscal rules by defining quantitatively what a 'significant deviation' from the medium-term objective (MTO) for the structural fiscal balance, or the adjustment path toward it, means in the context of the preventive arm.

Moreover, the six-pack operationalizes the SGP's debt rule, so that an EDP may also be launched if the debt-to-GDP ratio of a member country exceeds 60 percent and is not declining toward the limit at a satisfactory pace (defined as at least by 1/20th of the excess per year). It also includes an expenditure benchmark, specifying that the growth of expenditures should not exceed that of potential GDP, but does not envisage sanctions for non-compliance with the rule.

Financial sanctions are imposed on non-complying EA members in a gradual way, from the preventive arm to the latest stages of the EDP, and may eventually reach 0.5% of GDP. The Six-Pack introduces reverse-qualified majority voting (RQMV) for most sanctions, thereby increasing the likelihood of their implementation.

To ensure an effective implementation of these fiscal rules, the Six-Pack sets out a number of broad recommendations to make medium-term budget frameworks more binding, prepare budgets in a more top-down sequence, report more frequently, timely, and comprehensively on fiscal developments and risks, and give a bigger role to independent fiscal councils for the preparation of budget assumptions as well as the assessment of compliance with the rules.

2. The Fiscal Compact

The Treaty on Stability, Coordination and Governance (TSCG), the fiscal part of which is referred to as the Fiscal Compact, requires contracting parties to approve higher, preferably constitutional-level national legislation to ensure convergence (at paces to be agreed with the EC) toward the revised SGP targets, namely structural deficits no higher than 0.5 percent of GDP,[2] nominal deficits no higher than 3 percent of GDP, and public debt no higher than 60 percent of GDP.

The national legislations have to include automatic correction mechanisms for deviation from the MTO, or the adjustment path toward it, with escape clauses for exceptional circumstances. Compliance with the rules is to be monitored by independent institutions. The European Court of Justice (CoJ) may impose financial sanctions (0.1 percent of GDP) if a country does not properly implement the new budget rules in national law and fails to comply with a CoJ ruling requiring it to do so.

3. The Two-Pack

The so-called Two-Pack legislation, which entered into force at the end of May 2013, contains different initiatives aimed at strengthening economic coordination and surveillance in the EA. It subjects the area's members experiencing severe financial instability, or receiving financial assistance on a precautionary basis, to a new form of enhanced surveillance. It seeks to better articulate any financial assistance provided outside the framework of the EU (e.g. under the European Stability Mechanism, ESM) with the Treaty. For this purpose, it sets out specific procedures for ensuring the consistency of ESM-supported adjustment programs with the EU's reformed macroeconomic and fiscal framework. The legislation also creates a system of post-program surveillance for countries that have received financial assistance, until at least 75 percent of the latter have been repaid.

The Two-Pack also includes provisions aiming to increase accountability and transparency. In particular, this regards the involvement of the national and the European parliaments, as well as the involvement of other relevant stakeholders, in the new procedures set out in the legislation.

Notes

1. This Appendix is largely based on Schaechter et al. (2012); and on EC documentation available at: http://ec.europa.eu/economy_finance/articles/governance/2012-03-14_six_pack_en.htm.
2. 1.0 percent of GDP for Member States with a debt ratio significantly below 60 percent of GDP.

2. Political economy of information generation and financial management for sub-national governments: some lessons from international experience[1]

Ehtisham Ahmad

POLITICAL ECONOMY OF MULTI-LEVEL INFORMATION GENERATION AND LIABILITY MANAGEMENT

The issue of managing sub-national liabilities is not only important in the EU, but is also a major concern in other parts of the world, including South Asia, China and Brazil, as much of the public investment needed for sustainable development is taking place at the sub-national level. Different countries and regions have used alternative mechanisms to control sub-national liabilities, ranging from the fiscal rules in the EU and Brazil, to administrative control mechanisms in China, cooperative arrangements in Austria and market-based controls in North America (see Ter-Minassian, Chapter 1 in this volume). Although coordination and control mechanisms vary from country to country, none will work effectively without full and timely information on the nature and timing of the liabilities. Indeed, effective management of the liabilities is critical also to ensuring a better buy-in from the private sector and a more credible environment for greater stability for contracts (Minervini and Vinella, Chapter 13 in this volume).

Many of the problems seen in the EU, and now in China, arise because there is incomplete recognition of the magnitude of the liabilities, or which level of government is eventually liable for meeting them. This is often because of game-play by State-Owned Enterprises (SOEs) and lower levels of government, seeking to circumvent scrutiny or debt limits. But some of this is also due to the asymmetric nature of contracts, e.g., for public–private partnerships (PPPs),[2] where the different parties try to maximize the rents that they are able to extract (including from the state and higher levels of government), or from the private parties concerned. And as seen in countries as diverse as Mexico and Ireland, a buildup of private debt, without state guarantees, can be rapidly transformed into public debt in times of crisis or exogenous shocks that begin to affect the banking system. While country-specific mechanisms to handle sub-national liabilities reflect differences in institutional arrangements and legal constraints, including differing constitutional perspectives and foundations, incomplete information in an increasingly complex world can negate many, if not all, of the control mechanisms, including in the most advanced countries.

Ter-Minassian (Chapter 1 in this volume) provides an update of the various control mechanisms that are operational at the present time in the EU – identifying (1) market-based; (2) cooperative; (3) administrative; and (4) fiscal rules-based approaches to the management of liabilities. We argue that the distinctions between the alternatives blur into irrelevance if there is insufficient information available on the buildup of liabilities. Indeed, Escolano et al. (2012) illustrate the ineffectiveness of fiscal rules in the EU. In the Brazilian case, monitoring and reporting requirements, facilitated by the Fiscal Responsibility Act of 2000, have led to subsequent sub-national responses for independent budget information management systems. However, the reporting requirements have been tightened by the requirement to adopt the IMF's GFSM standards at all levels of government as part of the Chart of Accounts from 2015.

The need to impose clarity on standards for information generation is now seen in many countries, including Portugal. And in the Mexican case, local autonomy prevented the adoption of uniform standards, and even at the federal level it has been difficult to adopt the IMF's GFSM standards or establish a Treasury Single Account (TSA). At the sub-national level, the implementation of a uniform framework for the generation of information has only just begun.

Section 1 also presents some insights and lessons from the recent experiences in the EU, particularly Portugal. It suggests that sub-national governments may react to controls or limits on indebtedness by parking liabilities in difficult to monitor activities or vehicles, often adopting more opaque budget management systems as a response. The response of the Fiscal Council is instructive. In contrast, the more measured management of sub-national liabilities in China over the past decade again emphasizes the importance of timely management together with the establishment of appropriate incentives and information at the sub-national level. In the Chinese case, this involves a reform of intergovernmental relations, including assignments and own-source revenues, to generate a credible basis for sustainable access to credit.

Section 2 examines the different mechanisms to control incentives to cheat on sub-national debt, including those related to public sector enterprises, from a 'political economy perspective', given imperfect information. It builds on the scope for 'game play' in relation to the usual mechanisms for controlling debt. With incomplete information, some of the options are not workable, and there needs to be a resort to a possible combination of the ideal type policy options.

Section 3 concludes with an examination of some standards that are needed to make the debt management workable, without negating the need to maintain the autonomy of sub-national governments in both federal and unitary states, in order to ensure the effective delivery of local services.

1. POTENTIAL GAME-PLAY ACROSS JURISDICTIONS

In order to ensure macroeconomic stability, the central government has the responsibility of ensuring that overall risks, including debt, are kept within prudent limits. As discussed below, this places a responsibility on the center, even within federal systems, to ensure that prudential debt limits are not exceeded in aggregate – this poses difficult problems of determining the overall sustainable debt limits and then apportioning the agreed limits among the different levels of government. This issue is reflected even in supranational administrations, such as the European Union's Stability and Growth Pact.[3]

Poterba and von Hagen (1999) examined the experience in Europe and view the set of rules and regulations according to which budgets are drafted, approved, and implemented as an important determinant of public sector deficits and debts. A similar result was found by von Hagen and Harden (1994); countries with more transparent budget procedures exhibited greater fiscal discipline in the 1980s and early 1990s. In practice, the efficacy of fiscal rules for sub-national governments (or for national governments in a supranational economic area, such as the EU) depends critically on the ability to measure and monitor the generation of debts and other liabilities. The literature in the US generally has a favorable assessment of debt management in US states.[4] However, as suggested above, more recent work suggests that in the EU case the rules have not worked that effectively (Escolano et al., 2012).

In the absence of any limits on sub-national borrowing, the central government faces the risk that local governments may try to free-ride on its efforts to stabilize the economy – effectively passing the costs of excessive borrowing on to other jurisdictions or future generations. Larger sub-national governments that are 'too big to be ignored' could hold the central government to ransom by bargaining for debt write-offs and other fiscal advantages.

Local governments' efforts to conduct anti-cyclical policies – if left unchecked – could also result in ratcheting up public spending. Policy makers are likely to borrow when the economy is slowing down, but may be reluctant to repay the debt when the economy is recovering. In addition, during recoveries voters and vested interest groups often put pressure on local authorities to increase the provision of public goods or decrease the tax burden, reducing any fiscal surpluses available for debt repayment (Buchanan et al., 1987). Local politicians may even use to their advantage the possibility that taxpayers might not correctly discount their future tax liabilities, and pursue increasing borrowing strategies to mitigate the current tax bill (Moesen, 1993).

But above all, the need to control local borrowing arises from the common pool problem and the soft budget constraint it implies. The common pool problem stems from the separation of costs and benefits of public spending. If a certain public project predominantly benefits a particular jurisdiction but is financed through a common pool of taxes collected from all over the country, this jurisdiction will pay only a small fraction of the costs of the project while enjoying a large fraction of its benefits. This lack of full internalization of the costs of a project will result in excessive spending[5] and create a clear incentive for the regions to compete for federal transfers to finance their projects out of a common pool. Ideally, regions should compete on the basis of the quality of their proposed spending projects. Alternatively, they could signal that they are in particular need of federal assistance by running large budget deficits or accumulating unsustainable debts, and hope that the central government will eventually bail them out.

The possibility of a bailout does not stem from the existence of a common pool per se, but from the way in which it is administered. When transfers are allocated on the basis of ex post financial needs rather than ex ante characteristics, regions experiencing financial difficulties could be bailed out by the central government. In this case, the budget constraint faced by the sub-national government becomes 'soft'. Thus sub-national agencies have an incentive to under-collect taxes, and overspend, or even default, on accumulated debts, as they expect the federal government to cover the financing gap. Moreover, lenders also lose incentives to police regional governments as they view their investments as protected by a federal government guarantee.[6]

These problems would not exist if central governments could credibly commit to never revising transfer allocations ex post, that is, to a no-bailout policy. Unfortunately, such a policy stance, arguably optimal in the long run, is difficult to commit to in the short run especially if it involves a painful local default or a reduction in the provision of basic public services with schools being closed and pensions left unpaid. Thus, the sanction of not providing funding or transfers for basic services may just not be credible. Persson and Tabellini (1996) and Bordignon et al. (2001) show formally that even a national government maximizing the federation's social welfare is likely to find it beneficial to bail out a financially distressed region. In addition, a default by one region can increase the cost of borrowing for all other regions in a federation, so neighbors themselves may be interested in providing the defaulting region with a bailout transfer.

Mourmouras and Rangazas (Chapter 12 in this volume) and Minervini and Vinella (Chapter 13 in this volume) illustrate the incentives for sub-national governments and entities to renege on contracts or be 'economical' with the exchange of information on the buildup of liabilities. There are issues related to whether increasing the number of tiers (e.g., the supranational level in the EU), or multiple levels in China, diffuses the responsibilities for spending, makes it harder to impose budget constraints given the limitations on the potential own-source revenues, and complicates the exchange of information.

1.1 The Case of Madeira

An interesting example of evading fiscal rules in the EU appeared in the case of the Portuguese autonomous region of Madeira during the fiscal crisis in Portugal in 2011. A number of 'hidden' liabilities surfaced – some were related to disagreements with Lisbon in relation to who should bear the burden of meeting 'social standards', particularly for health care. But a considerable proportion was due to arrears on construction and other supplies. These were likely linked to an over-supply of tourist facilities that were badly affected by the downturn in demand following the crisis in Europe.

The total hidden liabilities of €1.1 billion led to an overall debt of €5.8 billion, amounting to 126 percent of regional GDP, or 927 percent of annual revenues – and almost half of this was due to SOEs – see Paixão and Baleiras (2013). This pattern of obfuscation of liabilities was repeated, to a lesser extent, in the municipalities on the mainland, and indeed at the central level. The extent of adjustment needed was quite severe but the Portuguese government entered into an adjustment program with Madeira, paralleling the arrangement that it had with the Troika.

It is interesting that the Portuguese Fiscal Council recommended that:

1. The Budget Coverage needs to be inclusive of the liabilities being generated by SOEs;

2. There needs to be proper accounting for the liabilities in keeping with international standards, including for PPPs;
3. There needs to be a proper Chart of Accounts (COA) – this was required by the Portuguese government in 2007, but was not implemented; and that
4. There needs to be a Treasury Single Account, in order to track the cash.

As we discuss below, the budget coverage issue is critical. To ensure comparability across jurisdictions, it is advisable that the full coverage reflects the standards incorporated in the IMF's Government Financial Statistics Manual (GFSM) 2014 that is also synchronized with the System of National Accounts. In addition, the accounting framework should permit recognition of liabilities, conforming, e.g., to the IPSAS standards for PPPs.

Consequently, one of the key messages of the Portuguese Fiscal Council that resonates elsewhere is that the policy framework must be implementable. In other words, that there may have to be an overlapping set of rules that generate the incentives to comply, but that these should not be too complex to render the system un-implementable. In addition, there has to be sufficient assurance that the information on budgets and budget execution cannot be manipulated – in order to minimize the possibility of 'game-play'.

2. LIMITING INCENTIVES TO CHEAT[7]

A key element in responsible management of liabilities is clarity as to the responsibility for spending. As discussed in Ahmad (2015), this involves not just the function carried out by a particular level of government, but also whether it was on behalf of another level, e.g., through earmarks or mandates. Moreover, it is important to be able to distinguish between the 'economic' components – such as whether or not the wages are set nationally – and whether different levels of government hire the workers. It is also critical which level of government authorizes and finances the requisite investments against which liabilities are being generated (Dafflon 2015). Note that liabilities may also arise due to arrears on account of current and not just capital spending. These distinctions are rather important, and imply that greater care needs to be taken in generating data and defining variables carefully, and rather more than the IMF's GFSM 2014 categories or the OECD/UN's Classification of Functions of Government is likely to be needed – and this is now being attempted systematically by the OECD

(Blöchliger, 2015). There is a spate of literature drawing conclusions on intergovernmental issues erroneously relying on incomplete data from the IMF's GFS yearbook – this should be treated with extreme caution.

Similarly, in examining incentives on the revenue side, it is important to distinguish between own-source revenues over which a level of government may have control at the margin, and shared revenues that might accrue to the jurisdiction like a transfer. Thus, the tax policy element involving jurisdictional controls over rates or bases at the margin is critical in ensuring whether or not a future liability can be financed or whether a sanction is credible (Ambrosanio and Bordignon, 2015). Similarly, whether or not the system of transfers automatically meets deficits greatly influences the incentives to incur and manage liabilities effectively.

An equally important issue is whether there are national or international standards in effect, and whether a local government has the mechanisms to circumvent these, e.g., with information systems under its control.

The international standards for the economic classification of public activities (the IMF's GFSM 2014, together with the UN's functional classification (COFOG)) provide a key for the tracking and reporting of expenditures, and for determining whether there have been any diversions of public monies for unauthorized purposes. This is essential even if there has been appropriation at a fairly aggregate level, in order to present consistent and comparable information to the policy makers or the public at large – particularly the markets that have to judge the relative ability of sub-national entities to service the buildup of liabilities that may span several political cycles or decades.

In some cases, especially in unitary countries, the central government is responsible for establishing standards for the accounting and reporting systems of all levels of government, and is usually also responsible for their enforcement. The development of sound budget, accounting and reporting systems is a complex and time-consuming process and it would not be efficient or cost-effective for sub-national governments to develop bespoke accounting and information reporting systems on their own. Besides, if sub-national governments were to establish their own government financial information management systems (GFMISs), it opens up the possibility of 'game-playing', particularly in response to a tighter control over liabilities, e.g., as implied by the Fiscal Responsibility Legislation or debt management rules that might be imposed at the national or supranational level (as in the EU). The key to generating standardized information then becomes a standard chart of accounts that tracks the budget process in a common manner – facilitating comparisons across jurisdictions.

This standardized information is critical in establishing the effective operations of yardstick competition between jurisdictions within a country, and also across countries. It is not enough to be able to rely solely on easily observable 'outcome indicators' that reflect standards of living. Let us assume that jurisdictions A and B within a country (say Länder) or countries within a common currency area, such as the EU, have similar observable standards of living. However, jurisdiction A has managed to meet its obligations within the agreed Fiscal Responsibility framework including recognition of all future liabilities (e.g., Maastricht). Jurisdiction B also appears to have met the criteria, but has in fact done so only on a cash basis, i.e., not recognizing all the liabilities generated, or parked them in state-owned enterprises or even private companies (e.g., through PPPs, on which more later).

Relatively few countries utilize the full format of the IMF's GFSM 2014 for both the central as well as the sub-national governments (in this regard the BRICS countries do better than the OECD, including the EU countries). The format is designed to ensure conformity of the financial information with the System of National Accounts.[8] Multiple formats in Mexico at the federal level and across the states make it difficult to generate standardized information for general government. This makes it problematic to ensure comparability across sub-national entities or engender accountable competition across states. Brazilian states, while not (yet) conforming to the GFSM 2014, perform better than Mexico in that the Federation requires a standardized format to receive and report on federal resources as well as their own resources. Recognizing the dangers of game-play, Brazil has required the use of the GFSM 2014 standards for all sub-national transactions by 2015 – this will require adjustments to the Information Systems (SIAFIs in Brazil) and their associated Chart of Accounts that will have to be standardized. Mexico has now also legislated standardized reporting and a common Chart of Accounts for sub-national operations. This is an issue that should also be addressed at all levels in the EU.

The likelihood of 'game-play' by various levels of government or government agencies cannot be ruled out without a complete and standardized format to categorize the cycle of revenues and expenses, in conjunction with a tracking of the cash flows. A typical problem is the inconsistent treatment of budget coverage – with the frequent exclusion of spending of government agencies or liabilities parked in public enterprises, especially at the sub-national level. This has been problematic in several EU countries during the crisis, including Portugal and Greece.

Standardized information is critical for any serious implementation of fiscal rules in multi-level countries/currency unions. This should be based on the consistent and systematic generation of information in the overlapping manner described above.

The importance of the GFSM 2014 cannot be over-stressed for the efficient management of finances in multi-level countries and in common markets/currency unions. The more complete agenda for the generation of accurate, complete and standardized information will have consequences for developing countries, and also for countries in the EU (such as Portugal and Spain) as they struggle to get to grips with the discovery of liabilities in the extended public sector as well as at the regional and sub-national levels.

PPPs have been encouraged, including by international finance agencies, as a means of leveraging 'private sector' expertise for public investment projects, and also bypassing bureaucratic bottlenecks. This is believed to generate efficiencies, and improved value for money, especially at the subnational level. The expectation is that this will generate additional growth through the efficiencies and additional private finances that would be utilized.

The problem is that governments often see PPPs as a means of circumventing budget constraints, especially although not exclusively at the subnational level. This could generate legal obfuscations, and relevant official agencies or governments are not fully aware either of the liabilities or of the ability of the private partner to meet them. Sometimes, the issue of liability for full costs is avoided, often with respect to public infrastructure (highways and hospitals in Europe); and local governments only include the annual contractual cash payment on the budget, and generally only during the tenure of the local government concerned. Often, there is no provision for the eventual reversion of the assets to the public sector. Further, there is usually a continuation of public interventions with respect to prices or distribution.

There is also incomplete and asymmetric information, with costs and efforts for projects generally known only to the private partner, and significant incentives for either the private contractor or the government to renege (Danau and Vinella, 2012, Ahmad et al., 2014). An example of a growing recognition of limited commitment comes from the UK (which was in the forefront of the PPP revolution). In the 2002–03 upgrading of the London Underground, Metronet, the contracting consortium, could not borrow the full amount of funds needed for the project. Consequently, Transport for London, the decentralized agency responsible, guaranteed 95 percent of Metronet's debt obligations. Metronet failed, and the UK Government (Department of Transport) had to pay Transport for London a sum of £ 1.7 billion to enable it to meet the guarantee (House of Lords, 2010). The direct cost to taxpayers was estimated to be as high as £410 million. Other examples from the UK, e.g., for wind farm projects, show that in these cases the private contribution was financed by complex financial instruments that are tantamount to debt – which has eventually to be taken over by the state.

As a result of the difficulties noted above, the International Accounting Standards Board (2011) has issued a new set of guidelines (IPSAS 32)[9] that forces an upfront accounting for PPPs, and would significantly affect deficits and recognition of liabilities for general government – i.e., for both central and sub-central governments and related agencies. This ensures that the operator is effectively compensated for services rendered during the period of the concession. It requires the government or granting public agency to recognize assets and liabilities in their financial statements, when the following are met:

- The government or granting public agency controls or regulates the services to be provided, the target beneficiaries or the price; and
- The grantor controls, through ownership, beneficial entitlement or otherwise, a significant residual interest in the asset at the end of the arrangement.

A full assessment of liabilities avoids the situation where neither the public sector nor the private partner recognizes the asset/liability at the end of the period. Of course, as has been seen in Ireland and Spain recently (and with Mexican roads in the early 1990s), even if there are no explicit guarantees by the federal or state governments, if there is sufficient pressure on the banking system, it is likely that the state will assume a significant portion of the liabilities. EU governments resisted following the new IPSAS rules, as it would have led to an immediate increase in the measured debt, breaching Maastricht limits in some cases. However, this type of 'satisficing' rules weakens the overall framework under which governments and markets operate.

While cash-based systems are generally deemed insufficient to cover all aspects of budget execution, relatively few developing countries have the capability to operate accrual accounting. Nonetheless, many countries try to monitor the generation of arrears by registering commitments and recognition of liability. This usually entails the utilization of government financial information systems. These have been relatively expensive, but simpler versions are now becoming available for use in smaller jurisdictions – thus in principle permitting sub-national administrations to also operate in an environment as conducive to overall accountability as at the center – however, these systems require standardized generation of information (such as through the common budget classification and Chart of Accounts described above).

The standardized generation of information was a major feature of the reform of sub-national finances carried out in Brazil in the late 1990s, with substantial benefits for the management of the consolidated public finances. A Fiscal Responsibility Law for Brazil was approved in May 2000, which (1) introduced a golden rule provision; (2) imposed new uniform accounting, planning, and transparency requirements on all levels of government – states and municipalities are now required to submit multi-year plans and reports on the use of resources from privatization, social security funds, and contingent liabilities; (3) attempted to enhance the credibility of the central government's no bailout commitment by prohibiting the central government from bailing out any member of the federation and the central bank from exchanging the debt securities of the states for federal public debt securities; and (4) increased the role given to the judiciary and the penal system in the enforcement of certain of its provisions, mandating prison sentences for illegal efforts to issue bonds and stipulating the dismissal of a mayor or governor if debt limits or personnel expenditure ratios are exceeded. However, it is becoming apparent that Brazilian states are moving quickly to establish their own GFMISs (see below). Consequently, the possibility of game-play is reintroduced, and the Fiscal Responsibility Legislation may degenerate into a system that effectively relies on administrative controls by the federal government, based on more aggregate information. Consequently, the new requirement that all sub-national governments must use the IMF's GFSM 2014 format as an integral part of their Chart of Accounts is a sensible measure that also merits consideration in other multi-level countries.

In Germany, all policy is made at the federal level and implementation is by the Länder, both for revenue and spending. The decentralized tax administration with central policy making creates inefficiencies in the operation of taxes, such as VAT (the Court of Accounts regularly publishes estimates of leakages that result – running into several billions of euros annually). Moreover, it prevents major 'own-source' of revenues at the sub-national level, except by variations in administration that in turn generate further inefficiencies. On the spending side, a federal law governs budgetary management at all levels of government, mandating the use of a detailed budgetary classification, a uniform cash-based accounting system, as well as multi-annual financial planning. The law also obliges all levels of government to provide the Financial Planning Council with all necessary information to monitor fiscal developments for the nation as a whole. Länder must provide all relevant information on behalf of their municipalities (Lienert and Jung, 2004). However, the sub-national administration opens up possibilities of non-standard applications of the rules, and the debt brake legislation now requires that the standardized reporting must be complete by 2020. However, as discussed in this chapter, the incentives appear to be moving in the opposite direction (see also Spahn, Chapter 4 in this volume).

In other federal countries, however, sub-national governments can define their own budget and accounting systems. In some cases, lower levels of government are committed to follow internationally accepted budgeting and accounting standards. All US states, for instance, are free to determine the way their budgets are prepared, adopted, executed and reported. There is no constitutional or legislative requirement to harmonize accounting standards. However, state and local governments follow accounting standards developed by the private non-profit Governmental Accounting Standards Board (GASB) in line with generally accepted accounting principles (GAAP). Similarly, Canadian provinces have voluntarily adhered to the standards of the Public Sector Accounting Board, the independent and authoritative standard-setting body for the public sector in Canada.

Some other countries, such as China, have established treasury single accounts at the local level as a mechanism not only to enhance cash management and prevent diversion of government resources and accumulation of arrears but also to improve financial discipline and transparency of local government operations.[10] Despite a technical ban on direct sub-national borrowing, and strict allocations of credit by the Central Government, liabilities at the sub-national level have risen sharply due to borrowing by investment companies owned by the local governments. Initial excitement about PPPs was tempered by the realization that this also involved a buildup of liabilities that would eventually end up at the doors of the Central Government as most local administrations (provinces and below) lack the own-source revenues to service the liabilities, except through inefficient land sales. Consequently, China is now moving from an administrative control mechanism to a more rules-based system permitting access to credit, but with a strong emphasis on the generation of information and aligning sub-national incentives to make it work. This framework has become even more important as the State Council in 2014 relaxed the borrowing constraints, with the establishment of a framework for local governments to issue bonds (State Council Communiqué, September 26, 2014).

In Australia, Commonwealth States and Territories report a minimum amount of financial information in a uniform presentation framework (UPF). While many states and territories continue to prepare their budgets using different budget classification and accounting standards, each jurisdiction attaches data in the UPF format to their budgets.

In some other federations, such as Mexico and Argentina, sub-national governments have been free to define their own budget and accounting systems – although this is changing in Mexico. As a result, local fiscal data is characterized by large inconsistencies in terms of how revenues and expenditures are reported in public accounts. In addition, the lack of an agreed framework or guidelines for presenting state-level fiscal data makes it very difficult to consolidate fiscal accounts at the national level.[11] In the absence of uniform budget and accounting standards, at a minimum a uniform reporting system should be in place at the local level. Credible sanctions for either non-compliance or untimely reporting should be introduced. However, the increasing practice has usually been to reach agreements with lower levels of government on financial reporting requirements. Agreements that do not result in specific sanctions or penalties for breaches of the agreement are generally ineffective. As mentioned above, Mexico is moving towards the standardization of budget processes and reporting at the state level (under an agreement with the States in 2014). But in the absence of an alignment of the information systems, or state-level GFMISs, agreement on the IMF's GFSM 2014 standard (not implemented even at the federal level), and operation of a common chart of accounts by the independent GFMISs, it is hard to see how the new arrangements will be effective, even if sanctions are involved.

All of the above factors affect whether the consequences of sub-national spending can be shifted to higher levels of government, or across generations, and whether there is an absence of a hard-budget constraint at a junior level of government (Rodden et al., 2003). This generally translates into weak or non-existent control over borrowing. The borrowing might be explicit, e.g., through issuance of debt or contracting of loans, or indirect, such as through the buildup of arrears or accounts payable. Under different constitutional arrangements, policy responses vary from enforced controls over sub-national borrowing (generally in unitary states) to voluntary agreements or rules (in federations, as well as in supranational conglomerations of states, such as the EU), to sole reliance on the strictures of the market.[12]

3. CIRCUMVENTING BORROWING LIMITS AND EFFECTIVENESS OF SANCTIONS

The key elements of circumventing administrative controls, binding rules, and cooperative agreements arise through the weaknesses in information on the spending and liabilities being generated. Indeed, weaknesses in the intergovernmental structure may make it hard to implement the sanctions or even recognize the imbalances until there is a serious macroeconomic problem (as has been the case in the crisis in the EU).

Often the credibility of a system of sanctions depends on the relative political power of a jurisdiction in relation to the level of government imposing it – e.g., the EU was unable to impose the Maastricht limits on Germany or France. Similar issues may arise in the context of large and important entities within countries – e.g., Catalunya – that may also harbor separatist tendencies.

The initial success of the Brazilian Fiscal Responsibility Legislation (FRL) lay in the fact that the federal government had a GFMIS (known as the SIAFI) together with a TSA that allowed it to monitor the spending of the sub-national entities in a coordinated and systematic manner – even if they did not fully comply with the GFSM framework to record and manage liabilities. However, increasingly the Brazilian states have chafed at the constraints and have invested in their own GFMISs. Consequently, with the absence of a GFSM format agreed for all states, the Brazilian government would have been faced with a progressive deterioration in quality and timeliness of the information needed to make the FRL work effectively. The new legislation requiring the use of the GFSM 2014 standards by 2015 is a step in the right direction, and recognition of the dangers of a proliferation of standards and systems. Of course a meaningful reform would involve cleaning up spending and revenue assignments to remove distortions and internal barriers to trade. This is part of the fundamental reforms in intergovernmental fiscal relations (especially the tax assignments) needed in Brazil to remove obstacles to sustainable growth.

The Brazilian example has some lessons for the operation of the German Debt Brake that was introduced through a Constitutional Amendment in 2009, in the light of a sharp increase in municipal debt.[13] The 'debt brake' (*Schuldenbremse*) amounts to a full injunction on incurring new debt for the States from 2020 on. This establishes a requirement for structurally balanced budgets, at all levels of government, although the federal government is permitted a margin of 0.35 percent of nominal GDP for macroeconomic stabilization.

As pointed out by Spahn (Chapter 4 in this volume), the impact of the debt brake will be felt most severely at the State level, which, together with the local levels, amounts to 80 percent of all spending on public sector investment at present.[14] True, the debt brake does not imply a total ban on municipal debt, which would conflict with the European Charter,[15] but it will be a considerable constraint, mainly over the longer run. An incentive will also be created for the Länder to push responsibilities and liabilities down to the municipal level.

The only alternative to local borrowing to finance new local infrastructure appears to be increased local taxation (or higher state grants[16]), since reducing social spending does not appear to be an option. Even preserving the level of replacement investments will be difficult under the debt brake in the light of escalating federal standards. Consequently, to make the debt brake work, there will need to be a better application of standards to measure and account for the buildup or change in liabilities. However, the resulting compression should lead to renewed debate about the reforms of the German intergovernmental system that were renewed in the later years of the last 'grand coalition' but were not taken to completion.

CONCLUDING REMARKS

In the final analysis, it is clear that full information is needed for any system of controls or coordination to work. However, this is a necessary and not a sufficient condition, and a policy framework that leads to a hard budget constraint is equally important. This involves the operation of own-source revenues and incentive-compatible transfers.

The own-source revenues are critical in providing the basis for sustainable and accountable access to credit for sub-national investments. And a transfer system that permits similar levels of services to be provided at similar levels of tax effort is critical in ensuring balanced structural change. Thus, any effort to effectively control the buildup of liabilities needs to be placed in the context of a fundamental reform of intergovernmental fiscal relations in many countries, in order to ensure that the preconditions for sustainable growth are met.

NOTES

1. Paper presented at a Conference on the Crisis in Europe and Multilevel Finance, held in Moncalieri in July 2014. Helpful comments from Teresa Ter-Minassian, Ruth Kattumuri and Georg Milbradt are gratefully acknowledged. All errors are mine.
2. There is a growing literature on the incentive problems associated with PPPs – see Danau and Vinella (2013); Ahmad et al. (2014).
3. Indeed, as seen with the recent discussion of the debt limits in countries such as Germany, penalties under the pacts must be implemented to be credible; and there should also be a corresponding capability to monitor compliance with the stipulations (as has recently been illustrated in the case of Greece).
4. See, for instance, Bohn and Inman (1996), Inman (1996), and Poterba (1997).
5. Also see Weingast et al. (1981) who show that bargaining in a legislature comprised of regional representatives will lead to overprovision of spending programs with benefits concentrated in particular regions.
6. For more detailed discussion of soft budget constraints and their consequences see Kornai et al. (2003).
7. This section draws extensively on Ahmad (2015).
8. A number of countries use transition matrices for the reporting of central or general government information to the IMF in the GFSM2001/2014 format. Pakistan, for example, reported data only for the budgetary central government in the latest issue

of the GFS Manual. This is inadequate, as much of the social spending takes place at the sub-national level. As seen in Ahmad et al. (2014), even OECD countries do not conform to the standards – and this may be a factor in the current crisis.
9. See IASB (2011), IPSAS 32. This standard is also likely to affect the guidelines of Eurostat that are not so tightly defined.
10. The creation of a pure TSA implies that all government revenues must flow to the TSA and all spending must be made out of the TSA.
11. Mexico promoted higher transparency and publication of debt and fiscal statistics at the sub-national level by states, by introducing in 2000 a requirement for states of holding credit ratings. Though to date, all states (with the exception of Campeche) have obtained at least two credit ratings from international credit rating agencies, the Mexican authorities recognize that more work remains to be done in the harmonization of accounting and reporting information by the states.
12. See Ter-Minassian and Craig (1997) for a typology, described in greater detail below.
13. The borrowings of municipalities have increased dramatically over the last decade, from €6.9 billion in 2000 to €40.5 billion in 2010.
14. The impact of the debt brake on local governments is indirect through the constraint on state finances including municipalities. How to coordinate and control local sector borrowing is left to state legislation.
15. The European Charter stipulates in Article 9 (8): 'For the purpose of borrowing for capital investment, local authorities shall have access to the national capital market within the limits of the law.'
16. Higher state grants to municipalities would imply higher federal grants to the states, since the latter are severely constrained on the spending side of the budget (wage bill) and have practically no own taxing powers.

REFERENCES

Ahmad, E. (2015), 'Governance and institutions: the role of multilevel fiscal institutions in generating sustainable and inclusive growth', in E. Ahmad and G. Brosio (eds), *Handbook of Multilevel Finance*, Cheltenham, UK and Northampton, MA, USA: Edward Elgar, pp. 200–230.

Ahmad, E., A. Bhattacharya, A. Vinella and K. Xiao (2014), 'Involving the private sector and PPPs in financing public investment', G24 Group of Countries.

Ambrosanio, F. and M. Bordignon (2015), 'Normative versus positive theories of revenue assignments in federations', in E. Ahmad and G. Brosio (eds), *Handbook of Multilevel Finance*, Cheltenham, UK and Northampton, MA, USA: Edward Elgar, pp. 231–63.

Bhattacharya, A., M. Romani and N. Stern (2012), 'Infrastructure for development: meeting the challenge', LSE in collaboration with G24.

Blöchliger, H. (2015), 'The challenge of measuring fiscal decentralization', in E. Ahmad and G. Brosio (eds), *Handbook of Multilevel Finance*, Cheltenham, UK and Northampton, MA, USA: Edward Elgar, pp. 617–32.

Bohn, H. and R.P. Inman (1996), 'Balanced budget rules and public deficits: evidence from US States', *Carnegie-Rochester Conference Series on Public Policy*, **45** (1), December, 13–76.

Bordignon, M., P. Manasse and G. Tabellini (2001), 'Optimal regional distribution under asymmetric information', *American Economic Review*, **91** (3), 709–23.

Buchanan, J., C.K. Rowley, and R.D. Tollinson, (1987), *Deficits: The Political Economy of Budget Deficits*, Oxford: Basil Blackwell.

Dafflon, B. (2015), 'The assignment of functions to decentralized government: from theory to practice', in E. Ahmad and G. Brosio (eds), *Handbook of Multilevel Finance*, Cheltenham, UK and Northampton, MA, USA: Edward Elgar, pp. 163–99.

Danau, D. and A. Vinella (2014), 'Public–private contracting under limited commitment', *Journal of Public Economic Theory*, **17** (1), 78–110.

Escolano, J., L. Eyraud, M.M. Badia, J. Sarnes and A. Tuladhar (2012), 'Fiscal performance, institutional design and decentralization in European countries', IMF Working Paper WP/12/45.

European Union: The Maastricht Treaty, http://eur-lex.europa.eu/en/treaties/dat/12002E/pdf/12002E_EN.pdf.

House of Lords (2010), 'Private finance projects and off-balance sheet debt', First Report of Session 2009–10, Volumes I and II, Report and Evidence, HL Paper 63, I–II.

Inman, R. (1996), 'Do balanced budget rules work? U.S. experience and possible lessons for the EMU', NBER Working Paper No. 5838.

Kornai, J., E. Maskin and G. Roland (2003), 'Understanding the soft budget constraint', *Journal of Economic Literature*, **41** (4), 1095–136.

Lienert, I. and M.-K. Jung (2004), 'The legal framework for budget systems: an international comparison', *OECD Journal on Budgeting*, Special Issue, **4** (3).

Moesen, W.A. (1993), 'Community public finance in the perspective of EMU: Assignment rules, the status of the budget constraint and young fiscal federalism in Belgium', in Commission of the European Communities (ed.), *The Economics of Community Public Finance*, Luxembourg: Office for Official Publications of the European Communities, pp. 167–90.

Paixão, M. and R. Baleiras (2013), 'Analysis of debt limits in the regional and local finance bills', CFP Occasional Paper 01/2013.

Poterba, J. (1997), 'Do budget rules work?', in A. Auerbach (ed.), *Fiscal Policy: Lessons from Economic Research*, Cambridge, MA: MIT Press, pp. 53–86.

Poterba, J. and J. von Hagen (eds) (1999), *Fiscal Institutions and Fiscal Performance*, Cambridge, MA: National Bureau of Economic Research.

Persson, T. and G. Tabellini (1996), 'Federal fiscal constitutions: risk sharing and moral hazard', *Econometrica*, **64** (3), 623–46.

Rodden, J., G.S. Eskeland, and J. Litvack (eds) (2003), *Fiscal Decentralization and the Challenge of Hard Budget Constraints*, Cambridge, MA: MIT Press.

Ter-Minassian, T. and J. Craig (1997), 'Control of subnational government borrowing', in T. Ter-Minassian (ed.), *Fiscal Federalism in Theory and Practice*, Washington, DC: International Monetary Fund, pp. 156–72.

von Hagen, J. and I. Harden (1994), 'National budget processes and fiscal performance', *European Economy – Reports and Studies*, **3**, 311–418.

Weingast, B., K. Shepsle and C. Johnson (1981), 'The political economy of benefits and costs: a neoclassical approach to redistributive politics', *Journal of Political Economy*, **89**, 642–64.

3. History of the constitutional debt limits in Germany and the new 'debt brake': experiences and critique

Georg Milbradt

1. THE SITUATION IN POST-WAR WEST GERMANY

To understand the reasons behind the concept of the German debt brake,[1] which was subsequently introduced in a modified form at the European level, we have to look to history. The German population lost its monetary assets twice in the twentieth century. The first time was after the hyperinflation crisis of 1923 that followed World War I, when currency inflation resulted in an incredible exchange rate of 1 trillion old Marks: 1 RM (Reichsmark).[2] The second time occurred after World War II, when the currency reform of 1948 resulted in an exchange rate of 100 RM: 6.5 DM (Deutsche Mark)[3] in the West, and greater losses in other German territories. A West German bailout helped to avoid a third sharp devaluation after the fall of communism in East Germany.[4] The reason behind these drastic devaluations of currency was that German governments financed their expenditures primarily via debt, and used the printing press directly or indirectly. The resulting hyperinflation caused great hardship and is often considered a key element in the ascent to power of the fascist government. Therefore, aversion to debt financing and inflationary policy is deeply enshrined in German collective memory.

Because of our turbulent modern history, German economic thinking and policy after World War II was deeply influenced by Ordoliberalism, an alternative liberal answer to the new fiscal challenges, developed and embraced by a group of German scholars and politicians. Among the most prominent advocates was the famous father of the DM and the economic miracle, the federal economic minister Ludwig Erhard, who later became chancellor. One of the main political demands of proponents was 'fiscal and monetary stability', which was politically interpreted as the wish for an independent central bank and a deficit limit for the public budgets. Both principles were enshrined in the 1949 constitution (known

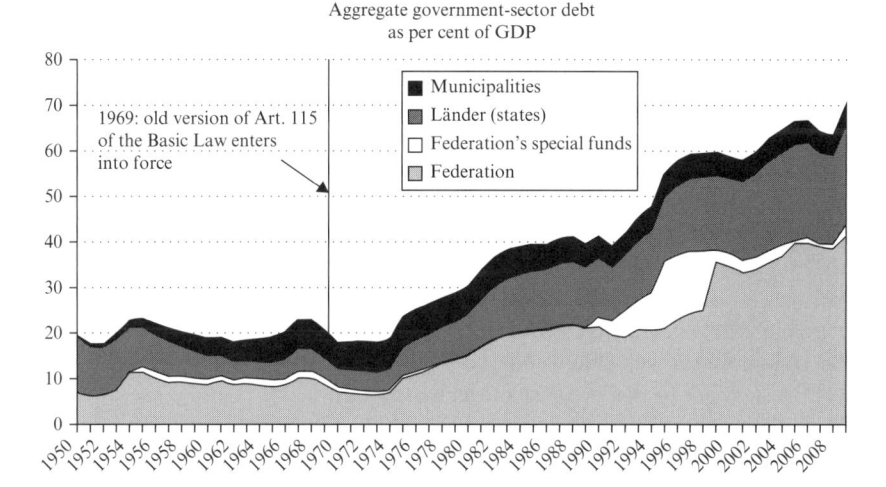

History of the constitutional debt limits in Germany 67

Figure 3.1 *Aggregate government-sector debt (as a percentage of GDP)*

Source: Federal Ministry of Finance (2012), *Compendium on the Federation's Budget Rule as Set Out in Article 115 of the Basic Law*, Berlin.

as Grundgesetz, abbreviated GG, or Basic Law) of the new Federal Republic of Germany.

The constitutional debt provision in Article 115 GG allowed borrowing only for extraordinary purposes and usually only for profitable ones.[5] This is in accordance with the classical opinion that borrowing is acceptable for capital expenditures if the return on investment covers amortization. Similar provisions existed for the German states and municipalities. Under the influence of Ordoliberalism, legal scholars interpreted this clause strictly.

The currency reform of 1948 had reduced the ratio of all public government debt to around 20 per cent of GDP. For the following 25 years, the overall ratio remained more or less stable. However, as is shown by Figure 3.1, after 1950 the share of the municipalities' debt rose, which indicates that this development was in accordance with the debt provision because German municipalities executed around two-thirds of all public investments.

2. THE FIRST RECESSION AND THE 'GREAT PUBLIC FINANCE REFORM' OF 1969

Times changed when West Germany had to endure its first, relatively mild, recession in 1966/67. GDP decreased by 0.2 per cent and the unemployment rate rose from 0.7 to 2.2 per cent. In comparison to the current economic climate, these figures may seem negligible, but for a nation that had experienced an economic miracle in the years following the end of World War II, it was a shock. For the first time, Keynesian recipes were discussed and enacted.

A special law passed in 1967 allowed the federation and the states to adopt countercyclical fiscal policies, especially debt-financed expenditures or tax cuts to increase macroeconomic demand. It also stated, however, that surpluses should be made during periods of economic boom. Initially, politicians used the new measures very cautiously. As Figure 3.1 shows, the debt ratio increased to over 20 per cent from 1966 to 1968 but in 1969 the public sector was able to balance its budgets. In the following years, the debt ratio sank to the pre-crisis level once again.

The recession, the implementation of Keynesian ideas, and the general dissatisfaction with the post-war federal structure led in 1969 to the first extensive constitutional reform, known as the 'Great Public Finance Reform', which came into force on 1 January 1970. This profound change was made possible by the accession of a grand coalition government to office after the fall of Chancellor Erhard in 1966. It was able to lean on the two-thirds majority – which is necessary for constitutional amendment – that it enjoyed in both houses of parliament.

The 'Great Public Finance Reform' changed fiscal relations and competences between the federation and states. It called for greater cooperation between the levels of government, made a number of changes in relation to, among other things, tax distribution and fiscal equalization, and introduced new debt limits. Borrowing was no longer restricted to extraordinary needs and profitable expenditures, but could be used more widely.

Now the deficit limit of Article 115 GG was defined as 'the sum of planned investment expenditures in the budget', but exceptions were allowed 'to avert disturbances of macroeconomic equilibrium'. The majority of the states enacted similar constitutional debt provisions, although changes on the municipal level were not so extensive. Additional financial regulations expanded the debt limits further: the respective federal and state laws defined investment expenditures as gross expenditures but borrowing as net borrowing.

During and after the oil crisis of 1973, the federal governments, now led by social democratic chancellors, used these new measures extensively. Due to rising unemployment, which became more and more structural, the federal government pursued an expansionary budget policy and enlarged the welfare state. Due to high deficits, the debt–GDP ratio rose from under 20 per cent to around 40 per cent at the beginning of the 1980s (see Figure 3.1).

Motivated by the economic difficulties and other political problems, the

Free Democrats abandoned their old coalition partners in 1982 and formed a new government alongside the Christian Democrats under Chancellor Helmut Kohl. The new government returned to a more traditional economic and fiscal policy that would stabilize the economy and the debt level, but which still retained a relatively high level of structural unemployment.

The majority of German states pursued similar policies. Operating on the basis that they had to avert a disturbance of macroeconomic equilibrium, signified by the high unemployment rates, they ran higher deficits. The state debts rose as well. However, the municipalities only increased their indebtedness along the lines of GDP growth so that their level of debt remained more or less unchanged, as Figure 3.1 shows.

However, at the same time as deficits and the debt ratio were rising, the public investment to GDP ratio was falling dramatically – net investments after 2000 fell nearly to or below zero, see Figure 3.2. That leads to the

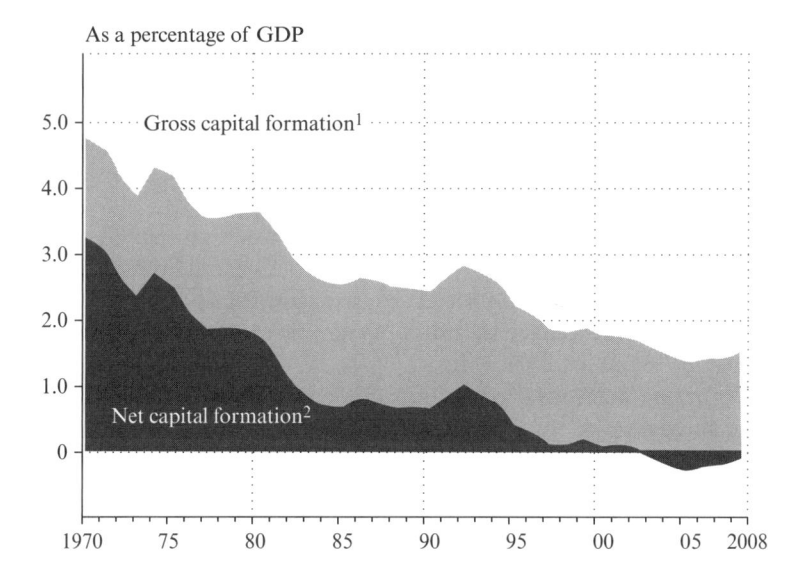

Notes:
* As defined in the national accounts; central, state and local government and security funds. Until 1990, Western Germany.
1 Gross fixed capital formation, changes in inventories and acquisitions, less disposals of valuables.
2 Gross capital formation less consumption of fixed capital.

Source: Federal Statistical Office and Deutsche Bundesbank (2009), 'The development of government investment', *Monthly Report*, **61** (10), 15–34.

Figure 3.2   Government gross and net capital formation (as a percentage of GDP)

conclusion that the increase in debt was not used primarily to increase investment, but to finance current expenditures, particularly the welfare state.

The negative experiences of Keynesianism and demand-side economics caused a shift in the public debate once again. The focus was now placed on the supply side, economic reforms, and privatization.

3. REUNIFICATION AND THE BEGINNING OF THE EUROPEAN CURRENCY UNION

In 1990, after the Berlin Wall came down and the Iron Curtain fell in Europe, Germany was able to reunify. It soon became apparent, however, that the East German economy was in a critical condition and that huge differences existed in relation to wages and productivity. The introduction of the DM in the East and the trade unions' policy of adjusting East German wages to the Western level led to massive unemployment in the East. High expectations in the East, which were encouraged by West German politicians in the first federal elections after unification, could only be fulfilled via the use of an enormous financial aid package, and even then the hopes of East Germans could be met only partly.

It was self-evident that such a programme, which amounted to more than a hundred billion DM per year, could not and should not be financed through increasing taxes and social security contributions alone, but also via debt. The extraordinary situation of reunification provided ample justification for increased borrowing.

The other momentous event to impact German debt policy in the 1990s was the agreement of the EU member states to establish a currency union and prepare for its introduction. For Germany, an absolute precondition for participation and success was that this currency union emulated the German DM tradition. Therefore, the primary rules for the ECB and the Euro system were copied from the old Bundesbank, in particular those relating to independence and the explicit legal prohibition of state financing. To strengthen this position, two important clauses were inserted into the Maastricht treaty: debt and deficit limits of 60 per cent and 3 per cent of GDP respectively (the latter underpinned by sanctions); and a prohibition of a bailout by one member state of another.

When the talks on the euro began in 1990/91, the newly united Germany underestimated the burden of reunification and believed that fulfilling the proposed debt and deficit criteria would be simple. At that time, politicians did not realize how expensive the unification process would eventually become and that the merger would increase public debt from 40 per cent to 60 per cent of GDP by the end of the '90s. The German government did not anticipate problems with the deficit criterion either. When parliament ratified the Maastricht Treaty, the government neglected to introduce national legal provisions to secure the fulfilment of the debt and deficit criteria within the German federal system, which is based on financial autonomy and independence between the federation and the various states.

4. CONSTITUTIONAL REFORM OF FEDERALISM AND THE NEW DEBT BRAKE

At the end of the '90s, it became evident that the German system had to be fundamentally overhauled. Reform was needed to adapt not only to a now united and more heterogeneous country, but also to competitiveness challenges, to the introduction of a common currency, and to globalization. The main topics under discussion were the federal system and the welfare state, as both seemed to be no longer sufficient to cope with the emerging challenges, and would in their current state become financially unsustainable in the future due to demographic developments.

The constitutional provisions of 1969 did not guarantee fulfilment of the EU deficit criterion. Germany failed to meet it during the recession between 2001 and 2005 and the EU Commission began a deficit procedure. The increase in the level of debt and the deficit to above the Maastricht criteria, and the implicit hidden debt in the non-funded social security system (demographic change!), made a reduction of debt and a reform of the constitutional deficit limits of 1969 politically compelling.

As the limit of borrowing stipulated under the clause of 1969 was set as the amount required for planned investment expenditures, parliaments often passed budget bills with an artificially high amount of capital expenditure and a high level of borrowing. Governments subsequently used the entire credit amount but could not or did not intend to execute all planned capital expenditures. Consequently, at the end of a fiscal year the deficit surpassed investment expenditures. In many other cases, governments justified exceeding the deficit limit by arguing that this was necessary to avert disturbance of macroeconomic equilibrium, even in cases of an economic boom.

Federal and state governments often circumvented or even broke the debt provision, despite the many judgments passed by the constitutional courts at the request of the respective parliamentary opposition. The main purpose of the reform of 1969 was to allow anticyclical demand policies, but experience demonstrated that the conditions which justified such policies were ill defined, misused, and de facto asymmetrical. Surpluses and a reduction of debt in boom times hardly ever occurred – never at the federal level and very seldom at the state level. Before 2009, a high growth rate for a number of years reduced the overall GDP debt level.

With the prediction of a shrinking population in Germany, there was no longer a clear justification for the financing of public investment expenditures via debt, especially gross investments. With intergenerational equity in mind, future generations should be relieved of debt burden.

Another pertinent issue was how to enforce the deficit limits. Through sanctions or even automatic sanctions? Via supervision? Who would be responsible for enforcement? Independent bodies? How could this process be organized in a federation with a high degree of budgetary autonomy? It is no coincidence that the German debate of the late '90s and early 2000s closely resembled much of the European debt discussion that accompanied the financial crisis nearly a decade later.

5. THE NEW 'DEBT BRAKE'

Shortly after the turn of the new millennium, in 2002, the Swiss Federation introduced new debt limits under the title of 'Schuldenbremse' or debt brake, via a referendum. Some Swiss cantons had already passed similar legislation, and others followed suit.

Shortly before the passing of the Swiss national debt brake, Leukerbad, a very small municipality in Vallais, had become insolvent. The creditors, in particular banks, sought a bailout from the canton or the confederation. Both of these levels of government refused and the creditors lost a great deal of money. Therefore, banks began to examine the financial situation of Swiss public debtors more closely, and with this came the threat of interest rate rises. In this situation, it was very much in the interest of those cantons which had no debt brakes before to introduce them in order to enjoy lower interest rates. Under the Swiss federal system the federation, the cantons, and the municipalities finance their expenditures primarily through fees, individual taxes, or tax surcharges. Therefore, it is not only in the interest of financing banks that their creditors be solvent, thereby limiting losses linked to insolvency, but is also in the interest of the electorate, for whom an unsound fiscal policy may lead to higher taxes.

The Swiss example extensively influenced the German debate[6] on how to reform the debt rules. The implementation of a constitutional reform became easier as the second grand coalition government to have a two-thirds majority in both houses, required to amend the basic law, entered office in 2005 (and held office until 2009). The first part of the reform was enacted in 2006 under the title Föderalismusreform I (Federalism

History of the constitutional debt limits in Germany 73

Reform I). This amendment mandated a stricter separation of competencies and the reduction of co-financing. The second part of the reform, Föderalismusreform II (Federalism Reform II), was passed in 2009 with the new debt rules at its core. In contrast to the Swiss example, the German debt brake was top-down (the federation obliged the states to introduce debt brakes) rather than bottom-up (the cantons introduced the limitations voluntarily), which can be attributed to the important differences in the constitutional structure of federalism in both countries. Whereas in Switzerland there is a clear separation of the federal levels and units and the principle of responsibility, liability, and tax autonomy, the German system is still based on a cooperative model with closer interdependencies in relation to taxes, expenditures, and overlapping competencies.

During the discussion of new debt limitations, the 2008 global financial crisis broke out. To combat the recession of 2008/09 the federal government increased expenditures and cut taxes, resulting in high deficits. To stabilize the banking system the government was required to bail out a number of private and state banks and transfer their toxic assets to government-backed 'bad banks', increasing the debt ratio dramatically, eventually to over 80 per cent (see Figure 3.3). To justify this huge increase, politicians promised to limit public deficits more strictly through the new reform and to avoid the mistakes of the past.

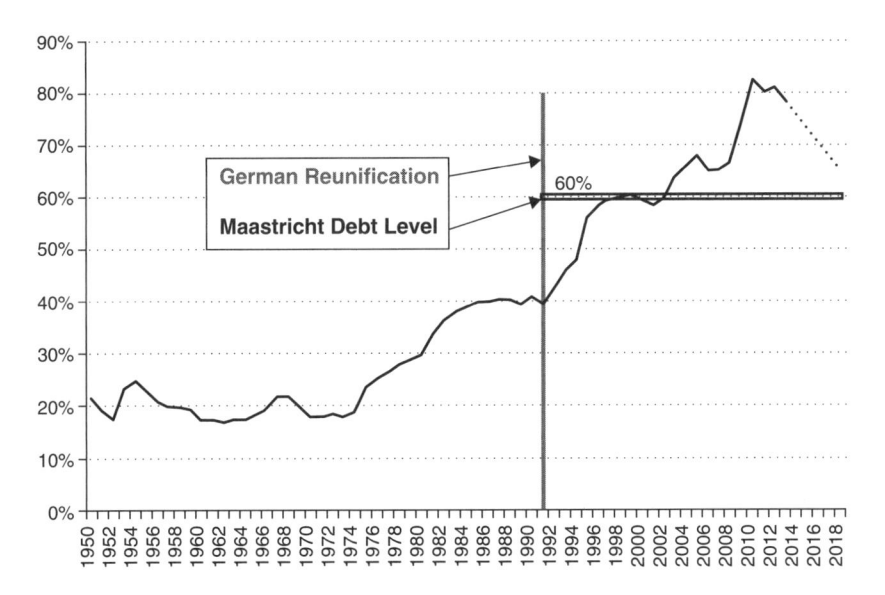

Figure 3.3   GDP–debt ratio and the Maastricht debt level criterion

The new debt-limiting provisions of article 109 and 115 GG, often referred to as the 'debt brake', are very detailed and extensive, quite unusual for a constitution. They are, like their predecessors, deficit limits only and therefore indirect debt limitations. At the heart of the provisions is a strict general balanced budget rule that allows annual deficits at the federation level of a maximum of 0.35 per cent of GDP from 2016, and no deficit at all for states from 2020. The new articles do allow for deviations from this for reasons of macroeconomic fiscal policy. Deviations, however, may only occur symmetrically, and are controlled by a special account – the so-called control account – in order to level out deviation over the business cycle. Moreover, the planned amounts were no longer the decisive factor, but instead the figures realized.

The new provisions also allow for exceptions in the event of natural disasters and 'unusual emergency situations beyond governmental control and substantially harmful to the state's financial capacity', providing an absolute majority of the Bundestag approve and there is an amortization plan which is different to the EU fiscal compact.[7]

The reform also established a stability council to control the new provision and monitor financial performance. The council consists of the federal finance minister and his state colleagues plus the federal economic minister. But, unfortunately, this is a purely political body. Because of the European fiscal compact the lawmakers also created an independent committee, responsible for assessing the application of the European provisions and preparing reports for the stability council and the public.[8]

Alongside this, specific transitory clauses were added to regulate the time between the introduction of the constitutional amendments and the date of strict application. This measure was taken to assist those states in particular financial distress to consolidate their budgets up to 2020.

6. EVALUATION

As the new rules will not be fully implemented and operational for some time, currently there is limited experience of working under them. The real test will come when the whole system experiences real financial and political stress. Therefore, a final evaluation is not yet possible. However, when compared with the old provisions of 1970 that were often misused and circumvented, the rules have been improved.[9]

A number of important unresolved issues and questions remain, however, because the debt brake rules are founded on great deal of compromise and unrealistic expectations. This is often the case in politics, especially under the cooperative German system.

6.1 Enforcement of the Debt Brake

Ultimately, Germany was unable to solve the fundamental question of how to enforce rules in a federation with a high degree of financial autonomy. In the past, the majority of the rulings of the federal and state constitutional courts were declaratory judgments. The courts declared several budget laws unconstitutional because of violation of the old debt limits. They ruled in many cases that a claimed macroeconomic disequilibrium had not existed. These judgments had little impact, however, because the ruling came after the budget year and could not influence the execution of the budget.

More recently, however, the courts appear to have adopted a different attitude. In late 2010 the opposition in the North Rhine-Westphalian state parliament applied for a preliminary injunction of the state constitutional court against a supplementary budget that had been adopted by the parliament but which violated the old deficit limit. The court granted the injunction and prohibited the extra borrowing.[10]

The court confirmed its ruling a few months later in the main proceedings.[11] The crucial point was that the court issued its judgments very quickly. This could indicate a new policy for the courts in future.

As a result of past experience, Germans tend not to trust politicians because they believe they can be tempted to misuse their power, especially in relation to public debt. Germans believe more in the efficacy of rules than in discretionary actions by politicians, and not only in the sphere of economics. Therefore, the existence of the independent central bank and strong and independent constitutional courts, especially the federal constitutional court with its lofty reputation, is unsurprising. Nevertheless, enforcing the debt brake through legal actions is no general solution.

In the public debate that preceded the constitutional amendment, many participants argued that the existence of a clear rule, a critical press, and public scrutiny would oblige politicians to obey the rule or risk losing office in the next election. I doubt that this self-regulating process will work under conditions of real stress in the German federal system, with its nearly unlimited spending autonomy of the states, because of the danger of moral hazard inherent in our specific federal construction.

In legal practice the states de facto guarantee debts at the local level to enable them to borrow money at low rates of interest. Usually the rating of the municipalities is similar to that of the respective states. To avoid moral hazard issues, the municipal codes of the different states restrict the financial autonomy of the local level. State institutions act as supervisors. They review the local budgets, and debt financing in particular, to prevent over-indebtedness and illiquidity. They can intervene in the municipalities through special instructions and prohibitions to oblige the local authorities to act responsibly in financial matters. As ultima ratio (or the last resort), they can remove the mayor and the local council from office and appoint a commissioner to govern the municipality. So in this case, reducing autonomy ultimately solves the conflict between autonomy versus solidarity.

The legal situation at the state and federal levels is very different. The basic law establishes no hierarchy in budget matters.[12] In principle, the federation and the states govern themselves autonomously in this field. No effective supervision or sanctions could be introduced in the debt brake constitutional amendment, only by the aforementioned stability council, which can provide advice but has no enforcement powers. The only exception to this is that the stability council can cut the aid granted to distressed states if they do not comply, but then only during the transition period that ends in 2020.[13] The reason for this very limited power is that those states that experience financial problems have at least a one-third minority, or even a majority, in the Bundesrat, thereby enabling them to block constitutional amendments that are seen as inconvenient or harmful. In the past, states have rejected stricter budget constraints and have demanded or anticipated more money from the federation or the other states.

The legal situation of indebted states improved as a result of a constitutional court ruling in 1992. This ruling stated that in the case of an extreme budget crisis distressed states could sue for aid. This is because in the German federation a principle of communality (bündisches Prinzip) exists which is not written explicitly into the constitution. To avoid insolvency and over-indebtedness, the federation and the other states must bail them out as ultima ratio.[14] This ruling opened the door to moral hazard problems.

In a new decision taken in 2006 in relation to Berlin, the constitutional court moderated its earlier verdict and dismissed the case, judging that the city-state had not made every effort to help itself.[15] Therefore, the conflict between solidarity versus autonomy remains unsolved. If you want unlimited solidarity and a bailout, you are required to relinquish autonomy, which contradicts the basic idea of federalism. The states find themselves under the supervision of the federation, just as the municipalities are under the supervision of their respective state, which ultimately grants them a bailout. Some would accept this solution because, when compared with other federal countries, German federalism is unique, with only limited autonomy of the states outside the budget.

I do not share this view because I am in favour of federalism as a suitable form of government for Germany. The great advantage is that autonomy increases competition and freedom. If one accepts this argument, then the principle of communality (based purely on court rulings) which led to bailouts should be abolished, as in many other federations. The examples of Switzerland and the USA demonstrate that this is possible and it works. If one favours autonomy and freedom, one must accept responsibility, liability, and default, as in the private sector. Consequently, states must have sufficient tax autonomy, which they have lacked in the past and remains insufficient. If one favours solidarity and wishes to avoid insolvency, greater central powers are required.[16]

It is unlikely that the German debt brake alone will be able to resolve this problem. Germany has copied Switzerland, but has neglected to properly take into account the differing federal structure of its neighbour. On the state level in particular, the risk of moral hazard may hinder Germany's ability to permanently reach a balanced budget.

6.2 Circumventions

While the new debt rules are more precise than the older 1970 provisions, a number of other problems still remain. The EU definition of deficit, which Germany applies for its debt brake, can be manipulated. Typically a deficit (an annual figure) is a representation of a change in debt over the year. Therefore, a deficit represents an increase in the level of debt, and a surplus represents a reduction. In other words, the sum of the deficits and surpluses over time defines the level of debt. However, the EU is currently amending its definition of deficit and excluding certain items from the deficit which do increase the debt level, such as non-recurrent effects, but which will no longer form part of the deficit definition. This definition is a gateway to manipulation or creative bookkeeping. As the German debt brake is a deficit limit, it may not necessarily be able to guarantee a fall in absolute or relative levels of debt in times of stress.

Closely connected to this problem is the issue of defining what constitutes the public sector. We must avoid the practice of hiding public debt and counting it as private debt in statistics; i.e., private institutions execute public expenditures and borrow money under a direct or indirect public guarantee.

Public accounting can lead to another loophole. How can the issue of governments deliberately building arrears to avoid official deficits be addressed? These types of arrears were a significant problem in a number of distressed Euro countries such as Greece and Italy. Until now, this practice has not been undertaken in Germany, perhaps because a functioning court system can enforce due payments and penalties for non-performance.

6.3 Municipalities and the Social Security System

Municipalities do not fall under the scope of the German constitutional debt brake provision but their finances do constitute part of the national public debt.[17] In the past, the traditional balanced budget rules, which were not changed in substance, guaranteed that debt at the local level as a whole was kept under control and that no specific debt problem existed. However, this does not apply to individual municipalities. Structural problems, ill-conceived fiscal equalization schemes, bad local management, or careless state supervision have resulted in cities in some areas such as the Ruhr district in North Rhine Westphalia accumulating illegally unsustainable debt.

Under the German system the state is eventually required to bailout these indebted cities, and in turn this can lead to a deficit which is no longer permitted and which increases the overall level of debt. If these bailout activities are excluded from the deficit because they are non-recurrent effects under the Eurostat definition, this demonstrates the aforementioned problem: that the debt brake alone cannot guarantee a real limitation of debt. The hope is that the states to whom the municipalities belong will find a solution to this problem, but, unfortunately, the states with the highest municipal indebtedness are also the states that possess the highest levels of state debt. When North Rhine Westphalia, economically the most important German state, has neither the ability nor the will to solve the problem, this might be an indication of moral hazard.

Just as with the municipalities, the German debt brake does not apply to the finances of the social security system, which is supervised by the government. In some distressed countries, Greece in particular, the public health sector had considerable hidden debts, which ultimately increased the national debt. As long as the principle that deficits and surpluses lead to a more or less automatic adaptation of the contribution rate governs the system, this exclusion cannot endanger the debt brake.

7. CONCLUSION

The German debt brake is the latest attempt to avoid deficits and limit public debt. It is better designed and much more precise than its predecessor, but is far from perfect. As rules, which can be circumvented or cannot be enforced, often seduce political actors, it is likely that even these new rules will require further amendment to achieve their objective.

Probably we will face similar problems on the Eurozone level as well, as the European rules are not so strict as the German ones. The Europeans,

History of the constitutional debt limits in Germany 79

with no central state, would not be able to solve the problem of autonomy and sovereignty of countries versus solidarity (including bailouts) within its existing structure either.

NOTES

1. Due to be implemented by the end of the decade.
2. From 1873 on the mark (M) was the official currency unit of the Germany and corresponded to 0.358423g of gold. Unofficially it was known as the Goldmark. With the beginning of WWI the gold standard was abandoned. The RM (Rentenmark, later Reichsmark), with an initial exchange rate of 4.2 US$, was legal tender from 1923 until 1948.
3. The Western powers introduced the DM in their occupation zones, which later became the Federal Republic of Germany. The Soviets followed on with a separate currency in their zone of occupation, also initially known as DM, but later renamed Mark der DDR (Mark of the GDR).
4. Under the terms of the currency union of 1990 between East and West Germany that preceded the political reunification, the DDR Mark was exchanged into the Western DM with a basic rate of 1:1, and 2:1 for larger amounts of money.
5. The respective provision of the Weimar Constitution of 1919 was very similar, but did not prevent the use of the printing press for government purposes, especially for war and post-war financing.
6. See Sachverständigenrat zur Begutachtung der gesamtwirtschaftlichen Entwicklung, *Staatsverschuldung wirksam begrenzen, Expertise im Auftrag des Bundesministers für Wirtschaft und Technologie*, March 2007.
7. This chapter does not address the differences between the German debt brake and the somewhat weaker European provisions of the Fiscal Compact. See H.T. Burret and J. Schellenbach (2013), 'Implementation of the Fiscal Compact in the Euro Area Member States', German Council of Economic Advisers, Working Papers 08/2013, November, partly updated 2014, pp. 14ff.
8. Gesetz zur innerstaatlichen Umsetzung des Fiskalvertrags (FiskVtrUG) of 15 July 2013, BGBl. I S. 2398, Article 2, Number 2.
9. Nevertheless the fundamental critique advanced by politicians, trade unionists and Keynesian scholars is that the idea behind the German debt brake (and therefore the debt brake generally) is based on an erroneous concept. Critics argue that it reduces legitimate policy options and endangers full employment and growth policies. The real problem is a long-lasting deficit of macroeconomic demand. See G.A. Horn, A. Truger and C. Proaño (2009), 'Stellungnahme zum Entwurf eines Begleitgesetzes zur zweiten Föderalismusreform BT Drucksache 16/12400 und Entwurf eines Gesetzes zur Änderung des Grundgesetzes BT Drucksache 16/12410', Policy Brief, Institut für Makroökonomie und Konjunkturforschung, May, available at: http://www.boeckler.de/pdf/pb_imk_05_2009.pdf.
10. Verfassungsgerichtshofes des Landes Nordrhein-Westfalen, VerfG 19/10 (18 January 2011).
11. Verfassungsgerichtshofes des Landes Nordrhein-Westfalen, VerfG 12010 (15 March 2011).
12. Article 109, section 1 GG.
13. Article 143d, section 2 GG.
14. BverfGE, Vol. 86, p. 148 ff.
15. BVerfG, Urteil, 2 BvF 3/03 (19 October 2003), available at: http://www.bverfg.de/entscheidungen/fs20061019_2bvf000303.html.
16. The same unsolved problems also exist on the European level. The Maastricht Treaty

introduced the famous no bailout clause within the Euro zone. Under the pressure of the financial crisis, this clause was neglected and rescue funds introduced to avert a break-up of the Euro zone. The ECB is supporting the rescue initiative by its monetary policy with the same result, a hidden bailout. As a central European state with real supervisory powers does not exist, it is impossible to properly enforce the European debt rules. Nor has new legislation like the 'Six Pack' and the Fiscal Compact solved the moral hazard problem yet either. The member states are not willing to transfer enough budgetary sovereignty to Brussels. Therefore, there are two solutions available to the EU. The Euro zone can create a powerful central state with supervision and sanction powers with the ability to oblige the member states to respect the debt rules of the Euro zone and to avoid its break-up. The alternative to this centralized solution (more centralized for example than the USA or Switzerland) is to return to the pre-crisis no bailout rule and accept state insolvencies.
17. Therefore, the debt brake of the European fiscal compact includes the municipal debt.

PART II

Incipient Problems in the Biggest Countries in Europe

4. Multi-level finance and the Euro crisis: the German experience
Paul Bernd Spahn

1. PORTRAYING THE IMPACT OF THE CRISIS ON THE OVERALL ECONOMY

The financial crisis of 2008/09 had a severe and immediate impact on the German economy because of its high export dependency. Exports, which had grown by more than 10 per cent per annum in 2006 and 2007, produced a comparably weak rate of growth in 2008, and fell by 15 per cent in 2009. This resulted from financial uncertainties and poor growth performance in the economies of Germany's trading partners. But export growth resumed vigorously after the peak crisis year, to level out only more recently – again mirroring the dynamics of growth in important economies, notably in Asia and the European Union. What is often overlooked, however, is the fact that exports and imports of goods and services are positively correlated in Germany. From 2004 to 2012 the import elasticity of export growth was 1.095, indicating that German exports trigger a more than proportional response of imports from its trading partners, both positive (when growing) and negative (during crisis). True, German net exports, which had reached an all-time high in US dollar terms just before the crisis, experienced a sharp decline in 2009, but they recovered strongly afterwards.

Export growth is intimately related to the investment cycle in Germany. Gross fixed capital formation moved almost in tandem with exports, which exacerbated the negative impact on overall economic growth during the crisis. Other components of domestic absorption could counteract the external shock to some degree. Private consumption remained rather flat during the peak of the crisis, while public consumption produced some intended counter-cyclical effects, especially in 2008/09, albeit being insufficient to compensate the fallout produced by foreign trade and gross investment. Overall the growth rate of GDP dropped by 5.1 per cent in 2009, but recovered quickly thereafter (with 4.0 per cent in 2010 and 3.3 per cent in 2011, respectively).

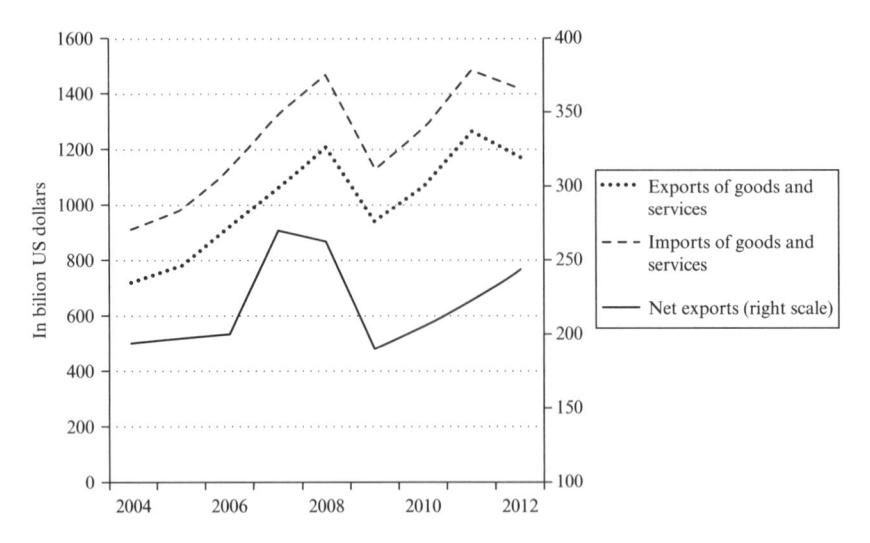

Source: World Bank, *World Development Indicators.*

Figure 4.1 Exports and imports of goods and services; net exports

In order to cushion the impact of the crisis, the federal government initiated two programs, the second of which (January 2009) was rather far reaching.[1] Among other things, it released about 10 billion euros for local public investments in addition to 4 billion euros for federal government investment. The latter assumed 75 per cent of the costs for local public fixed capital formation, which leveraged roughly 13.5 billion euros of additional local spending. The focus was on education (especially kindergartens, schools and universities) and infrastructure (especially transport, hospitals, urban development, information technology and energy efficiency). Moreover the government was able to facilitate and accelerate the spending on public investments through deregulation, and by simplifying the procurement procedures.

The policy was combined with a number of measures to stimulate private demand of both households and companies. Inter alia, it reduced the marginal tax rate for low incomes from 15 to 14 per cent and increased the tax-free income threshold; it provided one-time support for families with children; it launched a subsidy for public health insurance; and it paid a singular environmental bonus to car owners deciding to scrap their car (which, to qualify for the payment, had to be at least nine years old) in exchange for a new, environmentally friendly vehicle.

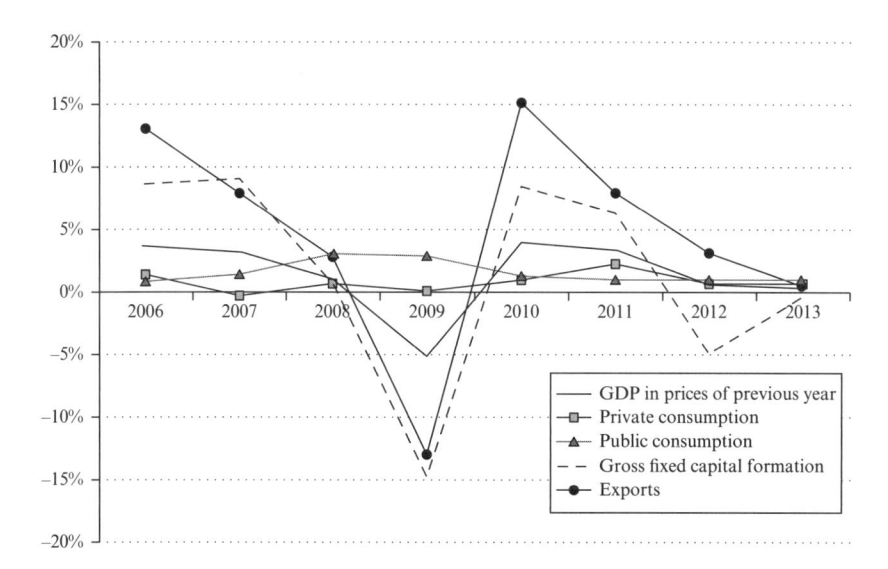

Source: Statistisches Bundesamt; Volkswirtschaftliche Gesamtrechnungen, Wiesbaden, 2014.

Figure 4.2 Annual rates of real GDP and its components in Germany

Most importantly it introduced a support scheme equivalent to 50 per cent of the employer's social security contributions to be paid to the Federal Employment Agency for employees working on a reduced work schedule. This proved to be extremely successful because it provided an incentive to shorten work hours rather than to dismiss staff. The number in employment could thus be stabilized, which supported household consumption while avoiding new claims on public agencies for social protection. Following the shock of 2009, real private consumption expanded, reaching 2.3 per cent per annum in 2011, which is unusually high for German standards, and the expansion rate of private consumption remained slightly above the overall growth rate until recently. However the main contribution to leveraging the German economy out of the slump was, again, real exports, which grew by 15.3 per cent in 2010 and 8 per cent in 2011, to flatten out only more recently. Exports triggered the usual investment cycle, which, initially, supported growth, but gross fixed capital formation quickly lost momentum and even fell by almost 5 per cent in 2012.

It is significant to note that the cyclically motivated actions of the federal government did not simply follow Keynesian guidelines, but were combined with structural policy measures to enhance the competitiveness of German companies. For instance, an additional special program of the KfW banking group provided loans and guarantees to large enterprises (totaling 100 billion euros); the funds of the Central Innovation Program for SMEs for research and development projects were enlarged and the eligibility threshold extended;[2] there was additional support for the expansion of wired and wireless-based high-performance networks; an 'electro mobility' loan program of over 500 million euros from KfW was launched for hybrid, fuel cell and storage technologies; and, by 1 July 2009, the motor vehicle tax was put on an emission-related tax base.

All these measures, while simultaneously targeting the supply-side of the economy, contributed to the recovery of the economy, although with a time lag, which could not fully avoid the decline of GDP in 2009. The decrease of GDP and its impact on government resources affected all public budgets, not only that of the federation, but also those of states and municipalities. This is a consequence of the high degree of revenue sharing of all major taxes among levels of government, which is characteristic of the German federal arrangements. As to the performance of local finances at the sub-national level, the federal support program for municipal investments was a key element in sustaining local budgets, which resulted in higher public sector deficits and debt.

At the same time, there were, and are, strong tendencies to consolidate public budgets both at the national and sub-national levels. The balance of the consolidated general government budget, which had reached −3.1 and −4.2 per cent of GDP in 2009 and 2010 (from a more or less balanced budget situation in 2007–08), improved in 2011 to reach a more comfortable level at −0.8 per cent, returning to balance already by 2013. Compared to the overall fiscal position of EU member governments, Germany's public sector was in much better shape as regards its fiscal deficit. Nevertheless, the fallout drove the debt to GDP ratio to an all-time high of 82.5 per cent in 2010, which could however be stabilized and even reduced somewhat thereafter (78.4 per cent in 2013).[3]

Moreover, on the recommendation of the Commission on Federalism,[4] and in view of the level of consolidated public debt, a 'debt brake' was introduced in the German Constitution (*Grundgesetz*) in 2009 (see below). Its purpose is to ensure that sub-national public budgets are financed without any structural deficits from 2020 on, with only a small structural deficit allowed for the federal budget (0.35 per cent of GDP). In addition, a new instrument, the Stability Council, was instituted to survey all public budgets on an annual basis using common benchmarks, to monitor public borrowing and to coordinate medium-term financial planning within multilevel government.

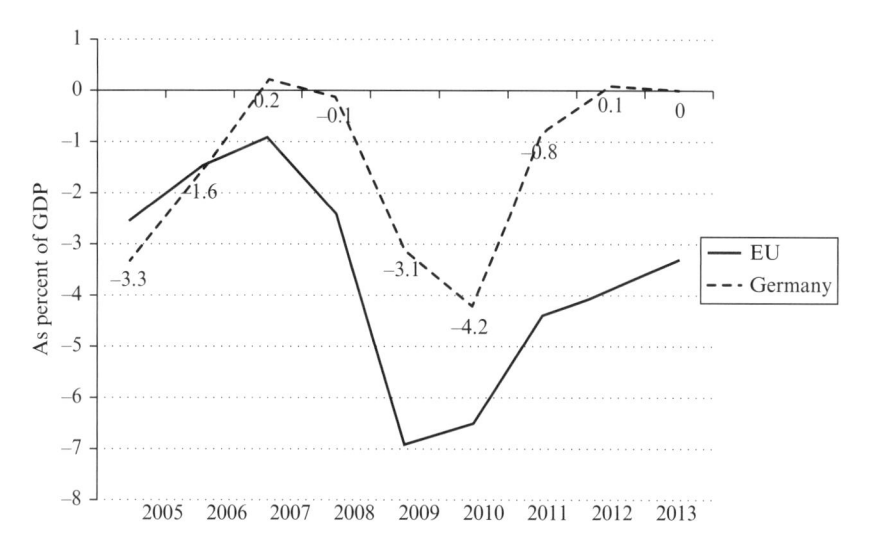

Source: Eurostat; according to the European System of National Accounts.

Figure 4.3 Public sector deficit: the European Union and Germany

2. MULTILAYER FISCAL POLICY DURING THE CRISIS

The impact of the fiscal crisis on public budgets at various levels of government is depicted in Figure 4.4. It is obvious that the federal government, but also the German states, bore the brunt of macroeconomic adjustment as mirrored in fiscal deficits.[5] The policies adopted to cope with the crisis were reasonably successful in cushioning the impact on the local sector, which plays a dominant role in securing fixed public capital formation in Germany. Nevertheless, it could not avoid the financial distress of some municipalities, in particular some larger cities in the western part of the country. These difficulties are of a structural nature and basically unrelated to the fiscal crisis, but the crisis was to expose the underlying weaknesses of the local government sector, putting them on center stage of the policy agenda.

The response of the revenues side of public sector budgets in Germany was as expected: After vigorous rates of increase of 10.6 per cent in 2007 and 4.4 per cent in 2008, taxes (excluding contributions to the EU budget) declined substantially by 6.5 per cent in 2009 and were only slightly above that level in 2010 (+0.8 per cent). As said, the shares of the various levels of government in current revenues remained basically unaltered due to a

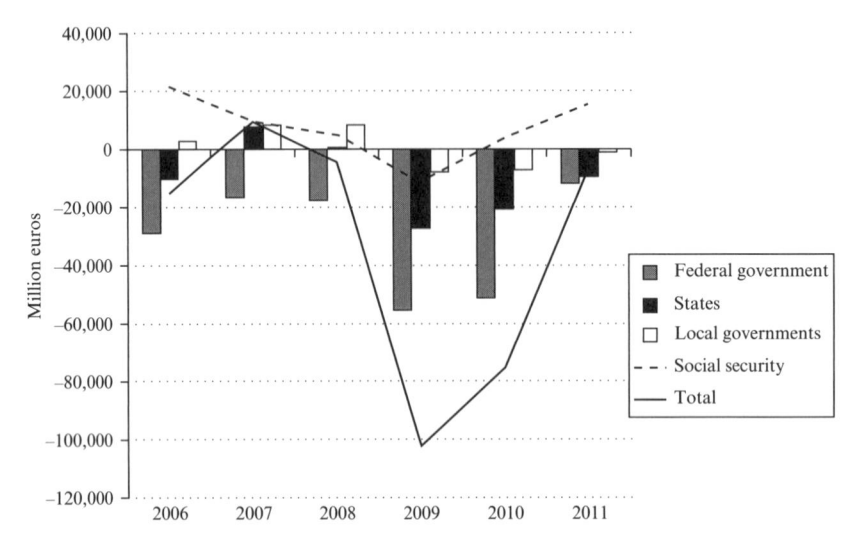

Source: Statistisches Bundesamt, Wiesbaden.

Figure 4.4   Fiscal deficits at various levels of government in Germany

high degree of revenue sharing and the workings of intergovernmental grants, with only a slight improvement of the federal government's budget at the expense of the states.

The compensating role of intergovernmental transfers during the crisis played the decisive part however. Measured in terms of the index of the share of grants received in current revenues, the states benefited, relative to 2007, from an increase of 11.2 and 19.0 per cent in 2009 and 2010, respectively. For local governments the comparable figures are 9.7 and 8.9 per cent, although their level of grant support was already substantially higher than that of the states (54 per cent of current revenues in 2007 compared to 16.8 per cent for the states).

The development of current revenues within multilevel government in Germany during the crisis is depicted in Figure 4.5. It also exhibits the shares of grant support in current revenues as measured by an index based on 2007.

In retrospect it is remarkable how fast and resolutely multilevel fiscal policies in Germany responded to the challenge of an unforeseen crisis in order to secure the steadfast provision of public services closest to citizens: at state (wage bill) and municipal (public investment) levels.[6] At the same time, the federal government took care of macroeconomic stabilization, which implied a higher level of public spending and debt. Social security

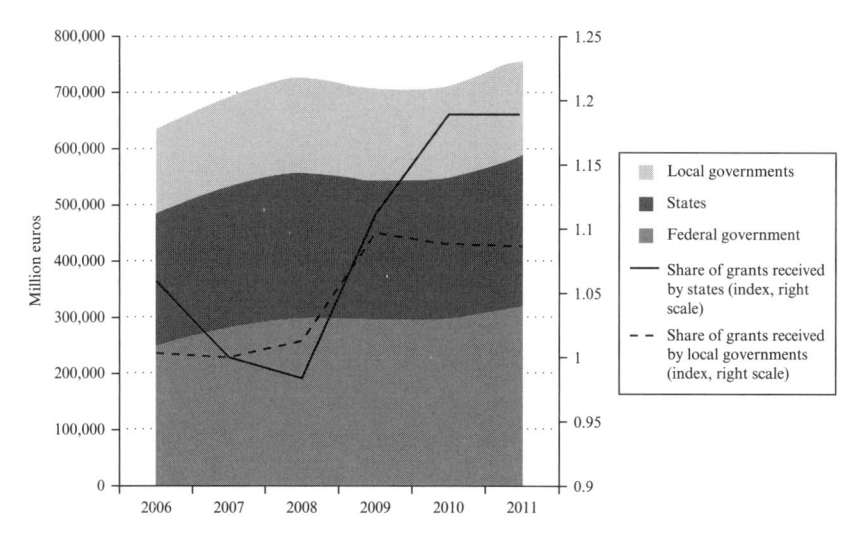

Source: Statistisches Bundesamt, Wiesbaden; own calculations.

Figure 4.5   The development of current revenues and the shares of grant support

institutions could rely on their savings to cushion the impact of the crisis on social security contributions, which avoided additional social hardship.

The smoothing effects of intergovernmental fiscal arrangements during the crisis are best demonstrated by looking at the development of current spending (excluding intergovernmental transfers) and expenditures for fixed capital formation by levels of government. As to the former, current spending, the impact of the crisis is hardly noticeable for local governments; state expenditures experienced acceleration from 2009 on; and only the federal government saw its expenditures reduced after the crisis year (Figure 4.6).

As to the latter, fixed capital formation, the development during the crisis exhibits a clear anti-cyclical pattern for all levels of government, most notably for the federal government, albeit from a comparably low level (share of investment expenditures about 20 per cent of total). The impact on public fixed capital formation is strongest at the local government level because of its higher relevance for this spending category (about 60 per cent).

Whatever fiscal policies could do to attenuate the impact of the crisis on public budgets in the short run, the crisis exposed, and accentuated, existing structural imbalances that had emerged over the years requiring more

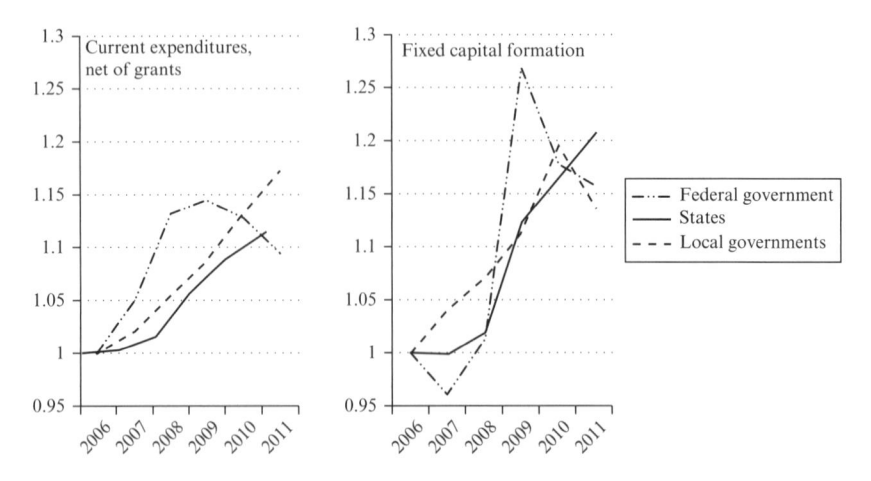

Source: Statistisches Bundesamt, Wiesbaden; own calculations.

Figure 4.6 The development of current expenditures and fixed capital formation, by level of government (index, base year 2006)

fundamental adjustments of intergovernmental fiscal relations. This is best illustrated by focusing on the local government sector.

3. THE CRISIS AND STRUCTURAL IMBALANCES: THE LOCAL GOVERNMENT SECTOR

Apart from their dominant role in public fixed capital formation, local governments in Germany are also strongly committed to spending on social assistance. These expenditures tend to expand not only organically, but also as a result of unfunded mandates heaped upon local governments by federal legislation (for instance, the newly introduced right of a kindergarten place for each child of a certain age group). And as a rule, local taxes and state transfers could not, over a longer term, keep pace with social spending at local levels.[7]

The crisis enlarged this type of expenditures exposing structural weaknesses of the local government sector. In 2009/10 local social spending increased by 8.8 per cent, and the deficit of the local government sector more than doubled.[8] It triggered a sense of urgency for political action.

In 2010 the federal government set up a Commission for reforming local finances with the intention of strengthening their command over public resources and fiscal self-rule (*Gemeindefinanzkommission*). In the context of this endeavor, a 'Working Group on Standards' was set up to

- Look into standards imposed by federal legislation that would have financial implications for local budgets;
- Estimate the volume of the financial implications and propose measures to reduce them through more flexible standards;
- Evaluate the proposed measures from a technical point of view and sketch appropriate legislation for implementation.

It is interesting to note that three-quarters of the complaints by municipalities about undue standards imposed by federal legislation did *not* entail financial implication for higher tiers of government at all. Among the revenue-neutral measures, municipalities expected significant savings from procedural changes, the easing of norms, and – to a lesser extent – changes in the fee structure.

The remaining quarter of the proposed measures entailed a shifting of financial burdens onto other layers of government, in particular onto the Federation. These proposals, if implemented, would potentially have had significant bearing on local budgets at the margin, which is why much of the discussions concentrated on these propositions – mainly in the sphere of social spending. However, little was achieved in this regard and the reforms concentrated mainly on the easing of norms, the reduction of costly higher-level interventions, and on the local fee structure. Municipal governments, though, are suspected of applying, in varying degrees, relaxed standards when implementing local social policies, which, for some, would still leave room for maneuver in constraining this type of expenditure.

As to reforming local finances more fundamentally, the federal government presented a model that included a higher municipal share of sales tax and the replacement of the business tax by local income and corporate taxes with locally variable rates, while the municipal associations aimed at strengthening the trade tax by income-based additions and the inclusion of the liberal professions. This controversy over the modes of financing proved to be insurmountable, and the main structural weaknesses of local government finances linger on unabatedly.

In order to bridge the gap between expenditures and revenues, more and more local governments have taken recourse to financing through short-term cash credits rather than longer-term borrowing for their investments. During the crisis years 2009/10, the level of short-term debentures reached unprecedented levels, since the fallout of tax revenues could not be easily compensated for on the expenditure side, especially for spending on social assistance. Cash credits to local governments are an indicator of increasing structural budget imbalances within this sector, mainly resulting from poor state supervision of local budgets, and a low level of interest on short-term debt tends to fuel this trend.

Given the varying degrees of leniency in the states' supervising of their municipalities' budgets, it is noteworthy that there are significant differences between local jurisdictions. The phenomenon mainly affects West Germany (670 euros per inhabitant in 2011) rather than East Germany (190 euros). It varies significantly by state (with the Saarland, Rhineland-Palatinate and North-Rhine-Westphalia leading the train). And there are obvious differences between cities and counties. The overall development of short-term cash borrowing of German municipalities as well as its distribution by states is depicted in Figure 4.7.

The trend in financing also affects local fixed capital formation over time. Local governments in Germany used to carry about two-thirds of total public investment, but this is now on a declining trend. The crisis year 2009 saw the fall of local investment below the 60 per cent mark, which only recovered somewhat due to the policy measures of the federal government described above.

The structure of financing fixed capital formation in the public sector is depicted in Figure 4.8. It clearly demonstrates the anti-cyclical response to the crisis of the government sector as a whole, which maintained, and even increased, spending on public fixed capital formation (especially during 2010). But it also depicts the declining trend in the share of local government spending in this area.

Unfortunately the continuation of the fall in local investment appears to be unavoidable, especially when a recently introduced constitutional instrument for public budget consolidation cuts in: the so-called 'debt brake'.

4. CONTROLLING PUBLIC BUDGETS: THE 'DEBT BRAKE' AND THE STABILITY COUNCIL

The quest for fiscal discipline and budget coordination to reach international norms, for instance the Maastricht criteria for comprehensive public borrowing and debt, as well as concerns about the unbridled expansion of government debt and short-term municipal borrowing in particular,[9] had led to a national debate in Germany on intergovernmental coordination of public debt, which resulted in a self-imposed new constitutional norm (which has also influenced state constitutional law, for instance in Schleswig Holstein and Hessen): the 'debt brake' (*Schuldenbremse*). Article 109 (3) of the Constitution (*Grundgesetz*) establishes the principle of structurally

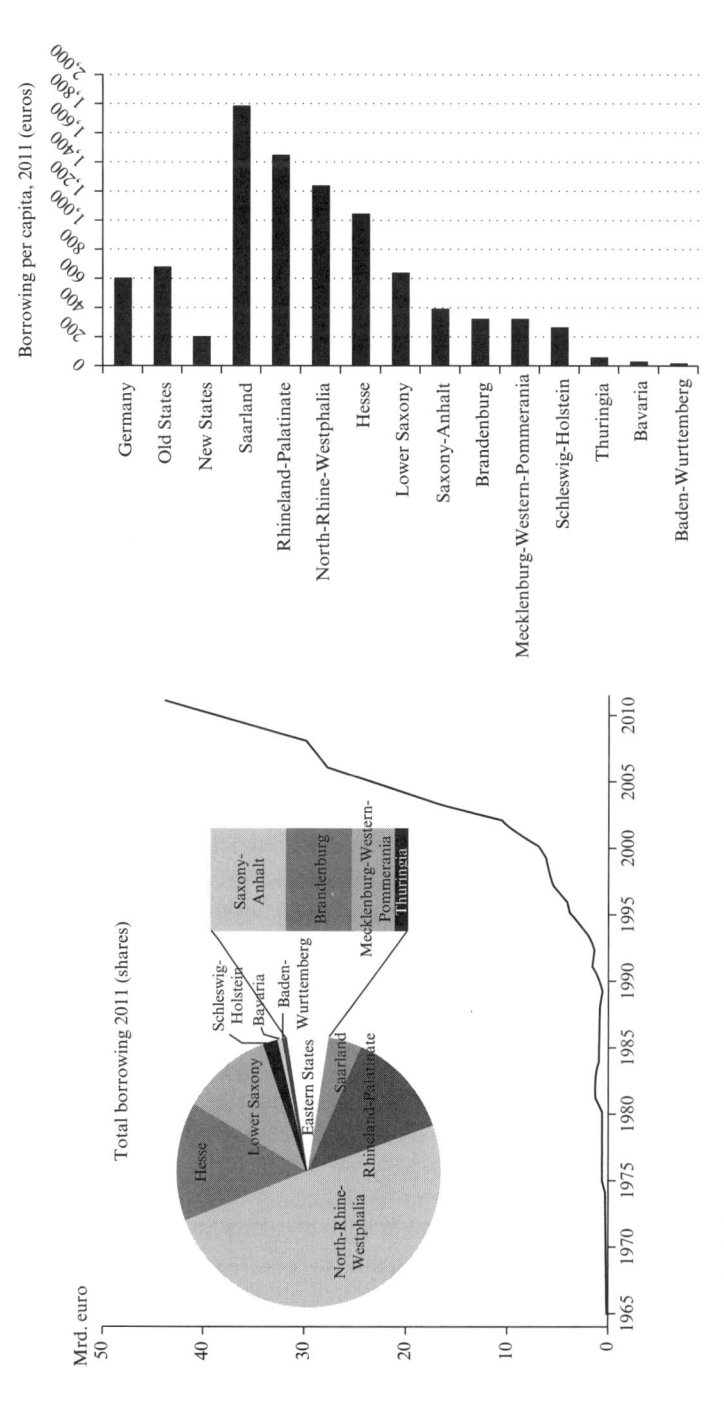

Source: Statisches Bundesamt; own representation of the BBSR 2012 and Bundesministerium der Finanzen, Monatsbericht September 2012; own representations.

Figure 4.7 Short-term cash borrowing of local governments (except city states)

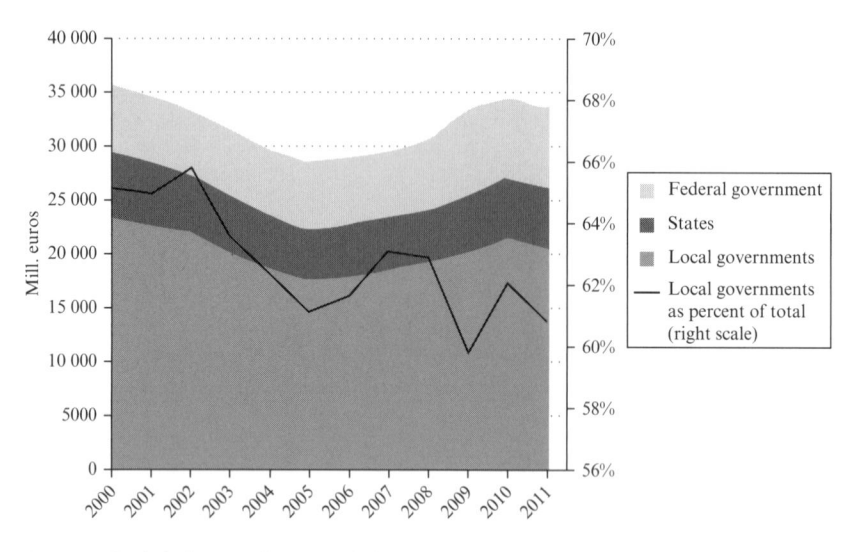

Source: Statistisches Bundesamt, Wiesbaden; own calculations.

Figure 4.8 Fixed capital formation by level of government and the share of local public investment in total

balanced budgets for the Federation and the states. Consequently deficits can no longer be financed through borrowing, except for the federal budget where a margin of 0.35 per cent of nominal GDP is tolerated in view of the Federation's responsibility for macroeconomic stabilization.[10]

The local sector is not constrained by the Federal Constitution since it consists of territorial units that enjoy local autonomy, according to Article 28 'to regulate, within the law, all the affairs of the local community on their own responsibility'. Hence, they do not form part of the state administration, but are subject to state supervision. The Federal Constitution conveys the responsibility for the debt brake to state constitutional law, as to the state budget, in a narrow sense. The provisions for the debt brake are thus incomplete. There are fears that the states could aim at balancing their budgets by pushing burdens of financing down to their local jurisdictions. Formally, the state constitutions exclude this through the so-called connectivity principle (*Konnexität*), which is supposed to avoid unfunded mandates at the local level, but this principle can easily be undermined for non-specific local expenditure functions (and was even violated for specific services such as mandatory kindergartens).

The impact of the debt brake will be felt most severely at the state and, most likely, also at the local level, which, together, carry nearly 80 per cent of all spending on public sector investment at present.[11] Although the constitutional debt brake does not yet carry with it direct consequences for local finances, it could conflict with the European Charter,[12] and it could become a considerable constraint, mainly in the longer run. If exercised through State supervision, it would allow municipalities, as it would for the State itself, to borrow only when retiring old debentures. In other words: borrowing would be allowed only for replacement investments, *not* for expanding the existing capital stock. The only alternative to local borrowing for creating new infrastructure appears to be increased local taxation (or higher state grants[13]), since reducing social spending appears to be a difficult option.[14] Even preserving the level of replacement investments would be difficult under a state and/or municipal debt brake in the light of escalating federal standards, e.g. in the area of energy conservation and the concomitant refurbishment of public buildings. Even if there were no growth, the real value of replacement investment allowed via borrowing would decline with inflation over time since the real value of retired debt will erode. All this would pose severe restrictions on state and local budgets, which are conjointly responsible for a substantial share of infrastructure development within a, hopefully, further growing economy.

During the negotiations between representatives of the federal government and the states it became clear that a number of states are currently not in a position to comply with the norms set by the debt brake. Therefore the five financially weakest states (Bremen, Saarland, Berlin, Saxony-Anhalt and Schleswig-Holstein) now benefit from a consolidation grant (*Konsolidierungshilfe*) during the transition phase up to 2019. This grant is co-financed by the Federation and the states at par.

It remains to be seen what the constitutional norm of the debt brake will mean in practice. Of course it could be a device to mobilize local taxation and relax self-imposed constraint on revenue policies, for instance as regards a long-term stagnating local property tax. First signs of increasing local taxation are already apparent since the impact of the crisis. But the debt brake clearly appears to interfere with the principle of budget separation between tiers of government and the autonomy of their budgets. And, German attitudes vis-à-vis fiscal discipline and rectitude have begun to impact on fiscal policies within the European Union, notably the Euro zone (see below).

In order to prevent future imbalances in multilevel public finances, the German federal legislature instituted a cooperative early warning system under the newly created Stability Council. It consists of the finance ministers of the Federation and the states as well as the federal minister of economics, and is supposed to monitor budget policies of all governments down to the state level. It does not comprise representatives of local governments, which are subject to monitoring by their respective states.

The main tasks of the Stability Council can be sketched as follows:

1. It forms a coordinated view on the state and development of the economy as a whole, on the convergence of its constituent economies, and facilitates agreements on joint fiscal policy actions.
2. It coordinates the federal government's and the states' budget policies within a medium-term framework in order to maintain macroeconomic stability and growth, to preserve sustainable public budgets, and to achieve economic convergence.
3. It examines the conditions and the procedure for determining threatening budget crises (*Haushaltsnotlagen*).
4. It identifies the need for public borrowing, and monitors public debt levels and budget deficits to achieve responsible budget performance at all levels of government and, perhaps, allocates EU fines resulting from violations of the Maastricht budget criteria to individual public entities.

During a transition phase the Stability Council is also bound to control progress in consolidating the budgets of the five states that benefit from consolidation grants, and it decides on possible sanctions.

5. GERMAN 'FISCAL RECTITUDE' AND THE EUROPEAN MECHANICS FOR BUDGET CONSOLIDATION

The strong German penchant for fiscal consolidation has produced significant spillover effects at the supra-national level, which affect the budget policies of member countries of the European Union more generally. Already at the time when preparing for the common currency, the German government was advocating for a Stability and Growth Pact (SGP) for the EU's then 27 members. It was adopted in 1997. The aim of the SGP was/is to establish fiscal discipline based on two 'convergence criteria': public debt and deficits. These criteria are defined comprehensively and encompass general government, i.e., all levels of government as well as social security. They mainly serve as benchmarks, but meeting them is compulsory for those members that wish to join the Euro zone. There is even a formal mechanism for sanctioning treaty violations, the multiple-steps 'Excessive Deficit Procedure' (EDP), which was invoked, ironically, first against Germany (2002) and then France (2003), but did not entail sanctions.[15] Punitive proceedings were started (but fines never applied), e.g. in the cases of Portugal (2002) and Greece (2005). These political considerations, together with deficiencies in the definition of the criteria in the first place,[16] undermined the credibility of the SGP.

The sovereign debt crisis resulting from the recent economic and financial upheavals has re-emphasized the need for taking collective action to secure macro-fiscal stability and enhance the fiscal governance of EU Member States more generally. At the end of 2011, 23 out of 27 Member States were in the EDP.[17] With this aim in mind, and at the instigation of the German government, the EU Member States signed, in March 2011, a 'Euro-Plus Pact' (EPP) within the EU's Open Method of Coordination (OMC)[18] that commits Member States to a set of political reforms intended to foster competitiveness and employment; to enhance the sustainability of public finances (including through national fiscal rules); to reinforce financial stability; and to engage in a structured discussion on tax policy issues. Not all EU Member States signed this treaty, however, criticizing it as an infringement, in certain aspects, of their sovereignty.[19]

On 13 December 2011, a reinforced Stability and Growth Pact (SGP) entered into force with a new set of rules for economic and fiscal surveillance. These new measures, the so-called 'Six-Pack', are made of five regulations and one directive proposed by the European Commission, and were approved by all 27 Member States and the European Parliament. Member States, in the excessive deficit procedure, are to comply with the specific recommendations of the Council addressed to them to correct their excessive deficit. In case a euro area Member States does not respect its obligations, the Council, on the basis of a Commission recommendation, can impose a financial sanction unless a qualified majority of Member States votes against it ('reverse qualified majority').[20] The surveillance mechanism established is also known as the Macroeconomic Imbalance Procedure (MIP) (see Box 4.1).

Finally, an intergovernmental treaty, the Fiscal Compact, was signed on 2 March 2012, to become effective from 2013 on.[21] It requires all parties introducing national legislation to bring consolidated national budgets in balance or in surplus, similar to the 'debt brake' of the German Constitution. The 'structural deficit' (adjusted for the business cycle) must not exceed 0.5 per cent of GDP – except for countries with a debt/GDP ratio that is significantly lower than 60 per cent. The rules have to be incorporated into national legislation at constitutional or similar level. It must also provide automatic readjustment mechanisms in the case of deviation. Member States in the EDP must submit an economic partnership program (to be endorsed by the Commission and the Council) that details the necessary structural reforms to ensure an effectively durable correction of

BOX 4.1   MACROECONOMIC IMBALANCE PROCEDURE (MIP)

The MIP is a surveillance mechanism that aims to prevent and correct macroeconomic imbalances within the EU. It relies on an alert system that uses a scoreboard of indicators and in-depth country studies, strict rules in the form of a new Excessive Imbalance Procedure (EIP), and enforcement in the form of financial sanctions for euro- area Member States that do not follow up on recommendations.

Preventing and Correcting Macroeconomic Imbalances

Over the past decade, the EU has registered serious gaps in competitiveness and major macroeconomic imbalances. A new surveillance and enforcement mechanism has been set up to identify and correct such issues much earlier: the Macroeconomic Imbalance Procedure (MIP), based on Article 121.6 of the Treaty. It will rely on the following main elements:

An early warning system: an alert system is established based on a scoreboard consisting of a set of ten indicators covering the major sources of macroeconomic imbalances. For each indicator, alert thresholds have been set to detect potential imbalances. . . .

Preventive and corrective action: the new procedure allows the Commission and the Council to adopt preventive recommendations under article 121.2 of the Treaty at an early stage before the imbalances become large. There is also a corrective arm in more serious cases, and an excessive imbalance procedure (EIP) can be opened for a Member State. In cases of serious imbalances, the Member State concerned will have to submit a corrective action plan with a clear roadmap and deadlines for implementing corrective action. The Commission will step up surveillance.

Rigorous enforcement: a new enforcement regime is established for euro-area countries. The corrective arm consists of a two-step approach:

- An interest-bearing deposit can be imposed after one failure to comply with the recommended corrective action;
- After a second compliance failure, this interest-bearing deposit can be converted into a fine (up to 0.1% of GDP);
- Sanctions can also be imposed for failing twice to submit a sufficient corrective action plan.

The decision-making process in the new regulations is streamlined by prescribing the use of reverse-qualified majority voting to take all the relevant decisions leading up to sanctions. This semi-automatic decision-making procedure makes it very difficult for Member States to form a blocking majority.

Source: EU Commission: http://ec.europa.eu/economy_finance/economic_governance/macroeconomic_imbalance_procedure/index_en.htm.

excessive deficits. The European Court of Justice is acknowledged as an arbiter, and as judge in the case of applying fines.

True, the Fiscal Compact and in particular the enforcement procedures of the Six-Pack have strengthened awareness of the importance of fiscal discipline. Even if formal sanctions are not applied, political and reputational effects will matter under these circumstances. However the experience with the SGP demonstrates that the decisive point may still be the political will, or lack thereof, to apply sanctions, especially vis-à-vis sovereign states, which is decidedly counterproductive in the wake of a country's economic and fiscal crisis. It remains to be seen whether the Fiscal Compact and MIP will be more successful in establishing fiscal discipline than its predecessor.

Moreover, the concomitant initiatives to support flagrant budget deficits through collective funding instruments such as the European Financial Stability Facility (EFSF), the European Financial Stabilization Mechanism (EFSM) or the European Stability Mechanism (ESM) all run counter the idea of financially sanctioning violations of the Fiscal Compact. Even worse: they may provide incentives for moral hazard. Financial discipline is always and everywhere achieved only where the issuer of new debt has to bear its costs 'at the margin'. This marginality principle is put on its heads by some of the institutional arrangements and German proposals intended to resolve the present sovereign debt crisis.[22]

Finally, the Fiscal Compact requires that national government reconsiders its financial relations with sub-national authorities and assures that the macro-fiscal signals are appropriately transmitted to, and incorporated in, sub-national fiscal policy making and budgeting. This must revive the interest of national governments in mechanisms such as the Domestic Stability Pacts, or comprehensive Financial Responsibility legislation. Some lessons could be drawn from the experience of Germany in this respect, in particular the measures relating to the creation of the Stability Council.

6. SUMMARY AND KEY FINDINGS

The key findings can be summarized as follows:

- The impact of the crisis on GDP growth was severe (−5.1 per cent in 2009) and the consolidated budget deficit of the German public sector reached −3.1 and −4.2 per cent of GDP in 2009 and 2010, respectively.
- The policy response to the crisis was Keynesian, albeit combined with supply-side elements. Fiscal interventions were successful in

overcoming the recession, assisted however by strong export growth and induced fixed capital formation.
- The federal anti-cyclical program was not only instrumental for reinvigorating the economy, although with a time lag, but also for protecting sub-central budgets from adverse immediate financial shocks.
- As a result, sub-central budgets managed to consolidate their current budgets, even during the crisis, by controlling current spending (pay freeze) while avoiding the dismissal of staff.
- Due to an early recovery of the economy, public revenues rebounded from 2011 on, which helped to restructure sub-central budgets through tax sharing and grants.
- Capital spending bore the brunt of the shock, but was reasonably maintained by capital transfers of the federal government and the European Union, whose share in sub-central discretionary spending is substantial.
- In 2011 most German states had restored their cyclical budget balances. However structural deficits remain, especially in the local government sector where infrastructure investments tend to be financed with short-term borrowing, albeit to strongly varying degrees.
- Municipalities experienced an erosion of their fiscal positions, which was more moderate in the new states, where municipalities maintained a consolidated budget surplus, while local governments in the old states went into deficit. Again this points to structural imbalances among regions of the nation.
- Importantly, it was possible to successfully blend anti-cyclical policy with longer-term structural objectives, and hence avoid a simple flash in the pan.
- The crisis has enlivened the already strong propensity to consolidate public budgets in Germany. A new constitutional instrument for controlling public-sector debt in a multilevel environment was introduced: the debt brake. It will severely restrict the management of state and, perhaps, local government budgets from 2020 on.
- To monitor and control multilevel government finances, a new institutional framework was created for coordinating federal and state budget policies within a medium-term framework. This is to maintain macroeconomic stability and growth, to preserve sustainable public budgets, and to achieve economic convergence.
- Last but not least, the German penchant for budget consolidation has had consequences for the coordination of fiscal policies at the European level where, in response to the sovereign debt crisis, a reinforced Stability and Growth Pact (SGP) was introduced, with a new set of rules for economic and fiscal surveillance, including sanctions.

NOTES

1. It was implemented through the Law on Investments into the Future (Gesetz zur Umsetzung von Zukunftsinvestitionen der Kommunen und Länder of 2 March 2009).
2. The Central Innovation Program for SMEs (ZIM) is a funding program of the Federal Ministry of Economics and Technology (BMWi) to foster innovation and the competitiveness of small and medium enterprises (SMEs), including craftsmanship and professionals. The promotion is not limited to specific industries or technological fields.
3. Eurostat, April 2014 (Stability and Growth Pact).
4. There were in fact two commissions on reforms of the federal system in Germany: the Kommission zur Modernisierung der bundesstaatlichen Ordnung (2003–04), and the Kommission zur Modernisierung der Bund-Länder-Finanzbeziehungen (2007–09).
5. Deficits are shown according to the Financial Statistics, which are cash-based and differ from the standard definition as adopted for National Income Accounting.
6. Where there were disruptions in the delivery of local public services, these were of a structural nature and not so much related to the crisis, although the crisis sometimes worked as a trigger.
7. From 2001 to 2010 the average yearly rate of increase in local taxes and grants received was about 3 per cent; the average yearly rate of increase of local social spending was 5 per cent (Bundesinstitut für Bau-, Stadt- und Raumforschung (BBSR), Bonn 2012).
8. Bundesministerium der Finanzen, *Monatsbericht*, September 2012.
9. The cash credits of municipalities have increased dramatically over the last decade, from €6.9 billion in 2000 to €40.5 billion in 2010 – which is an annual rate of increase of 19.4 per cent.
10. There are other exceptions that apply: (i) borrowing to cope with natural catastrophes and other emergencies; and (ii) anti-cyclical borrowing to mitigate the business cycle, whereby incurring and retiring of debt must be symmetrical and balance over the cycle. For the exemptions an appropriate repayment procedure must be introduced.
11. The impact of the debt brake on local governments is indirect through the constraint on state finances, including municipalities. How to coordinate and control local sector borrowing is left to state legislation.
12. The European Charter stipulates in Article 9 (8): 'For the purpose of borrowing for capital investment, local authorities shall have access to the national capital market within the limits of the law.'
13. Higher state grants to municipalities would imply higher federal grants to the states, since the latter are severely constrained at the spending side of the budget (wage bill) and have practically no own taxing powers.
14. Contrary to this view the German Minister of Finance, Mr Schäuble, expects the main repercussions to lie on the expenditure side of public budgets. 'Recipients of corporate welfare, as well as civil servants, must share the sacrifice. German corporations will have to contribute to fiscal consolidation through reductions of subsidies and additional taxes on major energy companies, airlines and financial institutions. Similarly, civil servants must forego promised pay increases, and the government is looking for annual savings in the federal armed forces of up to €3 billion.' (OECD, *Budget deficits: What Governments are Doing – Germany: Hitting the Debt Brake*).
15. In fact the SGP was relaxed in 2005 as it became obvious that the pact could not be enforced against powerful members such as France and Germany.
16. The deficit criterion does not account for variations due to the business cycle, for instance. The debt criterion does not account for productive assets of the public sector. Both criteria are related to GDP, while average tax revenue is likely to be more appropriate as the denominator.
17. European Commission, http://europa.eu/rapid/pressReleasesAction.do?reference=MEMO/11/898.
18. The 'Open Method of Coordination' (OMC) is a form of EU soft law, a process of policy making, which does not lead to binding EU legislative measures nor require

Member States to change their law. The open method of coordination (OMC) aims to spread best practices and achieve greater convergence towards the main EU goals and was initially used for employment policies and the European Social Dialogue. http://www.eurofound.europa.eu/areas/industrialrelations/dictionary/definitions/ openmethodofcoordination.htm.
19. Four members opted out of the EPP: Hungary, the Czech Republic, Sweden and the United Kingdom.
20. European Commission, http://europa.eu/rapid/pressReleasesAction.do?reference=MEMO/11/898.
21. Among the 27 Member States of the EU, only the Czech Republic and the United Kingdom abstained from signing.
22. For instance, the German Sachverständigenrat zur Begutachtung der gesamtwirtschaftlichen Entwicklung (*Jahresgutachten 2011/12 'Verantwortung für Europa wahrnehmen'*, November 2011) recently proposed a Eurobond on a pool of sovereign debt that exceeds the 60 per cent of GDP margin. This would 'socialize' excess deficits. Yet only the reverse complies with the marginality principle: debt up to 60 per cent of GDP (or corresponding tax base) could be pooled into a common first-class Eurobond, while all excesses would have to be financed as second- and third-class tranches of a specific country.

5. French sub-national public finances: on the difficulty of being a decentralized unitary state
Pierre Garello[1]

1. DEFICIT, DEBT AND DECENTRALIZATION: HOW DO THEY INTERACT?

Two facts can hardly be missed when studying French public finances. Firstly, the country has one of the highest reported ratios of general government public spending to GDP (57.1 per cent in 2013 according to INSEE – the French National Institute for Statistics, second only to Denmark among OECD countries); a high public-sector deficit (4.3 per cent of GDP in 2013 and probably slightly more in 2014), and a rapidly increasing national debt that could reach 100 per cent of GDP in the coming years. Secondly, France has followed a systematic policy of decentralization for the past 30 years, the first law for decentralization dating back to 1982. This chapter looks into a potential link of causality between those two observations, focusing more specifically on the impact of the recent crisis on the budgets of the various layers of government. Indeed the crisis provides us with a good test for assessing the quality of our institutions. Did the decentralization, as it is designed and operated in France, soften the impact of the crisis? Or did it make things worse due to, for instance, the inability of sub-national governments to control their expenditures? Did the crisis lead to a rolling back of decentralization, making the various levels of government less accountable, or did it, on the contrary, help improve the French model of decentralization?

An attempt to answer these questions must rely on a good understanding of the mechanisms of decentralization in France. Accordingly, the next section will provide an overview of French territorial organization and the main steps of the decentralization process. It will be followed with a section that presents data on the evolution of public finances at all levels of government in the long term and during the years of crisis until now. The next, and main, section of the chapter offers a detailed study of the process through which budgets are built and executed at sub-national levels of government. This will be done by juxtaposing an explanation of the budgetary and fiscal legal rules with a presentation of what local governments have actually been doing during the crisis. A final section will draw lessons from that analysis. It appears that, although local governments are closely monitored and controlled by the central government and various fiscal rules limit their freedom, the present state of decentralization is far from satisfactory and repeated attempts to fix problems have generated legal insecurity as well as a dangerous game-play between local and state representatives. Unless greater coherence is brought to the decentralization mechanism and unless cooperation and confidence are restored between layers of government, the state of public finances will continue to deteriorate. A golden rule for central government's fiscal policy could help establish the right direction.

2. FRANCE'S ADMINISTRATIVE ORGANIZATION: AN EVER-CHANGING *MILLEFEUILLE*

The French decentralization process has been and continues to be very chaotic and sometimes confusing. The metaphor of a 'millefeuille'[2] is often used to describe this territorial organization. Indeed, as of today, the population of 65.1 million is divided between:

- 36,767 municipalities[3]
- 101 *départements* (including five *départements* overseas)
- 27 regions (22 for the metropolitan territories including Corsica and 5 overseas).

To this must be added, of course, the central government. It is also important to note that 99.8 per cent of the municipalities cooperate within associations, which, for some of them, have the power to tax and can therefore raise their own revenues (*Etablissements publics de coopération intercommunale*, henceforth EPCI). As of 2014 there were 2,145 such associations. Municipalities are also often gathered in associations (*syndicats*), most often deprived of fiscal power.[4] There are 13,402 cooperating bodies of the latter kind between municipalities, but their number is decreasing in favor of the EPCI. This territorial organization is clearly complex, frequently changing and therefore unstable, as a quick look at the modern history of French legislation will confirm.

The division of the national territory into municipalities and *départements* dates back to the 1789 revolution (with greater competences granted to both levels of government toward the end of the 19th century),[5] while regions were formed more recently and in successive steps. Firstly, a law of 5 July 1972 gave the regions the status of public institutions with specific missions. Ten years later, in 1982, a law (known as 'decentralization law' or *loi Defferre*) was voted granting those regions the statute of autonomous territorial entities. Since then, more laws have amended the so-called decentralization process without, as we will see, following a clear pattern. An important step was the law of 1999 (*loi Chevènement*[6]) that led to a sharp increase of inter-municipality cooperation. It created the EPCIs mentioned above; a level of governance that has come to play an increasing role in local governance. If the economic justification for such horizontal cooperation between local jurisdictions is well known,[7] a byproduct of this new structure was, however, an increasing lack of transparency in local governance since the representatives at the council of the inter-municipal administration were not directly elected (they were appointed by the council of the municipality),[8] making it very difficult for taxpayers to understand exactly which entity was managing what and who was fixing which rates. It is not uncommon, for instance, for a municipality to freeze its tax rates while at the same time voting in favor of an increase of those rates that are decided at the EPCI's level. It is hence difficult for taxpayers to figure out who is accountable for what, especially since there are incentives to maintain this opacity of the governance of the municipality.

This confusing situation partly explains why an ambitious reform of the territorial organization of the country was passed into law in 2010.[9] Among the novelties introduced at that time was the fusion of two mandates – the mandate to the council of the *département* and the mandate to the council of the region – so that each elected representative, to be named a 'territorial councilor', would systematically sit in both chambers. Another important innovation was the election of the members of the EPCI council by direct suffrage. These new electoral rules were to be implemented for the first time during the March 2014 local elections. But the change of majority following the presidential election of 2012 led to a dismantlement of the 2010 reform and gave a somewhat new direction to the decentralization process.[10] This new direction materializes in particular with (i) a return to separate elections for the region and the *département*, (ii) an acceleration of the development of *métropoles*,[11] and (iii) the return of the 'general competence' clause. This last issue is an important one that deserves attention in so far as good governance requires clear missions.

2.1 Allocation of Responsibilities between Various Levels of Government

Since 1884, municipalities have benefitted from a general responsibility clause (*clause de compétence générale*), meaning that they are 'in charge of any business that concerns the municipality'.[12] But a gap has always existed between the words of the law and reality itself for the following reasons:

1. Firstly, the constitution of 1958 states in its article 34 that 'the law shall fix the general principles of the free administration of local communities, of their responsibilities and of their resources'. Hence, the freedom granted to the local governments is clearly conditional upon the decision of the national parliament who, at any moment, can reduce it.
2. Beside this, the Constitution limited the power for municipalities and departments to levy taxes (more on this below).
3. Local governments had, and continue to have, many missions forced upon them by the central government (such as providing medical assistance, taking care of the elderly or paying salary and accommodation to primary school teachers).[13] In that sense, again, local governments are not autonomous.
4. Finally, prior to the law of 2010, the same responsibility was sometimes given to *départements* and regions: since their territories overlap, those clauses were always difficult to interpret and, consequently, often criticized.

As a result, the Law of 2010 proposed to abolish the clause of 'general competence' and to replace it with a list, for each level of administration, of its 'missions', that is, the fields for which that level had authority. Two years later, however, the law of 2014 reintroduced the famous clause for the regions and the *départements*.[14] But that's not over: a new proposition for a reform of territorial law dating from June 2014 suggests that the clause be abolished again. Interestingly, this reform that is presently being discussed in parliament also proposes to bring the number of regions down to 13. Indeed the road toward decentralization has been a rather bumpy and curvy one since 1982.

3. THE PRESENT STATE OF PUBLIC FINANCES

As explained above, when discussing fiscal and budgetary policies there are at least five major layers of administration to be considered: municipalities, associations of municipality, *départements*, regions and central state.

In public accounting and common discourse, the expression 'local public administration' is used to refer to the four lowest levels, that is to say, to everything but the administration of the central state and of the social security system. The same terminology will be used here.[15]

3.1 Public Deficits: Long-Term Trend and Recent Evolution

Clearly, French public finances today are in dire straits. On 27 April 2009, the European Council addressed a formal recommendation to the French government on the basis of the deficit observed for 2008 (around 7.5 per cent of GDP – see Table 5.1). France was given until 2013 to bring the deficit below 3 per cent. In 2013, the government asked and obtained permission to postpone this deadline to 2014. But the deficit is still expected to be around 4.4 per cent in 2014 and 4.3 per cent in 2015, so that France could, even if this is unlikely for political reasons, be the first EU member state to endure the sanctions written in the fiscal compact (up to €4 billion according to the Excessive Deficit Procedure). This situation is nothing but the latest episode in a long series. For each of the last 40 years, the consolidated account of all the branches of the French public administration has been in deficit (1974 was the last time a budget surplus was realized).[16] A 2006 report to the government prepared under the supervision of Michel Pébereau (former CEO of BNP Paribas) recalls that: 'for the

Table 5.1 Deficit of public administrations (Maastricht definition)

	2007	2008	2009	2010	2011	2012	2013
	\multicolumn{7}{c}{In billions of euro}						
All levels included	−49.2	−61.1	−140.7	−135.7	−103.1	−98.7	−87.6
Central government	n.a.	n.a	−119.8	−110.5	−89.2	−82.1	−65.9
State	*n.a.*	*n.a*	*−117.1*	*−120.8*	*−88.8*	*−80.2*	*−67.6*
Various central agencies	*n.a.*	*n.a*	*−2.7*	*10.3*	*−0.5*	*−1.9*	*1.6*
Local public administration	n.a.	n.a	−6.0	−1.7	−0.7	−3.7	−9.2
Social security administration	n.a.	n.a	−14.8	−23.5	−13.2	−12.9	−12.5
	\multicolumn{7}{c}{As % of GDP}						
All levels included	−2.6	−3.2	−7.5	−7.0	−5.2	−4.9	−4.3
Central government	n.a.	n.a.	−6.4	−5.7	−4.5	−4.0	−3.2
State	*n.a.*	*n.a.*	*−6.2*	*−6.2*	*−4.4*	*−3.9*	*−3.3*
Various central agencies	*n.a.*	*n.a.*	*−0.1*	*0.5*	*0.0*	*−0.1*	*0.1*
Local public administration	n.a.	n.a.	−0.3	−0.1	0.0	−0.2	−0.4
Social security administration	n.a.	n.a.	−0.8	−1.2	−0.7	−0.6	−0.6

Source: INSEE – National accounts as of 31 March 2013.

Figure 5.1 Evolution of deficits at various levels of government in billions of euros

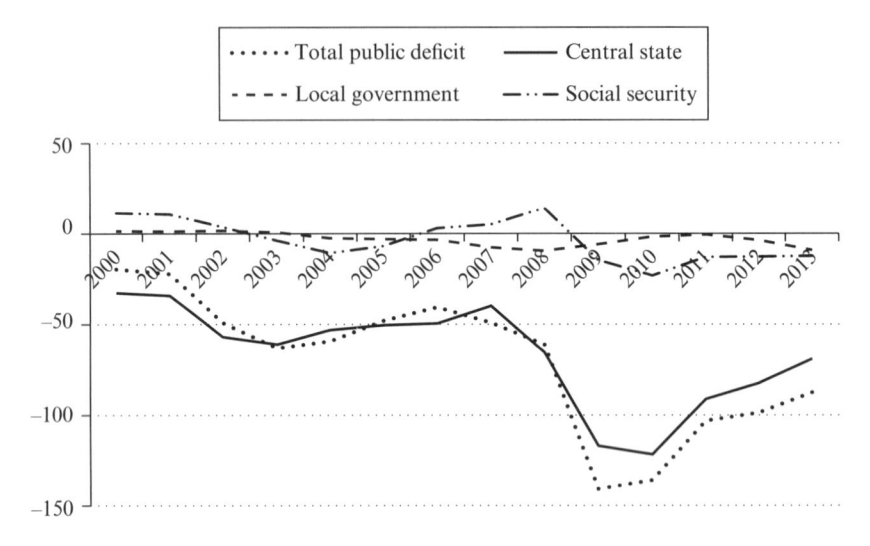

Source: Computed from INSEE database.

last ten years expenditure of public administrations have been each year in average 7 per cent above their revenues. Expenditures of the central government itself have been on average above 18 per cent.'[17]

Unsurprisingly, Figure 5.1 and Table 5.1 show that the 2008 crisis did not help reverse that trend. The total deficit soared between 2007 and 2009 from some €49 billion to over €140 billion. Interestingly, the figure also shows that during that period the deficits of central and local governments evolved in opposite directions. The impact of the crisis was first on the central government (with a record high deficit, both as percentage of GDP and in absolute value for the year 2009). But after 2010, while the situation for the central finances improved, local governments started to fare poorly. In 2013, the deficit of local governments more than doubled, climbing from €3.7 billion in 2012 to reach €9.2 billion a year later – a phenomenon we try to explain below.

3.2 Public Debt: Long-Term Trend and Recent Evolution

At the end of 2013, total debt reached €1,904.4 billion or 91.8 per cent of GDP. Six months later, it reached €2,023.7 billion and amounted to 95.1 per cent of GDP. A large portion of the debt (80 per cent) comes

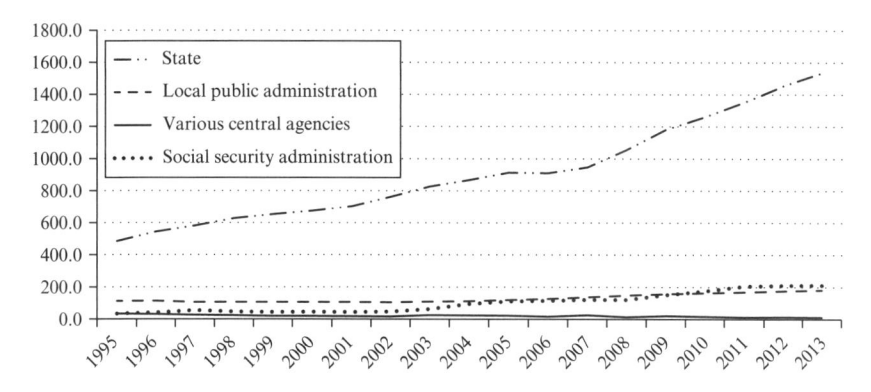

Source: National account, Base 2010, INSEE.

Figure 5.2   Long-term evolution of public debt by level of administration

from central government (€1,546.4 billion). The second-largest contributor to national debt is social security administration, with €211.7 billion (11 per cent), closely followed by local governments: €182.3 billion, representing 9 per cent of the total.

Any concern that this situation may legitimately cause will be reinforced when taking a long-term perspective (Figure 5.2). Indeed, 2002 was the last time national debt was below the 60 per cent threshold and public debt is growing rapidly, more or less doubling every ten years for the last two decades.[18]

Sub-national debt reached a turning point in the first years of the century. The debt remained stable over the 1990s (it was at €96.8 billion in 1995 and almost at the same level ten years later: €97.8 billion in 2004); it then reached €170 billion in 2013, almost doubling in ten years. The situation is likely to remain tense, since transfers from central government (see below) have been cut by €1.5 billion in 2014 and a €3.67 billion cut is announced for 2015 (but with a special subsidy for energy transition of €423 million).

3.3   Beyond the Data: The Real Importance of Local Administrations

The data above suggest a rapidly deteriorating situation for all levels of government. It could also wrongly give the impression that local governments play only a small role in this story, accounting for only 10.5 per cent of general government deficit and 9 per cent of gross public debt in 2013 (see Table 5.1 and Figure 5.2). Those opinions tend to be confirmed after a quick look at the evolution of public spending by level of government over

110   *Multi-level finance and the Euro crisis*

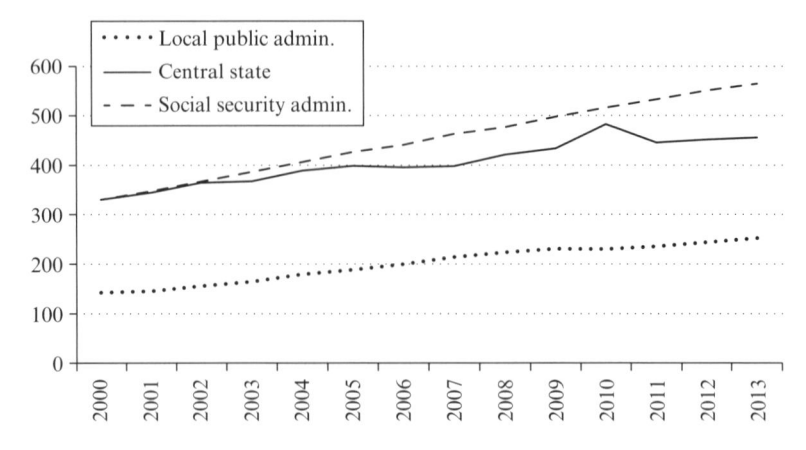

```
600 ┐    ····· Local public admin.
         ───── Central state
500 ┤    ─ ─ ─ Social security admin.
400 ┤
300 ┤
200 ┤
100 ┤
  0 ┼──┬──┬──┬──┬──┬──┬──┬──┬──┬──┬──┬──┬──┬──
    2000 2001 2002 2003 2004 2005 2006 2007 2008 2009 2010 2011 2012 2013
```

Source: INSEE.

Figure 5.3   Public spending by level of administration (in billion euros)

the last decade (Figure 5.3): both central and local governments' spending levels appear to move more or less along parallel lines. More precisely, local public expenditures have been increasing just slightly faster than central government expenditures and at a slower pace than social security. The share of local public expenditures in total public expenditures was at 17 per cent in 1982, 18 per cent in 1990, and 20 per cent in 2004. It reached its maximum in 2008 (21.1 per cent) and, after a modest decline, was back at 20.9 per cent in 2013.

Those impressions, however, are misleading for various reasons.

1. First, as already mentioned, the recent evolution of central and local deficits has diverged since the start of the crisis.
2. Second, almost three-fourths of public investment is done at the local level (71 per cent in 2012), so that the budgets of local governments have a 'non-marginal' impact on the economy of the country.
3. Third, the *effective* budget of local governments is greater than those figures suggest due to large transfers from central to local governments. Hence, in 2010 local governments' budget reached €220 billion while central government had a budget of approximately €450 billion, but the central government transferred that year some €150 million to other entities, including local governments, so that the effective budget of the latter was closer to €300 million, that is to say, approximately the same as that of the central government.

These remarks justify a closer examination of the sources of revenues for local governments as well as of the nature of their expenses.

4. DETAILED ANALYSIS OF LOCAL GOVERNMENTS' BUDGETARY RULES AND POLICIES

As noted above, the tax freedom granted to local governments comes with many legal constraints, including monitoring and controls from the central state.

4.1 General Constitutional Framework

Article 72 of the 1958 Constitution bears on the administration of territorial jurisdictions. It clearly establishes control of local decision making by the law, stating in particular that:

> Local authorities (in the text: *les collectivités territoriales*) benefit from resources that they can freely use as long as they remain in the framework imposed by the law ... They can receive the whole or part of the revenues from all forms of taxation. The law can authorize them to choose the tax base or the rate of those taxes inside pre-determined limits.

The law, that is to say, the parliament of the country, is hence supervising the whole process. Clearly France remains a unitary state.

Later, Article 72 of the Constitution was amended by the Constitutional Law of 28 March 2003. This is often seen as a milestone in the history of decentralization. The new law redefines the relationship between the central and local jurisdictions. In particular, it restates the principle of free administration outlined in the original Article 72 of the Constitution by confirming the financial autonomy of local authorities, on both revenue and expenditure sides, and by raising the principle of equalization to a constitutional level.[19]

- Autonomy in spending is illustrated by two provisions. First, local governments can freely dispose of their budgetary resources. Second, the principle according to which any transfer of responsibilities between the centre and local jurisdictions must be linked to the necessary transfer of resources is now transposed in the Constitution and is accompanied by a clarification: a transfer of resources must also take place whenever some existing responsibility is extended or a new one is imposed by law.

- In terms of revenues, the Constitution now provides that the resources of local authorities must necessarily include a tax component. It also establishes that 'tax revenues and other own-source revenues of local governments should represent, for each layer of government, a crucial (in the text: *déterminante*) part of their total resources.' Article 72-2 of the revised Constitution also specifies the types of taxes that may be levied for the benefit of local communities and gives greater freedom to local public decision makers. In stipulating that communities can 'receive all or part of the proceeds of taxes of any kind,' the new constitution also paves the way to a sharing of taxes between the state and local authorities. By providing that the authorities may, within the limits set by law, not only vote the rates of taxes they levy, but also set their bases, Article 72-2 extends the power of local assemblies in tax matters.[20]
- To correct inequalities between communities, particularly due to the uneven geographical distribution of tax bases, but also to unequal burdens imposed on territorial communities, Article 72-2 provides that 'the law establishes equalization arrangements in order to promote equality between local jurisdictions.'

To implement such 'controlled freedom' is not an easy task. In practice, the mechanisms prevailing in the allocation of resources as well as the constraints imposed on spending are so complex that local administrators are all too often lost and simply follow the 'recommendations' provided by the central government. This state of affairs has the direct consequence that local decision makers have very little visibility as regards their future resources, and tend to opt for a myopic management.

Incentives to manage efficiently are also hampered by the formulation of the equalization mechanisms on actuals (known as écrêtement) rather than incentive compatible 'standard' factors. The local administration that reaches a surplus will see its transfer diminished to the benefit of poorly managed territories. Indeed, the law establishes two equalizing mechanisms: a vertical equalization mechanism implemented essentially through the general transfer allocation from the centre to sub-national governments (a mechanism which is supervised by the Committee for local finances), and a newly introduced horizontal equalization mechanism based on transfers from richer to poorer EPCI and municipalities.[21]

4.2 The Sources of Revenues

The law, that is to say, the central government, fixes the rules governing tax-bases and tax-rates as well as the rules governing the collection of all taxes, regardless of their nature.[22] Also, as has been recalled above, the Constitutional reform of 2003 (Article 72-2, paragraph 3) establishes that 'a critical part' of the revenues of local governments must consist of own-source revenues. It was left to the organic Law of 29 July 2004 to specify what is meant by own-source revenues and by 'critical level'.

Own-source revenues are those that local governments, at least partially, control, as opposed to those that depend entirely on the center, e.g. transfers from central government. What are counted as own-source revenues include income from services rendered, income from the property of the local entity, revenues from financial instruments, private donations and legacies. On the other hand, grants, and in particular central state grants, resources delegated by the state, resources associated with a temporary and experimental objective and, most importantly, resources from borrowing are not considered as own-source revenues. The goal of these rules and definitions is clearly to push local administrations toward sustainable budgetary and fiscal policies: a sound budget should be built around resources that the jurisdiction can control. As for the definition of a 'critical level' of own-source revenues, Article 3 of the organic law of 2004 stipulates 'the share of own resources is crucial when guaranteeing the free administration of local authorities, given the powers entrusted to them. That share cannot be lower than the level recorded for 2003.' In 2003, the ratios of own resources were at 60.8 per cent for the municipalities and EPCI, 58.6 per cent for the *departments*, and 41.7 per cent for the regions.

Looking at actual sources of revenues for local governments, one can see that local tax revenues account today for approximately 55 per cent of their total revenues (€124.32 billion in 2014), the rest, as we will see, essentially represent transfers from the central government (€101.2 billion in 2014).

4.3 Own-Source Revenues and the Professional-Tax Revolution

Without going into the details of the various tax mechanisms, five features of local taxation deserve attention:

1. In many instances the tax base is common to various levels of government. Hence, the very painful residential property tax is shared between the municipality, the association of municipalities and the *département*.
2. The rates of the various taxes cannot be fixed by local jurisdictions to suit their own needs. The law provides upper and lower bounds for those rates and imposes rules regarding the changes (for instance, the municipality cannot increase the residential property tax without increasing non-residential property tax).

3. Almost all local taxes are direct taxes (unlike the central government that derives a large part of its revenues from indirect taxation). As is well known, those taxes have a stronger impact than indirect taxes, making increases politically difficult.[23]
4. The tax base is often the value of the property (land and residence), which makes those taxes very progressive. In some cities half of the inhabitants do not pay the council tax.
5. The value of property changes over time. To take those changes into account the law of 18 July 1974 specifies that the base should be the rental value of those properties and that this value should be reassessed every two years, with a complete revision every six years. In practice however this has never been done. Instead, the center imposes every year a uniform adjustment for rental values. This adjustment process of course is a source of inequity. If, for example, a building has been renovated since the last assessment of the rental value, this is not taken into account and its owners will pay much less tax than owners of a building that was new around the time of the assessment period, but is now in poor condition.[24]

Table 5.2 gives the detail of the various tax revenues. In 2012, taxes on businesses accounted for 19.71 per cent of total tax revenues (€23.86 billion out of €121.03 billion).

Table 5.3 shows that proceeds from local business taxes was much higher prior to 2011. As a matter of fact, until 2010 approximately 40 per cent of fiscal revenues were from the so-called 'professional tax' (*taxe professionnelle*). This tax, introduced in 1975 to replace the '*patente*' which was introduced in 1791, was levied on all undertakings having some economic activity in the local jurisdictions. The base was computed from the wage bill of the company and the value of its real estate and physical assets. The *taxe professionelle* has long been criticized, in particular for taking the wage bill as a determinant of the tax base. In a country with a high level of unemployment, to tax labour-intensive establishments was rightly seen as paradoxical. A first reform introduced in 1999 took out of the tax base the wages paid; the lost revenues being replaced with a direct transfer from the central government.

In 2010, the professional tax was further reformed and replaced with the so-called Territorial Economic Contribution. This new tax is made mainly of two contributions: the undertaking's property tax (based on the rental value of its real estate property) and a 'Contribution on Value-Added'. To those two elements must be added a specific tax for network companies (energy, telecommunication, transportation) and another levied on large retailers (with shops of over 400 square meters). As shown in Table 5.3,

Table 5.2 Local government tax revenues in 2012 (billion euros)

	Municipalities (includes EPCI)	Departments	Regions	Total
Direct contribution	48.11	19.18	4.44	71.73
Revenues from the 3 'household taxes'	36.28	11.58		47.86
Council tax	19.53			19.53
Residential property tax	15.78	11.58		27.36
Non residential property tax	0.98			0.98
Revenues from taxes on business	11.82	7.60	4.44	23.86
Tax on Business Real-estate	6.66			6.66
Tax on Business added-value	4.02	7.36	3.80	15.18
Tax on network companies	0.49	0.24	0.64	1.37
Tax on large retailers	0.65			0.65
Other taxes	18.96	22.34	8.00	49.30
Including:				
Garbage collection	6.09			6.09
Tax on property transfer	2.22	7.97		10.19
Consumption tax on energy product		6.54	4.36	10.89
Contribution for public transportation	6.85			6.85
Tax on insurance contracts		6.63		6.63
Total	67.07	41.53	12.44	121.03

Source: DGFiP.

the combination of those new 'local economic taxes' or 'local business taxes' was not sufficient to generate revenues equivalent to those raised previously through the now-abolished professional tax. Some five to nine billion euros were missing. As a result the central state created a special allocation to compensate for those losses, hence reducing the proportion of own-source revenues and increasing the role of transfer payments.

4.4 Transfers from the State

Table 5.4 shows the level of transfers from central government to lower levels of administration between 2010 and 2014. With the exception of 2013, the total amount transferred by the center has been slowly increasing. Since expenditures have been increasing at a faster pace, the share of transfers is slightly decreasing (43 per cent in 2010, 40 per cent in 2013).

Table 5.3 *Revenues from the taxation of businesses 2009–13 (million euros)*

		2009	2010	2011	2012	2013
Municipalities	All business taxes	4,547	4,282	2,792	2,811	2,705
	Professional tax	4,547	4,282			
	Tax on Real-estate			1,461	1,466	1,353
	Tax on Added-value			1,045	1,063	1,080
	Tax on network companies			155	148	143
	Tax on large retailers			132	134	129
Association of municipalities with their own resources (EPCI)	All business taxes	13,496	14,514	8,466	8,981	9,751
	Professional tax	13,496	14,514			
	Tax on Real-estate			4,833	5,165	5,560
	Tax on Added-value			2,845	2,961	3,246
	Tax on network companies			312	340	367
	Tax on large retailers			477	514	579
Other organisms of cooperation between municipalities	All business taxes	18,092	18,831	11,292	11,822	12,478
	Professional tax	18,092	18,831			
	Tax on Real-estate			6,327	6,662	6,934
	Tax on Added-value			3,890	4,024	4,325
	Tax on network companies			467	488	510
	Tax on large retailers			609	648	708
Départements	All business taxes	9,239	9,396	7,356	7,602	8,165
	Professional tax	9,239	9,396			
	Tax on Added-value			7,130	7,363	7,916
	Tax on network companies			226	239	248
Regions	All business taxes	2,922	3,042	4,317	4,438	4,736
	Professional tax	2,922	3,042			
	Tax on Added-value			3,675	3,795	4,081
	Tax on network companies			643	643	655
All local governments	All business taxes	30,253	31,269	22,966	23,862	25,378
	Professional tax	30,253	31,269			
	Tax on Real-estate			6,327	6,662	6,934
	Tax on Added-value			14,695	15,182	16,323
	Tax on network companies			1,370	1,370	1,413
	Tax on large retailers			609	648	708

Source: DGFiP.

Table 5.4   Transfers from the central state to local administrations

	2010	2011	2012	2013	2014
Total expenditures	229,200	235,290	242,490	252,000(*)	–
Total of transfers from State	98,040	98,813	100,769	100,256	101,237
Including:					
DGF (global transfer)	41,093	41,265	41,390	41,505	40,121
Compensation for paid VAT	6,228	6,040	5,507	5,627	5,769
Compensation for tax relief	16,380(**)	11,128	10,310	9,805	9,744
Share of state tax receipts	22,629	25,430	27,297	27,461	29,942

Note: (**) The transfer compensating for the abolition of the local business tax was particularly high in 2010, the year of the transition to a new set of local business taxes.

Source: DGFiP 2014 (table 6-1) and (*) INSEE (table t_3205) for 2013 expenditures.

The table also gives a hint of the complexity of the matter. If the main transfer (the DGF – *Dotation Globale de Fonctionnement*) has been decreasing throughout this period together with the compensation for the local tax relief granted by the parliament, other transfers such as the share of state tax receipts given to local administrations in order to cover their new missions have been rapidly increasing.

To this already tense situation must be added the fact that, in order to meet the requirements of the European Union fiscal compact, the center is imposing for the period 2014–17 a special effort involving local governments. The block grant from the state (DGF) has been cut by €1.5 billion in 2014 and will be reduced further by €3.6 billion every year in 2015, 2016 and 2017, so that the transfer in 2016 should be €12.3 billion below its 2013 level. Combined with the rule that forbids local jurisdictions to borrow in order to pay for their current expenditures (see below) and with an already high level of local taxes, the outlook for local public finances is definitely grim.

4.5   The Nature of Spending and the Budgetary Procedures

The budget of a local administration is strictly controlled by the central state via its local representatives, the *préfets*, and the local courts of auditors (*chambres régionales des comptes*). The law fixes a precise procedure to be followed for the vote and execution of the budget, the main steps being:

1. Year t: the National Parliament votes the financial law for the year t + 1, thereby setting the maximum and minimum tax rates for local

administrations. The Parliament also votes the amount of money that will be transferred to local administrations for year t + 1. The largest share of those transfers is known as the *Dotation Générale de Fonctionnement* (DGF, the general transfer for functioning).
2. Year t: debates in the local assemblies around the budgetary objectives for the coming year (t + 1).
3. Year t or t + 1 (preferably after the vote of the financial law by the Parliament): discussion of the first draft of the budget for year t + 1 presented by the local executive body. It must be (i) a consolidated budget (all actions and liabilities of the local administration must be presented), (ii) a balanced budget (see below) and (iii) a 'sincere' budget (regarding in particular expected revenues).
4. Year t or t + 1 (preferably after the vote of the financial law by the Parliament and not more than two months after the local debate): the budget is voted and then sent to the *préfet*. It can be executed immediately, without waiting for feedback from the local representative of the central government.[25]
5. After receiving the budget, the *préfet* can require further explanation and, if not satisfied, ask the regional court of auditors to provide an in-depth analysis of the budget and eventually sanction the local administration (administrative court).
6. In extreme cases, the *préfet* will reject the budget and the regional court of auditors will temporarily manage the local administration.[26]

To this must be added that each and every expense must be approved and executed by a local official accountant, paid by the central state, who checks compliance with the budget voted. At the end of the year, the accountant presents the budget as it was executed and reports once again to the préfet, with the possibility of sanctions in case of mismatch between the voted and the executed budget.

Whether this procedure is effective is an open question, but it surely did not prevent the rapid increase in total expenditure since 2000 (by approximately 70 per cent over the period), even if that trend has somehow been slowing down since the early days of the crisis. This rapid increase in spending was due in large part to the steady growth of the number of employees and consequently of the payroll (Table 5.5). Keeping in mind the privileged status of civil servants (they cannot be dismissed), such an increase in the labor force creates a serious constraint on future budgets.

During the same period the debt of local governments more than doubled (Table 5.5). This is surprising since, as we will see, those administrations can only borrow for the purpose of investment. But, predictably, investment kept increasing, including during the crisis.

Table 5.5 Local expenditures, debt and deficit (in billions €)

	1994	2000	2007	2008	2009	2010	2011	2012	2013
Operating expenses	50.4	74.0	102.3	107.6	113.3	117.4	120.2	124.3	128.6
Including payroll	*30.2*	*41.9*	*60.2*	*64.3*	*67.0*	*68.9*	*70.3*	*72.5*	*74.8*
Interest	7.2	3.6	5.0	6.2	3.9	2.7	3.4	3.4	3.0
Benefits paid and other transfers	28.6	30.0	57.1	59.0	63.1	62.9	63.4	65.1	67.0
Investment	28.7	34.7	49.4	50.4	50.4	46.8	48.4	51.0	53.4
Total expenditures	115.0	142.3	213.9	223.2	230.7	229.8	235.3	243.8	252.0
Total revenues	110.7	143.7	206.1	213.7	224.7	228.1	234.7	240.1	242.8
Deficit	−4.3	1.3	−7.7	−9.5	−6.0	−1.7	−0.7	−3.7	−9.2
Debt (*)	–	*88.9*	*125.4*	*136.8*	*145.8*	*151.3*	*156.5*	*163.7*	*170.0*

Source: INSEE (table t_3205 except for the debt taken from t_3101).

4.6 Balancing the Local Budgets

The law requires that the budget of a local administration be organized in two sections: the operating budget (*budget de fonctionnement*) and the investment budget. The operating budget covers all those annual recurring expenses such as salaries, maintenance of public buildings and roads, paying social benefits. On the other hand, investment expenditures are supposed to be discrete (e.g. building a new school). Art. L 1612-4 of the General Code for Territorial communities (CGCT) states that:

> The budget of the local authority is really balanced (*réel équilibre*) when both the operating section and the section of investment are voted as balanced budgets, when revenues and expenditures have been assessed in a sincere way, and when the levy on the revenues of the operating section transferred to the investment section, added to the own-source revenues for investment, excluding the proceeds of loans, grants and possibly accounts for depreciation and provisions, provides sufficient resources to cover the repayment of capital annuities of the accruing debt during the year.

A quick look at the consolidated budget of municipalities and EPCI for 2013 will help illustrate how this rule functions (Figure 5.4). For that year, the operating budget was balanced with a gross saving of €16.9 billion. That amount was transferred to the investment section. Adding that amount to other investment resources (€4 billion), municipalities and EPCI had largely enough to cover the repayment of the debt for that year (€7.9 billion). In that sense, the budget was safe and complied with the rule.

120   *Multi-level finance and the Euro crisis*

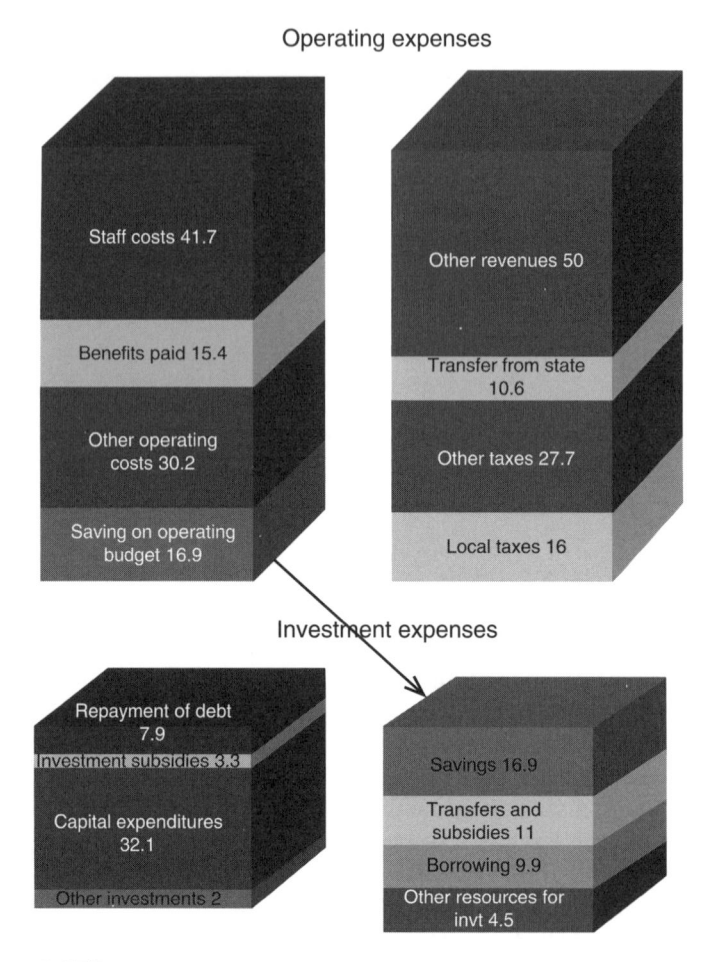

Operating expenses

- Staff costs 41.7
- Benefits paid 15.4
- Other operating costs 30.2
- Saving on operating budget 16.9

- Other revenues 50
- Transfer from state 10.6
- Other taxes 27.7
- Local taxes 16

Investment expenses

- Repayment of debt 7.9
- Investment subsidies 3.3
- Capital expenditures 32.1
- Other investments 2

- Savings 16.9
- Transfers and subsidies 11
- Borrowing 9.9
- Other resources for invt 4.5

Source: DGFiP.

Figure 5.4 Budget of municipalities and EPCI in 2013 (billions €)

Furthermore, investment for that year reached €37.4 billion while loans amounted to only €9.9 billion.

This confirms that the greatest share of investment is financed with savings and specific transfers (from the state or the EU). Considering that part of the €9.9 billion borrowed was used to repay the accruing debt (€7.9 billion), then only €2 billion of the borrowed money was used to finance investment (this is the figure found in Figure 5.5, if you add up the borrowing from EPCI and municipalities).

French sub-national public finances 121

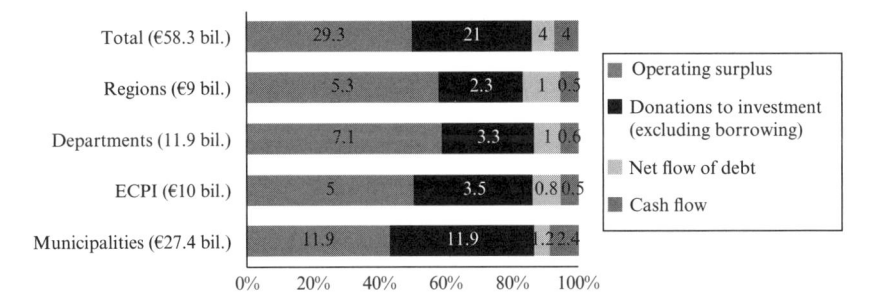

	Operating surplus	Donations to investment (excluding borrowing)	Net flow of debt	Cash flow
Total (€58.3 bil.)	29.3	21	4	4
Regions (€9 bil.)	5.3	2.3	1	0.5
Departments (11.9 bil.)	7.1	3.3	1	0.6
ECPI (€10 bil.)	5	3.5	0.8	0.5
Municipalities (€27.4 bil.)	11.9	11.9	1.2	2.4

Source: DGFiP – Table from Observatoire des finances locales (2014), p. 34.

Figure 5.5 Financing of local public investment in 2013

4.7 Borrowing for Local Governments

Before 1982 and the start of the decentralization process, the central government controlled the entire borrowing process. Local governments had to combine borrowing with central subsidies and to borrow from one of two centrally controlled agencies (*Caisse des Dépôts et Consignations* or *Caisse d'aide à l'équipement des collectivités locales*-CAECL later renamed *Crédit local de France*). These controls entirely disappeared after 1982, however, with the above-mentioned rules of balanced budget and borrow-only-to-invest (Article L.1612-4 CGCT). Despite this new freedom, borrowing is neither the only nor the main source of financing. As a matter of fact, borrowing covers only a small share of local public investment. Local governments use three sources to finance their investments:

- self-financing (the difference between operating revenues and operating costs),
- specific transfers (from central government, the EU or the sale of its own assets),
- borrowing, and
- cash flow surpluses (reducing their treasury balances).

Figure 5.5 clearly shows the residual role played by borrowing. But, taking a long-term perspective leads to a somewhat different assessment of reality. Indeed, the level of the debt has been steadily increasing since the turn of the century (see Figure 5.2 and Table 5.6) to reach €137 billion in 2013, due in part to the record deficit of €9.2 billion for 2013.

Municipalities and regions are the big borrowers. One should not

Table 5.6   Financing for municipalities, EPCI, départements *and regions*

	2005	2006	2007	2008	2009	2010	2011	2012	2013
Financing needs	−3.3	−3.1	−7.7	−8.3	−6.3	−1.8	−0.7	−3.7	−9.2
Debt repayment	12.4	12.4	11.2	11.6	12.0	12.0	12.4	13.0	12.8
Borrowing	16.3	17.1	17.6	19.1	19.3	16.1	15.9	17.9	16.8
Total debt (on 12/31)	93.7	98.8	105.2	112.7	120.0	124.3	127.6	132.4	137.0

Source: INSEE from DGFiP (Table NATTEF08340).

conclude however that *départements* have been more virtuous; the explanation for their lower level of borrowing is rather due to a lower level of investment.

4.8   Sources of Borrowing

Today, most of the borrowing is done, not directly on the market, but through banks.[27] In 2011 and 2012, local administrations encountered some difficulties in borrowing (see below and Table 5.7). This situation was the result of two factors. Firstly, banks were weakened by the financial crisis and hesitant to lend. Secondly, the Franco-Belgian bank Dexia, leader in the financing of local governments in the EU, went virtually bankrupt. The central government reacted by nationalizing the French branch of Dexia and opening, for those two years, a credit line of €5 billion.

Since 2013, the situation has been improving due to: (i) the creation of a new bank for local governments as a substitute for Dexia (this new bank is backed by Banque Postale and Caisse des Dépôts et Consignations); (ii) an increase in the credit line of the European Bank for Investment (from €4 to 7 billion); (iii) a new credit line of €20 billion at the Caisse des Dépôts for long-term projects. Also, in October 2013 a new agency was created on the model of *Agence France Trésor*, the Department of the Finance Ministry managing the debt of the central government. This new entity, named '*Agence France locale*', will borrow directly on the financial market and then grant loans to local governments. This will allow small municipalities to indirectly access the financial market and be less dependent on banks; something that was so far only possible for the largest municipalities.

Table 5.7 shows how local administrations went through the crisis. The crisis did not have a significant impact on the budgetary sustainability of local administrations. The structural deficit was nonetheless contained at 1.77 per cent of revenues (fiscal + state contribution) in 2012.[28] The table also confirms that local authorities met some difficulty in borrowing,

Table 5.7 Borrowing and debt of local administrations (billion euros)

	2008	2009	2010	2011	2012
Total expenses	206.82	214.23	212.82	219.38	225.87
Total revenues	206.03	215.15	215.10	222.11	227.01
Total expenses net of debt payments	195.24	202.19	200.81	206.95	212.84
Total revenues net of borrowing	186.93	195.85	199.04	206.23	209.14
Investment (excluding debt payment)	55.23	56.68	52.03	54.00	55.20
Deficit	8.31	6.34	1.77	0.72	3.70
Borrowing	19.10	19.30	16.06	15.88	17.87
Total debt	112.74	120.04	124.35	127.58	132.45
Ratios					
Current saving/revenues (*)	18.9%	17.8%	19%	20%	19%
Net saving (**)/revenues (*)	16.2%	15.4%	16.8%	17.7%	16.6%
Debt/revenues (*)	67.5%	69.8%	69.5%	68.7%	70.1%
Annual debt payment/revenues (*)	9.7%	9.4%	8.9%	9.0%	9.3%

Note: (*) Revenues net of revenues from investment – see previous table; (**) current saving – interest on debt.

Source: DGFiP.

starting in 2010–11. Borrowing dropped by 17.7 per cent between 2009 and 2011.

4.9 Toxic Loans

Not all local governments were impacted the same way by the crisis: the shock was tougher on those who had contracted so-called 'toxic loans'.[29] Many of them reacted by initiating lawsuits against the banks. This resulted in interesting legal battles. The first battle ended with a partial victory for both sides: the loans were maintained but the rates were brought down considerably on the basis that banks, and in particular Dexia, in violation of the law, did not communicate the 'effective rate' of the loan to the borrowers (Court of first instance – Tribunal de Grande Instance de Nanterre). This was fraught with dramatic consequences for the state, which now owns the French subsidiary of Dexia. Potentially it could have cost the state some €17 billion. While banks decided to appeal the decision, the state, via the parliament, decided to pass a law (July 2014) that simply makes local governments responsible for those loans, hence reversing the decision of the court.[30] In the meantime, another law was passed that makes it virtually impossible for local governments to contract similar toxic loans in the future (law 2013-672 of 26 July 2013).

4.10 Public–Private Partnerships: A New Threat?

Introduced in 2005 (ruling of 17 June 2004), PPPs initially grew rapidly in France, with 544 projects (as of 1 October 2014), 24 per cent of them coming from the state and the rest from local governments. Two-thirds of these projects involved amounts below €30 million, and only 9 per cent are related to amounts above €150 million.[31] However, PPPs have been criticized for endangering the solvency of local governments, the latter finding that PPPs provided an easy way to get around the borrowing limits. It was also pointed out that sometimes there was a 'toxic' aspect to those contracts, the local governments not being always fully aware of what it would really cost them: repayments having to be paid until the end of the, often long-term, contract.

Those worries were addressed by the introduction of a new rule on 1 January 2011. The rule establishes that public–private partnership contracts must be integrated into the budget of the local governments following standardized reporting procedures fixed by decree (Decree of 16 December 2010). Does this explain the steep fall observed in the number of contracts since the start of 2013, especially on the part of local governments (Figure 5.6)? This is very likely, and it is to be hoped that future PPPs will bring new opportunities for local administrations, but without bringing with them new and uncontrolled risks. Meanwhile, it will be necessary to deal with some of the ongoing 'toxic' contracts, which, it must be recalled, are typically long-term contracts.

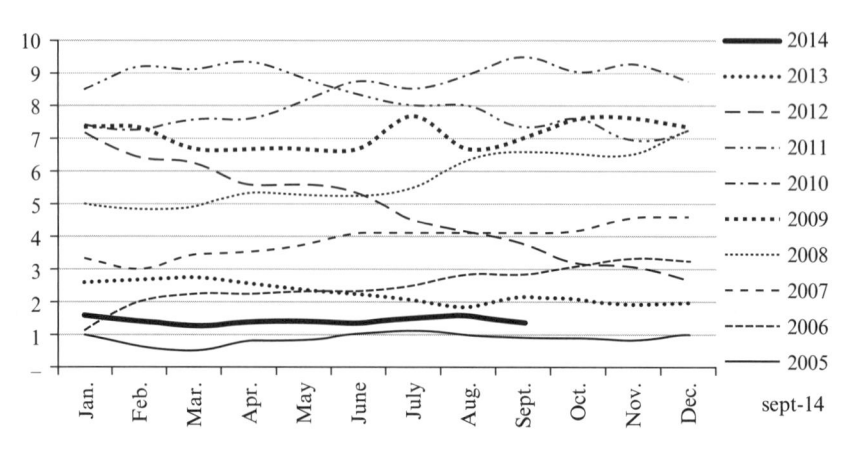

Source: MAPP.

Figure 5.6 Number of new PPPs started each month

4.11 Efforts to Develop New Public Accounting Standards

Article 115 of the finance law of 30 December 2008 created a '*Conseil de normalisation des comptes publics*' (National Council for Standardization of Public Accounting). The council has been active since 7 September 2009. Besides being the relevant partner for IPSAS (International Public Sector Accounting Standards), its role is in particular to reflect on the prospects for improving the transparency of financial statements in local government operations. In this context, the work will consist in putting together a model to be used for financial statements (balance sheet, income statement and annexes) that would be simple and readable; a statement that could also be, for the entities concerned, submitted for some state certification of accounts still to be implemented.

This project follows recommendations by both the General Inspectorate of Finance (December 2012 report on the Regions, proposition No. 12) and the Court of Auditors (October 2013's report concerning all levels of local government) to have a unique financial account and reporting. It also follows on some suggestions included in a new bill on territorial development (the bill mentions the certification of accounts for some municipalities). It is, finally, in line with European ongoing reflections on the harmonization of accounting standards across all public sectors.

5. CONCLUSIONS

Sub-national levels of government were already under the strict control of central government when the crisis unfolded in 2008. Indeed, despite a strong wind of decentralization that had been blowing since the early 1980s, the central government had always kept a strong hand on local public finances. If the constitutional law of 2003 had increased at the margin the financial autonomy of territorial jurisdictions, it also confirmed the rules imposing a balanced budget and forbidding them to borrow except for investment purposes. It also required that a 'critical level' of own-source revenues be retained. In summary, France remains a country where fiscal sovereignty entirely belongs to the central government, as reinforced by a 2009 ruling from the Constitutional Council:

> It does not follow from article 72-2 of the constitution, nor from any constitutional work that local authorities (*collectivités territoriales*) are granted fiscal autonomy.[32]

This explains that local public finances were not too badly impacted by the crisis. The level of public investment was maintained (something that could be explained by the local election of 2014), very few local governments have been in total distress so far and the potential problems stemming from liabilities built in public–private partnerships or from toxic loans were quickly dealt with through the legislative channel.

Still, one should not be in a hurry to conclude that there is nothing to worry about. As a matter of fact, it has been shown that signs of weaknesses are easy to detect. Hence, the level of local deficits reached unprecedented levels in 2013 (€9.2 billion); EPCIs – a form of cooperation between municipalities that was favored by decentralization laws and was supposed to rationalize local spending by the pooling of some activities – have so far led to disappointing results: competencies were transferred to ECPIs without transferring the staff, thereby bringing higher payrolls and little economies of scale. On top of this must be added the fact that the levels of local taxation have been steadily increasing over the last decades and, given the record level of the overall tax burden in France, a further increase in these rates will be politically difficult, affecting the competitiveness of French enterprises, and well-being of households. Local authorities, in particular, are at an impasse since the central government must meet the requirements of the EU fiscal compact and will do so by reducing transfers to sub-national levels of government.

In a way, the true crisis of public finances, at both central and local levels, could well be yet to come, and it could come soon. To avoid, or to mitigate, that possibility surely requires a more serious examination of spending plans at each level of government. But the above analysis shows that it is equally necessary and urgent to fix once and for all the rules of the game between the various levels of government; to clarify the responsibilities devoted to each level and to allocate resources in a way that makes each level accountable. As an illustration of the prevailing confusion, in 2012 the operating budget of the central state showed a deficit of €63.2 billion. But the same budget specified that €49.9 billion was taken from central government's revenues to be transferred to local governments and €18.9 billion to the EU. Hence, it could be – and has been – argued that the central government deficit is due to the fact that its budget is used to balance the budgets of supra- and sub-national governments. To which, sub-national governments will probably reply that the central government has taken away from them some of their own fiscal resources (Oliva, 2013, p. 15).

This situation must be sorted out, and this would require that left and right, local and central representatives work together and stop passing a new law every other year that gives a new direction and meaning to the decentralization process. To regain the visibility indispensable for sound public management, that bumpy road toward decentralization must be leveled once and for all.

NOTES

1. The author wishes to thank Vesselina Garello as well as participants to the Turin conference on multi-level finances (Collegio Carlo Alberto, Moncalieri, July 2014) for their helpful comments on earlier drafts of this work.
2. The *millefeuille* is a cake made of many layers of puff pastry alternating with layers of cream. It is also known in some countries as the Napoleon.
3. In France, the word 'municipalité' refers to the executive branch of the 'commune': the mayor and his/her team. In this text we translate the French word 'commune' by the English terminology of municipality, keeping in mind that the latter does not have exactly the same meaning in French.
4. There exist two types of *syndicats*: the SIVU (Syndicat communal à vocation unique) and the SIVOM (Syndicat communal à vocation multiples). The responsibilities taken by those associations are often linked to network services: water supply, electricity, urbanism, garbage collection, etc.
5. On this evolution see, for instance, Douat and Badin (2006), pp. 407–32.
6. Law 99-586 of 12 July 2009 'concerning the simplification and strengthening of inter-municipality cooperation'.
7. Spillover effects, economies of scale, etc. See for instance Gilbert and Picard (1996) or Garello (2003).
8. This rule, we will see, has been changed twice since 1999.
9. Law no. 2010-1563 of 16 December 2010.
10. Law no. 2014-58 of 27 January 2014 'for the modernisation of public territorial action and confirmation of *métropoles*'. Among the provisions of the previous law that were not amended is the direct election of members of the ECPIs' council.
11. *Métropoles*, forming a new administrative layer, were introduced with the law of 16 December 2010 modified by the law of 27 January 2014. It concerns highly populated areas. Nice Côte d'Azur is the only existing *métropole* so far but, pursuant to the law of January 2014, Aix-Marseille, Lyon and Paris will soon acquire this status. Interestingly, in the case of Aix-Marseille the project has run into fierce opposition from many municipalities, concerned that the merger was imposed on them by central government.
12. It must be stressed that, at the same time as the law was entrusting greater power to local governments, the control over the budget of those local governments was reinforced and the local representative of the central government, the *préfet*, was asked to approve all local budgets. This remains the rule as of today, although the laws of decentralization have reduced the power of *prefets*. See below, section 4.5.
13. To further illustrate that point, a law of 1 January 2002 made regions responsible for regional transportation, and another law of 1 January 2004 entrusted to *départements* the payment of a minimum income to all citizens (RMI).
14. The table listing the responsibilities for each level of government can be found here: http://www.collectivites-locales.gouv.fr/files/files/tableau_repartition_competences_valideCILapublier%281%29.pdf.
15. The budget of the administration of the social security system is included in public accounting and comes under the definition of gross public debt and general government. As the following tables show, this administration alone outweighs all the other administrations combined and has been lately increasing its debt at a rapid pace. Furthermore, the separation between the budget of the social security system and the central government budget is not that clear. As an illustration of this lack of transparency, the 'contribution sociale généralisée' (a flat tax on all incomes, which was introduced in 1991 with a rate of 1.1 per cent and reached in 2014 rates that vary between 6.2 and 15.5 per cent, depending on the type of income) is a major source of financing for the social security system. Interestingly, the control of the social security budget by the parliament is only recent and remains loose (the reason being that the system is supposedly managed by the social partners, that is, essentially, the labor and employers' unions). This state of affairs clearly calls for attention (from the perspective of sustainable public finances),

and two roads are open to the parliament: one implying stricter control, the other greater liberalization.
16. http://www.insee.fr/fr/themes/comptes-nationaux/tableau.asp?sous_theme=3.1&xml=3.106prov.
17. Pébereau (2005), p. 47.
18. During that period, the French public treasury was able to borrow at historically low interest rates, a consequence being that in terms of debt financing, things can only get worse for the French Treasury Agency, the exposure to interest risk being high.
19. This 'freedom to administrate itself' has been transposed as art. L. 1111-1 of the *Code Général des Collectivités Territoriales* (General Code for Territorial Jurisdictions).
20. In practice, however, the power to fix the base remains very limited.
21. The Committee for Local Finances was created by a law of 3 January 1979. It is composed of 32 elected representatives coming from the various local assemblies (municipalities, *départements* and regions) and 11 members appointed by the central government. This mini-parliament is consulted on all matters related to the various transfers from central state to local governments. It was one of the suggestions from that committee to create a special entity that would collect revenues to be distributed through a mechanism of *horizontal* equalization. The mechanism, named FPIC (*Fonds national de péréquation des ressources intercommunales et communales*), was set up in 2012. It should redistribute around €1 billion by the time it is fully operational in 2016.
22. This is a direct consequence of article 34 of the constitution just discussed and of the fact that, de facto, a conflict between the parliament and the executive is unlikely in France.
23. Historically, it started the other way around: local jurisdictions from the Middle Ages to the French Revolution were essentially using indirect taxation. After the revolution, the state progressively introduced direct taxes on property. Then indirect taxation was taken away from local jurisdictions and became the privilege of the central state, while direct taxation on property was transferred from the state to local government (see Douat and Badin, 2006).
24. For the purpose of the present study it should be recalled that, contrary to what happened in some European countries such as Spain, the French real estate market was not much impacted by the 2008–11 crisis.
25. Article 72 of the constitution states: 'In *départements* and territories, the government's delegate [i.e., the *préfet*] is in charge of national interest, of administrative supervision and of compliance with the law'. Since the decentralization of 1982, however, the *préfet* only checks the legality (compliance with all relevant laws) of the budget but not the budget policy.
26. For exceptional circumstances (natural disasters and the like), and when the regional court of auditors cannot find a way to balance the budget, Article 2335-2 of the General Code (CGCT) makes it possible for the center to directly subsidize the local government. Those subsidies remain marginal, not exceeding €2 million, and are triggered in circumstances other than poor management.
27. Banks do not manage the treasury of local governments, the latter being forced to put their cash with the Central State Public Treasury, which hence benefits from free liquidities.
28. Structural deficit is here defined as total expenses net of debt payments minus total revenues net of borrowing.
29. See Portal (2013).
30. The matter will probably be brought to the Constitutional court.
31. Those data are provided by the MAPP: http://www.economie.gouv.fr/ppp/suivi-l'ensemble-des-contrats-partenariat.
32. Conseil constitutionnel, Déc. No 2009-599 DC, 20 December 2009.

REFERENCES

Benetti, Julie (2012), 'La constitution au secours des finances publiques ? Questions autour de la "règle d'or"', in Benetti Julie and Hervé Groud (eds), *Les finances publiques nationales et locales face à la crise*, Paris: L'Harmattan, pp. 53–64.
Benetti, Julie and Hervé Groud (eds) (2012), *Les finances publiques nationales et locales face à la crise*, Paris: L'Harmattan.
Bramoullé, Gérard (2006), *Finances et libertés locales: pourquoi l'explosion des impôts locaux?*, Aix-en-Provence: Librairie de l'Université d'Aix-en-Provence.
Buisson, Jacques (2012), *Finances Publiques*, Paris: Dalloz.
Conseil de normalisation des comptes publics (2014), 'Rapport d'activités 2013', at: http://www.economie.gouv.fr/files/files/directions_services/cnocp/Activite/Rapport_CNOCP_2013_web.pdf.
Douat, Etienne and Xavier Badin (2006), *Finances publiques*, 3rd edn, Themis, Paris: Presses Universitaires de France.
Dussart, Vincent (2009), *Finances publiques*, Orléans: Paradigme.
Garello, Pierre (2003), 'The dynamics of fiscal federalism', *Journal des économistes et des études humaines*, **13**: 421–40.
Gilbert, Guy and Pierre Picard (1996), 'Incentives and optimal size of local jurisdictions', *European Economic Review*, **40** (1): 19–41.
Groud, Hervé (2012), 'Les finances publiques: cause ou victime de la crise?', in J. Benetti and H. Groud (eds), *Les finances publiques nationales et locales face à la crise*, Paris: L'Harmattan pp. 11–52.
Groud, Vivien (2012), 'Les finances locales sous tension', in J. Benetti and H. Groud (eds), *Les finances publiques nationales et locales face à la crise*, Paris: L'Harmattan, pp. 113–28.
Guyon, Thibault and Stéphane Sorbe (2009), 'Solde structurel et effort structurel: vers une décomposition par sous-secteur des administrations publiques', *Les Cahiers de la D.G.T.P.E.*, No. 2009/13.
Josselin, Jean-Michel, Fabio Padovano and Yvon Rocaboy (2012), 'Fiscal rules vs. political culture as determinants of soft budget spending behaviors', HAL Id: halshs-00706980, https://halshs.archives-ouvertes.fr/halshs-00706980.
Observatoire des finances locales (2014), 'Les finances des collectivités locales en 2014', downloaded at http://www.collectivites-locales.gouv.fr/files/files/OFL2014_00.pdf.
Oliva, Eric (2013), 'Equilibre budgétaire et constitution: l'équilibre des budgets locaux', *Revue Française de Finances Publiques*, no. 123, September, 31–4.
Pébereau, Michel (2005), 'Rompre avec la facilité de la dette publique – pour des finances publiques au service de notre croissance économique et de notre cohésion sociale', La documentation française. Collection des rapports officiels.
Portal, Eric (2013), 'Risques et maîtrise de la dette volatile des collectivités territoriales françaises,' Revue Française de Finances Publiques, no. 123, September, 73–84.
Warsmann, Jean-Luc (2011), 'Rapport sur le projet de loi constitutionnelle relative à l'équilibre des finances publiques', Assemblée Nationale, Rapport no. 3333, April.

PART III

The Troubled Countries of Southern Europe

6. Economics and politics of local Greek government

Georgios Chortareas and Vassileios E. Logothetis

1. INTRODUCTION

The effects of the 2008 global recession were delayed in spreading to Greece, and in 2010 the country still displayed a higher growth rate compared to the Eurozone. The crisis in Greece reflected a number of macroeconomic and institutional weaknesses that had built up over the preceding decades. These weaknesses included structural deficiencies and lack of competitiveness, which were reflected in both the budget and current account deficits. The country for a long period had experienced a high growth rate along with falling competitiveness. Institutional weaknesses included a lack of clarity about local and municipal functions – with contracting arrangements for local services implying that wages are paid by the central budget, and liabilities parked in enterprises and off-budget entities. As we discuss below, this led to a lack of clarity in information flows, as well as diffused accountability. It also makes it extremely hard to adhere to adjustment targets, and also to evade rigid conditionality.

The economic crisis has had a severe impact on Greece's economy: the country's GDP has contracted approximately 25 percent since the beginning of the crisis, while unemployment has surged from 10.5 percent in 2004 to 24.2 percent in 2012. Greece, during the 2010 financial turmoil, faced increased borrowing costs and consequent inability to re-finance its debt. To avoid default, Greece entered the European Financial Stability Facility (EFSF) in May 2010 and agreed on an extended fiscal adjustment program. This included reforms in the institutional framework of the economy to tackle long-standing inefficiencies and bring the economy back to a sustainable growth path. Greece's primary deficit decreased from approximately −10 percent of GDP in 2009 to −1.3 percent of GDP in 2012. As a result of the adjustments, in 2013 Greece experienced a primary surplus of 1.45 percent of GDP. Similarly the deficit in the current account

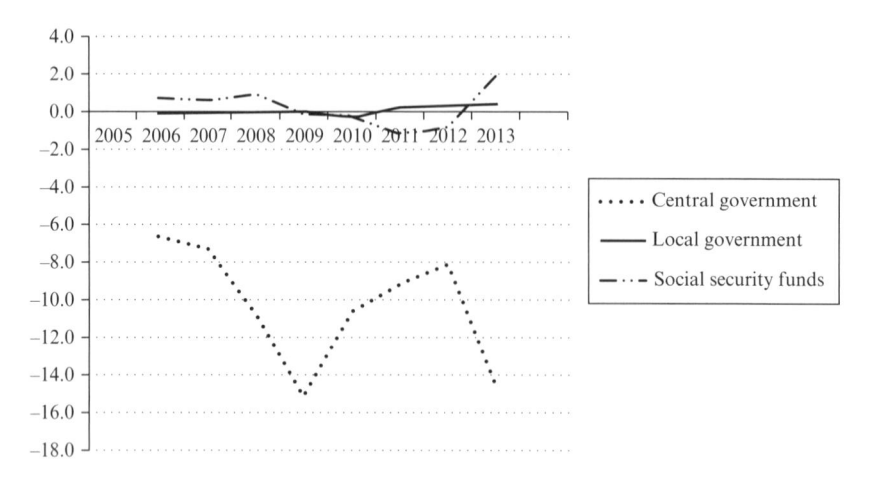

Source: Eurostat, Statistical Database.

Figure 6.1 Deficit (% of GDP)

balance turned to surplus in 2013. Nevertheless Greece's debt had skyrocketed to approximately 168 percent of GDP in 2013.

Throughout this period, local governments' deficits remained low, as in the era prior to Greece's admission to the EFSF, ranging from −0.1 percent in 2006 to a surplus of 0.4 percent in 2013 (see Figure 6.1). The healthy position of the local governments is misleading, however. As suggested above, this partly reflected the inappropriate assignments of functional and economic responsibilities. Consequently, the burden of adjustments has been laid primarily at the door of the central government, and successive governments have paid the political price for the steep adjustments required under the adjustment programs.

2. GREECE'S LOCAL INSTITUTIONS

2.1 Electoral Process, the Number of Municipalities and Responsibilities

For most of the 20th century, Greece's political environment has been characterized by relatively weak democratic institutions, with recurrent periods of political instability. Extended political polarization has been present since the restoration of democracy in 1974. Numerous rent-seeking activities permeate almost all aspects of economic activity and take place against the background of immature democratic institutions dominated by the presence of powerful interest groups (Mitsopoulos and Pelagidis, 2011).

Local politics in Greece, to a large extent, reflects national politics and is characterized by the same inadequacies as the ones present at the central level. Until 2014, elections for mayors and municipal councils occurred every four years. A two-stage system applies to determine the outcome of elections. The two strongest participants of the first round compete in the second only if no candidate has obtained a majority in the first round. Candidate mayors put together and lead their electoral list. Winning lists elect both the mayor and the majority of municipal council members, as the latter are allocated according to the electoral results. The municipal council is the decisive body in Greece's local politics, operates under a majority rule, and bears the ultimate responsibility for the main issues concerning each municipality. Mayors lead the municipal administration and are responsible for implementing decisions taken by the municipal council. Mayors in Greece are, in effect, the principal agents in local politics as they decide on the selection of municipal council candidates when they put together their list, and thus can exert influence on the decisions taken at the level of municipal council in the aftermath of elections.

The number of Greek municipalities has changed several times during past years, as it has been at the epicenter of the various reforms introduced to enhance administrative efficiency. As the number of municipalities decreased, their responsibilities broadened. Areas that were under central government's responsibility have gradually moved to become the responsibility of the elected municipal councils and the mayor. The map of Greece's local governments included thousands of municipalities and communes that constituted a complex administrative system with very few checks and balances, especially in the case of very small administrative entities. The reform act of 1997 reduced the number of administrative entities to 910 municipalities, and 124 smaller communes.

The current economic crisis has imposed further restrictions on the number of municipalities. After Greece's submission to the joint IMF–EU–ECB bailout plan, special provisions for municipalities were included in the memoranda that the Greek government signed with its creditors. Among these was a further reduction in the number of municipalities. The latest reform act of 2010 completely eliminated the communes and initiated extensive mergers that further reduced the number of municipalities to 325. This reduction primarily aimed at creating economies of scale to increase local government efficiency and at reducing the number of elected officials. These provisions were part of the first Memorandum of Understanding (MoU) that Greece signed in 2010 and explicitly stated that parliament should adopt legislation 'reforming public administration at

Source: Chortareas et al. (2014a).

Figure 6.2 Evolution of Greece's administrative divisions, municipal level

the local level, notably by merging municipalities, prefectures and regions with the aim of reducing operating costs and wage bill.' The reduction in the number of municipalities has not passed without resistance as both the 1997 and the 2010 reforms have been the subject of political controversy in local and central politics. The effects of the consecutive administrative reforms on the number of municipalities can be seen in Figure 6.2.

As far as municipal responsibilities are concerned, there has been an increasing shift from central to local government assignments. The latest reform act has been the most 'generous' in increasing the responsibilities of local governments in the fields of public health, social welfare, urban development, environmental supervision and public education. These areas were mostly under central government supervision, with municipalities having only a limited capacity to adapt policies. The 2010 reform strengthened the ability of municipalities to plan and execute policies.

2.2 Municipal Finances

The economic crisis has also played an important role in reshaping municipal finances, an area that has traditionally been less transparent than central government finances. Municipal finances in Greece are subject to uniform budget rules with municipal councils deciding upon the allocation of resources. The latter primarily come from central government's budget in the form of direct transfers (subsidies) and especially levied taxes in favor of municipalities, and secondarily through a system of local compensatory taxation. Residents and businesses operating in each municipality contribute to the local government's budget typically by a small amount on a regular basis, mainly for maintenance of basic infrastructure and for public services provided to them by that municipality. In addition municipalities have the ability to borrow, typically from government-controlled financial institutions and private banks. The 2010 reform has placed various limitations on the ability of a municipality to borrow from financial institutions, as the amortization should not exceed 20 percent of a municipality's regular revenues and the stock of the debt should not exceed the total revenues that a municipality has. The aforementioned brakes were imposed as an answer to Greece's excessive indebtedness, even if municipal debt has been relatively small and lower than the EU27 average – although as explained below, not all local spending is recognized as part of their respective budgets.

Nevertheless, several individual municipalities were in a position in which their annual revenues were not sufficient to service their debt and they were unable to keep up with their (interest and amortization) payments. By 2011, municipalities in Greece owed approximately 1.8 billion euros to banks, while several questions were raised over the legitimacy of some loans undertaken by certain municipalities. Table 6.1 presents the 10 most-indebted municipalities by July 2013 and the respective sums that they owe, while Table 6.2 presents the percentage of total debt relative to municipal regular income.

After the MoU signing, municipal finances fell under extensive monitoring by central government, while specific rules were introduced to increase transparency and enhance supervision. Municipalities are now required to publicize their budget plan statement before the new fiscal year begins. Every trimester, special reports are drafted that show how the budget is executed. Moreover, municipalities are also obliged to transmit their financial records to the Ministry of Interior. Failing to meet these requirements results in losses of direct transfers from the central government's budget, as specific budget-cutting plans were incorporated in the MoU. The MoU stated that governments should start implementing legislation reforming

Table 6.1 The 10 most-indebted municipalities in Greece by July 2013 (in thousand euros)

Municipality	Debt
Filis	52.152
Kalamarias	21.894
Acharnes	29.026
Rhodes	21.467
Amarousion	19.142
Nicea-Rentis	15.760
Corfu	15.064
Kordelio-Evosmos	14.289
Larissa	11.686
Ioannina	11.640

Table 6.2 Municipal debt as percentage of income in Greece (July 2013)

Number of Municipalities with Total Debt *above 150%* of their Regular Income	24
Number of Municipalities with Total Debt *between 120–150%* of their Regular Income	12
Number of Municipalities with Total Debt *between 100–120%* of their Regular Income	22
Number of Municipalities with Total Debt *between 80–100%* of their Regular Income	45
Number of Municipalities with Total Debt *between 50–80%* of their Regular Income	82
Number of Municipalities with Total Debt *up to 50%* of their Regular Income	140
Total	**325**

Source: Ministry of Interior.

public administration and reorganizing of local government with the aim of reducing costs by at least EUR 1,500 million from 2011 to 2013, of which at least EUR 500 million in 2011.

2.3 Municipal Hiring and Employment

Many aspects of municipal hiring have been rather obscure and constitute a long-debated issue in Greece. Institutional reforms introduced during the 1990s have reduced political pressures in the process of hiring civil servants. The Supreme Council for Civil Personnel Selection (ASEP) was established in 1994 as an independent authority to ensure transparency and meritocracy in the selection of public employees. Nevertheless, certain aspects of public employment did not fall under its jurisdiction, especially in municipalities. Consequently, during Greece's current economic crisis municipal employment has been at the epicenter of the fiscal adjustment process, with special provisions made for the reduction in the number of municipal employees.

Municipal employment broadly consists of two categories that represent the employment relationship between the municipality and its employees, i.e., permanent workers and contract workers. Since 1994, the former category was selected through procedures supervised by the Supreme Council for Civil Personnel Selection (ASEP), while the latter included both employees who were selected under the supervision of ASEP and others who were not. ASEP's responsibility was confined to selection of the most appropriate personnel based on requirements specified by municipalities when posting job announcements. In some cases, as explicitly mentioned in ASEP's 2004 report for its 10 years of operations, job requirements demanded by municipalities were so narrow and specific that they were, in effect, pinpointing specific candidates.

The second category of contract employees consisted of those hired as part of specific municipal operations via procedures not supervised by ASEP. Mayors had an increased role in the hiring process, while the selection criteria were not always clear. Contract employees were hired under fixed-term contracts that could vary from months to years or until the completion of the specific project. These contracts were often repeatedly renewed[1] and the employees' salaries, in many cases, were only partially paid from the municipal budget as another part could come, for example, from European Union or central governments funds. In effect, through this procedure, mayors created permanent or semi-permanent ties with parts of the electorate that were depending on them to have their contracts renewed. This also 'hid' the true extent of local financing and deficits.

As procedures for hiring this specific category were obscure and in most cases under the direct control of the incumbent mayor, several allegations regarding clientelism were publicly made regarding those hired outside the ASEP procedures. The aforementioned reality for contract employees and their ties with mayors or politicians was a key issue in the 2004 general election. The conservative opposition party suggested that contract employees who fulfilled core work in municipalities should be given the status of permanent workers. The relevant presidential decree issued in 2004 was proposed by the new conservative government, and stated that contract employees with more than 24 months of service and who in addition worked in core municipal operations could be given the status of permanent employees.

Court rulings in many cases decided which contract employees were fulfilling basic municipal operations or not, and thus would have the right to have their employment relationship with the municipality changed from temporary to permanent. Court rulings in many cases also decided which of the various categories of contract employees fell within the boundaries of the aforementioned presidential decree and thus would have their working relationship status changed from temporary to permanent.

Consequently, a large number of municipal employees have made use of the presidential decree to get a permanent employment position in municipalities. From 2004 to 2009 the number of public sector employees who changed their status from contract employees to permanent staff was 35,239. More than half of them, around 18,000, were local government employees, while another 6,000 were employed at the central administration and around 11,000 in the broad/extended public sector, including the local-government-owned enterprises. In terms of single entities, the Ministry of Culture emerges as the 'champion', with 1,720 employees becoming permanent staff, followed by public television (1,506), while the corresponding number for the largest municipality in Greece, the Municipality of Athens, is 575. The effects on local governments were spread out over many entities.

The aforementioned policy of transforming employees from contract to permanent status fuelled a heated debate following the outbreak of the Greek economic crisis, as the fiscal consolidation program included extensive public sector layoffs. The number of municipal employees was reduced by not renewing contracts, by layoffs, and by introducing a lower replacement rate for employees retiring. Layoffs were mostly concentrated among a pool of low-skilled workers employed in the areas of municipal police, school building guards and other low-skill positions, while the replacement rate was set at 20 percent of the employees retiring. Nevertheless, during the current economic crisis municipalities adopted temporary employment schemes as a way to tackle rising long-term and youth unemployment. Incidentally, in the aftermath of the January 2015 elections the minister of the interior, who was in office during the introduction of the presidential decree that changed the working status of the aforementioned contract workers to permanent, was elected president of the Hellenic Republic, after being proposed by the incumbent party of the radical left.

2.4 Municipal Enterprises

Municipal enterprises in Greece constitute another part of the potential administrative inefficiencies at the level of local governance. On a number of occasions multiple allegations regarding financial mismanagement and widespread clientelistic practices have been made, especially following the introduction of the IMF–EMU–EU bailout plan. Municipal enterprises have been one such area because large parts of their operation have been rather opaque.

Information available both to the central government as well as to the general public was limited because, for instance, the finances of municipal enterprises and the number of their employees had not been systematically reported, with available data being limited and of low reliability. To address the aforementioned reality, special provisions were made in the most recent municipal reform act in 2010.

Following the reduction in the number of local-level administrative entities, municipal enterprises in Greece were established by the thousands and served various local functions, ranging from providing water and sewage services, to transportation, local media, or even public relations.

The number of municipal enterprises increased between 1997 and 2004, reaching about 1,800 in number, with some of them being inactive. The total number of employees during the same period exceeded the 30,000 mark, while approximately 10,000 people served as board members. Financing for these enterprises was around 500 million euros, a large part coming from the European Union's structural funds and programs. Financially, the aforementioned enterprises were not sound and on average they generated increasing losses. Gekas and Mitsou (2004) report that from 2001 to 2004 losses increased by 65 percent, while the number of loss-generating municipal enterprises increased from 52 percent to 59 percent of the active municipal enterprises. On many occasions, debts generated from municipal enterprises were taken over by municipalities that they owned. The number of employees of municipal enterprises more than doubled from 1997 to 2004, and because the hiring criteria were largely undisclosed, this generated a series of allegations of clientelism. The Supreme Council of Civil Personnel Selection did not supervise this hiring process, as was the case for the rest of public hiring.

On the eve of Greece's financial crisis, the municipal reform act of 2010 contained special provisions to reduce municipal enterprises and to ensure that they would operate in a financially sound manner. The act places tight and binding restrictions on the number of enterprises that a municipality can establish, while at the same time it explicitly states that if an enterprise generates losses for three years concurrently, it is obliged to shut down its operations. At the present time, because three years have passed since the law was enacted and municipalities are faced with increased liabilities and debt stemming from their enterprises, the issue of shutdown of municipal enterprises is coming to the fore in Greece's public debate.

The central government has lately tried to ascertain the exact number of employees in these municipal entities, but reliable data are still not available after more than three years of effort. Casual estimations indicate that approximately 12,000 people are employed in the remaining 700 municipal enterprises.

3. PUBLIC SECTOR EMPLOYMENT, CLIENTELISM AND THE BUSINESS CYCLE

The size of the public sector, along with clientelistic practices, suggests that the electoral process may possibly affect employment. The role of elections in macroeconomic policy decisions in Greece has been considered in various contexts. In a more traditional political business-cycle framework Alogoskoufis and Philippopoulos (1992) consider the 'rational partisan' and 'exchange rate regime' models of inflation in the case of Greece. Milas (2000) considers a model with traded and non-traded goods and identifies a long-run labor demand equation with employment being proportional to relative output and prices. Testing the model with Greek data reveals that the effect of partisanship and the political business cycle affect the short-run employment decisions. More recently Skouras and Christodoulakis (2014) provide empirical evidence from Greece showing that electoral effects may manifest themselves in indirect ways. In particular, misgovernance may be more pronounced around elections, which are seen to be responsible, in turn, for a more pronounced manifestation of tax evasion, and even a significant increase in wildfires. These phenomena in turn have important economic implications, which can lead to the destruction of property or loss of government revenue, estimated at around 8 percent of GDP.

The more recent literature on Political Budget Cycles considers the implications of elections for local government finances (e.g. Sakurai and Menezes-Filho, 2010; Veiga and Veiga, 2007). Along these lines Chortareas et al. (2014a) examine for the presence of political business cycles in Greek municipalities using a new dataset that covers 109 municipalities from 1985 to 2004. They find strong evidence of pre-electoral manipulation not only through the traditional channel of increased expenditures but also through excessive borrowing. Moreover, the results appear robust to a number of controls, including the exclusion of small municipalities from the sample,

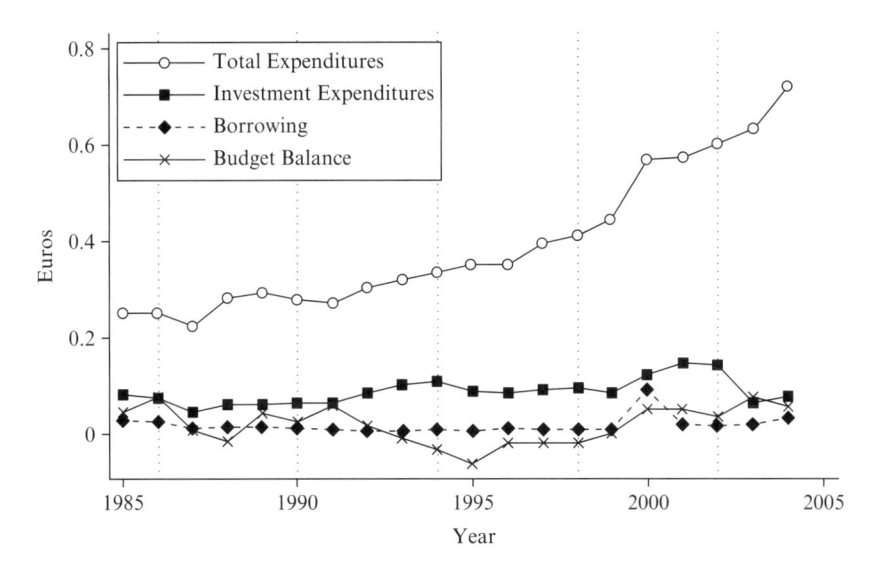

Note: 2005 euros per capita; vertical lines correspond to election years; 109 Greek municipalities, 1985–2004.

Source: Chortareas et al. (2014a).

Figure 6.3 Averages of fiscal variables in Greece's municipalities

considering whether the incumbent runs for re-election and so on. The results are also robust when the authors confine their focus only to the post-Maastricht period. It is also worth noting that the period covered does not include the years of macroeconomic and fiscal decline in the run up to the crisis. Moreover, empirical evidence produced shows that opportunistic excesses around the election year are electorally rewarded. Figure 6.3 shows the evolution of total expenditures, investment expenditures, budget balance and total borrowing for Greece's municipalities.

Municipal employment in Greece follows a pattern consistent with the opportunistic electoral cycle hypothesis. That is, employment in local governments increases around elections. The evidence is based on a dataset covering the period corresponding to Greece's participation as well as the run up to the Eurozone (1996–2009) and estimated using a two-step system GMM (Generalized Method of Moments) estimator for dynamic panel data. Interestingly the main result is driven by contract employees, suggesting that contract renewal is typically conditional on a successful electoral outcome for the incumbent mayor.

The emergence of an electoral cycle is not that surprising. There have

144   *Multi-level finance and the Euro crisis*

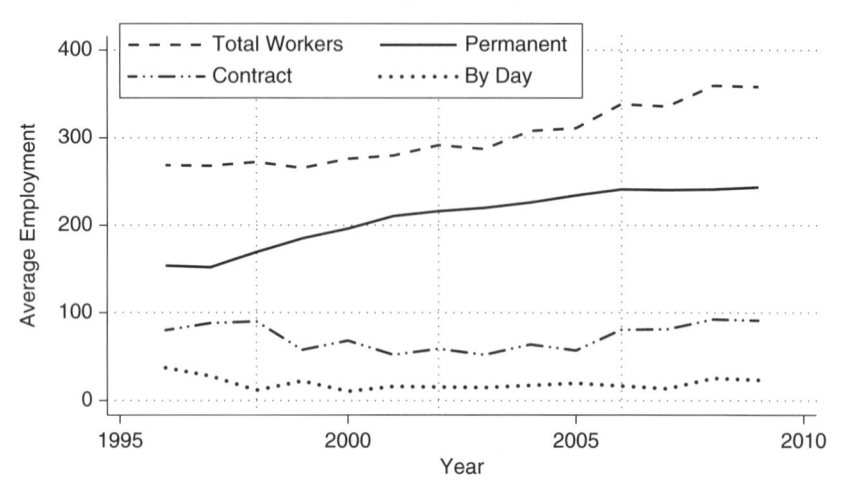

Average Employment for 109 Greek Municipalities
(1996–2009)

[Chart: Average Employment vs Year, showing Total Workers, Permanent, Contract, By Day]

Note: Vertical lines indicate the election years for Greece's municipalities in the sample.

Source: Chortareas et al. (2014b).

Figure 6.4   Average employment by types of municipal employees

been a few attempts to consider how elections may motivate incumbents to engage in opportunistic hiring, and indeed they manage to uncover evidence to support this hypothesis. For example, Coelho et al. (2006) show that opportunistically induced cycles exist in Portugal's municipal employment. Dahlberg and Mörk (2011) find similar results when they consider municipalities in Finland and Sweden, while Tepe and Vanhuysse (2009) find that the hiring of new teachers increases during election periods in the 16 German States they consider. Figure 6.4 shows the evolution of various types of municipal employment and the election years within the sample. The increase in the number of total employees around elections is more pronounced in small-sized municipalities. This is possibly because their operations are less visible and thus more difficult to be scrutinized.

4.   THE CRISIS AND BEYOND

The economic crisis has led to the abandonment of almost all of the fundamentals that prevailed since the restoration of democracy in Greece.

Criticism of the inadequacies of the past has risen widely, with clientelistic and rent-seeking practices being at its epicenter.

Despite some positive signs observed in the Greek economy lately, prior to the 2014 municipal and European parliament elections that were held simultaneously, a surge in political business cycle practices was also observed. By 2014, the stabilization of public finances observed, along with fulfillment of the goal for a primary fiscal surplus and the successful issuance of a five-year bond in the international markets with an interest rate below 5 percent, had formed the belief, at least to a part of society and political parties, that Greece was exiting the worst part of the crisis, albeit only at a slow pace. This in turn refueled a tendency toward practices of electioneering in an economy characterized by high and sustained levels of unemployment.

Among the most notable reappearances of such practices was the announcement by the Ministry of the Interior, made a few months before the elections, in which it stated its decision to hire thousands of seasonal employees to fill vacant positions, and asked incumbent mayors to indicate where and in which areas these positions should be allocated. This incident came at the same time as a series of similar ones that demonstrated Greece's inability, politically, to handle the burden of fiscal adjustment any longer. As reforms mostly occur against the background of an economic crisis that renders the status quo much more expensive to maintain, the first sign of any departure from the most acute point in the crisis will support the case for a reform reversal in some of the policy areas. Given the surge in unemployment and the extended wage and pension cuts, it is not surprising that in these areas a clear electioneering shift can be observed. The depth of the crisis was so great that this attempt did not sway the result in favor of the ruling coalition government – and so the populist Syriza party was swept into office on the promise of reversing job losses and other austerity measures.

Municipalities in Greece have come a long way since their establishment toward taking over responsibilities that once belonged to central government. Faced with acute financial problems that will probably persist into the immediate future, the great challenge will be to fulfill their responsibilities in a financially sustainable way, providing the most effective services for their citizens. Such a task requires a departure from the rent-seeking and extensive electioneering practices that dominated local politics prior to the crisis.

As Europe moves toward a more integrated system where regions will be more important as administrative units than in the past, Greek municipalities need to transform themselves in order to keep up with the prospective changes and fiscal pressures. A better linkage between better service delivery may also affect the willingness of citizens to pay municipal and income taxes (Ahmad et al., 2015). There is, however, much work to be done in this area for Greece.

Viable local finances and well-managed public services, both of great importance, are only the first necessary step toward the much-needed transformations that have to take place. Central politics are now more transparent than in the past and a shift in the same direction is likely to be observed at municipal level too. The maturing process of Greece's democratic institutions ensures that phenomena belonging in the area of political cycles will probably be of a smaller magnitude that the ones of the past leaving room for more public oriented policies. This is the ultimate goal of a well-functioning and sustainable local government.

NOTE

1. Cases have been reported where contract employees were working under this employment relationship for more than 10 years.

REFERENCES

Ahmad, E., G. Brosio and C. Pöschl (2015), 'Local property taxation and benefits in developing countries: overcoming political resistance?', in Ehtisham Ahmad and Giorgio Brosio (eds) (2015), *Handbook of Multilevel Finance*, Cheltenham, UK and Northampton, MA, USA: Edward Elgar, pp. 389–409.

Alogoskoufis, G. and A. Philippopoulos (1992), 'Inflationary expectations, political parties and the exchange rate regime: Greece 1958–1989', *European Journal of Political Economy*, **8**, 375–99.

Chortareas, G., V. Logothetis and A. Papandreou (2014a), 'Political budget cycles and reelection prospects in Greece's municipalities', Working Paper, University of Athens.

Chortareas, G., V. Logothetis and A. Papandreou (2014b), 'Political cycles in Greece's municipal employment', Working Paper, University of Athens.

Coelho, C., F.J. Veiga and L.G. Veiga (2006), 'Political business cycles in local employment: evidence from Portugal', *Economics Letters*, **93**, 82–87.

Dahlberg, M. and E. Mörk (2011), 'Is there an election cycle in public employment? Separating time effects from election year effects', *CESifo Economic Studies*, **57**, 480–98.

Gekas, R. and K. Mitsou (2004), *Municipal Enterprises in the European Union*, Institute of Local Administration (in Greek).

Hellenic Statistical Authority (various years), 'Municipalities and communities income-expenditure', http://dlib.statistics.gr/portal/page/portal/ESYE/category years?p_cat=10008058&p_topic=10008058.

Milas, K.C. (2000), 'Employment, output and political business cycle effects in the Greek non-tradable sector', *Applied Economics*, **32** (2), 123–33.

Mitsopoulos, M. and T. Pelagidis (2011), *Understanding the Crisis in Greece: From Boom to Bust*, Basingstoke, UK: Palgrave Macmillan.

Sakurai, S. and N. Menezes-Filho (2011), 'Opportunistic and partisan election cycles in Brazil: new evidence at the municipal level', *Public Choice*, **148**, 233–47.

Skouras, S. and N. Christodoulakis (2014), 'Electoral misgovernance cycles: evidence from wildfires and tax evasion in Greece', *Public Choice*, **159** (3–4), 533–59.

Tepe, M. and P. Vanhuysse (2009), 'Educational business cycles', *Public Choice*, **139**, 61–82.

Veiga, L. and F. Veiga (2007), 'Political business cycles at the municipal level', *Public Choice*, **131**, 45–64.

7. Portugal's multi-level finance adjustments within the sovereign debt and Euro crises

Mário Fortuna

1. INTRODUCTION

Portugal's multi-level government organization has undergone substantial changes since the democratic revolution of April 1974. From a highly centralized regime based on districts with little power, and municipalities with even less power, the country's governance model evolved into a more decentralized system with empowered municipalities and disempowered districts, and the simultaneous creation, in 1976, of two autonomous regions – Azores and Madeira.

The asymmetric arrangements are linked, in the second half of the 1970s, to the fast decolonization process that detached Portugal from its African possessions under strong local and international pressure. This paved the way for the concession of ample autonomy to the two Atlantic archipelagos adjacent to the continent.

A strong leftist orientation of the central government was key to the strong separatist sentiment that developed in the more conservative communities of the islands. An unstable political environment within the central authorities also facilitated the establishment of regional governments outside the continental territory. In a country with little decentralization experience and against an unstable political background, it is no surprise that the new decentralization processes were guided mostly by political sentiments rather than structured governance objectives.

This is the setting that led to major reviews of the governance system, characterized by the empowerment of two regions and a little over three hundred municipalities and the phasing out of districts led by purely decorative civil governors, which were abolished in 2012. An attempt to regionalize continental Portugal was rejected in a referendum undertaken in 1998.

Meanwhile, Portugal went through various and very significant moments that impacted, or were impacted by, the ongoing fiscal decentralization. These moments were: the sovereign debt crises, in 1978 and 1983, which prompted the intervention of the IMF in Portugal; joining the then European Economic Community in 1986, which created a new scenario of intensive external aid and prompted a new matching grant strategy on the part of public authorities; the adoption of the single currency that started major financial governance changes as of the beginning of the 1990s, before completion of the process in 2002; the excessive deficit struggle since the inception of the single currency; and the 2008 financial crisis which prompted the Euro area crisis and led to the sovereign debt crisis of 2011, summoning an array of issues on its own.

Poor fiscal management coupled with easy credit and aggressive party politics led to a generalized leveraged overspending at all levels of government in spite of supposedly strict debt restrictions. One should recall, however, that the Euro area itself was going through a process of relaxation of the tight fiscal rules foreseen in the stability and growth pact. In fact, besides Portugal's inauguration of the excessive debt procedure of the Stability and Growth Pact, Germany and France were also, from the start, at risk of overshooting the 3 percent deficit limit and 60 percent debt limit on GDP, which led to the softening of the rules of the pact in 2005.

In this chapter we focus on how sub-national government behavior, directly and through local municipal enterprises, has impacted on the financial crisis over the past decades. Another objective is to assess to what extent the established information flows in relation to incomes, assets and liabilities contributed to the depth of the crisis, and how these issues have been subsequently addressed. Finally we illustrate how the crisis has impacted on local service delivery, taxation and on the configuration of the intergovernmental relations system itself. The memorandum of understanding signed in 2011 by the Portuguese central government and the EC/ECB/IMF will be recalled in all aspects relevant to the topic of the chapter.

We first review, in Section 2, the national setting that led to the 2011 Memorandum of Understanding (MoU) and the contribution of regional and local jurisdictions. Section 3 reviews the evolution of decentralization to local government, identifying the main landmarks. Section 4 does the same analysis of decentralization, but with respect to the regions of Azores and Madeira. The final section presents some concluding remarks about the management and reorganization of intergovernmental relations in Portugal.

2. SOVEREIGN DEBT CRISES AND THE AGENDA FOR CHANGE – IMPACTS OF THE 2011 MOU

Since the new political regime instituted by the constitution of 1976, as a consequence of the 1974 revolution, Portugal has continuously struggled with excessive budget deficits and external disequilibria.

The first crisis arose in 1977 as a consequence of twin deficits in the external balance and the national budget. Portugal lost competitiveness due to factors such as excessive salary increases, strikes, loss of the colonies and nationalizations in a revolutionary environment. Reserves were rapidly depleted and the IMF was called upon for a standby agreement to help correct public policies. Some initial improvements were quickly annulled by circumventing actions such as the international indebtedness of public companies. Again, a second intervention of the IMF was required in 1983, to last until 1985.

In 1986 Portugal joined the then European Economic Community and became the beneficiary of substantial transfers. Later, in 1993, with the Treaty of Maastricht, nominal conversion was brought into the forefront of the economic policy agenda and for more than a decade the focus was on a national consensus to prepare the country to join the single currency. As a result of the new economic setting the country experienced a fast growth period boosted by wide access to international credit, low interest rates and the inflow of structural funds.

Some structural problems such as weak external competitiveness and excessive budget deficits were not resolved by the time of the introduction of the euro. New challenges were posed by the fact that Portugal could no longer resort to nominal devaluation to adjust for external imbalances.

In fact, Portugal initiated the excessive debt mechanism of the stability and growth pact. Budget deficits remained close to or in excess of 3 percent (2.8 percent in 1999, 3.1 percent in 2000 and 4.2 percent in 2001), justifying continuous monitoring. This scenario was never overcome, with deficits floating above the limits, in turn strongly impacting political cycles. In December 2001, the prime minister resigned and new elections dictated a change of political control and renewed attention focused on the deficit.

Figure 7.1 shows how the deficit evolved in the decade to 2014. The depressions in 2005 and 2009 coincide with national elections, with the accounts of these years being closed by newly elected governments (this was also the case in 2001).

Portugal confronted the 2008 financial crises in a very fragile structural position and quickly found its public finances at an unsustainable level. The setting of the Euro area crisis made the situation even more difficult.

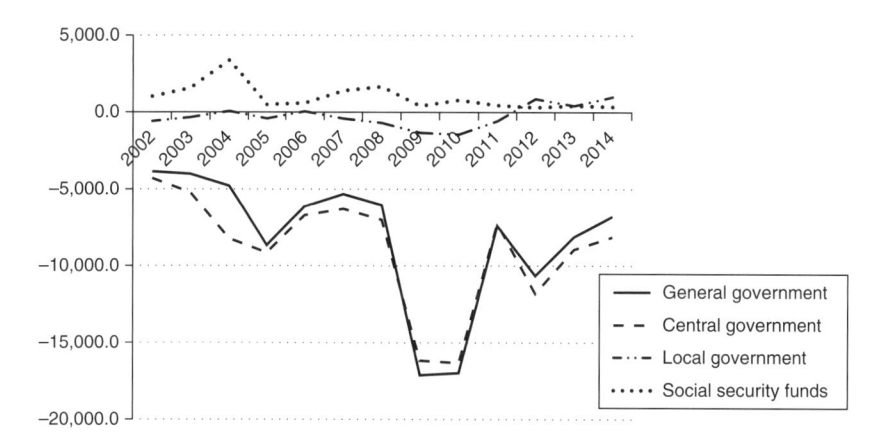

Figure 7.1   Budget deficits by government level

Profound adjustments became a must in a new context with no currency devaluation.

The total national debt was mostly the responsibility of the central government, even though one might question the extent to which fiscal transfers contributed to the national fiscal deficits. In a study of US and German state governments, Potrafke and Reischmann (2014) concluded that intergovernmental transfers have implicitly subsidized debts.

Figure 7.1 also shows that the general government budget deficit is mostly affected by the central government budget deficit. Social security is a positive contributor, while local and regional governments have been, on average, slightly negative contributors, with definite positive contributions after the MoU of 2011.

Looking at the disaggregated sub-national deficits, one can identify some interesting differences between municipalities and the Azores and Madeira regions (Figure 7.2). All seemed to be largely controlled until 2008, with municipalities showing some tendency to diverge from equilibrium. After 2008, municipalities ran larger deficits but quickly recovered to show surpluses; the Azores kept a stable trajectory with very low deficits, but Madeira seemed to collapse after 2008. In fact Madeira ran into a deep crisis when 'hidden' deficits of the government and of publicly owned entities become a clear budget problem. The regional government resorted to its own memorandum of understanding with the central government to finance its deficits in 2012. The problem involved about €1,100 million of commercial debt of which about €67 million came from arrears in medication bills, €42 million from the health system, €690 million from construction companies, and about €290 million from other smaller suppliers.

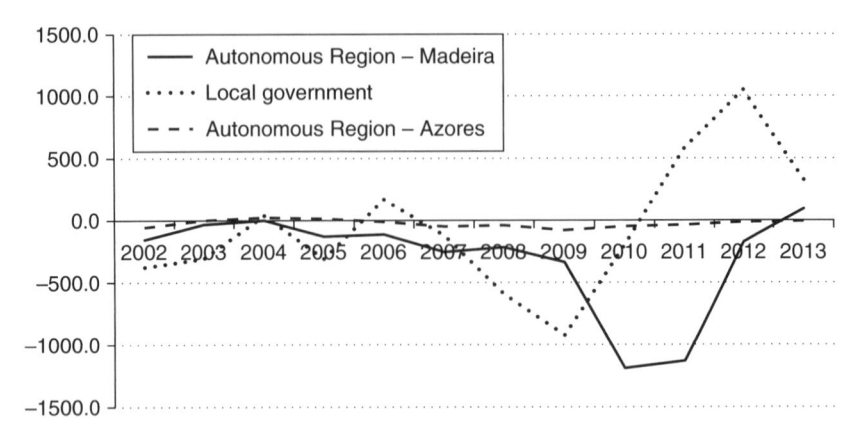

Figure 7.2   Sub-national budget deficits

The Azores region stands out as a particularly stable situation for the full period of analysis, while municipalities and the region of Madeira show very irregular behavior, as of 2008. The explanation rests in the fact that many public operations were being undertaken outside the public budgets, through public entities that are only included in the budget perimeter for analysis after 2008.

In 2012 the Azores also had to resort to a mild MoU with the central government to refinance €180 million in 2012 and 2013, mostly of debt that was due for reimbursement, since the markets were not accessible for that purpose.

The recourse to entities outside the public budget can be traced back to the restrictions put on regional and local governments in 2002. In fact the national government, through the annual budget, forbade local and regional increases in net debt. Confronted with this restriction, the local and regional governments resorted to public companies that were not included in the budget and to other off-budget financial mechanisms such as public–private partnerships (PPPs).

At the level of local jurisdictions, the predominance was of local public companies totally or partially owned by the municipalities. In 2012, for the 308 municipalities there were 281 municipal companies held by almost 50 percent of the municipalities (Carvalho et al., 2013a). Between 2009 and 2012 these companies owed, on average, €1,700 million to banks, the state and various suppliers.

The use and abuse of these entities led to the introduction of regulatory clauses in the law restricting these mechanisms. At the regional level, public companies or development companies and PPPs were widely used to circumvent the financing restrictions. This approach has been rendered gradually useless since the definition of the budget perimeter started to include all entities that depended mostly on revenues from the public budget. The most common situations are found in health, roads and other costly infrastructure. In many instances, instead of adjusting service delivery levels and quality the sub-national governments resorted to off-budget solutions.

Various restrictive policies were implemented to stop or to revert the adverse effect of these strategies, mostly at the municipal level. At the level of the two autonomous regions, not much was done beside the definition of the budget perimeters, relegating other policies to the regional authorities and to MoUs with the central government.

The following two sections review in some detail the landmarks of change in the local and regional finance laws that incorporate most of the policy reactions to sub-national undesirable practices.

3. LANDMARKS OF DECENTRALIZATION TO LOCAL GOVERNMENT

Until the revolution of April 1974, local finances in Portugal were guided by an administrative code, which restricted the municipalities to being more of an extension of the central administration than a true autonomous jurisdiction (Nabais, 2007). Municipalities were a mere vehicle of the will of the central government (Campos, 1988). According to Bilhim (2004), until the revolution, municipalities were simply administrative institutions politically diminished and discredited, the consequence of a centralized model that characterized the administrative organization of the 'Estado Novo' (new state) period.[1]

In the 1976 constitution, municipalities acquired new relevance with their powers and autonomy clearly defined. In a process of administrative decentralization, they were attributed regulatory power, own assets and own finances, This was implemented through successive changes in their attributions and in the Local Finance Law that established their revenue sources, first published in 1979 and, since then, modified six times (1984, 1987, 1992, 1998, 2007 and 2013).

According to Zbyszewski (2006), the local finance law established the financial autonomy of local government by assuring stability of own revenues, reduced dependency on discretionary transfers from the central budget, and vertical and horizontal equalization. This is generally done in two steps: the first determines the value of the resources to be allocated to municipalities; the second determines how these resources are distributed among them.

The successive local finance laws defined own revenues, the budget for shared revenues, the way these shared revenues were distributed, as well as the limits of access to debt financing. Accounting harmonization was an objective set out from the first law, but reporting and off-budget operations was not an issue in the early stages of the decentralization process.

In the first law (Law no. 1/79), revenues of municipalities were organized in two main categories: 1) own revenues from local taxes and fees and 2) shared revenues. The own revenues included fees, fines, own piggy-back taxes, credit and several other minor categories of taxes. Shared revenues were: (1) the totality of the revenues from local vehicle taxes and property taxes; (2) shared projected revenue from income and corporate taxes as well as from inheritance taxes and the tax on contracts (Sisa); (3) shared other revenues, on the basis of current and capital expenditures of the national budget as financial equilibrium fund.

The shared revenues were to be at least 18 percent of the projected revenues from corporate and personal income taxes, whereas the shared other revenues were 18 percent of the projected current and capital expenditure of the national budget. These two sources implied that in a balanced budget situation, 36 percent of the projected national budget was to be shared with the municipalities.

In addition to defining the revenue sources, this first law also established that municipalities were allowed to contract debt of all maturities from public lending organisms, limited to 1/12 of their investment budget to cover temporary treasury needs; and 20 percent of the same indicator to cover medium- and long-term needs. A ceiling of debt services was fixed at 10 percent of the investment budget. This formulation created a bias in favor of the investment budget.

Having defined the total amount of funds allocated for municipalities, the second step was to find criteria for the distribution of the values from each of the shared sources – personal and corporate income taxes and expenditures.

The shared income taxes were distributed among municipalities: a) 50 percent depending on the number of inhabitants; b) 10 percent as a function of the land area of the jurisdiction; c) 40 percent as a direct function of the per capita direct taxes collected in the municipality.

The shared expenditures were distributed: a) 35 percent depending on the number of inhabitants; b) 15 percent as a function of the land area; c) 15 percent as a function of the number of parishes; and d) 35 percent as a function of needs assessed on the basis of electricity and water consumption, sewerage coverage, road network, number of children below six years of age, number of adults above 65. This model of revenue sharing has since undergone six changes (in 1984, 1987, 1992, 1998, 2007 and 2013).

The first review of the law occurred in 1984. The main change introduced was to eliminate the revenue-sharing component of the financing formula restricting all financing to a percentage of national expenditures to be defined in each budget law. According to Bilhim (2004) municipalities were at the mercy of whatever the government decided to grant them. In spite of this change in the transfer formula, Campos (1988) concludes that transfers increased at a pace higher than the inflation rate in the period 1985 to 1987.

Zbyzsewski (2006) further points to two new norms pertaining to the possibility of obtaining financial bailout contracts or contract-programs with the central government. These new mechanisms were prompted by the occurrence of several cases of financial unsustainability.

Yet another set of changes introduced by the law was the financing rules. Short-term credit was limited to be a maximum of 5 percent of government transfers while for longer-term credit, debt service could not be higher than 20 percent of government transfers or investments of the previous year. The bias toward investment expenditures was maintained.

Finally, the law contemplates penalization for arrears relative to other public non-financial institutions, with retention of transfers to pay for the values due. The occurrence of unpaid commitments or arrears was becoming a significant problem.

The first major review of the law took place in 1987. Transfers from the national budget became determined by a formula whose argument is the projected VAT for each year. This allowed for an annual adjustment to changing economic conditions, but did not provide any safeguard against poor VAT projections. In addition, the transfers were not made a function of needs, but of potential revenue. Credit-financing limitations were relaxed, since the limit of short-term obligations rose from 5 percent to 10 percent of government transfers, and the limit on longer-term obligations rose from 20 percent of transfers or investments to 25 percent of transfers or 20 percent of investments. We should recall that Portugal had just joined the EU and was the recipient of considerable development funds for which many jurisdictions had to budget and provide matching funds. Recourse to credit was fostered by the drive to take full advantage of all the funds made available.

A penalization for arrears vis-à-vis public entities was maintained, but no provision was considered for arrears to the private sector. This would later become a significant problem.

A new version of the local finance law was enacted in 1992 through the budget law. The allocation of funds was changed to include a three-step procedure: in the first, the overall transfers budget was determined; in the second, the budget was distributed between continental Portugal, the

Azores and Madeira; in the third, the budget for each of the three regions was distributed among municipalities. The Azores and Madeira were allowed to adapt some of the distribution criteria.

The fourth review was undertaken in 1998 and lasted until 2006. The base for calculating transfers was changed from a percentage of budgeted VAT to a percentage of the sum of VAT and corporate and personal income taxes collected in year $t - 2$.

The budget for transfers was itself broken up into three funds: a General Municipal Fund, to cover basic expenditure obligations; a Municipal Cohesion Fund, to redistribute funds to the poor municipalities; and a Locality Financing Fund, to finance parishes.

The final result of these changes was that transfers to municipalities were considerably increased. In fact, Cunha and Silva (2002) compare transfers through the new formula with transfers through the old one to conclude that the new formula implied considerably greater increases between 1999 and 2002. Zbyszewski (2006), on the other hand, concludes that the new law led to the doubling of transfers between 1998 and 2002.

By 2002, Portugal had been a member of the EU for 16 years and had begun its single currency era. The country was already at the limits of the excessive debt procedure of the Stability and Growth Pact, and in desperate need of fiscal consolidation. The central government fell (December 2001) as a consequence of unfavorable local elections, and new concerns over the excessive debt became a central issue of the political agendas, even though the perception of the seriousness of the situation was not generally accepted as critical. The last two reviews of the law were undertaken in 2007 and 2014, one before and the other after the MoU signed in 2011.

The main changes implemented in 2007 focused on specifying principles and on changing both the own revenues and the shared revenues. The principles focused on financial control and discipline and on cooperation with the national government. Portugal was at this point well into a very stressful financial situation.

The changes introduced in the specification of own revenue included the creation of new local taxes, namely those connected with property, real estate transactions and vehicles. The piggy-back tax on corporate income was also changed to allow a 1.5 percent surtax.

With respect to the revenue-sharing component, a main change was to reduce the percentage of participation in revenues from VAT, corporate and income taxes from 33 percent to 25.3 percent (Vilarinho, 2010).

New debt controls were introduced as well as limitations and penalizations for non-compliance. Debt limits were also changed to link to the stock of debt (net debt was not to exceed 125 percent of revenues for the previous year). This criterion replaced the previous one that was linked to the flow variable of interest and reimbursements (Fernandes, 2007).

The 2013 changes, introduced to become effective as of 2014 (Law no. 73/2013, 3 September), recognized, for the first time, the existence of inter-municipal communities and metropolitan areas. New principles were also explicitly introduced to include budget stability, transparency, reciprocal solidarity and dependence on inspections. New debt controls were introduced not only in terms of their limits but also in the way they were contracted, in order to avoid postponement of obligations. An example is the imposition that in no year could the reimbursement of loans be 80 percent lower than the average reimbursement.

The most recent law (2013) maintains a revenue-sharing mechanism that allocates 19.5 percent of revenues at $t - 2$ from VAT, corporate and personal income taxes to be distributed among municipalities. This percentage has been reduced in the context of the recent national budget consolidation process. Formulas determine the distribution of these funds among municipalities as a function of various indicators such as population, characteristics of the population, and land area, among others.

Other important characteristics of the law are budget principles (which are, in some aspects, a redundancy relative to the national budget framework law), debt limitations, debt sustainability alerts, financial recovery procedures, budget perimeter, and accounting and reporting obligations.

The tendency of the changes introduced in the financing of municipalities evolved significantly since the third quarter of the 20th century along the following lines: 1) improvement of the specification of revenue sources, both from revenue sharing and own revenues; 2) improvement of the fiscal capacity through transfers and fiscal autonomy, both in credit contracting and the levy of own taxes; 3) improvement of central control mechanisms, both directly and through the framework laws; and 4) clarification of the separation between national and local finances.

In addition to the local finance law, legislation was passed to regulate local public entrepreneurial entities (Law no.50/2012). According to this law, local public companies should be closed within six months if one of the following circumstances occurs: a) sales of goods and services during the last three years are less than 50 percent of total expenditures of the fiscal year; b) current subsidies, for the previous three years, represent more than 50 percent of revenues; c) current income net of amortizations and depreciation is negative for three consecutive years; d) net income is negative in three consecutive years. Applying these criteria to the 2010–12 income reports would lead to the closing of 111 of 266 local public companies (Carvalho et al., 2013a). This is evidence of the extent of off-budget activities that were being undertaken through these companies.

Carvalho et al. (2013b) further highlight what is considered to be a serious problem with municipal revenue budgeting. In fact, between 2007 and 2012, budgeted revenues were consistently overestimated by more than 30 percent. The motivation for this practice can be associated with other regulations that allow spending of up to 100 percent of budgeted expenditures, regardless of revenue performance.

This problem, widespread in public entities, was later tackled by means of a new law (DL No. 127/2012) that regulated payments of compromises and arrears. It became mandatory that before assuming new expenditure commitments, revenue had to be previously assured. It was no longer enough that expenditures were merely budgeted.

For the 2014 budgets, an additional norm was introduced to prevent budgeting more revenues than it was reasonably expected would be collected. Budgeted revenues were to be equal to the revenues of 2012 (year t − 2). Other values would have to be adequately justified.

Some interesting questions have been posed with respect to the equalization characteristics of the transfer system to local governments (Fortuna et al., 2014c) and issues of fiscal sustainability (Fortuna et al., 2014b).

Using panel data for all the Portuguese municipalities, for the 1997–2010 periods, Fortuna et al. (2014c) test and evaluate whether there has been an equalization effect in the system of transfers to the municipalities. They also test whether the various changes introduced over time improved or worsened the equalization effects. Their results showed that on average the municipalities with the highest GDP per capita and own revenues per capita receive more transfers per capita, which suggests that the system does not contribute to equalization. It is also concluded that the successive changes of the system, namely those undertaken in 1998 and 2007, were significant in improving the equalization impact of the system.

This study suggests that municipalities still have, on average, significantly different levels of resources to undertake, on a per capita basis, their service delivery functions. This might put significant stress on poorer municipalities to keep up with the others, increasing the risk of excessive debt.

The main objective of Fortuna et al. (2014b) was to evaluate the sustainability of the local public finances of the Portuguese municipalities using the primary gap indicator suggested by Buiter (1995) and by Ianchovichina and Liu (2008). The work measures the distance between the current ratio and the sustainable ratio, that is, the values that would keep the debt ratio invariant. In this study, the indicator was calculated using two public expenditure criteria: paid expenditures (with data for the period 1996 to 2012) and accrual expenditure (with data for the period 2005 to 2012). The results were significantly different, suggesting marginal sustainability when using cash accounting with liabilities falling below 20 percent of regional

GDP by 2012. But an accruals basis showed liabilities remaining above 80 percent of regional GDP, well above permitted levels.

In Fortuna et al. (2014b), using the calculated indicators, tests were performed to assess the impact on the successive changes in the local finance law and of the electoral periods, and to test if municipalities of the Portuguese autonomous regions were different from the national average. In the first case, it was found that local finances tend not to be sustainable and that the successive changes, except that of 2007, have aggravated the tendency. Controlling for election years, it was found that, on average, sustainability was worsened and that, looking at each election year, only 2005 can be associated with some improvement. The test of the hypothesis of no difference in the average sustainability indicator for the autonomous regions leads to the conclusion that the Azorean municipalities exhibit a significantly lower average, while those of Madeira exhibit no significant difference.

This study highlights the fact that there are significant differences in the sustainability analysis depending on whether one uses the concept of cash expenditures or accrued expenditures (which includes arrears). For the 2005–12 periods, arrears seem to have been significant since they change the results obtained. The existence of significant arrears is consistent with the reaction of the municipalities that, having seen their budgets controlled, resorted to other strategies to spend, among which is the delay of payments or even of non-recognition of expenditures.

Along broad lines, local governments gained considerable relevance in Portugal in the last quarter of the 20th century, in a process that continued into the first decade of the 21st century. Increased decentralization toward municipalities and the use of new financial instruments led to widespread lack of sustainability of many local governments. If the problem started to gain shape before the turn of the century, restrictive policies implemented after 2002 put a break on a faster degradation course of local public finances.

While local expenditures represent about 30 percent of public expenditures, the local financing deficit and the local accumulated debt is a small percentage (less than 4 percent) of the national values. Nevertheless, maintaining the financial situation under control has required strict rules, which, for some time, were circumvented by a set of uncontrolled off-budget vehicles that, at the regional and local levels, created significant negative impacts.

4. LANDMARKS OF DECENTRALIZATION TO THE REGIONAL GOVERNMENTS

The autonomous regions of the Azores and Madeira were instituted in 1976 with the approval of the new constitution and the subsequent approval of the political and administrative statutes of each region.

The competences of the regional governments were specified in the political and administrative statutes and abided by the subsidiarity principle and the unity of the state. Except for a few cases, these competences have been fairly stable since 1976. The regional authorities, comprised of a legislature and a government, are responsible for most government functions that can be considered within the subsidiarity principle. This means that the regional budget takes into account, for example, most administrative functions and development policies and excludes national security, courts, social security and higher education.

The main issues that have arisen refer to the determination of revenues and of debt financing. Other issues pertain to the control mechanisms, which regional political forces tend to reject given that there are regional control institutions such as the regional parliaments.

The revenue sources of the regional governments have always included the totality of taxes generated in the regions as well as transfers from the national budget, transfers from international accords and, since 1985, transfers from the EU.

Technical issues of arriving at own revenues aside, the volatility of revenue sources arose only from the various transfer sources and especially from transfers from the national budget. With no experience in regionalization, the process evolved from very rudimentary criteria of transfers to the more elaborate current system.

The first rule for determining transfers attributed the financial proceeds of international accords to the regions, and established that each region would get additional funding equal to a per capita value of the central government budget deficit. This meant that transfers from the central government were only based on the idea that each region would share the proceeds of national deficits. This rule was applied in 1976 and 1977. In 1978 and 1979 the rule was changed to a per capita share of public expenditures excluding non-regionalized services. As of 1980, these criteria were suspended and transfers were based on political negotiation, which resulted in very uncertain and subjective processes. Later, as of 1988, due to the need for extra resources to match funds from the EU, the regions were compelled to resort to debt financing.

The first law that regulated transfers and other fiscal regional competences was only published in 1998. The new law: (1) clarified what were own revenues; (2) contemplated the ability of the regional governments to adapt the national tax system through rate changes in VAT, corporate taxes, income taxes and special consumption taxes; (3) defined a transfer mechanism; (4) defined debt limits; and (5) determined that the central government would assume part of the debts (about €550 million each) of the two regions.

Before publication of the law, in 1989, Madeira had already been the subject of a national aid program to deal with its excessive debt. In fact, in 1989, the accumulated debt led to 38 percent of the budget being allocated to debt services. A program for the financial recovery of Madeira was approved by the central government in September of 1989. It implied strict budget options on the part of the regional authorities and financial coordination with the central authorities.

Between 1989 and 1993 the government of Madeira subscribed to the following objectives: to keep growth of current expenditures, without interest costs, at a maximum of 1 percent per year; to raise fuel prices to the national levels (except for fuel supplied to the electric power company); to keep the budget in balance or in surplus.

The central government, in turn, would assume 50 percent of the interest cost of the consolidated and renegotiated debt and the national share of subsidies to the productive sector financed by EU programs.

Transfers from the central government were to be based on the per capita national investment effort adjusted by a factor of 1.66 and subtracted from the national direct investment in the region.

The relevance of this formula is that it became, independently of its nature, the first objective rule to determine transfers from the central budget.

Within the agreement, the national budget for 1990 also determined that Madeira was not allowed to increase its net debt, the central government was forbidden from increasing its guarantees on Madeira's debt, and that if the Treasury was to pay some of its guarantees to Madeira the central government could retain transfers until payment of the full amount due.

In 1998, with the publication of the first law that regulated financial relations between the national and the regional governments, the national budget assumed close to €550 million of debt from each region and later, in 2002, it assumed another €100 million from each region.

An important function of the new law was, aside from the debt assumption by the central government, which was an effective bailout, to establish a stable rule for transfers.

To this effect, the law adopted a formula that was, in essence, equal to what had been established in the first recovery program for Madeira, with different adjustment weights for the two regions. Madeira had an additional 2/3 and the Azores a 9/10 adjustment factor. More important, however, was the safeguard rule, which stated that in any year the transfers were not to be smaller than those of the previous year, adjusted for the growth rate of current expenditures in the national budget. Since the national government had made a discrete transfer adjustment in 1998, before the new law came into effect, the formula was never applied and the safeguard rule became fundamental in determining the transfers, pegging them to the growth of the national budget expenditures.

In addition to the base transfer, each region was attributed an extra 35 percent of transfers in the form of a cohesion fund that was not dependent on any indicators.

Notably, these rules were static in the sense that, for an extended period of time, transfers were only a function of the transfers for 1998, adjusted for the growth of the current expenditures of the national budget. No consideration was taken of effective need or of the fiscal capacity of each region.

A note should also be made with respect to VAT. This tax was established in the 1980s after Portugal joined the EEC. From the beginning, in the Azores and Madeira, it was set at 70 percent of the national rate, but own revenues to the regional governments were set according to the national per capita value. This meant there was an implicit transfer to the regions, particularly to the Azores, given the lower per capita income.

This rule was changed in the first review of the law, in 2006, effective as of 2007. There were three main changes: (1) VAT revenues were to become the effective collections for each region; (2) the total transfers were to be fixed in the national budget, after adjustment for the change in the VAT imputation methodology; (3) there would be a formula to determine the split of the budget between the two regions; and (4) the cohesion fund was to be indexed to the gap between per capita income and the national average.

One important item introduced in this revision of the law was that the state was not allowed to assume any of the regions' responsibilities, meaning that, contrary to what had happened in 1999 and 2002, the central government was not to take upon itself any of the regions' debt.

The split of the central budget transfer fund between the two regions was made according to a formula that weighted population ratios, age ratios, distance to the national capital, dispersion of islands, fiscal effort and a discrete adjustment factor.

In addition to the values obtained through this methodology, the regions were eligible for a cohesion fund contribution attributed as a percentage of the transfers depending on the gap between per capita GDP and the national average. Negative differences justified additional transfers

(20 percent if < 90 percent; 12.5 percent if ≥ 90 and < 95 percent; 5 percent if ≥ 95 percent and < 100 percent; 0 percent if per capita GDP was greater than the national value).

Sanctions were to be applied as reductions in transfers, should the regional governments exceed the stipulated deficit finance ceilings. For the greater part of the period under analysis, the restriction was a balanced budget. In 2009, Madeira surpassed the authorized debt and the stipulated sanctions were applied.

This law was strongly contested by the government of Madeira since it implied a reduction in that region's share of the transfer budget. The impact on the Azores was made neutral through a discretionary factor of the distribution formula. In 2010, taking advantage of a minority government, the law was changed by the parliament in the following main aspects:

- The state was authorized to provide guarantees for loans contracted by the regions;
- Debt limits could be surpassed if projects co-financed by European funds were at stake;
- Debt should only be limited by reference to established debt service indicators.
- The transfers fund was to be determined as the sum of an initial VAT compensation value of €165 million (to be updated annually by the bigger growth rate of current expenditures or public servants' salaries), 29 percent for Madeira and 71 percent to the Azores, plus an additional adjustment to make VAT, plus the compensation equivalent to the average per capita national revenue, plus €355.8 million (to be updated annually by the bigger growth rate of current expenditures or public servants salaries), plus 35 percent of the transfers as a cohesion component of transfers.
- The distribution formula was similar to that of the 2007 law except for the weights and the elimination of a discretionary factor.

$$R_{,t} = T_{RA,t} \left[0.725 \frac{P_{R,t-2}}{P_{RA,t-2}} + 0.05 \frac{P65_{R,t-2}}{P65_{RA,t-2}} + 0.05 \frac{P14_{R,t-2}}{P14_{RA,t-2}} \right.$$
$$\left. + 0.125 \frac{IU_R}{IU_{RA}} + 0.05 \frac{EF_{R,t-4}}{EF_{RA,t-4}} \right]$$

- After the first year of application of this formula, the total amount of transfers could not be lower than the value obtained in the previous year.

This configuration of the law was clearly more favorable for the regions, but demanded more from the national budget. Because of a special law passed to help Madeira's reconstruction following an episode of flooding, the law was suspended, until December 2013, in all norms that implied a change to the previous transfer formula. There was, in fact, a retreat from a situation that would certainly have led to greater central government expenditures at a time when the country was already dealing with excessive debt and Madeira needed extra help to recover from a natural catastrophe.

In 2013, the new law passed (Lei Orgânica no. 2/2013) incorporated features that were included in the MoU with the IMF/ECB/EC. In fact, the MoU set that the maximum tax rate reductions that the regions were allowed to make in VAT and income taxes would be reduced from 30 percent to 20 percent. It was also understood that desirable budget practices would be included in the new law, in accordance with the new budget framework law. The Portuguese Public Finance Council (2013) provides a discussion of some of the aspects of the proposed law. Paixão and Baleiras (2013) analyze the impact of the new law on debt rules and conclude that a considerable number of municipalities and the two autonomous regions would be on the limit of or beyond the admissible debt limits.

The new law included the following main attributes:

- Reinforcement of the role of the accompanying Council for Financial Policies, to identify early warnings of budget deviations;
- Specification of the principles that were to guide the financial autonomy of the autonomous regions to include, namely, the principles and rules of the national budget framework and, specifically, the principles of coordination and the balanced budget rule;
- VAT revenue to be determined on an adjusted per capita basis where the adjustment factor was the ratio of the regional VAT rate to the national VAT rate (this rule penalizes revenues when rates are lower but can still have an implicit subsidy if per capita transactions are lower in the region);
- Procedures established for requests for national aid on the part of the regions if they run into financial difficulty;
- New debt incurred by the regions to be approved by the national legislature and must not impact on external debt or negatively influence the national ratings. The regional debt limit is fixed at 1.5 times the average of actual revenues in the last three fiscal years;
- The transfers to regions to start, in 2014, with a provision of €352.5 million, to be adjusted annually by the lesser of the growth rate of current expenditures and GDP. Additionally, the regions are eligible for transfers, as a percentage of the other transfers, from a

Cohesion Fund (55 percent if GDP is < 90 percent of the national value; 40 percent if ≥ 90 and < 95 percent; 25 percent if ≥ 95 percent and < 100 percent; 0 percent if per capita GDP is greater than the national value, all in year t − 4);
- The state is not allowed to assume the regions' debt responsibilities;
- Maximum tax rate differentials are reduced from 30 percent to 20 percent;
- The municipal variable income tax revenue from taxes collected in each municipality becomes the responsibility of the regional budget. The central authorities will, therefore, subtract that amount from transfers and hand them to the municipalities.

As can be seen from the above, successive changes in the intergovernmental financial relations were centered on the amounts of transfers, with some marginal improvements to the principles underpinning the law, and coordination and control mechanisms. The most recent review was, in part, forced by the requirements of the MoU signed in 2011 and expanded on the controls and the mechanisms of assistance should the regions require financial help. This was the case in Madeira, which in 2012 had to sign its own MoU with the central government in order to refinance its excessive debt.

Between 1989 and 1997, the two autonomous regions of Portugal received from the national budget €1,073 million representing, on average, 0.14 percent of the national GDP (Fortuna et al., 2014a). Figure 7.3 shows how the numbers evolved.

For this period, transfers from the national budget contributed to 12 percent of the regional government budgets each year. The Azores seem to receive more support than Madeira, but if we account for the help Madeira kept on receiving from the 1990 financial adjustment program (50 percent of interest on the renegotiated debt was supported by the central government), the relation is inverted.

The change of the transfer system in 2007 led to higher explicit transfers, but it also took into consideration that the regions would receive the VAT actually collected instead of the national per capita value. For the Azores, this led to making explicit a considerable number of transfers that were implicit in the way VAT was attributed to the region. The impact on Madeira was not as great as in the Azores because that region has a much higher per capita income and the effective own revenues from VAT were, accordingly, much higher and incorporated less subsidization.

One way of correcting for this peculiarity is to calculate a series that adds transfers and VAT. These results showed that transfers plus VAT follow very similar paths for the two autonomous regions.

166   *Multi-level finance and the Euro crisis*

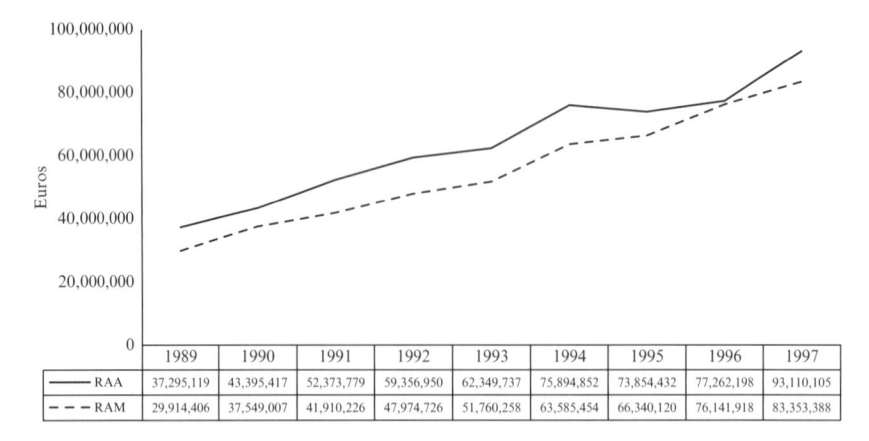

	1989	1990	1991	1992	1993	1994	1995	1996	1997
—— RAA	37,295,119	43,395,417	52,373,779	59,356,950	62,349,737	75,894,852	73,854,432	77,262,198	93,110,105
- - RAM	29,914,406	37,549,007	41,910,226	47,974,726	51,760,258	63,585,454	66,340,120	76,141,918	83,353,388

Note: RAA: autonomous region of the Azores; RAM: autonomous region of Madeira.

Source: Fortuna et al. (2014a).

Figure 7.3   Transfers to the Azores and Madeira, 1989–97

Fortuna et al. (2014a) analyze the sustainability of the budget deficits of each region calculated through the Buiter (1995) one-period primary gap indicator. The authors calculate the indicator for each region, project it into the future, and test whether the changes in the laws that regulate transfers impacted on the sustainability indicator. From the historical values they conclude that the sustainability indicators are substantially different for the two regions.

The values calculated for the Azores lead to the conclusion that only in 1999 and in the period 2003 to 2007 was the primary gap sufficient not to worsen the debt level. In 1999, the central government assumed part of the regional debt and in the period 2003–07 the regional governments were not allowed to contract new debt due to the explicit restrictions of the national budget law. In the period from 1993 to 1997, the stock of debt in the Azores increased rapidly and interest rates were higher than the growth rate of GDP. The annual growth of debt was, on average, 26.3 percent.

The values calculated for Madeira show a different scenario.

One should recall that, in 1990, Madeira was subjected to a financial recovery program, and that in more recent years there was a further intervention by the central government due to the excessive debt accumulation. For 1990, the primary balance would have to be 14.9 percent of regional GDP for sustainability using the Buiter criteria. In 2012, the primary balance would have to be 19.3 percent of regional GDP to attain sustainability.

Projecting the sustainability indicators under the assumption that the current debt would be maintained and for scenarios of 1 percent and 3 percent GDP growth and interest rates of 2 percent, 3 percent and 4 percent, Fortuna et al. (2014a) conclude that, except for 2013 to 2015, the Azores would achieve sustainability with a 1 percent GDP growth rate and 4 percent interest rate. For Madeira, sustainability is only achieved if we assume a GDP growth rate of 3 percent and an interest rate of 1 percent. Any scenario less favorable implies that debt will increase in an unsustainable manner.

Fortuna et al. (2014a) also ran a test of the hypothesis that changes in the regional finance laws changed the average Buiter indicator. The conclusion for the Azores is that the 1998 law did improve sustainability, but not the 2007 and 2010 revisions. For Madeira there was no significant impact for any of the revisions.

Regional finances in Portugal have been always subjected to the idiosyncrasies of the Madeira governments. The same politician and political party were in office, leading to a path of successive periods of overspending and ensuing 'bailouts'. The Azorean governments, on the contrary, have been much more conservative and displayed prudent behavior as far as indebtedness is concerned. Nevertheless, debt has grown in a fairly unsustainable fashion in both regions, with Madeira's debt levels becoming a severe problem.

The successive reviews of the regional finance law, published for the first time in 1998, centered mostly on the definition of transfers and on the expenditure control mechanisms. The most recent version incorporated several new dispositions associated with the rules of the stability and growth pact in regard to debt controls.

The regional governments, like the central government and municipalities, also resorted to various off-budget financial arrangements and outright arrears, which justified the extension of stricter rules to this level of government also.

5. REVIEWING INTERGOVERNMENTAL RELATIONS IN PORTUGAL – STRUCTURE AND PRACTICE

Intergovernmental relations in Portugal have undergone substantial changes since the governance changes introduced with the 1974 revolution. Municipalities gained power and two new autonomous regions were created.

The first two decades of empowerment of local and regional governments brought with them new experiences: some financial autonomy, and with that the need to establish financial controls for sub-national governments. There have been unfortunate incidents of poor budget control since then, leading to the expectation that the central government would always bail out bankrupt jurisdictions. This is what in fact happened both in the two autonomous regions and in several municipalities.

In 1990, the central government helped Madeira re-program its excessive debt and assumed part of the interest costs involved. In 1998 and 1999, with the publication of the first regional finance law, the central government assumed a considerable portion of the debt of the Azores and of Madeira. Municipalities in financial distress could also resort to several assistance mechanisms in order to regain sustainability. One critical aspect of these interventions was that citizens of the jurisdictions affected were not called upon to pay – in any significant or perceptible manner – more taxes in order to compensate for the excessive expenditures of government. The adjustments were made mostly through reducing expenditures for the essential functions of government.

The 21st century brought about some changes due to three very important facts: by joining the euro, Portugal subscribed to the Stability and Growth Pact and was bound to abide by the control rules it implied; because of failure to control the national budget, the 2011 MoU set an agenda of considerable adjustments and structural reforms, including the review of the national budget framework law; in 2013 the budget treaty reinforced the restriction on budget targets, and thus on budget policy.

These changes affected the controls that were placed both on the regional and on the local governments. To deal with the persistent budget deficits at the turn of the century, the central government imposed a zero deficit restriction on regional and local governments, which was to hold until the onset of the financial crisis of 2008. This approach to financial control restricted the budgets of the sub-national governments to the limits of transfers and own revenues. This policy might be part of the explanation for the low volume of local and regional debt in total national debt in Portugal. Including commitments generated through public companies and PPPs does not significantly impact on this conclusion. The hard budget restriction, however, led regional and local governments to engage extensively in off-budget operations.

Changes in the regional and local finance laws, as well as other complementary legislations, introduced more controls and more reporting requirements for all levels of government and for public entities not included in the public budgets.

The obligations of the Stability and Growth Pact were the main driving factors for change in the local finance law in 2006 and in the regional finance law of 2007. One important norm was the prohibition of the national authorities to assume regional or local government obligations, debt controls, and even the norm that contemplated the possibility that the national budget law change established transfers if national obligations within international treaties rendered it necessary.

As a consequence of the international financial crisis and of the Euro crisis that ensued, renewed attention was devoted to the budget process and to equilibrium targets. This led to various changes in the national budget framework law, which was made applicable to all public budgets with the necessary adjustments.

The MoU provided a new fast track agenda for change in Portugal, impacting significantly on regional and local governments through the mere reductions in transfers and through the changes in the regulatory set-up. The MoU addressed changes in the relation with local and regional authorities when it specified, for example: reduction of the staff and wage bill of regional and local administrations by 2 percent per year, in 2012 and 2013; reduction of transfers to local and regional authorities; introduction of a standstill rule on tax expenditures at the central, regional and local levels; amendment of the regional finance law to limit the reduction of VAT and of income taxes to 20 percent, as opposed to 30 percent; streamlining of the budgetary process through the legal frameworks; enhancement of the existing monthly reporting on budgetary execution on a cash basis for the general government, including regional and local governments; expanding the tax expenditure report to include regional and local administrations; revising the local and regional finance laws to fully adapt the local and regional financing framework to the principles and rules adopted by the budgetary framework law in what concerns the inclusion of all relevant public entities in the perimeter of local and of regional government, the multi-annual framework with expenditure, budget balance and indebtedness rules; program budgeting; the interaction with the function of the Fiscal Council; reducing the number of municipal offices by at least 20 percent per year in 2012 and 2013; and reorganization of local government administration.

The revised budget framework law published in 2013 incorporated not only the changes included in the MoU but also those included in the Directive no. 2011/85/UE. This aligns the requirements imposed on the budgets of the member states and complies with what is contemplated in the treaty on stability and coordination of governance in the economic and monetary union.

The main changes of the law included: setting rules, in accordance with the Stability and Growth Pact, for the structural budget balance and for converging rules to its targets; multi-year budget planning; macroeconomic scenario specifications; budget execution information; inclusion of new principles – sustainability, efficiency and efficacy, and responsibility; debt limits, transposing the norms in Regulation (UE) no. 1177/2011; definition of what constitutes a significant deviation of the deficit from its long-term target; deviation correction mechanisms; and exceptions.

The regional and local finance laws published in 2013 have incorporated the main mechanisms of the budget framework law that applies equally to the local and regional budget processes.

In 2012 the central government signed a memorandum with Madeira to finance its excessive commercial debt and with the Azores to refinance part of its debt that was due that year. These agreements took into account the basic principles contained in the MoU, setting a considerable difference relative to what had been done in previous crises, with the central government assuming part of the effort of supporting the debt. In the case of Madeira, taxes had to be increased, even without review of the regional finance law, and expenditures reduced, with significant impacts on the citizens of the region. In the Azores, a mere case of difficulty of refinancing through the market led to a requirement for maintaining no deficits in the public companies included in the budget perimeter.

Evaluating critical local and regional issues such as sustainability and equalization, one concludes that the record in Portugal has been poor. Equalization at the local level was not clearly attained and sustainability was clearly not achieved, on average, as assessed in Fortuna et al. (2014c) and in Fortuna et al. (2014b). This topic requires further analysis, namely along the lines of Potrafke and Reishmann (2014), who find that fiscal transfers have significant behavioral impacts on sub-national governments.

Even though fiscal rules did not totally prevent overspending, they provided some containment of the problem. However, the benefits of fiscal controls were at least partially offset by the off-budget mechanisms in a system where municipalities do not have much tax autonomy. Foremny (2014) analyzes how fiscal rules and tax autonomy in European countries influence deficits, concluding that rules decrease deficits only in unitary countries and that deficits of sub-national sectors can be avoided through tax autonomy.

Yet another study, by Neyapti (2010), looks at the issue of fiscal decentralization and deficits. He suggests that the analysis of fiscal decentralization should consider both expenditure and revenue configurations since they affect motivations differently. Using the Government Financial Statistics of the IMF, the author concludes that there is a significantly negative effect of fiscal decentralization on deficits. He also concludes that country characteristics and institutional features significantly influence the effectiveness of fiscal decentralization in reducing deficits, and calls attention to social issues such as ethno-linguistic divisions and governance.

This brings to mind the conflicting positions of the regional governments vis-à-vis the central government, particularly in the case of Madeira. Arriving at a consensual transfer budget has always been an issue with Madeira. The longstanding regional president admitted resorting to indebtedness, by way of securing compensation for Portugal's long exploitation of Madeira since the 15th century. The regional government even went as far as to finance a history of the region to support its thesis. To a significant extent, this behavior on the part of one of the players did influence the others.

In the period under analysis Portugal made significant strides toward implementing better budget procedures, better control of contingencies, and better control of budget execution. The changes in the budget framework law, first because of the evolution of Europe's concern over excessive debts in the Euro area and the evolution of the Stability and Growth Pact mechanisms, and secondly due to the MoU, were considerable. However, these need continued attention in their application, and will probably still need further improvement in the near future.

The government's strategy to implement the new budget framework set as a law in 2011 (Law no. 64-C/2011) identifies the main concerns for implementation and the priority areas for action. The two main priorities set in 2011 were 1) the improvement of the budget's information quality and 2) the reinforcement of the control over the commitments assumed by all public entities. The document describes the Portuguese budget process as a mechanism based on cash accounting, annual limits, and lack of focus on results. In addition, the system is characterized as fragmented, without a multi-year setting to fix expenditures and lacking a complete system of accounting control and information for a critical appraisal of performance. Use of the cash accounting methodology does not comply with the accrual methodology contemplated in the Stability and Growth Pact. Even within the existing system, not all entities were complying with the established accounting rules adopted in 1997.

The strategy document also focuses on accounting procedures and reporting to stress the fact that procedures were designed 20 years ago and lacked adaptation to more recent international standards and to the capacity of producing adequate information for measurement and comparison of results.

One important aspect of control pertains to the public entities that are not directly contemplated in the budget. To this effect, two interesting aspects of the budget framework law are the zero base budget and the requirement that the budget report contain information on the debt of all public entities.

The zero base budget requires a complete revision and justification of a budget to assess the consistency of costs and outcomes, applicable to all public entities, including entrepreneurial public entities. The entrepreneurial public entities are totally owned by the government, pursue non-lucrative objectives and provide a service of public interest. This model is used mostly in hospitals. It is the responsibility of the minister of finance to determine which entities will have to present a zero base budget, and to provide the guidelines and evaluation criteria of its application to the autonomous institutes and to the entrepreneurial public entities.

The information requirement of the budget report implies the specification of global debt of the administration, of public companies, of public entrepreneurial entities, of PPPs, of regional public companies, and of municipal companies. These are much broader than the zero base budget, which is not applicable to the public companies, to the regional public entrepreneurial entities, or to municipal public companies. Aside from the rules for extinction of the municipal companies, there are no specific control mechanisms over the regional and municipal entrepreneurial sector.

Looking ahead, better controls are necessary for a wider spectrum of public entities, including companies that have systematically been used to circumvent budget restrictions. Part of the associated compromises can be tracked through the loan guarantees that are provided by governments and which can become a contingent liability. The Portuguese Public Finance Council (2013) provides an interesting discussion of both the local and the regional finance laws, pointing to aspects that that should have been corrected in these laws, namely: harmonization of debt definitions for all levels of government; inclusion of all entities that create potential liabilities in the debt rule of regions and municipalities; improvement in information for sub-national taxes and expenditures for more transparency; elimination of exceptions to rules that make them weaker; assurance of public financial coverage for municipalities in distress without market solutions when excessive debt corrective mechanisms have to be used; harmonization of central and regional financing mechanisms of municipalities; improvement in reporting systems; implementation of better local accountability rules with a clearer ownership of local taxes; assurance that earmarked funds are duly applied as they are intended. Even though most of the recommendations were not taken up in the regional and local finance laws, there is considerable room for improvement of current practice.

The law that regulates the Municipal Support Fund (Law no. 53/2014 of 25 August), designed to rescue local governments on the brink of bankruptcy, establishes that municipalities which require assistance have to increase local taxes to their maximum limits and undertake very restrictive labor policies. This is a major step toward making local elected officials more directly accountable for their spending and taxing policies.

In Portugal, the newly adopted norms tend to make sub-national governments more accountable but, except for extraordinarily bad circumstances, there is little assurance that citizens will understand the implications of local or regional spending options. More fiscal autonomy is one way of making sure that citizens are aware of the costs of public spending even when bailouts are not necessary.

Portugal has come a long way toward improving its fiscal processes, making citizens more aware of the implications of public policies and making politicians more accountable. The course of adjustments is not complete and continued attention needs to be devoted to marginal but nevertheless important adjustments to secure better results.

Faced with the need for continued financial consolidation, Portugal will also continue to receive financial resources to support development coming from the EU. As in the previous development programs, the 2020 horizon program will create pressure for local and regional governments to overcome budget limits in order to take full advantage of the significant contribution from these European funds.

NOTE

1. This designation is attributed to the authoritarian, autocratic and corporativist political regime that prevailed in Portugal between the Constitution of 1933 and that of 1976.

REFERENCES

Bilhim, J. (2004), 'A governação nas autarquias locais', *Coleção inovação e governação nas autarquias*, Porto, Portugal: SPI.

Buiter, W.H. (1985), 'A guide to public sector debt and deficits', *Economic Policy*, **1**(1), 13–61, DOI: 10.2307/1344612.

Buiter, W.H. (2003), 'Fiscal sustainability', paper presented at the Egyptian Center for Economic Studies in Cairo, 19 October.

Campos, B. (1988), 'Os Municípios, o Financiamento das suas Actividades e as Relações com o Poder Central', *Revista Crítica de Ciências Sociais*, **25**, 115–26.

Carvalho, J., Fernandes, M.J., Camões, P. and Jorge, S. (2012), 'Anuário Financeiro dos Municípios Portugueses – 2010', OTOC.

Carvalho, J., Fernandes, M.J., Camões, P. and Jorge, S. (2013a), 'Setor Empresarial Local-Atualização do Anuário Financeiro dos Municípios Portugueses, 2011–2012', OTOC.

Carvalho, J., Fernandes, M.J., Camões, P. and Jorge, S. (2013b), 'Anuário Financeiro dos Municípios Portugueses, 2011–2012', OTOC.

Carvalho, M.F. (2010), 'A governação local no Algarve no contexto de financiamento e responsabilidades'.
Carvalho, M.F. (2011), 'Gestão pública: um novo paradigma para a governação da administração local em Portugal'.
Da Cunha, J.C. and Silva, P. (2002), 'Finanças Locais e Consolidação Orçamental em Portugal', Boletim, económico, Banco de Portugal, March, 47–56.
Fernandes, M.J. (2007), 'Contribuição da informação contabilística para a tomada de decisão na administração pública autárquica', *Tékhne-Revista de Estudos Politécnicos*, 67–96.
Foremny, D. (2014), 'Sub-national deficits in European countries: the impact of fiscal rules and tax autonomy', *European Journal of Political Economy*, **34**, 86–110.
Fortuna, M., Vieira, J.C. and Mendes, M. (2005), 'Equalization effects of local financing models in Portugal', CEEAplA – Centro de Estudos de Economia Aplicada do Atlântico, Working Paper No. 03/2005.
Fortuna, M, Silva, F. and Borges, L. (2014a), 'A Sustentabilidade das Finançasdas Regiões Autonomas Portuguesas – 1990–2012', Centro de Estudos de Economia Aplicada, Working Paper No. 6/2014, University of the Azores.
Fortuna, M., Silva, F. and Camilo, J. (2014b), 'A Sustentabilidade das Finanças Locais em Portugal – 1996–2012', Centro de Estudos de Economia Aplicada, Working Paper No. 5/2014, University of the Azores.
Fortuna, M., Silva, F. and Carreiro, R. (2014c), 'Assessment of Equalization Effects of Government Transfers to Portuguese Municipalities Using Data Methodologies', CEEAplA Working Paper 02/2014, available at: http://www.ceeapla.uac.pt/uploads/pms/attachments/3669_paper02-2014.pdf.
Foremny, D. (2014), 'Sub-national deficits in European countries: the impact of fiscal rules and tax autonomy', *European Journal of Political Economy*, **34**, 86–110.
Ianchovichina, E. and Liu, L. (2008), 'Subnational fiscal sustainability analysis', *PREM Notes*, 117, Washington, DC: World Bank, available at: http://documents.worldbank.org/curated/en/2008/06/9731691/subnational-fiscal-sustainability-analysis.
Nabais, J.C. (2007), *A Autonomia Financeira das Autarquias Locais*, Almedina.
Neyapti, B. (2010), 'Fiscal decentralization and deficits: International evidence', *European Journal of Political Economy*, **326**, 155–66.
Paixão, M. and Baleiras, R. (2013), 'Analysis of debt limits in the regional and local finance bills. Portuguese public finance council', Occasional Paper No.1/2013. Lisbon.
Portuguese Public Finance Council (2013), 'Analysis of the legal proposals for new subnational finance laws', Report No. 1/2013, Lisbon.
Potrakfke, N. and Reishmann, M. (2014), 'Fiscal transfers and fiscal sustainability', CESifo Working Paper No. 4716 (accepted for publication in the *Journal of Money, Credit and Banking*).
Vilarinho, F.C.V. (2010), 'A nova lei das finanças locais e os seus impactes', Master's thesis, University of Aveiro.
Zbyszewski, J.P. (2006), *O Financiamento das Autarquias Locais Portuguesas*, Coimbra: Almedina.

8. Multi-level finance and governance in Spain: the impact of the Euro crisis

Santiago Lago-Peñas and Albert Solé-Ollé

1. INTRODUCTION

The recent economic crisis provoked in Spain a fiscal crunch without any precedent in recent history, with public deficits of around 10 percent of GDP over several years and a public debt approaching 100 percent. Although economic prospects are currently improving, the situation in public finances at different levels of government is going to be challenging in the coming years.

The main causes of this situation are external to the country, and related to the availability of 'low-cost' credit during the boom years and to the effects of the international financial crisis. However, some authors suggest that internal factors also played a role: the poor quality of institutions made it more difficult to provide an appropriate and speedy response to the housing bubble once the crisis appeared (e.g., Fernández-Villaverde et al., 2013). Santos (2014) provides a description of the role of government in dealing with the crisis of Spanish savings banks. And Solé-Ollé and Viladecans-Marsal (2013) examine the role of regional and local land-use policies in fuelling the housing bubble.

One of the possible internal causes of this crisis exposed in the public debate is the Spanish decentralized system of public finance and governance. For the supporters of this standpoint, Spanish regional and local governments were not prudent enough in managing windfall revenue gains during the boom, excessively increasing public spending and employment. And once the crisis hit, these governments resisted the implementation of the needed fiscal adjustment, adversely affecting the image of the country in international bond markets, making fiscal consolidation more difficult (see Jenker and Lu, 2014).

In this chapter we will try to identify which aspects of the multi-level framework of finance and governance might have helped reach this situation. As will become clear, although the Spanish fiscal decentralization process toward regional governments (i.e., the so-called Autonomous Communities, ACs from now on),[1] appeared to be initially successful (see, e.g., Solé-Ollé, 2010), there are several traits in its design that can partly explain what happened in recent years – these include: the assignment of volatile taxes to the ACs; reluctance to make the AC's tax autonomy deep enough; failures in the design of equalization transfers; and an inappropriate fiscal discipline framework. Similar arguments can be raised in the case of local governments.

We will also argue that the decentralization process has not paid sufficient attention to strengthening sub-national democratic institutions, resulting in low levels of accountability and, in the end, harming the quality of fiscal management and the legitimacy of decentralized institutions. Also, there are doubts regarding the effectiveness of the design of decentralized institutions in channeling the demands for greater autonomy of Spanish historical regions, as the current secessionist movement in Catalunya (Catalonia) shows.

This chapter is organized as follows. In Section 2 the basic facts about the recent economic cycle in Spain and its effects on the public finances of the several layers of government are described. Then, in Section 3 we describe the behavior of regional public finances during the boom and the crisis, showing that both the size of the shock experienced and the quality of government institutions matter. In Section 4 we analyze the institutional failures in the Spanish multi-level system of public finances that helped create this situation, focusing on multilayer financial arrangements and on the fiscal discipline framework. Section 4 focuses on an additional effect of the crisis, namely its impact on governance and territorial conflict. Section 5 concludes with suggested recommendations on intergovernmental reforms inspired by the lessons learnt in Spain.

2. THE SPANISH FISCAL BOOM AND CRISIS: THE MAIN FACTS

The recent crisis has had a deep impact on public finances in Spain. During the boom years, public revenues grew much more than in most European Monetary Union (EMU) countries, both in absolute terms and as a percentage of GDP (see Figure 8.1). Since spending was not growing faster than GDP a fiscal surplus was generated, giving the impression of good fiscal management. However, a large share of revenues came from taxes related to housing transactions and building activity. Hence when the housing bubble burst after 2007, tax collection plummeted. Add to this the

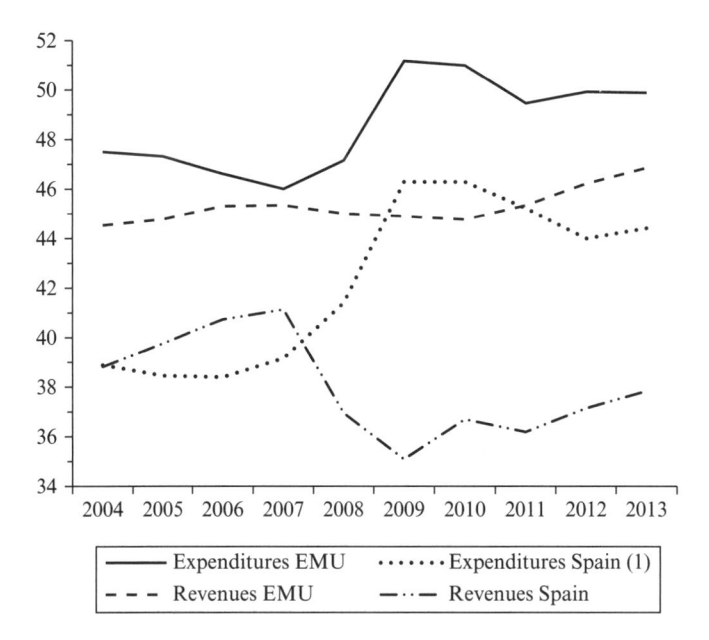

Notes: The expenditure figures for Spain exclude the one-off cost of the financial reform.

Source: Lago-Peñas (2014).

Figure 8.1   Revenues and expenditures, Spain and EMU as a % of GDP

effect of automatic stabilizers and of the large anti-cyclical measures taken at the beginning of the crisis, and the result was massive fiscal deficits from 2008 onwards.

The housing boom that preceded the crisis had a magnitude and duration not seen before.[2] It yielded huge windfall revenues for all Spanish layers of government. For example, regional governments obtain revenues from the stamp duty tax, which is one of the highest in the world, with a 7 percent tax rate on average. Local governments obtain revenues from a land transactions tax, from a construction tax (which is a percentage of contractor revenues), from developer's fees and from sales of land plots. Both national and regional governments obtain revenues from VAT, which also significantly depends on the construction sector. All these revenues proved to be highly volatile.

Figure 8.2 shows the evolution of selected regional taxes during the period 2002–12. Note that the revenues from the stamp duty tax more than doubled during the period 2002–06, but dropped to less than half the 2002 revenues by 2012. The revenues from inheritance tax also dropped

178 *Multi-level finance and the Euro crisis*

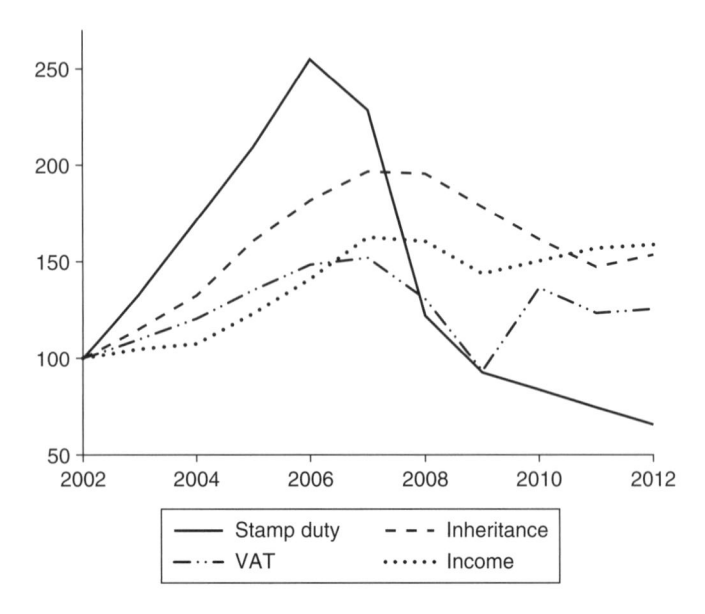

Notes: (1) Stamp duty: revenues from 'Impuesto de Transmisiones Patrimoniales y Actos Jurídicos Documentados'; (2) Inheritance: revenues from 'Impuestos de Sucesiones y Donaciones'; (3) Income: revenues from the 'Personal Income Tax'.

Source: Ministerio de Hacienda y Administraciones Públicas (several years).

Figure 8.2 Evolution of regional taxes, 2002–12 (2002 = 100)

during the crisis, although in this case it is difficult to know whether the effect is due to the housing bust or to the race-to-the-bottom in this tax, which started during the boom but continued during the first years of the crisis (see Solé-Ollé, 2014). The fall of VAT revenues during the first two years of the crisis was also huge. There is no official data on the share of VAT revenues coming from sales of new houses, but this had to be substantial. Given that the VAT is a shared tax, the drop had a huge impact on both the central and regional budgets. The impact should have been large, given the share of this tax in both central and regional budgets. However, the effect of the fall in VAT revenues was felt with some delay, both because collections started falling later than the other housing-related taxes (see Figure 8.2), and in the case of regional governments because of the system of cash advancements used by the central government to channel these revenues to the regional treasuries.[3] Revenues from personal income tax are also shared. Although PIT collection dropped slightly during the first years of the crisis, its dynamic was much more stable than that of the VAT.

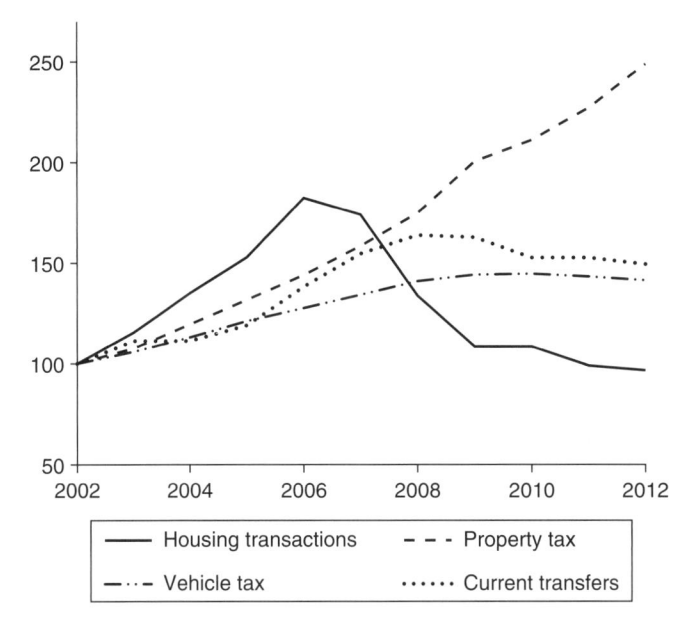

Notes: (1) Housing transactions: revenues from the tax on land transactions ('Impuesto sobre Incremento del Valor de los Terrenos de Naturaleza Urbana') + Construction tax ('Impuesto sobre Construcciones Instalaciones y Obras'); (2) Property tax: revenues from the urban property tax ('Impuesto sobre Bienes Inmuebles de Naturaleza Urbana'); (3) Vehicle tax: revenues from the 'Impuesto sobre Vehículos de Tracción Mecánica'; (4) Current transfers: transfers earmarked for current expenditures.

Source: Ministerio de Hacienda y Administraciones Públicas (several years).

Figure 8.3   Evolution of local taxes, 2002–12 (2002 = 100)

Figure 8.3 shows the evolution of the main municipal taxes. Note here that revenues from the two local taxes related to housing market activity (i.e., the tax on land transactions and the construction tax) nearly doubled during the boom, but returned to the previous level in 2012.[4] This evolution sharply contrasts with that corresponding to property tax, the revenues from which grew at a lower rate than the other housing-related taxes during the boom, but did not collapse during the crisis and, in fact, continued to grow at substantial rates. There are several explanations for this. First, property tax revenues are a function of the assessed value of the stock of property, which is much less volatile than the base of the land transactions and construction taxes – which depend on the annual number of transactions and also, to some extent, on prices. Second, due to the difficulties in performing locality-wide reassessments at the beginning of the 1990s, the central government envisaged a new system that allows the assessment increases arising from such a re-evaluation to be progressively incorporated into the tax base during a 10-year period (10 percent each year). This means that for municipalities reassessing at the beginning of the 2000s, the tax base continued to grow substantially during the first years of the crisis. Third, municipalities made use of their autonomy to adjust the property tax rate to compensate for other revenue losses during the first years of the crisis. Fourth, it seems that property tax delinquency has been at reasonable rates despite the huge bust in the housing boom. Note that the performance of the property tax in Spain has been remarkable, since other local taxes (mainly the vehicle tax) and current transfers (with its overall pot of revenues linked to the evolution of a basket of central taxes) also stagnated during the crisis.

So, the crisis hit the finances of all layers of government. The decline in social security contributions and the rise in unemployment payments had a strong and negative effect on the centralized social security budget. In the case of regional governments, the difficulties in cutting spending on key public services (i.e., education, health, and social services) implied that revenue drops were automatically translated to deficit increases during the first years of the crisis. This is probably a difference from previous crises, since at that time these services had only been devolved to a few ACs. In the case of local governments, the fall in revenues was partly compensated for by a drop in public investment, but deficits also soared during the first years of the crisis. See Figures 8.4 and 8.5 for a comparison of the levels of deficit and debt of the different layers of government.

It is evident also that the average effect of the crisis might actually mask wide differences between sub-national governments (see Figure 8.6). Some regional governments (e.g. Valencia and Catalunya) became virtually bankrupt and were bailed out by the national government, while others faced a lower level of fiscal stress (e.g. Galicia and the region of Madrid). Some municipalities also accumulated an unbearable level of debt (e.g. Madrid city) while others have been able to generate a substantial budget surplus (e.g. Barcelona – see also Chapter 10 on Barcelona and Turin in this volume). In the next section, we will provide some clues as to why the effect of the crisis has been so heterogeneous.

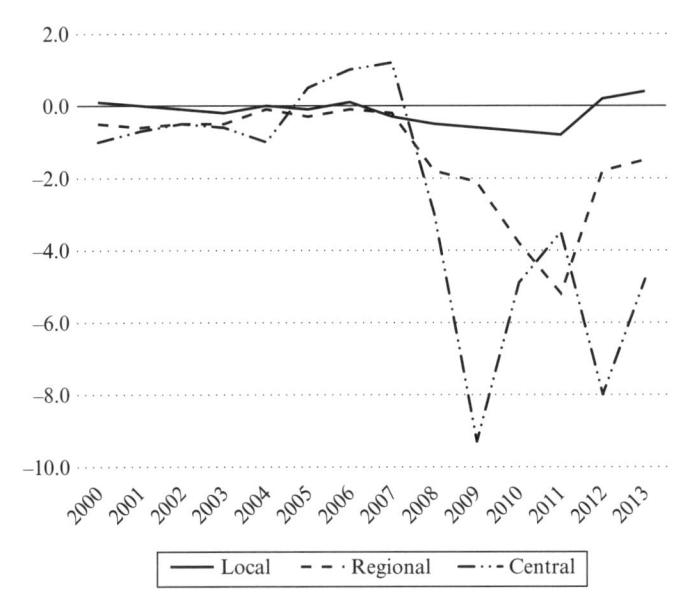

Notes: Deficit and surplus according to the excessive deficit procedure (EDP).

Source: The authors, based on data from Bank of Spain.

Figure 8.4 Fiscal surplus (+) or deficit (−) by layer of government as a % of GDP (2000–2013)

3. UNDERSTANDING PUBLIC FINANCE OUTCOMES

3.1 Fiscal Profligacy during the Boom

As explained above, during the boom regional and local governments experienced huge windfall revenues from housing-related taxes. It is important to note that due to the peculiar design of regional and local transfers, these windfalls were not equalized, so they fully accrued to the sub-national treasuries.[5] These revenues were clearly extraordinary, so it would have been prudent to save part, if not all, of them. Instead, regional and local governments, after experiencing positive windfalls year after year, ended up considering that these transitory revenues were permanent and decided to spend them.[6] We might then conclude that during the boom, regional and local governments overspent; i.e., they spent a too-high portion of the additional extraordinary revenues they received. In any case, one should

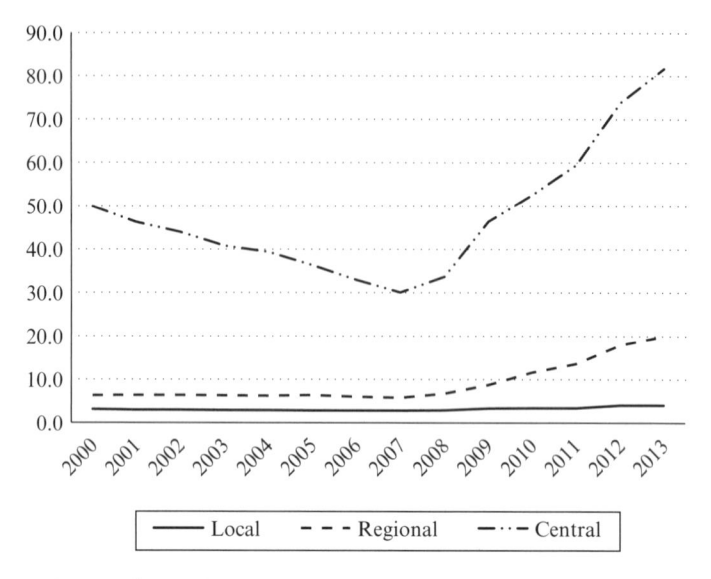

Notes: Debt according to the excessive deficit procedure (EDP).

Source: The authors, based on data from Bank of Spain.

Figure 8.5   Debt by layer of government expressed as a % of GDP (2000–2013)

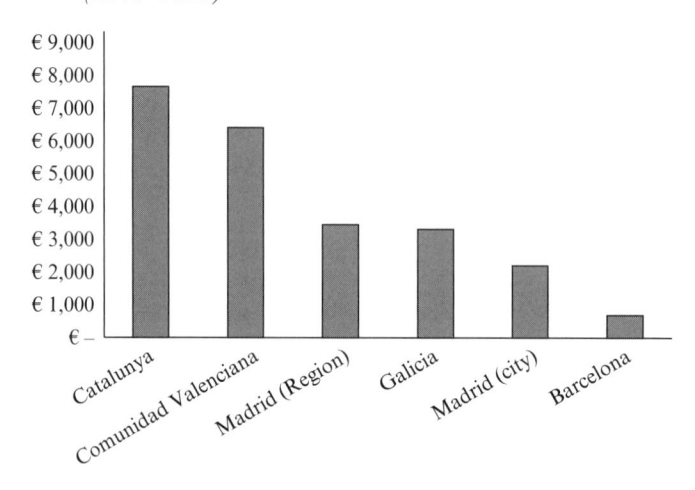

Note: Figures expressed in per capita euros.

Source: The authors, based on National Institute of Statistics and Bank of Spain.

Figure 8.6   Debt of selected regional and local governments, 2013

note that the central government also probably overspent during this period, given the large budget surplus generated.[7]

Other regional revenue sources (e.g. tax sharing and transfers) also grew at high rates during the boom years, due to the dismantling of dynamic equalization guarantees following the reform of the regional financing system in 2001 (see below).

Something similar happened to grants to municipalities. A reform in 2002 linked the global requirements for grants to the growth of central government's revenues, explicitly in order to increase the exposure of regional and local budgets to the evolution of the economy. It is unclear, however, whether regional governments were fully aware of the implications of this change. As a result, the higher rates of growth in these revenues also fuelled increases in public spending, creating thus another source of overspending.

Figure 8.7 shows that the average annual growth rate of public expenditure during the period 2002–07 was over 10 percent in most regions. Spending growth was also high in the case of local governments, especially in areas where the housing boom was more intense (Solé-Ollé and Viladecans-Marsal, 2011). Regional spending growth also continued at a high rate (around 8 percent) during the period 2008–09, in spite of the fact

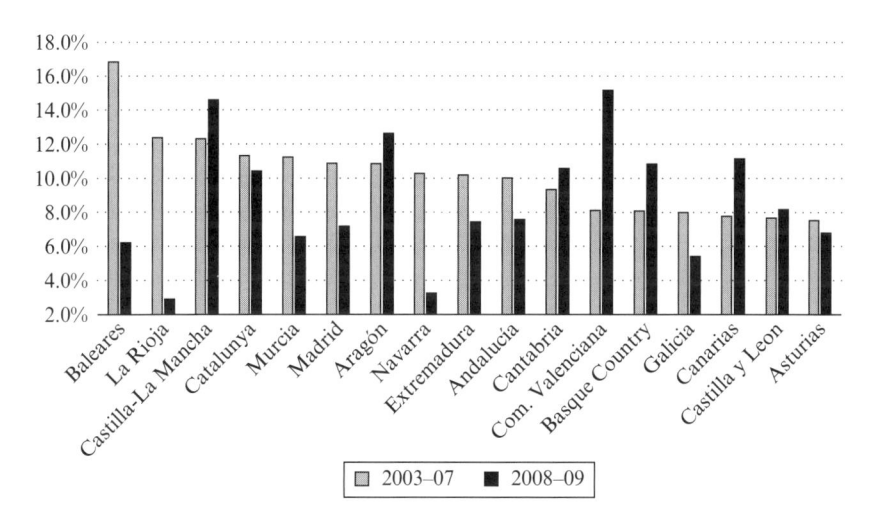

Source: The authors, based on data computed by Lago-Peñas and Fernandez-Leiceaga (2013).

Figure 8.7 Average annual growth rates of expenditures in 2003–07 and 2008–09

that tax collection was falling. Two main reasons explain this mismatch. First, the idea that the crisis would be much shorter and public expenditure rises would help to boost the economy. In fact, during those years, the central government was implementing powerful stimulus packages. Second, because the regional financing system is based on cash advancements, these were overestimated in both 2008 and 2009, generating thus an additional type of windfall. Again, something similar happened to municipalities during that period, first because the disbursement of local transfers is also based on the same system of cash advances, and second because a substantial part of the central government's stimulus program came in the form of capital transfers to local governments (see Utrilla de la Hoz, 2010).

While the growing spending trend was widespread, it was more intense in some regions than others. Compare Castilla-La Mancha or Aragón, with annual growth rates over 10 percent for the whole period 2002–09, against Galicia where spending growth was much lower (Figure 8.7). Obviously, the regions that experienced a higher growth in revenues also increased expenditure more. However, for a given amount of additional revenues some regions overspent more than others. Two different explanations can be provided for these differences. First, there was more overspending in places where the revenue windfalls were larger and more persistent. Sustained growth of revenues during several years might be the reason everyone in the region, from politicians to voters, from public employees to other stakeholders, ended up thinking that these revenues were secure. Figure 8.8 plots the average real annual growth rates of regional expenditures during 2002–07 against the real growth in regional revenues during the same period. In Panel (a) we split the sample into regions with low vs. high revenue growth. The idea is that overspending should be larger in regions with higher revenue growth because the persistence in revenue shocks might have fostered there a bubble-like mentality among voters and politicians. This is precisely what the figures show, with all the caveats related to sample size: the response of spending to revenue growth is small and statistically not significant in the low growth regime, and very high (on average a 1 percent increase in revenues triggered a 1 percent increase in spending) in the high growth regime.[8] It turns out that these regions are the ones that experienced a more intense housing boom. Something similar happened in the case of local governments, as has been shown in Solé-Ollé and Viladecans (2011).

Second, spending growth also tended to be greater in regions where the quality of government is lower. There are several theoretical arguments for this. One might argue, e.g., that in places with high levels of corruption and/or inefficient government citizens do not believe that politicians are going to make good use of revenue windfalls. Therefore, in these

Panel (a): Revenue growth

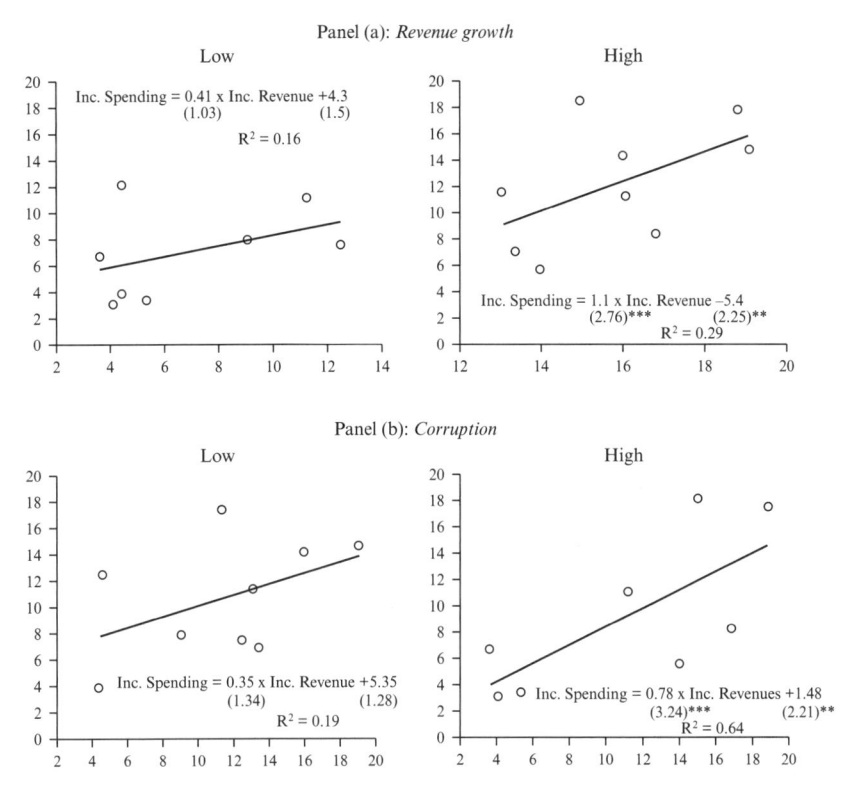

[Scatter plot "Low": Inc. Spending = 0.41 × Inc. Revenue +4.3, (1.03) (1.5), R² = 0.16]

[Scatter plot "High": Inc. Spending = 1.1 × Inc. Revenue −5.4, (2.76)*** (2.25)**, R² = 0.29]

Panel (b): Corruption

[Scatter plot "Low": Inc. Spending = 0.35 × Inc. Revenue +5.35, (1.34) (1.28), R² = 0.19]

[Scatter plot "High": Inc. Spending = 0.78 × Inc. Revenues +1.48, (3.24)*** (2.21)**, R² = 0.64]

Notes: (1) y-axis: growth rate of real regional revenues, x-axis: growth rate of real regional spending; source: Spanish Ministry of Finance and Public Administration (www.minap.gob.es) and National Institute of Statistics (www.ine.es). (2) Low vs. High Persistence: revenue growth rate below/above average. (3) Low vs. High Corruption level: number of corruption scandals during the period 1984–2014 per thousand inhabitants below/above average; source: Cercle Català de Negocis (www.ccncat.cat). (4) Line = regression line; in parenthesis t-statistic, ***,**, and * = statistically significant at the 99, 95 and 90% level. (5) The sample does not include the Basque Country and Navarra since they have a completely different funding system.

Figure 8.8   Overspending by Spanish regional governments (2002–07), conditional on the levels of revenue growth and corruption

jurisdictions, citizens demand that the government immediately spend any unexpected revenue (see Alesina et al., 2010). A similar argument posits that higher revenues provide social groups with additional incentives to fight for an additional slice of the pie, exacerbating the already existing common-pool problem (see Tornell and Lane, 1999).

The above discussion suggests that in places with a poor quality of government overspending will be above the average. Panel (b) provides some evidence for this hypothesis. Again, we plot the rate of growth of spending against that of revenues (both variables expressed in real terms and per capita), but this time we divide the sample according the prevalence of corruption (below and above average in terms of number of corruption cases per million inhabitants). The figures show that the amount of overspending (the sensitivity of spending to revenues) is much higher in the sample with high corruption. The elasticity is around 0.8 percent. In fact, the relationship is not even statistically significant in the low corruption sample.

Summing up, both experiencing a huge revenue boom and having a low quality of government might explain the degree of overspending during the boom. Actually, it is quite possible that both explanations interact: the trouble is to be expected where huge revenue windfalls meet bad governance.

3.2 Difficult Fiscal Adjustments

The economic downturn led to a precipitous drop in revenues. Figure 8.1 shows that the revenues/GDP ratio fell from 41 percent to 35 percent in just two years (2007–09), in deep contrast to the EMU countries' average. Moreover, the rise in the expenditure ratio was also significantly above the average, rising from 39 percent to 46 percent. As a result, the 2007 surplus become a massive deficit in 2009. Sustainability of Spanish public finances was at stake, and tax rises and expenditure cuts started in 2010.

The central government's budgetary strategy for the period 2014–17 is mostly based on additional cuts in the expenditure/GDP ratio (Table 8.1). Only one-fifth of the deficit reduction was to be on account of higher revenues. In contrast, one-third of the future fiscal adjustment is focused on employee compensation. Both further reductions in the number of public employees, and nominal wages freeze applied over an already shrunk wage bill, were to be the instruments.

According to the Labor Force Survey, the number of public employees in Spain at the end of 2013 was 2.91 million, down 12 percent from the peak achieved in 2010 (Figure 8.9). Because of the high expenditure decentralization in Spain, the local and regional tiers account for 75 percent of total public employees, so the downsizing of public employment basically affected those layers of government. As a result, by the end of 2013, public employment in Spain was similar to that in 2004. But spending needs had not been reduced. On the contrary, with mostly the same catalogue of public services, the Spanish population has increased by 10 percent and real GDP by +5 percent over this period. Also, according to the

Table 8.1 Actual and forecast change in the deficit and its main components for 2012–17 (figures as a percentage of GDP)

	2012	2013	2014(F)	2015(F)	2016(F)	2017(F)
Non-financial revenues	37.17	37.76	38.5	38.8	38.9	39.0
Non-financial expenditures	44.01	44.38	44.0	43.0	41.7	40.1
Total public deficit	−6.84	−6.62	−5.5	−4.2	−2.8	−1.1
Interests payments	3.06	3.43	3.5	3.6	3.7	3.8
Primary deficit (−) or surplus	−3.78	−3.19	−2.0	−0.6	0.9	2.7
Deficit of regional governments	−1.86	−1.54	−1.0	−0.7	−0.3	0.0
Deficit (−) or surplus of local governments	0.22	0.4	0.0	0.0	0.0	0.0
Real GDP growth rate	−1.6	−1.2	1.2	1.8	2.3	3.0
GDP deflator rate	0.0	0.6	0.5	0.8	1.2	1.5

Notes: The expenditure and deficit figures exclude the one-off cost of the financial reform. (F) means a forecast.

Source: The authors, based on *Ministerio de Hacienda y Administraciones Públicas* (2014a and 2014b).

government plans for the period 2014–17, the remuneration of public employees accounted for around one-third of the fiscal adjustment in GDP terms. Given the sharp cut in the number of employees and subsequent salary reductions over the period 2011–13, it is not at all clear how the government will be able to generate the anticipated savings to maintain the quality of services and incentives for public employees. And this is a matter of concern for Spaniards, whose opinions about the quality of public services (see Figure 8.10) have fallen during the crisis, reaching a minimum in 2012, the last year this information is available. Insofar as expenditure cuts have deepened in 2013 and 2014, the current opinions will probably be worse.

Instead of relying upon bargaining and cooperation, the central government has chosen the exercise of strict controls over sub-national treasuries, taking advantage of the extreme difficulties for regions in accessing financial markets and their subsequent financial dependence on the central government. For example, in 2012 the central government started to provide loans to the most indebted ACs, and conditioned this assistance to specific expenditure categories for payment of providers (e.g. contractors, hospitals, pharmacies, etc.), charging at times above market interest rates. In Table 8.2 we show the importance of these loans that should be openly qualified as 'bailouts': by the end of 2013 they represent nearly 30 percent

188   *Multi-level finance and the Euro crisis*

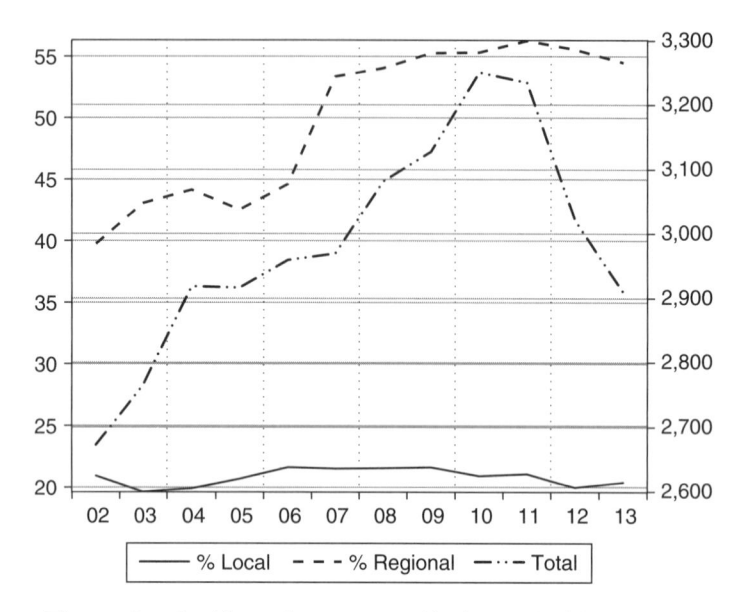

Notes: Figures of total public employees expressed in thousands (right scale). Shares of both local and regional tiers are expressed as a percentage (left scale).

Source: The authors, based on the Spanish Labor Force Survey.

Figure 8.9   The evolution of public employment in Spain (2002–13)

of the overall stock or regional debt, and this percentage reaches 50 percent for the most indebted regions (as, e.g., Catalunya).

Some ACs have explored the possibility of increasing taxes. However, they faced a sort of 'tax hostility' from the central government, which attacked many of the new regional taxes before the Constitutional Court (see Solé-Ollé, 2014). Also, the race-to-the bottom in wealth taxation, started during the boom, made it difficult to increase these taxes during the bust. At the same time, growth in intergovernmental grants has slowed so the ACs have been forced to adjust even more, or instead had to rely even more on central bailouts. The central government has not balked at passing more stringent national budgetary stability measures. The center has, however, paid the political price for a strategy many regional governments and nationalist parties perceived as a clear sign of political and financial recentralization in Spain (Lago-Peñas, 2013). While those political consequences are analyzed below, it is true that both regional and local governments have made a considerable effort in consolidating their budgets up to 2013. At the regional level, fiscal consolidation has been mostly based

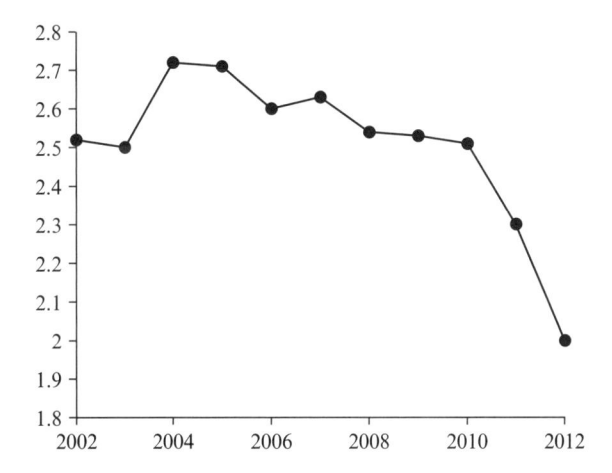

Notes: The index goes from a value of 4, reflecting the most positive opinion, to a value of 1, the most negative.

Source: Instituto de Estudios Fiscales (2013).

Figure 8.10 Average opinion on the evolution of public services in Spain over the last five years

on dramatic expenditure cuts affecting the main public services in Spain, including education, health care, and social services. In real terms, these basic services fell by more than 20 percent in most regions from 2009 to 2012 (see Figure 8.11).

The process of fiscal consolidation at the regional level has been quite effective, with a substantial reduction in the regional primary deficit. Moreover, local primary surpluses have arisen since 2013. Figure 8.12 shows that the ACs with higher debt stocks are the ones that made the greatest effort in reducing their deficits. Note also that the regional primary deficit could have been reduced even more had intergovernmental revenues been growing at the same pace as tax revenues. In some sense, either unintentionally or intentionally, the central government has been focusing the consolidation effort toward regional governments. This can be seen in Figure 8.13, which compares the evolution of revenues, spending, and of the primary surplus or deficit for the three levels of government.

In Figure 8.13 Panel (a) we can see that central government's revenues recovered over the period 2009–14; since expenditures were cut during 2010 and 2011, and the primary deficit of the central government was considerably reduced. In Panel (b) we show for regional governments that revenues continued to fall for the initial years, seemed to recover in 2012,

Table 8.2 Bailouts of Spanish ACs during 2013–14

	Bailouts (million euros)	Bailouts/Debt (in %)
Catalunya	24,039	41,31
Andalucía	12,230	50,04
Comunidad Valenciana	6,284	19,31
Castilla-La Mancha	5,834	51,43
Murcia	3,337	60,20
Baleares	2,755	40,02
Canarias	1,914	36,24
Madrid	1,346	6,09
Cantabria	791	36,32
Asturias	783	25,66
Aragón	513	9,55
Extremadura	392	14,90
Castilla y León	0	0,00
Galicia	0	0,00
Navarra	0	0,00
País Vasco	0	0,00
La Rioja	0	0,00
CCAA	60,218	28,69

Notes: (1) Bailouts: extraordinary loans provided by the Spanish central government during the period 2012–13; (2) Bailouts/Debt = bailouts expressed as a % of the stock of debt at the end of 2013.

Source: Ministerio de Hacienda y Administraciones Públicas and Banco de España.

and finally fell again in 2013. Note that the revenues sources of central and regional governments are quite similar as both layers get a share of the main taxes (PIT, VAT, Excises).

The discrepancies found in the growth of revenues of the two layers are due again to the systems of cash advancements. For instance, the excess revenues that regional governments received during 2008 and 2009 had to be returned in the following years, and the central government was reluctant until 2012 to delay these repayments. Also, throughout the entire period, the central government avoided cuts in own managed spending programs, instead adjusting down transfers to the ACs and local governments. The central government even decided in 2011 and 2012 to freeze the implementation of some of the complementary funds introduced during the reform of the ACs' financing system in 2009.[9] So, in practice, the system starves the ACs of the revenues needed to ensure a more successful consolidation strategy. Despite the huge cuts in spending,

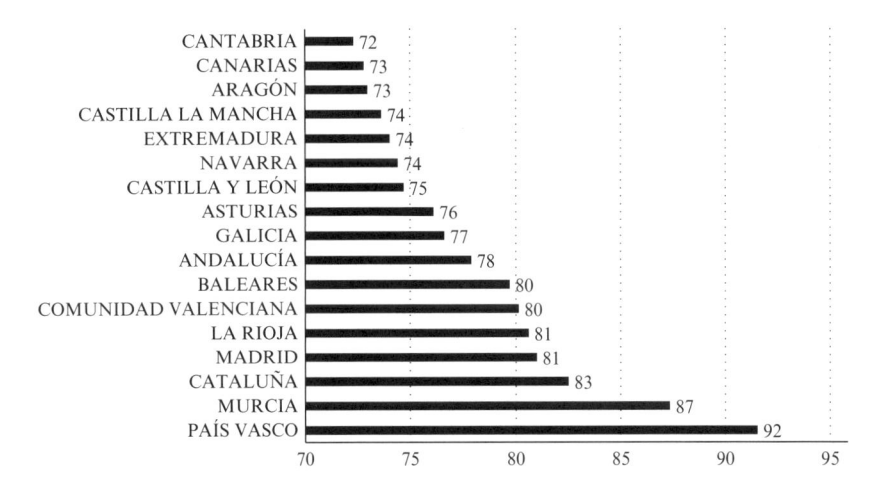

```
CANTABRIA      72
CANARIAS       73
ARAGÓN         73
CASTILLA LA MANCHA  74
EXTREMADURA    74
NAVARRA        74
CASTILLA Y LEÓN 75
ASTURIAS       76
GALICIA        77
ANDALUCÍA      78
BALEARES       80
COMUNIDAD VALENCIANA 80
LA RIOJA       81
MADRID         81
CATALUÑA       83
MURCIA         87
PAÍS VASCO     92
```

Notes: Spending in real terms (2009 Index value = 100).

Source: Lago-Peñas and Fernández (2013).

Figure 8.11 Dynamics of regional public expenditure from 2009 to 2012

it appears as though they are not putting in enough effort in adjusting their budgets.

The outcome in terms of the country's overall indebtedness is perhaps the same. The central government appears to have a lower deficit thanks to the reduction of intergovernmental transfers, while the regional governments appear to have a higher deficit, covered by loans from the central government. However, the social impact of the adjustment is probably very different, since the central government avoids any further cuts in centrally administered programs, while regional governments are forced to cut their socially sensitive programs, such as in health or education. One could argue that the central government avoids the most extreme outcomes by channeling the bailout moneys to cover its most pressing needs, but public services and its citizens are nevertheless being affected by the adjustment. Note also that it is not clear that this strategy can be sustained politically in the future, with the rise of the anti-Euro party in sync with a similar movement in Greece. Consequently, it will not be possible to fully stabilize Spanish debt without the central government accepting more adjustments in its own budget.

In Panel (c) we show what happened at the local government level. Note that revenues did not fall that much. At least on average, the possibility of using their tax autonomy to raise property taxes and user charges has

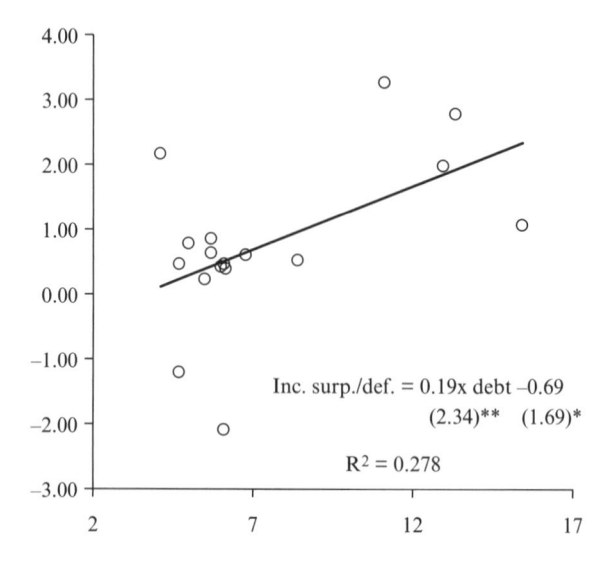

Notes: (1) x-axis: ACs debt stock/GDP, in %; (2) y-axis: increase in the ACs primary surplus (if +) or deficit (if −) over GDP during the period 2009–13; primary surplus/deficit = non-financial revenues − non-financial expenditures + interest payments. (2) Line = regression line; in parenthesis t-statistic, ***, **, and * = statistically significant at the 99, 95 and 90% level.

Source: IGAE, Ministerio de Hacienda y Administraciones Públicas, and INE.

Figure 8.12 Δ in primary surplus (+) or deficit (−)/GDP over 2013–09 vs. debt/GDP in 2009

avoided a fiscal catastrophe at the local level. Local governments also find it easier to adjust expenditures down, probably due to the larger share of capital spending in their budgets and to the fact that they do not deal with socially sensitive spending items, such as health or education. As a result, local governments have been even able to generate a substantial primary surplus. We have to conclude that local governments have been quite resilient in the face of a huge boom and bust in housing-related revenues – although the stability of property tax revenues was a big plus. Certainly, they also had to downsize, and this caused some deterioration in the quality of local services, but at least they did not put at risk the solvency of the entire country.

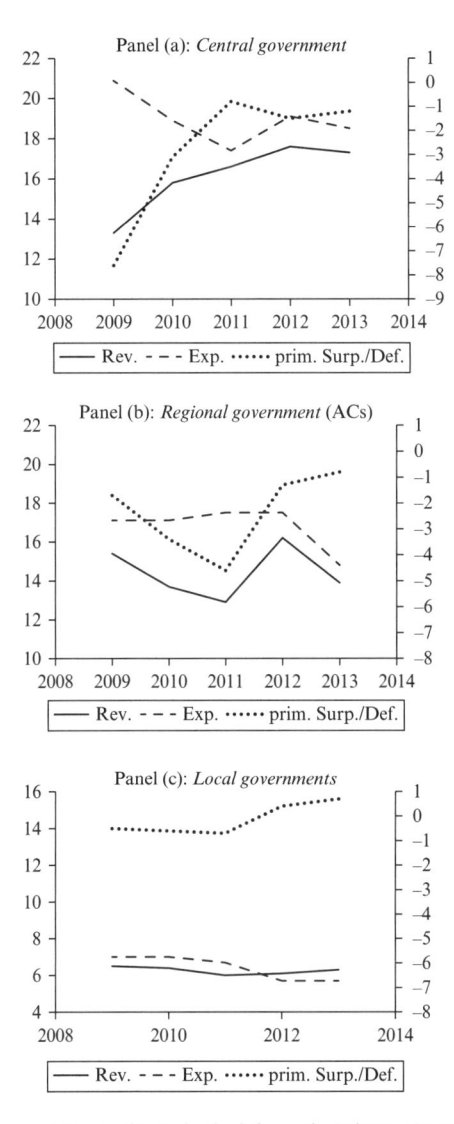

Notes: (1) Revenues and Expenditures in the left y-axis, Primary Surplus/Deficit in the right y-axis. (2) Revenues: non-financial revenues over GDP; Expenditures: non-financial expenditures – Interest payments – Bank bailouts/GDP.

Source: IGAE, Ministerio de Hacienda y Administraciones Públicas and INE.

Figure 8.13 Fiscal adjustment across layers of government: evolution of revenues, expenditures and primary surplus (+)/deficit (−) over GDP during 2009–13

4. FAILURES IN THE DESIGN OF FISCAL DECENTRALIZATION

Why did all this happen? Were these developments just consequences of cheap credit and the housing boom? The answer is partially yes. The Euro shock was simply too strong, and the windfall revenues that flew into public coffers during these years were too tempting, at least given the quality of Spanish governance.

But the answer is also partially no: the effects have been so strong because the Spanish multi-level fiscal and financial arrangements and fiscal discipline framework were not able to deal with such a shock. Spanish subnational governments were not well equipped to face a revenue boom and bust of such magnitude. The country was also not well equipped with institutions that could have helped address the process of fiscal adjustment in a different and less painful way.

4.1 Multilevel Financial Arrangements

There has been strong decentralization of spending powers in Spain toward the regional tier over the last three decades, and this is now similar to those of federal countries, such as the US and Canada. The regional share is over one-third of total public spending. Some authors have documented the positive effect of spending decentralization on the quality of public services and the adaptation of regionally differentiated needs and demands (see Solé-Ollé, 2010). Also, despite being feared at the beginning of the process, regional decentralization has not generated interregional inequality, thanks to strong equalization grants. Probably this helps to explain the wide, solid, and increasing support over time by most Spaniards for regional devolution. In fact, Spaniards were quite content with these arrangements before the beginning of the crisis.[10] Moreover, voter turnout at the regional level has increased over time to attain levels similar to those in general elections. The average turnout ratio between regional and national elections is now slightly above 0.9 (Blais et al., 2011).

Despite these positive aspects and successful developments concerning regional decentralization, a number of weaknesses remained unresolved. First, decentralization on the spending side has been much stronger than on the revenue side, as reported in Box 8.1. As is common in devolution processes, tax decentralization arrives late and when it does, it is done in a haphazard manner. For example, it is difficult to find good economic reasons to explain why the first taxes to be decentralized were the stamp duty tax, the wealth tax, and the property transactions tax. During the 1980s, the ACs were given competences to collect these taxes, while in

> **BOX 8.1 THE REGIONAL FINANCING SYSTEM SINCE 2001**
>
> The financing of Spanish regions (except the Basque Country and Navarra, see endnote 1) has evolved over time to the pace of periodic agreements between the central and regional governments. In 2001 a profound reform of the system involved a significant increase in tax decentralization and a reduction in the share of grants in total financing. Regions increased their capacity to modify the basic parameters of a number of taxes: net wealth tax, inheritance tax, gambling tax, stamp duty tax, and one-third of personal income tax. In addition, they were provided with some room in the special tax on motor vehicles, and the tax on retail sales of certain hydrocarbons, as well as a share of the VAT (equivalent to 35 percent of revenue) and of specific consumption taxes (40 percent). Setting aside tax sharing insofar as it does not provide tax autonomy, regions directly controlled about a third of their revenues on average after the reform. The following reform, approved in 2009, strengthened these changes, increasing the percentage of personal income tax under regional control (50 percent), and tax sharing on VAT (50 percent) and specific consumption taxes (58 percent). On average, the Autonomous Communities directly control half of their revenues.
>
> Progress in decentralization has been seemingly very substantial. But things change when one considers the use the regions have made of their tax powers. In short, there has been little meaningful use, and regions acted generally to reduce taxes despite widespread complaints of lack of resources by regional incumbents. The explanation lies in the inability to establish a hard budget constraint for the central government, and the high capacity to get into debt. The expected increases in grant resources makes regions reluctant to use their tax powers, and they choose to push the central government to increase grants. On the other hand, the possibility of borrowing postpones tax increases and the associated political costs. Even in the worst years of the crisis, when the fiscal adjustment was unavoidable and there were no additional resources coming from the central government, tax increases have been lower. On average, less than 10 percent of the fiscal adjustment has relied upon the regions' tax powers.

the 1990s they were granted nearly full autonomy. The decentralization of these taxes made difficult their use as a tool to improve collections of related taxes (i.e., the personal income tax), which continued in the hands of the central government. Moreover, in some of these taxes, the granting of full autonomy without a minimum of central regulation at the end of the 1990s (e.g. in the inheritance tax) involved a race to the bottom, like in Australia or Canada (see Solé-Ollé, 2014).

In addition, revenues from these taxes were also very cyclical since, as we explained, they closely follow the housing market. Moreover, because of difficulties in finding adequate measures of tax capacity, these taxes were never included in the fiscal capacity indicator used for equalization purposes.[11] Moreover, when other major taxes were decentralized (i.e., personal income tax, VAT and excises), they were centrally collected and then (a percentage of) the revenues transferred to the regional treasuries. To ensure fast disposal of resources by the ACs, the system was based on cash advances. The central government transfers resources based on the collection forecasts made at the beginning of the budget year and transfers (withdraws) an additional amount if forecasts were pessimistic (optimistic) when final collections are made, something that happens around two years after the cash advances are made. As can be easily understood, this system is very sensitive to wrong forecasts, especially because rainy day funds are marginal or non-existent.

Over-optimistic forecasts made by the central government in 2008 and 2009 were very harmful for fiscal stability. Figure 8.14 illustrates this problem in the case of VAT. The plot compares the evolution of the revenues from this tax with the cash advancements. It is evident from the figure that despite the fact that VAT revenues plummeted at the beginning of the crisis, the resource inflow for regional governments kept rising. In practice this created windfall revenues for the ACs. One could argue that the regional ministers of finance should have known that VAT revenues were falling and thus should have moderated spending growth. But the

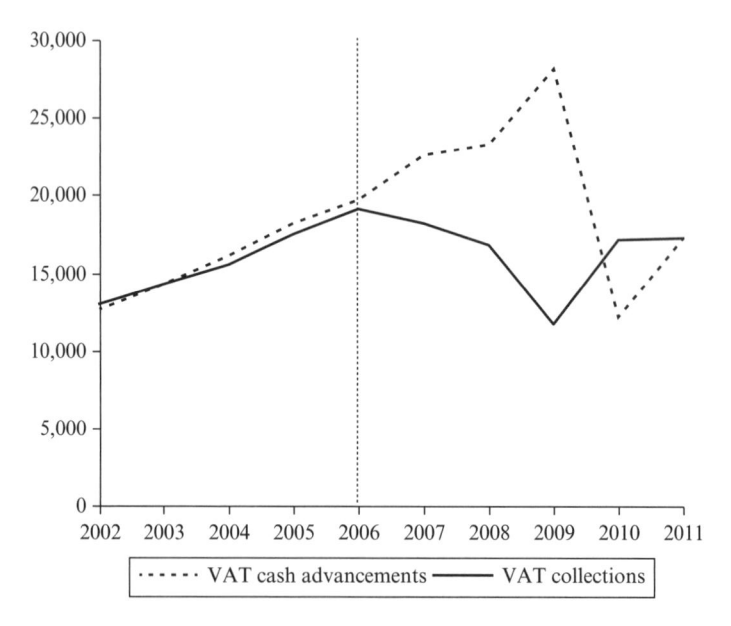

Source: Ministerio de Hacienda y Administraciones Públicas.

Figure 8.14 Effects of the system of cash advancements: VAT, 2002 to 2011

reality is that they did not have the tools to forecast the evolution of these revenues. They have no collection tools and they do not participate in the tax administration. Moreover, from a budgetary perspective, regional outlays from these sources were equal to the budgeted ones, since both are based on the VAT revenues as forecast by the central government. So, in practice, regional ministers of finance even seemed to be really virtuous fiscal managers.

Second, there has been a lack of an appropriate framework to deal with vertical imbalances. During the 1980s and 1990s the vertical component of equalization grants was very important, due to the fact that own taxes and tax sharing were marginal. The pool of resources allocated to those grants was expressed as a percentage of a basket of central taxes. This pool rarely grew with tax revenues, because the maximum growth rate was set to be equal to that of the growth of GDP, while the minimum growth rate was that of central government expenditure. This smoothed the cyclical fluctuations of the revenues of regional governments. Moreover, in order to be able to detect any inadequacies generated between the responsibilities and revenues devolved, the central government and the ACs sat down together every five years and bargained some adjustments to the transfer.

However, the 2000s reform ended this arrangement. The central government decided to substitute the vertical transfer for tax sharing in some of the major taxes (e.g. Personal Income Tax, VAT, Excises) and to increase tax autonomy in some of them (i.e., especially in the PIT). The equalization transfer was transformed into a horizontal one but was only computed for the base year. After that, tax-sharing revenues were to evolve differently in each region, and the equalization transfer was to be linked to national tax revenues. This increased enormously the exposure of regional treasuries to the economic cycle. The philosophy of the reform was that now the ACs had much higher tax autonomy, so they should be able to fully adjust their budgets in response to fiscal shocks. The new system did not generate much difficulty for some years, due to the buoyancy of revenues during the boom.[12] However, real tax autonomy was insufficient to balance the budget once the crisis hit, and taking into account the huge volume of expenditure decentralized.[13] It was thus an illusion to expect that the ACs could cope with the crisis without being able to act on consumption taxes, with the safety net of central government taxes dismantled, and with the central government not even willing to enter negotiations on how to cope with the crisis without adversely affecting the welfare state and basic public services, now in the hands of the regional governments.

Third, the previous experience of sub-national governments with respect to the periodical bargaining relating to the transfer system generates the well-known soft budget constraint problem. Bailout expectations explain why tax increases did not happen until very deep in the crisis. Several scholars have already shown that the budget constraint of the ACs was soft during the 1990s (see Sorribas-Navarro, 2011, and Esteller-Moré and Solé-Ollé, 2005). For instance, before the reform of the 2000s, it was customary that the ACs with health care responsibilities were periodically rescued by increasing the transfers earmarked for this type of spending. Also, the discussions regarding the reform of the ACs' financing system, held every five years, always ended with the central government adding resources to the vertical transfer. And there is evidence that the pre-Maastricht regional debt stabilization was possible in a great proportion thanks to the additional transfers from the central government (see Esteller-Moré and Solé-Ollé, 2005). At this point, while we want to be clear about the evils of the soft budget constraint syndrome, we also want to be clear about the responsibilities for this problem. It is the institutional framework that provides incentives to all the agents to behave in this way. Of course, regional governments will have incentives to spend more than the actual revenues if they expect that new resources will come in the future. But the central government also has incentives to starve regional governments (by making their revenues' growth less than national tax revenues) in order to strengthen its bargaining position in the future.

Last but not least, the lack of transparency concerning both expenditure and tax responsibilities involved confusion for citizens and other stakeholders. A considerable proportion of Spaniards cannot correctly identify the level of government responsible for providing services as important as health care and education. This means that citizens don't really know who is responsible for the provision of these services, making the current level of accountability far from acceptable for the standards of federations (see Lago-Peñas and Lago Peñas, 2010). This is also related to the soft budget constraint syndrome. The ACs blame central government for shortages in important services such as health care because they know central government is still seen by some Spaniards as having some responsibility in this regard, and central government blames the ACs for the situation because they know they will not have to bear all the political costs of the downward adjustment.

Things are a little bit different when it comes to local governments. In sharp contrast to regional public expenditure dynamics, the share of local governments in total public expenditure has remained between 10 and 15 percent over the whole democratic period. While the list of powers devolved to regions includes services with a high income-elasticity and demand (health care, education, and social services, among others) a significant proportion of local expenditure is devoted to non-mandatory services and very often to regional powers aiming at improving or complementing regional services. This asymmetry is relevant to understanding the response of both tiers to the fiscal crisis. Local expenditure has been easier to cut. Concerning revenues, while local tax revenues are overly dependent on property and construction activities, municipalities enjoy higher tax autonomy than the regions. As a consequence of the above, public deficit at the local level has not been as troublesome as the regional one. Also, financial markets, international institutions and the internal political debate have focused on the latter. Of course, this does not imply that we consider that the financial control and governance of local governments in Spain cannot be improved,[14] it is just that their behavior during that crisis shows that they have largely been able to pass the test.

4.2 Fiscal Discipline Framework

As summarized in Box 8.2, the legal framework ruling fiscal discipline in Spain was seemingly sound for all fiscal tiers. However, the economic crisis made clear the existence of mistakes in both design and implementation stages. First, it is evident that fiscal surveillance of sub-national governments failed. The crisis demonstrated that information on budget execution was insufficient, heterogeneous across regions, and in some cases misleading.[15] Given the large share of Spanish public expenditure managed by regional governments, those shortcomings affected the fiscal credibility and stability of general government in Spain.

Second, cyclical revenues boosted structural expenditures. Rainy day funds and expenditure ceilings would have involved moderation in expenditure, higher surpluses and lower debt stocks until 2007, and financial capacity to fill the gap between current revenues and expenditures since 2008. However, the existing contingency reserves available to face unforeseen needs do not match the aim of a rainy day fund, setting aside the issue of their small size. And – concerning the second instrument – in 2009 the regional government of Galicia introduced the first expenditure ceiling.

Third, financial bailouts implemented by the central government have been largely improvisations. As pointed out above, a constitutional reform on fiscal stability was passed in 2011, and major legal changes were introduced in 2012. In particular, the new Autonomous Liquidity Fund (see note 16) was quickly implemented in order to bail out regions facing extreme difficulties in accessing financial markets.

Fourth, the non-compliance with the rules by some regional governments has been widespread and substantial, partly due to the fact that penalties for non-compliance were unclear until recently. No region met the deficit targets in 2011. In 2012, five regions were unable to meet their targets: Comunidad

> **BOX 8.2 THE FISCAL DISCIPLINE FRAMEWORK**
>
> Since 2001 Spain has passed three organic laws (2001, 2006, and 2012), a number of ordinary laws and decrees, and a constitutional reform in 2011. The ordinary and organic laws on budgetary stability approved in 2001 went beyond what was required by the European Commission, and involved the zero-deficit principle for all fiscal tiers. Criticism was then made on the withdrawal of compensation powers of fiscal policy, an even more serious loss within a context of upward transfer of responsibilities in matters of monetary policy. In fact, those critiques founded and boosted the amendment of the legal framework by Law 15/2006 and Organic Law 3/2006. Commitment to budgetary stability was then made compatible with a maximum total deficit of 1.5 percent when the actual GDP growth was under 2 percent and at least 0.5 percent of this deficit was used to fund increases in productive investment. More than half of this deficit threshold was in the hands of regional governments (1 percent). While this reform softened the stringent ruling framework, it was still more exigent than the euro-related EU requirements.
>
> The economic crisis dramatically challenged this legal architecture in 2008–09. GDP plummeted, discretionary expenses increased, automatic stabilizers came into effect and extraordinary deficit levels were reached, which were, in fact, excessive for an output gap of the magnitude of Spain's. The concern for this imbalance, magnified by the well-known response from the international financial markets, led to an unprecedented agreement between PP (Partido Popular) and PSOE (Partido Socialista Obrero Español) to amend the 1978 Spanish Constitution in the summer of 2011, in order to raise fiscal stability to the category of constitutional principle. Finally, Organic Law 2/2012, which was passed in April, introduced substantial changes. The four main cornerstones of this reform are the introduction of a public spending ceiling, preventing an increase in spending above a moving average of the GDP nominal growth rate; the establishment of a cap on public debt expressed as a percentage of GDP (60 percent) to be distributed among different government levels (13 percent for the Autonomous Communities); the replacement of the concept of total deficit by that of structural deficit and a zero-level target (by 2020); and greater attention paid to the control and supervision of sub-national governments, at both regional and local levels, including severe sanctions and penalties. Legal changes are not cosmetic. Central government is applying them to the extent that it is being criticized by some regional governments and regionalist political parties for actions that are perceived as signs of political and financial recentralization.

Valenciana, Murcia, Andalucía, Catalunya, and Baleares. Finally in 2013, the deficit was over the limit in six regions: Aragón, Navarra, Castilla-La Mancha, and again in Comunidad Valenciana, Murcia, and Catalunya. Last, but not least, the most recent legal changes in 2012 involve less confidence on bargaining and intergovernmental agreements, and give preference to a hierarchical strategy to guarantee deficit control.[16] Recentralization in the definition and implementation of general government fiscal aims is one of the consequences of the crisis, including the unilateral setting of targets with no leeway for negotiation; the introduction of coercive measures by way of penalties, exclusion from funding lines and access to credit, and even the suspension of self-government.

5. FURTHER CONSEQUENCES – CRISIS IN GOVERNANCE AND TERRITORIAL CONFLICT

5.1 Governance Crisis

The boom and bust cycle brought another undesired outcome: corruption scandals. Prior to the 2000s, corruption was not a big issue in Spanish politics. However, the huge housing boom, coupled with a very rigid and completely decentralized system of land use regulations, generated a boom in corruption scandals at the local level. Most of these scandals involved acceptance of bribes in exchange for zoning modifications and building permits (see Solé-Ollé and Viladecans-Marsal, 2011). Although most of these corruption cases have their roots in real estate deals that occurred during the boom, scandals continued to break during the crisis. Given the slowness of the Spanish judiciary, some cases reached the trial stage during the crisis. There is also some evidence that several of the more recent cases are no longer related to land use regulations but to procurement and other irregularities. At this point, we can talk about an epidemic of corruption. Note, for instance, that in some regions the percentage of municipalities affected by a scandal up until 2014 is huge: 58 percent in Murcia, 40 percent in the Canary Islands, and 36 percent in the Balearic Islands (see Cercle Català de Negocis, 2014). Moreover, some of the most recent and prominent cases have involved vast networks of municipalities and regional governments across the Spanish territory, providing evidence of organized systems of illegal party financing.

The response of Spanish voters and institutions seems, at first sight, timid. Some research has found evidence of punishment of corrupt mayors during the 2007 and 2011 local elections (see Costas et al., 2012), although the effect was probably only enough to oust the incumbent in a handful of cases. Explanations for this leniency range from the willingness of citizens to trade off moral issues for jobs, the ideological polarization of Spanish voters, and the inability of the media and the judiciary to clarify the seriousness of each case. The judiciary has also been extremely slow: of the around 1,700 cases opened by the judiciary, involving around 500 accused politicians, only a few have reached the trial stage, and only around 20 people have ended up in jail up to now. Also, there is some suspicion that political parties are using all their means available to interfere with the judges' decisions in the most important of the cases (such as those affecting illegal party financing or the Royal Family) and in those on the watchdog role of the press. This situation has eroded the trust of citizens in political institutions. This was evident as early as 2009, as documented in a study that found that local corruption scandals reduced trust in those mayors accused (see Solé-Ollé and Sorribas-Navarro, 2014); nowadays this distrust has spread like an oil slick through all the Spanish territory. It explains why, according to official polls,[17] in 2014 corruption and politicians ranked for Spaniards as the second and fourth problems respectively out of more than forty items. Corruption was irrelevant in 2008 and politicians very secondary. This adds to the discontent related to fiscal adjustment – and to the politicians' failure to take responsibility for the crisis or for the austerity, as well as their dubious decisions in the case of bank runs (on savings banks or 'cajas'). This helps to explain the vote drain affecting the two main political parties in Spain (the Socialist Party and the Popular Party), the decline of voter turnout, and the rise of parties with more radical political discourses.

Is this effect independent of the crisis of public finances and governance? Not completely, for several reasons. First, note that this state of affairs is behind the huge economic boom that also impacted public finances. The same boom that generated enormous windfall revenues for governments at all levels created very powerful incentives that focused too much on the real estate sector. Recall that regional and local governments are the ones responsible for land use regulations. Also note that rezoning deals generate windfall revenues for the city council, funds to finance campaigns at all levels, and bribes for the intermediaries. Of course, weak financial and political institutions (e.g. excessive reliance on volatile taxes, weak and political media and judiciary) also facilitated this situation.

Second, citizens' discomfort with the situation interacts hugely with the suffering created by fiscal adjustment and from the effects of the crisis in terms of unemployment and foreclosures. For the citizens, these two last effects are not seen as different from corruption and public finances. Many unemployed had lost their jobs because of the collapse of housing-related economic sectors. People also blame the government for not fixing the social consequences of foreclosures, while at the same time using huge amounts of public funding to bail out banks, the officials of those institutions also being now involved in some of the most prominent scandals.

5.2 The Territorial Crisis

In recent years it has been commonplace in Spain to blame sub-national governments for the outbreak of the crisis and the difficulties in tackling it.

Newspapers published extensively on the scandals related to bad management (e.g. white elephants, over-hiring, etc.) and the corruption mentioned in the previous section. The central government also openly proclaimed that the ACs were the main source of the budget deviation (see, e.g., Stability Program of the Kingdom of Spain, 2012–15), at the same time accusing them of inefficiency and lack of accountability. Note, also, that the weak situation of the ACs (i.e., excluded from credit markets since very early in the crisis) contributed to giving the impression that the central government was the only body with the actual power and capability to confront this extremely pressing and complex situation.

It is not strange, therefore, that the opinion of the Spanish population regarding decentralization has deteriorated in recent years, as is shown by the responses citizens give to surveys. For example, between 1998 and 2005 over 70 percent of people surveyed expressed the view that the creation of ACs was positive, while this percentage had dropped to 56 percent by 2012 (see León, 2013). Also, the number of citizens in favor of recentralization of responsibilities has grown in most regions. In 1998, when confronted with different models of territorial organization, 50 percent of citizens chose to 'keep things as they are now' (i.e., compared to changing the status quo by giving more responsibilities to central government or to the ACs). This number increased to 58 percent in 2005 but had dropped to 32 percent by 2012. In contrast, the number of citizens that favored a recentralization (i.e., 'giving more responsibilities to the central government') rose from 8 percent in 2005 to 22 percent in 2012. The number of people in favor of an enhanced role for the ACs decreased from 28 percent in 2005 to 13 percent in 2012 (see also León, 2013).[18]

This state of public opinion backed the recentralization process undertaken by central government, ruled by the Partido Popular after coming to power in 2011. Actually, some scholars argue that this recentralization process began a while ago with an increase in the use of the possibilities of the government to regulate the basic aspects of services which are the responsibility of the ACs (see Viver and Martín, 2013). Also, there are deeper reasons other than the crisis that help in explaining this recentralization process. For instance, there is the belief, shared by social, political, and media sectors, that the decentralization process has gone too far and that the central government needs to regain responsibilities to coordinate the activities of the ACs. In any case, it is widely admitted that the process has quickened its pace and become more profound with the outbreak and subsequent aggravation of the economic crisis. In fact, it is well documented that an economic crisis tends to foster centralization in many countries (see Canavire-Bacareza and Martínez-Vázquez, 2013). The reasons are many: (i) the level of trust in sub-national governments is reduced, given their higher difficulties of coping with the crisis; (ii) the crisis might affect the proper distribution of resources across layers and thus the share of decentralized spending or revenues; or (iii) there is a demand for a more centralized and coordinated macroeconomic policy.

In Catalunya, the reaction to the current state of affairs took the form of increased secessionism movements. Clearly, secessionism was on the rise for some years prior to the beginning of the crisis. It has its roots in a very strong regionalist cleavage and in ongoing claims for more revenues and more tax and spending autonomy. For instance, from Catalunya it is argued that the regional financing system is unfair and that the direct spending of the central government (e.g., on the financing of infrastructure) is even more biased against the interests of the region. It does not help much that the other two rich regions with a history of self-governance (i.e., Navarra and the Basque Country) have a special financial arrangement which, in practice, means they do not have to contribute to the funding of the welfare state in the rest of Spain and end up with a much higher level of public revenues per capita than Catalunya.[19]

This conflict reached a point of no return after the 2010 ruling of the Spanish Constitutional Court, which abolished some important parts of the new Catalan Constitution (the so-called Statute of Autonomy). This new constitution was approved in referendum by the Catalan population and by the Spanish parliament in 2006 (so prior to the crisis). Also, during the crisis, national incumbents disregarded the application of some of the clauses included in the Catalan Constitution regarding equalization and inter-regional allocation of public investment, which were not amended by the Constitutional Court.[20] The conclusion from all this process by the Spanish elites and, particularly, by the right-wing party, Partido Popular, governing since 2011, has been that decentralization has gone too far and has not prevented but instead fuelled the demands of historic regions.[21] This in part explains the current recentralization movement and the shift in public opinion regarding the virtues of decentralization in Spain. The diagnosis from Catalunya is the opposite. Spanish institutions cannot be trusted. Not only is the system unfair to the region, but central governments show disrespect for laws and agreements, using all opportunities to encroach on the powers of ACs. In the eyes of many people and parties in Catalunya, the only solution is secession.

As we have already explained, this secessionist tendency started before the crisis. However, the current crisis might have worsened it, for several reasons. First, the argument that inter-territorial redistribution is excessive has more appeal during the crisis, given the shortage of public revenues and huge fiscal adjustment. Clearly, the allegedly excessive Catalan 'fiscal deficit'[22] is due in part to discrimination against the region in the allocation of discretionary spending (i.e., infrastructure spending) and partly to the operation of redistributive tax and transfer programs. However, the degree of support for these redistributive mechanisms in a rich region might decrease as a result of an economic and fiscal crisis, especially since the population probably cannot support further tax increases, and also given the high incidence of social problems.[23] Second, the high levels of corruption documented above and the inability of the Spanish political system to provide a solution to the current situation, or even to allocate fairly the costs of the adjustment, might have convinced many people that secession – which entails huge unknown costs that would deter many people in a normal situation – is the only solution. In some sense, secessionism is in Catalunya playing a similar role to the one played by social protest and voting for radical parties in the rest of Spain.

All of this means that besides the failures identified in the previous sections, the current financial and political institutions that govern the multi-layer system of government in Spain have also failed to keep the level of territorial conflict within reasonable limits. It is clear by now that the Spanish decentralized system cannot be qualified as federal in the same sense that this word is used in other countries. The level of fiscal decentralization in Spain is really high, and comparable to that in other countries. But the level of protection of this decentralization by the constitutional arrangements is quite low.[24] The Spanish central government can at any time use the means at its disposal to erode the real level of autonomy. Also, equalization mechanisms and other public spending programs with territorial effects are quite arbitrary, and non-transparent, and at the same time generate excessive levels of redistribution and of favoritism. A reform that tackles all of these points seems to be of paramount importance.

6. CONCLUDING REMARKS: ON REFORM PROPOSALS

The Spanish experience teaches us a number of lessons in several fields. Moreover, it demonstrates that the need for designing a robust institutional framework increases with the degree of decentralization. This section presents a combination of reforms required to avoid the several shortcomings and difficulties in the recent past in Spain. This set of recommendations may be also particularly useful for those countries designing decentralization processes or debating associated policy and institutional reforms.

Let us start with budgetary institutions. The implementation of both rainy-day funds and expenditure ceilings is the best way to manage the effect of cycles on public finances, especially in the case of strong and lengthy expansions often followed by deep recessions. Both instruments smooth the effects of business cycles on public finances and increase the margin of maneuver of anti-cyclical fiscal policies. This point is particularly relevant in the case of countries subject to fiscal stability pacts and deficit targets, like in the Euro area. Second, they avoid the temptation of relaxing cost–benefit appraisal, and then boosting inefficient public expenditure programs. Third, they preclude moral risk issues concerning the fight against tax evasion and electoral tax cuts. Tax evasion can be seen as a minor issue when both revenues and expenditure are growing at high rates. Moreover, strong revenue expansions trigger tax cuts potentially affecting the structural buoyancy of tax systems.

The Spanish case also highlights the distortions provoked by incorrect forecasts, especially in the case of multi-level governments, with sharing agreements involving the need for cash advances to sub-central governments. In this case, the accuracy of forecasts is crucial for agile adjustments of budgets to changes in the economic situation. In this respect, an independent fiscal authority may be a very useful tool to produce better forecasts. All in all, more sophisticated agreements between fiscal tiers concerning tax sharing are important. Monthly data on tax collection can be used to adjust cash advances if deviations from expected revenues surpass a previously defined threshold.

Concerning intergovernmental relationships, the first issue to deal with is vertical fiscal imbalances. While the optimal degree of tax and expenditure decentralization most often do not match, intergovernmental grants or tax sharing should guarantee a similar financial condition for all fiscal layers both in the short and the long run. The challenge is threefold. First, the evolution of revenues provided for in the tax basket of each layer of government may be significantly different. Second, expenditure cuts are more difficult to tackle for some fiscal tiers. The Spanish case is a good example. Regional powers include socially sensitive services, such as education, social services and health care. Cuts in local expenditures have been much easier by comparison. Second, and related to the previous point, sufficient tax power has to be provided to sub-central governments, taking into account their spending responsibilities. All fiscal tiers should enjoy the capacity to choose different ways of dealing with fiscal stress. Tax autonomy helps to maintain vertical balance. Third, hard budget constraints are fundamental to make the whole system work. A soft budget constraint involves lack of incentives with respect to using own-tax handles and a strong dependency on central governments. Moreover, if getting into debt is possible for sub-central governments, a soft budget constraint tends to involve higher deficits and the expectation of bailouts.

In the case of evolving federations, clarifying expenditure and tax responsibility has to be a serious concern. Lack of knowledge and experience of citizens and stakeholders in general may distort fiscal decisions, and political accountability is required. And this lack of accountability spoils some of the benefits from decentralization (Lago-Peñas and Lago-Peñas, 2010). Information campaigns and the definition of clear-cut responsibilities avoiding fuzzy and overlapping powers should be a central element of any decentralization package.

Discussions on equalization are usually one of the most contentious and difficult topics in federal or highly decentralized countries. The Spanish case demonstrates that asymmetrical federalism involving very different contributions to equalization for richer regions with the same per capita GDP is very dangerous for political stability. And this trouble is magnified when ad hoc criteria and political bargaining, in order to determine the amount of equalization grants received by each region, substitute for technical justifications and transparency. Current secessionist movements in Catalunya are partly explained by these reasons.

Last but not least, stronger formal federal institutions cannot be set aside. They are crucial to making a decentralized system work. Both vertical and horizontal bargaining and agreements require forums and political discussions to make developing the former and attaining the latter possible. The Spanish case also demonstrates that mismatched fiscal and institutional decentralization creates a weaker framework for the management of bad economic times and fiscal stress situations.

NOTES

1. The Spanish Constitution of 1978 created 17 ACs. Due to historical reasons, two of the regions (Navarra and País Vasco) enjoy an asymmetrically higher degree of autonomy and a radically different system of financing, which translates into a higher level of resources per capita than in the others. In short, they collect all taxes in their territories – business income tax, special excises, VAT and PIT among others – and transfer a yearly amount to the state.
2. During the period 1997–2007 housing prices grew 110 percent in real terms and in the peak of the boom (2006) nearly 660,000 housing units were built. The fall in the amount of housing construction was dramatic, with a minimum of 33,000 in 2012. Until 2012, the price of housing had also fallen by around 40 percent (see www.fotocasa.es).
3. Stamp duty tax and inheritance tax are taxes fully controlled by the regional governments: they autonomously decide on the tax regulations and they collect them directly. VAT and Personal Income Revenues are collected by the central tax administration and a share of the revenues is then transferred to the regional governments.
4. This pattern is even more acute if one also accounts for developers' fees and sales of land

plots. In this case revenues multiply by three during the boom and then drop to much less than 50 percent of the 2002 revenues by 2012. We have decided not to show this in the figure because, at least in theory, these other revenues are earmarked for capital spending.
5. See Section 4 below for more in-depth discussion of this point. See also Box 8.1 for a description of the main characteristics of the regional financing system before and after the 2001 reform.
6. Of course, one could argue that the bust in the housing market was impossible to predict. Also, regional governments had had no previous experience of dealing with a housing revenue boom. And for most local governments, this was indeed the first experience of managing these taxes. Before the 1988 reform of local government finances (effective 1990), only big cities had access to real estate related taxes (i.e., the tax on land transactions and the tax on construction activity).
7. The current housing boom-and-bust situation has led scholars and international organizations to reconsider how to deal with revenue windfalls in the computation of the fiscal deficit along the economic cycle (see, e.g., Morris et al., 2009).
8. In order to ease interpretation, the figure shows just a cross-section of data. However, the results also hold when using yearly data and controlling for year and region fixed effects (i.e., after subtracting the between and within averages). The results are also robust for scaling magnitudes by population. Results are available upon request.
9. These additional funds (i.e., the so-called 'fondo de cooperación' and 'fondo de competitividad') were additional vertical transfers introduced during the 2009 reform in order to make the redistribution created by the reform politically amenable.
10. The crisis and the current secessionist challenge in Catalunya undermined this state of affairs. We will try to provide a proper assessment of these factors in Section 5.
11. In these taxes, tax capacity was computed on the basis of collections in some year in the past, with the result that the increase in revenues during the booms was not accounted for in the calculation of fiscal capacity.
12. Fast-growing ACs also complained because failure to recalculate the equalization transfer meant that increasing populations were not taken into account. This was not an insurmountable problem during the boom because revenues were also growing a lot in these regions. However, they felt this was unfair because revenues also grew a lot in regions with lower (economic and demographic) growth (these revenues received, in practice, larger equalization grants and were linked to national tax revenues that also grew a lot on average).
13. Note, for instance, that the reform of the 2000s also involved the full decentralization of health and education to the ACs that still did not have these responsibilities.
14. For example, reducing the exposure of local budgets to the volatility of housing-related tax revenues would be a sensible reform. The fact that local governments had the incentive to adjust the budget does not mean that this adjustment nevertheless has not been painful (in terms of layoffs and reduction in the quality of services), so in the case of local governments, limiting the amount of windfalls during a boom in order to avoid these big adjustments during a crisis would also be useful.
15. The regional government of Madrid provides a good example of this lack of confidence. In February 2012 it claimed to be the regional government with the lowest deficit in 2011 (1.1 percent over regional GDP). Three months later, it had to recognize that the actual deficit was 2.2 percent, well above the accorded threshold (1.3 percent).
16. Financial support provided by the central government since 2012, by means of the new Autonomous Liquidity Fund ('Fondo de Liquidez Autonómica' or FLA), further strengthens this bias. First, it calls for the formulation or reformulation of adjustment plans, including spending cuts and tax increases designed under the auspices of the central administration. Second, information disclosure obligations in matters of budgetary management are broadened. Third, it increases the probability of sending control missions fully empowered to review the management in the relevant Autonomous Communities.

17. See: http://www.cis.es/cis/opencms/-Archivos/Indicadores/documentos_html/TresProblemas.html.
18. The situation has also become highly geographically polarized, with citizens in the Basque Country and Catalunya more favorable to decentralization and independence and citizens in the rest of the country more favorable to recentralization. In fact, one may argue that the demands for recentralization in one part of the country are a reflection of the increase in secessionism pressures in the other, rather than the result of the crisis. We will deal with this issue below.
19. In Spain, there are 17 regional governments (ACs) and two different regimes for regional financing. In the so-called 'common regime' (15 regions belong to it), regions get their revenues from own taxes, tax sharing and a vertical equalization transfer; the system is designed and managed by the central government but the ACs participate through a multilateral coordination organism (the so-called 'Consejo de Political Fiscal y Financiera'). In the so-called 'foral regime' (the one that applies to Navarra and the Basque Country), each of these regions collects all the taxes and bargains directly with the central government over the amount they have to pay to the center to help funding national public goods (e.g. defense, diplomacy); the computation of this bottom-up transfer does not include a contribution to the equalization transfer that funds public services in other ACs, meaning that in practice these regions have around 1.5 to 2 times higher per capita revenues than the 'common regime' ACs to fund more or less the same services (see Solé-Ollé, 2010).
20. The Catalan Constitution included for the first time in Spain the concept of 'partial equalization', which was then implemented in the new financial arrangements of 2009 and which consisted in equalizing only those fiscal capacity differences in the funding of 'fundamental services of the welfare state' (i.e., health care, education, and social services); in theory this should have meant the equalization of two-thirds of the difference in fiscal capacity (this was the weight of these services in regional budgets), although in practice it did not have any effect, owing to the introduction into the system of many other funds and to the lack of application of some of the clauses of the system by the incoming central incumbent.
21. See Spolaore (2010) and the survey by Dower and Weber (2015) for a discussion of whether decentralization prevents or fosters secession.
22. The so-called 'fiscal deficit' is the difference between what revenues were collected in a region by the central government and what expenditures allocated therein. The calculation of this concept and its use to claim a situation of excessive redistribution is very common in Catalunya, as it is also in rich regions with regionalist/secessionist movements, such as Flanders, Quebec or the north of Italy (see Bosch et al., 2010, for a review of selected cases, methodologies and interpretation).
23. That is, during a severe economic crisis like the current one, people might prefer to redistribute in favor of the poor in their own region but less in favor of the poor in other regions. See Balcells et al. (2014) for a study of regional redistribution preferences in Spain.
24. See Inman (2007) for the reasoning that federalism is needed in order to protect decentralization arrangements.

REFERENCES

Alesina, A., Campante, F.R. and Tabellini, G. (2010): 'Why is fiscal policy often procyclical?', *Journal of the European Economics Association*, **5**, 1006–36.

Balcells, L., Fernández-Albertos, J. and Kuo, A. (2014): 'Preferences for regional redistribution in multi-tiered politics: the role of information and survey evidence', IC3JM Working Paper, 2014/283.

Blais, A., Anduiza E. and Gallego A. (2011): 'Decentralization and voter turnout', *Environment and Planning C: Government and Policy*, **29**(2), 297–320.
Bosch, N., Espasa, M. and Solé-Ollé, A. (eds) (2010): *The Political Economy of Inter-Regional Fiscal Flows: Measurement, Determinants & Effects on Country Stability*, Cheltenham, UK and Northampton, MA, USA: Edward Elgar.
Canavire-Bacarreza, G. and Martínez-Vázquez, J. (2013): 'Fiscal decentralization and economic crisis', *IEB's Report on Fiscal Federalism '12*, IEB, Barcelona, 36–45.
Costas, E., Solé-Ollé, A. and Sorribas, P. (2012): 'Corruption, voter information, and accountability', *European Journal of Political Economy*, **28**(4), 469–84.
Dower, P. and Weber, S. (2015): '"Federalism and conflict" with Shlomo Weber', in E. Ahmad and G. Brosio (eds), *The Handbook of Fiscal Federalism II* (forthcoming).
Esteller-Moré, A. and Solé-Ollé, A. (2005): 'Estabilidad presupuestaria y financiación autonómica', *Hacienda Pública Española*, Special Issue on Budgetary Stability, 173–201.
Fernández-Villaverde, J., Garicano, L. and Santos, T. (2013): 'Political credit cycles: the case of the Euro zone', *Journal of Economic Perspectives*, **27**(3), 145–66.
Inman, R.P. (2007): 'Federalism's values and the value of Federalism', CESifo *Economic Studies*, **53**(4), 522–60.
IEF (2013): 'Opiniones y actitudes fiscales de los españoles en 2012', Working Paper 21/2013, Instituto de Estudios Fiscales, http://www.ief.es/documentos/ recursos/ publicaciones/documentos_trabajo/2013_21.pdf.
Jenker, E. and Lu, Z. (2014): 'Subnational credit risk and sovereign bailouts – who pays a premium?', IMF Working Papers 14/20.
Lago-Peñas, S. (2013): 'The new budgetary stability in Spain: a centralizing approach', *IEB's Report on Fiscal Federalism '12*, IEB, Barcelona, 74–77, http:// www.ieb.ub.edu/index.php?option=com_phocadownload&view =category&do wnload=402&id=5&Itemid=131.
Lago-Peñas, S. (2014): 'Fiscal consolidation in Spain: situation and outlook', *Spanish Economic and Financial Outlook*, **3**(3), 45–52.
Lago-Peñas, S. and Fernández, X. (2013): 'Las finanzas autonómicas, expansión y crisis: 2002–2012', *Papeles de Economía Española*, **138**, 129–46.
Lago-Peñas, I. and S. Lago-Peñas (2010): 'Decentralization and electoral accountability', *Environment and Planning C: Government and Policy*, **28**(2), 318–34.
León, S. (2013): 'Crisis, public opinion, and state of autonomies', *IEB's Report on Fiscal Federalism '12*, IEB, Barcelona, 68–73.
Ministerio de Hacienda y Administraciones Públicas (2014a): 'Déficit de las administraciones públicas en 2013', 31 March.
Ministerio de Hacienda y Administraciones Públicas (2014b): 'Actualización del programa de estabilidad. Reino de España 2014–2017', 30 April.
Morris, R., de Castro Fernández, F., Jonk, S., Kremer, J., Linehan, S., Rosaria Marino, M., Schalck, C. and Tkacevs, O. (2009): 'Explaining government revenue windfalls and shortfalls: an analysis for selected EU countries', ECB Working Paper 1114.
Santos, T. (2014): 'Antes del diluvio: the Spanish banking system in the first decade of the euro', Columbia Business School (http://www.gsb.columbia.edu/ whoswho/more.cfm? &uni=js1786&pub=6162).
Solé-Ollé, A. (2010): 'Evaluating the effects of decentralization on public service delivery: the Spanish case', in G. Brosio and E. Ahmad (eds), *Does*

Decentralization Enhance Service Delivery and Poverty Reduction?, Cheltenham, UK and Northampton, MA, USA: Edward Elgar, pp. 257–84.

Solé-Ollé, A. (2014): 'Regional tax autonomy in Spain: "words" or "deeds"?', in Kim, Lotz and Mau (eds), *Interaction between Local Expenditure Responsibilities and Local Tax Policy*, The Copenhagen Workshop 2013, The Korea Institute of Public Finance and the Danish Ministry of Economic Affairs and the Interior.

Solé-Ollé, A. and Sorribas-Navarro, P. (2014): 'Does corruption erode trust in government? Evidence from a recent surge of local scandals in Spain', CESifo Working Paper 4888.

Solé-Ollé, A. and Viladecans-Marsal, E. (2011): 'Local spending and the housing boom', IEB Working Papers 2001-27, Institut d'Economia de Barcelona.

Solé-Ollé, A. and Viladecans-Marsal, E. (2013): 'The influence wielded by land developers lobbies during the housing boom: recent evidence from Spain', *CESifo DICE Report*, **11**(2), 43–49.

Spolaore, E. (2010): 'Federalism, regional redistribution, and country stability', in Bosch, N., Espasa, M. and Solé-Ollé, A. (eds), *The Political Economy of Inter-Regional Fiscal Flows: Measurement, Determinants & Effects on Country Stability*, Cheltenham, UK and Northampton, MA, USA: Edward Elgar, pp. 329–50.

Sorribas-Navarro, P. (2011): 'Bailouts in a fiscal federal system: evidence from Spain', *European Journal of Political Economy*, **27**, 154–70.

Tornell, A. and Lane, P.R. (1999): 'The voracity effect', *American Economic Review*, **89**(1), 22–46.

Utrilla de la Hoz, A. (2010): 'El Fondo Estatal de Inversión Local: alcance y valoración', Informe IEB sobre Federalismo Fiscal en España '09, IEB, Barcelona, 36–45.

Viver, C. and Martin, G. (2013): 'The re-centralization process of the state of autonomies', *IEB's Report on Fiscal Federalism '12*, IEB, Barcelona, 46–59.

9. Economic crisis and fiscal federalism in Italy

Maria Flavia Ambrosanio, Paolo Balduzzi and Massimo Bordignon

1. INTRODUCTION

The 2008–09 crisis represented the worst recession and financial crisis that Italy had experienced since the end of the Second World War. The most effective way to describe the situation of regional and local public finances since then is best expressed as a 'war economy'. In an attempt to regain the confidence of markets, in the midst of the Euro crisis, the last Berlusconi government, and particularly the successor 'technical' government of Mario Monti in 2011–12, launched a massive fiscal adjustment program. This was meant to reduce public deficits and debt in a country already weakened by the recession. The fiscal stance of the succeeding governments was also tight, given the need to respect European fiscal rules, although less restrictive than the previous adjustments. The cumulate fiscal adjustment in the five years between 2008 and 2012 amounted to around 8 percent of GDP, mostly concentrated in the period 2011–13.

This massive adjustment significantly affected local governments, as in Italy regions and lower levels of government are responsible for large parts of public expenditure, and local tax bases are also significant. The national governments took a number of measures affecting local governments that would only have been possible and justified by a perceived situation of extreme risk for the country, analogous to an international conflict. Thus, local governments were not just simply 'squeezed' by the central government, but were also compelled to raise money, through enforced savings, to finance the general government budget. Indeed, the policies implemented or proposed by the national governments were so invasive of local governments' autonomy that they stretched to the limit the precepts of the Italian 'regional' constitution (reformed in 2001).

The European Fiscal Compact, which in Italy entered into force in January 2014 via a constitutional amendment, again imposes a continuous severe fiscal consolidation process on all levels of government. This is particularly severe for a country that is not yet growing (GDP real rate of growth in 2014 was still negative) and that has lost 10 points of GDP since the last pre-crisis year (2007). Most worryingly, the new budget rules leave little room for public investments at both national and local level, already drastically reduced during the crisis. Low public investments may impair future growth.

The crisis has changed the de facto balance of power between levels of government; and it appears increasingly likely that this new equilibrium will also be consolidated de jure, by a further constitutional reform, currently under review in parliament. The reform has the principal objective of overcoming the Italian 'perfect' bicameral system, by transforming the upper house into a Senate of local representatives.[1] But it also has the purpose of radically changing the number and responsibilities of sub-central governments, weakening the constitutional role of regions and eliminating one level of sub-regional government (provinces). In particular, not only will the functions of regions be reduced in number and importance, but the new constitution will also contain a 'supremacy clause' that gives the central government the upper hand in all cases of conflict with regions.

Yet, not all the proposed interventions should be judged negatively, even in the narrow perspective of intergovernmental relationships. The truth is that the system of fiscal federalism that evolved in Italy during the 2000s, as a result of the constitutional reform of 2001 and of a confused implementation, did not result in the expected efficient and responsive system of local governments. The 2001 Constitution's financial provisions were not implemented, leaving the regions and other levels of governments heavily dependent on the central government. And the (very large) category of 'shared' functions between the central and the regional governments, rather than becoming (as planned) an avenue for limited regional differentiation of policies inside a common national framework, has generated continuous conflict between the two levels of government, including before the constitutional court. This created uncertainty, and so limited economic activity and imposed additional costs on both citizens and firms, thus reducing popular support for decentralization, which had been strong in the 1990s. An apparently unending chain of political scandals and alleged misappropriations of public money by elected regional officials further reduced support, paving the way for a re-centralization of regional functions.

Moreover, as a consequence of the increased financial adjustment imposed on local governments, the central government was forced to increase tax autonomy at the local level, by reintroducing and enhancing municipal taxation on real estate, and by bringing forward the introduction of autonomous sources of financing for regional governments – stipulated in a 2009 'framework law' but over a longer period. Somewhat paradoxically, local governments are now more autonomous on their financing side than they were before the crisis – although this autonomy has been introduced in order to make local governments better able to collect resources for the benefit of general government deficit targets. The rationalization of the number of governments (with the elimination of provinces, the introduction of metropolitan cities and the forced aggregation of small municipalities in political 'unions' for the provision of all services, decided by law at the beginning of 2014), although still clearly not enough, is also a long overdue step in the right direction. Finally, the crisis and the need to strengthen budget discipline will also hopefully force the government to increasingly address the 'soft budget constraints' problems that still remain embodied in the Italian structure of local governments, in particular in the south of the country. As the financial emergency subsides, there is then at least the hope of rebuilding local finance on a more rational basis.

The rest of the chapter is organized as follows. Section 2 reviews the context of 'multi-level finance' in Italy before the crisis, summarizing the decentralization process in the '90s, its consequences in terms of financing and functions for local governments, the constitutional reform of 2001 and the problems of its implementation. Section 3 looks at the continuing crisis; the 'double dip' of the economic cycle during the period 2007–13 and the policies implemented to address the financial market confidence crisis; and the distribution of the burden of fiscal consolidation across levels of government. Section 4 discusses in more detail the institutional features of the policies that have been introduced during the crisis, in particular referring to the number of local governments, and to the financial relationships between levels of government, including taxes, transfers, fiscal rules and bankruptcy procedurals. Section 5 looks to the future: it first discusses the new financial relationships between levels of government that emerge from the Italian constitutional interpretation of the European Fiscal Compact. It then summarizes what it is implied by the proposed Constitutional reform currently under discussion in the Italian parliament. Section 6 concludes.

2. SETTING THE STAGE: FISCAL FEDERALISM IN ITALY BEFORE THE CRISIS, 1992–2007

2.1 Background: The Political and Economic Context of Decentralization

During the 15 years preceding the 2008 crisis, Italy experienced the strongest wave of decentralization reforms in its post-Second World War history (see Ambrosanio and Bordignon, 2007a and Ambrosanio et al., 2010). The rationale was both economic and political.

On the economic side, during the 1980s, Italy's public finances became unsustainable, with a staggering increase in public debt (at national and at local levels), to bring the debt/GDP ratio above 100 percent at the beginning of the 1990s. In 1992, moreover, Italy (together with several other European countries) experienced a severe currency devaluation, followed by the country's exit from the European Exchange Rate Mechanism. The financial crisis that ensued, and later the need to meet the Maastricht criteria for gaining access to the common currency in 1997, called for a strong fiscal consolidation, of which fiscal decentralization was thought of as an important part. On the political side, at the beginning of the '90s several corruption scandals put an end to the so-called 'First Republic', and an entire generation of politicians and political leaders underwent trials and were sentenced to prison. The old parties that had ruled the country for 40 years disappeared. Newer parties, some of which had a strong territorial constituency (e.g. Lega Nord), gained votes and took office.

Many of the new national governments at the beginning of the '90s – made up in large part of 'tecnici', meaning apolitical university professors and highly ranked public officials coming from top institutions (mostly, the Bank of Italy) – decided to grant regional and local authorities greater autonomy for taxation (along with additional functions), and to toughen their budget constraints. The objective was to respond to the demand coming from the new political forces for more local autonomy and to search for increasing efficiency and more fiscal responsibility at the local level. There was also a redistributive component; in particular, the Lega Nord's political agenda deliberately asked for a reduction in the financial flows channeled through the national budget – from the 'productive' North to the 'assisted' South (e.g., see Bordignon, 2005).[2] However, this never happened, not even when Lega Nord became the main partner of Forza Italia (later Partito della Libertà) in the long sequence of Berlusconi-led Center-Right coalitions that governed Italy for an entire decade, from the national elections of 2001 up until 2011.[3] Throughout this period, 'fiscal federalism' ranked high on the political agenda of all Italian governments, although its meaning became increasingly less clear over time.

As a result of this process, new local taxes were assigned in the '90s to regions and sub-regional levels of government. All these new revenues substituted previous grants and transfers from the national government and gave increased taxing power to local authorities.[4] As we will see, the same happened following the 2008 crisis, although under a completely different scenario.

2.2 New Financial Tools

As regards municipalities,[5] in 1992 a new municipal property tax (ICI) was created, with the tax base assessed by the national cadaster: municipalities could fix the tax rate within a range established by the national law, categorize the tax rate according to the use and nature of the building, and introduce tax rate rebates for owner-occupied residences. ICI soon became the main source of municipal revenue, generating on average more than 50 percent of the total tax revenues of municipalities. Because of the large differences in the tax base across municipalities, the new tax had however markedly different effects in different areas of the country. While in the rich north, ICI made municipalities almost totally autonomous financially (with a share of transfers on total revenues dropping below 20–30 percent of total revenues), the same was not true for the cities in the poorer South, which still remained heavily dependent on national grants to finance their expenditure (see Bordignon et al., 2013a). This affected their effective degree of autonomy.[6] ICI was reformed in 2008, when the tax on main residences was abolished, and then eventually cancelled in 2012 (see next section).

ICI was followed in 1998 by a municipal surcharge on the personal income tax (IRPEF), which is still applied by local authorities (see Bordignon et al., 2013b for further details). Originally, this surcharge was composed of a compulsory part (even though this was never applied) and a discretionary part of up to 0.5 percent. The central government later froze the tax rates in 2003 and 2004 (and again in 2005 and 2006, but only if the surcharge had already been used), and then again from 2008 to 2011. In the meantime, it also gave the mayors the possibility of increasing the tax rate up to 0.8 percent, to vary it according to IRPEF brackets, and to introduce tax exemptions for lower incomes.

Finally, in 2007 municipalities were assigned a new earmarked tax in order to co-finance capital investments. More precisely, this new tax could finance only a sub-set of investments, such as urban public transportation, roads, parks, public parking, schools, and so on. This tax could not collect more than 30 percent (later increased to 100 percent) of the total investment costs, could not be imposed for more than five years (later increased to ten years) and had to be given back to taxpayers in case the investment was not carried over. The tax base overlapped with the ICI and the tax rate could not be set above 0.05 percent.

With regard to regions, the other main sub-central level of government in Italy,[7] in 1992 these were assigned health contributions and a motor vehicle tax, followed in 1995 by a share of the excise on gasoline, in 1997 by a new tax on productive activities (IRAP), which substituted health

Source: Our calculations based on ISTAT data, *Spesa delle Amministrazioni Pubbliche per funzioni*, 2012.

Figure 9.1 Sub-national public expenditure as a percentage of total public expenditure

contributions and other minor taxes, and finally, in 1998, a surcharge on the personal income tax (IRPEF), with features similar to the municipal surcharge. IRAP is levied on entrepreneurs and firms (individual and companies, public and private) and its tax base is constituted by the net added value they produce within the region (sum of wages, passive interests and profits; see Bordignon et al., 1999). In 1997 the tax rate was established at 4.25 percent (later reduced to 3.9 percent in 2008), with a possible discretionary variation up to 0.92 percent, differentiated for sectors and categories. The regional surcharge on the personal income tax (IRPEF) is composed of a compulsory part (originally 0.9 percent, now 1.23 percent) and by a discretionary part (currently under revision).

Figures 9.1 and 9.2 summarize the effect of the decentralization period on both local expenditure and local taxation, respectively. As shown, the effect is robust in both cases, although much stronger on the revenue than on the expenditure side. Of course, the data must be interpreted with care. Local taxation also includes tax shares of national taxes,[8] where autonomy is by definition very limited and the total amount of local expenditure does not reflect the effective autonomy of local governments in managing this expenditure.

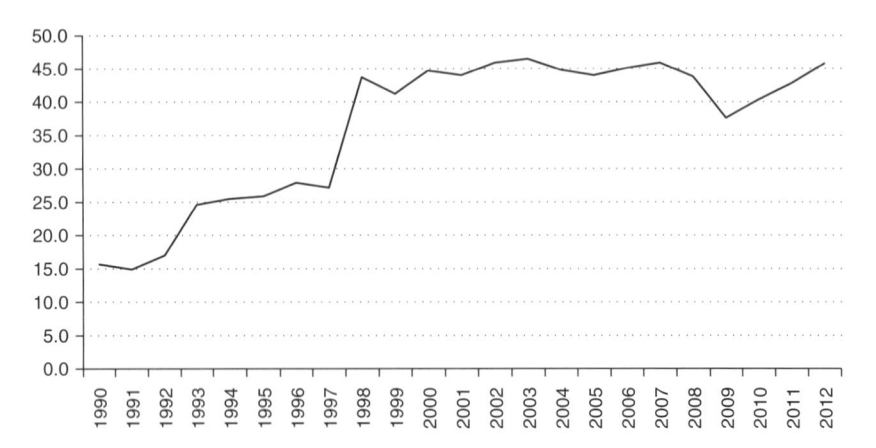

Source: ISTAT, *Conto economico consolidato delle Amministrazioni pubbliche, schema semplificato a due sezioni, 1990–2010.*

Figure 9.2   Own tax revenues as a percentage of total revenues of sub-national governments

2.3   The Internal Stability Pacts

As anticipated, during these years the national government also passed reforms to constrain financial irresponsibility at the local level and the consequent ex post bailing out of local and regional governments by the central government.[9] Hence, in 1999 explicit fiscal rules were introduced for regions, provinces and municipalities under the label of the *Internal Stability Pact*. Since its introduction, the Pact has been modified almost yearly with regard to subjects, targets, sanctions, monitoring procedures, and incentives. This approach caused extreme uncertainty for the activities of regions, provinces and municipalities. Rather than presenting a detailed list of interventions,[10] we briefly summarize the main reforms which occurred during the period (for more details, see Box 9.1).

2.4   The Local Political System and the New Constitution

Decentralization during the period not only affected financing tools and fiscal rules but also incentives facing local officials. With the idea of improving political accountability and financial responsibility, reforms were also introduced regarding the local political system. In particular, in the '90s new electoral laws were passed to allow for direct election of mayors and presidents of regions, and to move from a proportional-based system to a

> **BOX 9.1 THE EVOLUTION OF THE INTERNAL STABILITY PACT IN ITALY**
>
> **Subjects**: at the beginning, all municipalities were subject to the Pact; from 2001 to 2004 municipalities below 5,000 citizens were excluded; in 2005 and 2006 only municipalities below 3,000 were excluded, but in 2007 the threshold was set again at 5,000 citizens. Furthermore, since 2002, different rules have been introduced for regions, provinces and municipalities.[11]
>
> **Targets**: for regions, constraints were initially fixed in terms of overall budget balance, but in 2002 they were replaced by a constraint on expenditure growth. In addition, since 2000, regional health expenditures have been excluded by the regional pact and subject to different rules (the so-called Health Pact 'Patto per la salute').[12] As for local governments, targets have been usually defined in terms of pre-determined reduction of their deficits, except for 2005 and 2006, when a system of ceilings on the annual increase of nominal local expenditure (including investments) was introduced. Observe that, as long as local authorities have some tax autonomy, budget rules leave freedom to fulfill the goal by increasing revenues, cutting expenditures or a combination of both; whereas expenditure ceilings aim only at reducing the dimension of the (local) public sector. The definition of budget balance has also changed over time: initially it referred to cash current budgets only (with a number of exclusions both on the revenues and on the expenditures side); then, it referred to cash and accrual current budgets; in 2007 it was defined as the comprehensive financial budget (see next section).
>
> **Sanctions**: originally the Pact did not include specific sanctions for non-compliance of missed annual targets. Sanctions were introduced in 2003 and were differentiated for regions and local governments. They were also modified many times and often not applied. For regions, non-compliance with the Pact mainly led to an automatic increase in some tax rates (IRAP and the surcharge on IRPEF), and a loss in autonomy in managing health expenditure; for municipalities, non-compliance typically implied a reduction in grants and a freeze on hiring.
>
> **Monitoring**: since 2007, local authorities have been required to send information on cash and accrual accounts on a quarterly basis (recently, every six months) to the Ministry of Economy and Finance. The relevance of the monitoring process relies on the fact that if local governments do not submit to the Ministry of Economy and Finance certification about the compliance of targets relative to the previous year, they are then obliged to adopt all necessary measures to meet the targets if they do not want to incur sanctions. With regard to regions, monitoring of health spending is carried out in the context of a computerized system (the so-called *Tavolo di monitoraggio*), accessible by all participating entities and maintained by the Ministry of Economy and Finance.

more majoritarian one. The reforms were different for the different levels of government,[13] but all had the aim and effect of strengthening the political importance and powers of mayors and presidents with respect to their own majority and the political parties. The enhanced role assumed by heads of the regional and local executive was also determinant in leading to the main political reform in the decentralization process, namely the 2001 constitutional reform. This reform constitutes the apex of the Italian decentralization process of the '90s, and, somewhat paradoxically, it also marked a turning point toward a re-centralization of the system, given the difficulties faced in trying to implement it. The reform modified a number of articles (from 114 to 133) in Title V of the 1948 Constitution that concern the powers of sub-national governments and their financial relationships with the central government. The most important elements of this reform are summarized below.[14]

First (art. 117 of the new Title v), the central government retains the possibility to legislate solely in a limited sub-set of functions (defense, justice, public order, currency, international treaties etc.), while all other functions are handed to (ordinary) regions, to be legislated either only by regions (exclusive regional functions), or to be shared between the central government and regions (concurrent legislation).[15] In particular, the latter category is very large, including all main public activities (health, education, energy, transport, environment, regulation of markets, etc.).[16] In theory, the central government powers should have been limited to the field of shared functions for fixing the main principles, letting the regions legislate the details. However, the distinction between principles and detailed legislation has never been very clear, and the financial importance of the shared functions (excluding pensions and interests on public debt, about 80 percent of the remaining total public expenditure refers to functions included under this label) has made the central government unwilling to seriously consider giving up powers and responsibility in this field. The consequence has been a dramatic increase of litigation between regions and central government and of appeals to the Constitutional Court. Worse, the ensuing uncertainty as to which legislation applies, whether regional or national, has delayed economic activity, imposed extra costs on citizens and firms, and eventually reduced the popular consensus in favor of the decentralization process from the very high levels of support for it in the '90s.

The new Art. 119 regulates the new fiscal relations among the different levels of government. It has a strong flavor of decentralization: e.g., it establishes that local governments' activities should be financed totally by own revenues and tax shares, and that transfers from the central government can only be used to reduce differences in the fiscal capacity of the different regions or municipalities, without any strings attached (no earmarked grants). However, given the huge differences in economic activities and tax bases across the country, and the fact that central government still retains the power to set up uniform standards and levels for the provision of all fundamental services, Art. 119 turned out to be simply not implementable even in those fields the constitution assigns to the exclusive competence of regions. The contrast between the constitution and the true funding practices has negatively affected the transparency of the funding system of regional and local governments, and made largely inapplicable the last attempt to provide a plausible 'interpretation' of the constitution (in order to reduce the constitutional conflict between regions and central government), through the 2009 'framework law' (see below).[17]

The financial crisis erupted in 2008, while the institutional framework was already in a state of flux, followed by an even more severe sovereign debt crisis in 2011. What has been the impact of these shocks on Italian fiscal federalism? We look first at the economic consequences and then at the political/institutional ones.

3. FISCAL FEDERALISM IN ITALY DURING THE CRISIS: ECONOMIC CONSEQUENCES

Italy has been affected by two waves of the crisis. The first wave hit in 2008, causing a sharp fall in GDP in 2009 (-6 percent); then, after a small recovery in 2010, the Italian GDP collapsed again between 2011 and 2014, causing an impressive 'double dip' in economic activities.

While negative overall, the effect was differentiated across the country. In percentage terms the fall in economic activity was larger in the South than in the rest of the country; however, as the South was far poorer to begin with, the absolute distance between North and South was reduced during the crisis (ISTAT, 2014). Besides, the loss in GDP in the Center–North was mostly due to the fall in private economic activity (industrial production shrank by a fourth during the crisis), while the South suffered because of the reduction in public expenditure, which in relative terms is much more important in this part of the country.

One of the consequences of the fall in GDP was an automatic worsening of all the relevant fiscal indicators. Table 9.1 illustrates the evolution of debt-to-GDP ratio that hit the 100 percent threshold before the crisis and has been continuously rising since then, up to 133 percent in 2014. In contrast, debt of local governments, both in terms of GDP and as a percentage of total public debt, has been falling during the period, as a result of the fiscal consolidation measures adopted during the crisis (but see Section 4 on off-budget debts).

The downturn in GDP was intensified by the reaction of the national governments. Different from what happened in other countries, the public finance situation did not allow for counter-cyclical fiscal policy.

Table 9.1 General government debt

	Total (% of GDP)	Municipalities % of GDP	Municipalities % of total public debt	Regions and autonomous provinces % of GDP	Regions and autonomous provinces % of total public debt
2005	105.7	2.86	2.69	2.39	2.26
2006	106.3	3.08	2.90	3.04	2.86
2007	103.3	3.03	2.93	2.90	2.80
2008	106.1	3.04	2.86	2.64	2.49
2009	116.4	3.17	2.73	2.77	2.38
2010	119.3	3.14	2.63	2.64	2.21
2011	120.7	3.13	2.59	2.59	2.15
2012	127.0	3.11	2.45	2.61	2.06
2013	132.6	3.03	2.28	2.41	1.82

Source: Our calculations based on Bank of Italy data, *The Public Finances, borrowing requirement and debt.*

During the first crisis, the (Berlusconi) government initially denied any need for intervention and then eventually, with a delay, reacted in 2010. During the second crisis, the risk of a devastating financial crisis for the country led the governments (Berlusconi's first and then Monti's government) to impose an even harsher correction, in the hope of re-establishing trust in financial markets and gaining the support of the other European countries and the ECB. As a consequence, the government fiscal stance as measured by both total and primary deficit has been strongly pro-cyclical for all the period.

The cumulative effect of financial measures adopted during the crisis has been above 120 billion euros, namely almost 8 percent of GDP (Tables 9.2 and 9.3), particularly concentrated in the period between 2011 and 2012 (Berlusconi's and Monti's governments).

Fiscal consolidation was made up of almost 56 billion euros in additional fiscal revenues, 46 billion euros in current expenditure reduction[18] and 20 billion euros in capital expenditures cut. As regards the contribution of different levels of government to the fiscal adjustment, around 65 percent was due to the central government whereas around 25 percent was due to local governments. In 2012 a massive reform was also introduced in the public pension system, but as shown in Table 9.2, its short-term effects were limited.[19]

However, a more in-depth look at the characteristics of the fiscal adjustment shows that the contribution of sub-national governments to

Table 9.2 Cumulative effects of financial measures (percentage of GDP)

	2008	2009	2010	2011	2012	2013
Central administration	0.06	0.73	0.78	1.81	4.28	5.00
Local administration	−0.04	−0.08	0.34	1.09	2.09	2.10
Social security	0.00	0.00	−0.02	0.00	0.37	0.77
Total	0.02	0.65	1.11	2.91	6.73	7.87

Source: COPAFF (Technical Commission for Fiscal Federalism), *First Report*, 2014.

Table 9.3 Cumulative effects of financial measures (euro billions)

	2008	2009	2010	2011	2012	2013
Central administration	1.00	11.13	12.11	28.62	66.97	77.99
Local administration	−0.66	−1.21	5.34	17.26	32.75	32.78
Social security	−0.01	−0.03	−0.28	0.02	5.72	12.05
Total	0.34	9.89	17.17	45.89	105.44	122.83
of which:						
– current expenditures	1.55	−0.46	−4.78	−16.34	−30.34	−46.20
– capital expenditures	0.01	−3.60	−5.95	−17.35	−23.38	−20.83
– revenues	1.89	5.84	6.45	12.20	51.72	55.80

Source: COPAFF (Technical Commission for Fiscal Federalism), *First Report*, 2014.

the reduction of primary expenditure was slightly higher than the central government one (Table 9.4). More precisely, local administration (regions, provinces, municipalities and local health units, ASL) experienced a reduction of about 28 billion euros, around 52 percent of total primary expenditure reduction. This means that additional fiscal revenues were mainly granted to the central government.

The numbers in Tables 9.3 and 9.4 refer to savings with respect to predicted or forecast public expenditure (e.g., what would have happened to public expenditure growth in the absence of any interventions). General government current expenditure as a percentage of GDP actually jumped up in 2008–09 to about 50 percent of GDP as a result of falling GDP, and it has since fluctuated around this threshold ever since. Public investment instead dropped to around 1 percent of GDP, more than halving in nominal terms as GDP also collapsed.

What was the content of the national budget adjustment policies concerning local governments? For regions, the answer is quite simple:

Table 9.4 Cumulative effects of financial measures on primary expenditure by level of government (euro billions)

	2009	2010	2011	2012
Central administration	−6.13	−6.23	−16.47	−20.98
Social security	0.86	0.46	−0.42	−5.05
Regions	−1.52	−2.32	−8.17	−12.34
Provinces	0.24	−0.55	−1.28	−2.88
Municipalities	0.96	−1.74	−4.67	−8.41
Health units	1.42	−0.33	−2.50	−4.13
As % of primary expenditure				
Central administration	−3.2	−3.5	−9.4	−12.2
Social security	0.3	0.2	−0.1	−1.6
Regions	−4.0	−6.5	−24.2	−38.5
Provinces	2.0	−4.8	−11.7	−27.8
Municipalities	1.5	−2.8	−7.6	−14.3
Health units	1.3	−0.3	−2.2	−3.7

Source: COPAFF (Technical Commission for Fiscal Federalism), *First Report*, 2014.

transfers to finance health care were reduced to some extent, and more severely for other types of expenditure.[20] A series of relevant transfer cuts were imposed on municipalities as well; moreover, the Internal Stability Pact was also reformed in several aspects (see next paragraph).

All these measures had an impact on the financial distribution of resources across governments. The following tables help to clarify how the country has changed between 2007 and 2012. As regards municipalities (Table 9.5), current revenues increased from 2007 to 2012 by an average growth rate of almost 3 percent. This increase was totally driven by an increase in tax revenues (by almost 7 percent), only partially compensated for by a decrease in grants from regional and national governments. All main taxes increased between 2007 and 2012, despite the fact that ICI lost an important part of its tax base and the IRPEF surtax was often frozen by the central government. The raise in TARSU's revenues was due to the necessity, dictated by the law, of fully covering the costs of garbage collection and disposal.

Fiscal autonomy further increased (Table 9.6). Own revenues increased from 65 percent of total current revenues to almost 73 percent. In contrast, the share of non-tax revenues did not change much. Within tax revenues, it is easy to note the decrease in importance of ICI following the 2008 reform,[21] even if in 2012 (i.e., before Monti's reform discussed below) it still accounted for half of the municipal tax revenues.

Table 9.5 Municipalities' revenues (euro billions and percentage growth rate)

Revenues	2007	2012	Growth rate (%)	Average year growth rate (%)
Current revenues	52.6	60.4	14.7	2.8
Tax revenues	22.0	30.8	39.9	6.9
Current grants	19.0	16.4	−13.3	−2.8
IRPEF surtax	2.5	3.9	57.7	9.5
Property tax (ICI)	12.7	15.6	22.3	4.1
TARSU	4.4	7.3	68.3	11.0
Non-tax revenues	11.7	13.2	12.8	2.4

Source: Our calculations based on ISTAT data, *I bilanci consuntivi delle Amministrazioni Comunali*.

Table 9.6 Municipalities' revenues shares (%)

Revenues	2007	2012
Tax revenues as % of current revenues	41.8	51.0
Current grants as % of current revenues	36.0	27.2
Non-tax revenues as % of current revenues	22.2	21.8
IRPEF surtax as % of tax revenues	11.2	12.7
Property tax as % of tax revenues	57.9	50.6
TARSU as % of tax revenues	19.8	23.8

Source: Our calculations based on ISTAT data, *I bilanci consuntivi delle Amministrazioni Comunali*.

It is also interesting to detail these measures by the main areas of the country (Table 9.7). Despite showing a tiny convergence between 2007 and 2012, it is clear that municipalities in the North are characterized by a larger fiscal autonomy. The difference is striking with regard to tariffs too, which represent a rough measure of the ability to offer and finance additional services to citizens.

Grants are still a very important part of revenues for municipalities in the South (44.4 percent in 2012 versus 18.4 percent in the North). The relatively low importance of tax revenues in the South may be explained in two ways: on the one hand, there may be a lower propensity to use fiscal autonomy as traditionally grants have served as the main financing source of revenue. But on the other hand, the lack of a tax base may have had a

Table 9.7 Municipalities' revenues shares, by areas (%)

	Italy 2007	Italy 2012	North 2007	North 2012	Center 2007	Center 2012	South 2007	South 2012
Tax revenues as % of current revenues	41.8	51.0	44.3	50.3	43.1	57.7	37.4	47.2
Current grants as % of current revenues	36.1	27.2	29.9	18.4	31.2	21.3	48.2	44.4
Non-tax revenues as % of current revenues	22.2	21.9	25.7	27.1	25.7	21.0	15.0	14.5
IRPEF surtax as % of tax revenues	11.4	12.7	11.0	13.2	13.9	13.4	10.0	11.1
Property tax as % of tax revenues	57.7	50.6	61.7	57.5	63.4	50.1	46.7	40.2
TARSU as % of tax revenues	20.0	23.7	15.6	16.7	13.6	24.8	32.3	34.0

Source: Our calculations based on ISTAT data, *I bilanci consuntivi delle Amministrazioni Comunali.*

role (this should be particularly true for the IRPEF surtax). In the Center–North, it is interesting to observe that, while the municipalities in the North have compensated for the fall in grants by mostly increasing tariffs, in the Center, the compensation was achieved by mostly increasing taxes.

Regarding regions (Figure 9.3 and Table 9.8), netting the growth of tax revenues by VAT sharing and correctly relabeling it with current grants,[22] it emerges that between 2007 and 2012 tax revenues basically did not change (they grew by 0.5 percent in five years), whereas current grants grew by almost 20 percent (3.6 percent on average). Hence, regions seem to be less autonomous in 2012 than in 2007: the share of tax revenues over current revenues decreased from 56 percent to 52 percent and the share of grants increased from 43 percent to 47 percent. It is also worth recalling that in 2008 the IRAP basic tax rate was lowered from 4.25 percent to 3.9 percent, thus partially explaining the negative 3.3 percent average growth rate in the revenues from this tax.

Table 9.9 illustrates the dramatic fall in investments by all local governments (regions and municipalities). This is both a consequence of the crisis, which forced local governments to save (and it is easier to save on capital expenditure), and a consequence of the strengthening of the Internal Stability Pact, which during the crisis was extended to capital expenditure too (see next section for detail).

To counteract the fall in public investments, the central government introduced some incentives in the form of a 'flexible' pact. The general idea is to exploit the lumpy nature of investments by municipalities, to allow for more capital expenditure while still controlling aggregate local

Figure 9.3 Regions' revenues (euro billions)

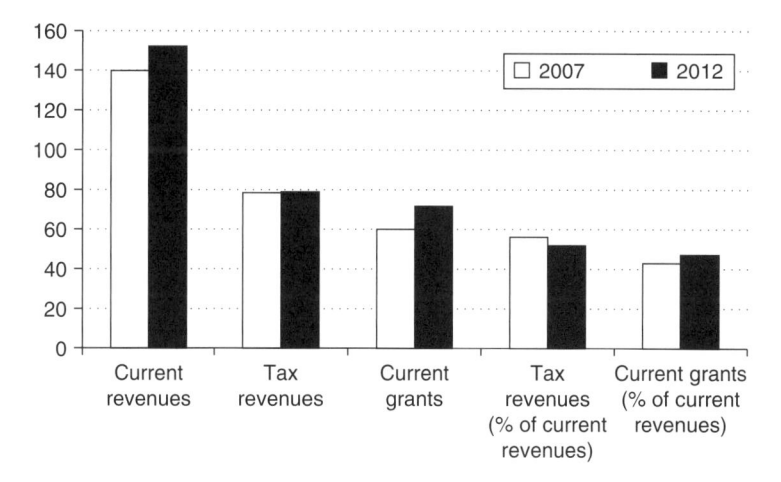

Note: Current grants are comprehensive of VAT sharing.

Source: Our calculations based on ISTAT data, *Conto economico delle Amministrazioni Regionali*.

Table 9.8 Regions' tax revenues (euro billions and growth rate)

Revenues	2007	2012	Growth rate (%)	Average year growth rate (%)
IRAP	39.4	33.2	−15.6	−3.3
IRPEF special regions	11.0	12.5	13.8	2.6
VAT special regions	5.4	6.3	16.5	3.1
Excise on mineral oils	3.4	4.0	18.7	3.5
IRPEF surtax	7.4	10.7	45.2	7.7
Motor vehicles taxes	7.6	8.5	11.3	2.2
Total	78.5	78.9	0.5	0.1

Source: Our calculations based on ISTAT data, *Conto economico delle Amministrazioni Regionali*.

public expenditure growth. More specifically, there are three possible forms of flexible pact: regional horizontal pact, regional vertical pact (in two versions: ordinary and incentivized), and national horizontal pact. In all cases, local governments subject to the pact that do better than their targets may lend their surplus to others (still subject to the pact) who

Table 9.9 Local administration expenditures (accrual, euro billions and growth rate)

	2007	2012	Growth rate (%)
Municipalities			
Current expenditures	49.4	54.3	9.9
Investment expenditures	27.8	13.0	−53.2
Regions			
Current expenditures	129.3	138.6	7.2
Investment expenditures	4.2	3.4	−19.0

Source: Our calculations based on ISTAT data, *Conto economico delle Amministrazioni Regionali e delle Amministrazioni Comunali.*

otherwise would not comply. With a regional horizontal pact, municipalities exchange financial resources within the region they belong to, whereas with a national horizontal pact, they can exchange resources with any other municipality in the country. Vertical pacts are different in the sense that a region simply gives some of its resources to municipalities, conditional on the fact that the region itself must have left enough resources to allow it to respect its own pact. Municipalities who lend resources obtain both a discount on their target for the next two years and get their money back after the same time period. Municipalities who borrow resources do the opposite, but they do not incur any sanction and are obliged to use these resources for capital expenditures only.[23] It is easy to understand why municipalities prefer vertical pacts (they do not need to refund the region), but national horizontal pacts could be useful whenever a region has insufficient resources left to create a vertical pact.

The experience with these flexible pacts was, overall, not positive. So far only the vertical pact (in the richest regions of the north) worked; there were very few examples of the horizontal pact, regional or national. Municipalities with a surplus, in a condition of crisis and continuous uncertainty, did not trust lending their resources; and rules were too rigid to allow for the development of a 'market' (in the rights of raising debt to finance investments) at the regional or national level. We will come back to this in Section 5.

Finally, one of the consequences of the fiscal consolidation in the period is a sharp reduction in the number of regional and municipal public employees, following both restrictions in the ability to hire new personnel and explicit rules to reduce turnover. The fall in local government employees is in line with that observed for the central administration, except for health units (Table 9.10).

Table 9.10 Public sector employees (thousands of units)

Administration	2007	2012	Diff.	Change (%)
Central administration	2,042.9	1,859.4	−183.5	−9.1
Local administration*	1,519.9	1,450.1	−69.8	−4.6
of which: regions, provinces, municipalities	619.1	568.4	−50.7	−8.2
Social security	55.5	47.3	−8.2	−14.8
Total	3,618.3	3,356.8	261.5	−7.2

Note: * Includes employees in the Regional Health Care Units.

Source: ISTAT, *Unità di lavoro delle Amministrazioni pubbliche per sotto-settore*, 1990–2012.

4. FISCAL FEDERALISM IN ITALY DURING THE CRISIS: INSTITUTIONAL AND POLITICAL CONSEQUENCES

Along with financial interventions, the central government also approved a number of different reforms which were not designed to directly collect or save public money, but rather to change, one more time, the relationship among the central and other levels of government. In this section we analyze the content and consequences of these political and institutional reforms.

4.1 Local Taxation

After 2007 the national government introduced a lot of reforms in connection with local taxation. For municipalities in particular, these reforms affected real estate taxation in a schizophrenic way.[24] First of all, in 2008, the Berlusconi government abolished ICI on the main (owner occupied) residence, which at the time represented a non-negligible revenue for municipalities, promising to compensate for the loss in local revenue by ordinary transfers.[25]

In 2012 a different government (Monti) reformed the ICI, now called IMU, by changing it quite substantially. First of all, the tax base was (approximately) doubled by revising cadastral values accordingly. Second, the tax could also be levied on the main residence.[26] However, while the proceeds of the tax on the main residence of the taxpayers went directly to municipalities, the central government *forced* municipalities to transfer back half of their revenues on the remaining buildings; more precisely, municipalities could choose a different rate on the value of these buildings, but they were anyhow obliged to transfer an amount equal to the tax base multiplied by 0.38 percent, i.e., half of the statutory tax rate.

Things changed again in 2013, when Letta's government once more abolished IMU on the main residence and established that, from 2014, there would be a 'single municipal tax' (IUC), composed of three parts: 1) IMU, levied only on land and buildings different from the main residence; 2) TARI, a service tax to finance garbage collection; and 3) TASI, a service tax to finance all the other indivisible services provided by the municipality. In 2011, municipalities were also granted a 'tourist tax'. This tax was discretionary, could vary from one to five euros per person per night, and could only be introduced in touristic cities, as nationally defined.

With regard to regions, the tax rate for the compulsory part of the surcharge on IRPEF was raised from 0.9 percent to 1.23 percent in 2012.

4.2 Transfer Mechanisms

The reform of local taxation resulted in the need to reform the transfer mechanism. The main innovation on these grounds is the introduction of standard costs and needs in order to compute municipal grants. Following the 2001 constitutional reform, in 2009 the Italian parliament delegated to the government the reform of the transfer system (framework law L. 42/2009).[27] The framework law contemplated the possibility of transferring funds to local governments according to two criteria: standard costs, to finance 'fundamental' activities, and fiscal capacity, to finance all other activities. To estimate standard costs on the basis of a 2011 decree implementing the framework law, very detailed questionnaires on the characteristics of the supply of all main services were sent to all municipalities. This information, coupled with budget data and other data on the territory and local prices, allowed the computation of minimal and average standard costs for the provision of services. Characteristics of the population were used to compute standard needs.[28]

The process of gathering and processing information lasted three years and standard costs/needs have just been made public (June 2014).[29] In principle, these standards could also be used to determine the total size of grants to be given to municipalities (the sum, over all municipalities, of how much more money in excess of standardized local taxation each municipality requires to cover standard needs when offering services at standard costs); in practice, and as long as public finances are at risk, the standards will be used to allocate savings across municipalities, revising Internal Stability Pacts and grants accordingly. A similar approach is used to determine standard costs and needs for health expenditures (and consequently transfers) for regions, though here the law is even clearer in stating that the total amount of resources will not be determined as the sum of regional needs, but on the basis of the overall constraints of the national budget.

The reform of the transfer mechanism was combined with several amendments of the Internal Stability Pact. First, since 2013 all municipalities with a population of over 1,000 have become subject to the Pact. Second, concerning targets: in 2008, a new concept of 'mixed accrual basis' balance to define the target was introduced. With this definition, the final balance is determined by the sum of an accrual current balance and of a cash capital balance, net of some exceptions. This definition is more consistent with European constraints, which do not allow for a golden rule, and make window-dressing operations for municipalities (re-labeling some items of current expenditure as capital expenditure eludes the Pact) more difficult. Nonetheless, as we saw in the previous section, this new comprehensive budget rule introduced a very strong incentive to reduce public investments for municipalities, adding to the usual practice of cutting capital expenditure during a crisis. Going back to targets, they are calculated as a percentage of the average current expenditures recorded three year earlier.[30] Percentages may vary according to the size and 'virtuosity' of each municipality (see below), whereas reference years vary with time. Third, along with sanctions a new system of premia was introduced.[31] However, it was only applied in 2012 as it soon became obvious that there were many difficulties in applying it.

An additional reform concerns the so-called Tesoreria Unica (a modification of a Treasury Single Account (TSA), see Ahmad, Chapter 2 in this volume), first issued in 1984, abolished in 1997, and finally re-introduced in 2012, in the midst of the financial crisis. According to the Tesoreria Unica regime, local authorities are no longer able to deposit the revenues they collect in their own treasurer's office (i.e., in commercial banks), but are obliged to do so in a specific interest-bearing account created by the Bank of Italy. Interest accrued is then paid back to the central government. Local governments can manage payments and deposits but cannot manage cash otherwise. In other words, interest payments did not accrue to local governments (not always the case with TSAs), but were assigned to the central government.

4.3 The Number of Governments

A well-known problem in the Italian system of government is the excessive number of local governments: too many regions and too many municipalities, many of a size too small to achieve efficiency in the provision of services. For instance, 75 percent of all municipalities (about 8,100) have fewer than 5,000 inhabitants; and although less than 17 percent of the Italian population live in these towns, mayors and councilors representing these small towns constitute more than 55 percent of the total municipal politicians. Plus, there are also too many levels of government, with the 21 regions, the 104 provinces, and the 8,100 municipalities and other aggregations insisting on the same territory, often with overlapping responsibilities.[32] The problem has been obvious for decades, but political resistance has always managed to abort any attempt at reform. On the contrary, as shown in Baldersheim and Rose (2010, see in particular their Figure 1.2) for municipalities (but the same could also be said for provinces), Italy is unique among European countries in having witnessed, up to the crisis, an increase in the number of local authorities, as splitting one territory into more governments has usually been a sure way to attract more central money and to increase the number of elected positions available for the local political class.

The economic crisis and the pressure of public opinion finally led to some progress in this area.

After several unsuccessful attempts, a law was passed in 2014 to reshape local authorities, with the specific aim of introducing and regulating '*Città metropolitane*' (metropolitan cities), redefining and reorganizing the role of provinces (in anticipation of a constitutional reform finally abolishing them; see Section 5), and providing new regulations for unions and mergers of municipalities.

The new government landscape that is emerging is still largely unsatisfactory, but some undeniable progress is evident. First, in the new law, the intermediate level between regions and municipalities, the provinces, has been definitively abolished as an autonomous level of government. Provinces still exist[33] – with reduced powers – but the provincial government is no longer directly elected by citizens and is composed of representatives of the mayors of the cities belonging to the territory of the same province. Small municipalities also still exist; but if below the threshold of 10,000 inhabitants, they are now forced to join forces in the provision of all services in 'unions', new political bodies whose mechanisms of representation and governance are similar to those of the new provinces. A straightforward merger for small municipalities would have been largely preferable, but unions are nevertheless likely to be an intermediate step in this direction.[34]

Finally, the law introduces the new '*Città metropolitane*', another important step toward rationalizing the structure of government, that has been under discussion for some considerable time (*Città metropolitane* are even mentioned in the current constitution, although none of them so far exists). In spite of the proliferation of local governments, Italy has always lacked an administrative/political body that could relate to the reality of its great urban agglomerates. Municipalities are usually too small,[35] and provinces have lacked the correct competences.

A rational reform would have also used this opportunity to discuss size and funding of the new *Città metropolitane*, but that would probably have amounted to wishful thinking. Thus, the new *Città metropolitane* inherited both the territory and the funding of the old province they replaced,[36] plus a number of extra powers, basically related to all networks (telecommunication, transport, utilities, etc.) serving the metropolitan city. The metropolitan mayor is the mayor of the main city and the metropolitan council is again made up by representatives of the mayors of all cities and towns belonging to the metropolitan area. Not surprisingly, while only five or six areas surrounding the main cities could qualify themselves as metropolises on the grounds of standard economic and social indicators (Iommi, 2014), 10 new metropolitan cities (nine plus '*Roma Capitale*') were in fact introduced, a compromise needed in order to reach enough political consensus for passage of the law.

4.4 Bankruptcy Procedures

Additional reforms passed during the crisis related to legislation concerning municipalities' financial distress. This is a condition under which a municipality can no longer provide its essential functions and services or when it is unable to pay back its own debts. Usually, financial distress is due to one (or more) of the following causes: bad accounting practices; liquidity crisis; excessive and out-of-control resort to off-budget debts; low and bad budget monitoring procedures; and so on. The legislation provides explicit support for municipalities declaring themselves as being in distress, but distress usually also calls for a suspension of the city autonomy. The mayor and the council need to resign, a central government commissioner takes all powers, debt and interest are frozen, assets are liquidated, tariffs and taxes are increased up to the maximum level etc.

Table 9.11 below summarizes all episodes of financial distress in the last 25 years, selected by region and by size of the municipalities. Notably, they are relatively few, are mostly concentrated in small towns and in the poorer South, and did not increase that much during the crisis, contrary to what one might have expected.

However, this should not be taken as an indicator of the Italian municipalities' sound financial health, or at least not of all of them. First, a side effect of the reform's tightening of national budget rules (up to the

Table 9.11   Financially distressed municipalities, by population, 1989–2013

	1–9,999	10,000–59,999	Above 60,000	Total
Piemonte	5	0	1	6
Lombardia	15	0	0	15
Liguria	4	0	0	4
Veneto	0	3	0	3
Emilia Romagna	8	0	0	8
Toscana	4	1	0	5
Umbria	3	1	0	4
Marche	6	0	0	6
Lazio	33	11	1	45
Abruzzo	19	1	0	20
Molise	15	0	0	15
Campania	89	35	4	128
Puglia	33	3	1	37
Basilicata	17	1	1	19
Calabria	134	11	0	145
Sicilia	20	11	0	31
Sardegna	2	1	0	3
Total	408	79	8	495

Source: Corte dei Conti, Sezione delle autonomie, *Relazione sulla gestione finanziaria degli enti locali, 2011–12*.

introduction of the European Fiscal Compact in the Italian Constitution) passed during the crisis is that central government is no longer allowed to help distressed cities with extra money. Thus, municipalities now have an incentive to engage in further window dressing of the budget,[37] in order to try to avoid or postpone the default as much as possible. Second, precisely in order to counteract this incentive and prevent the financial situation degenerating even further, a 2011 law allowed the Italian Corte dei Conti (the national auditing body) to make a direct pronouncement regarding the financial distress of a municipality (*guided distress*), while previously only the municipality itself had been able to do it.

But somewhat paradoxically, to avoid the just-introduced guided distress status (and thus openly acknowledge the fact that several Italian cities might be on the verge of bankruptcy), since 2012 (with some further adjustments in 2014), central government has offered municipalities the possibility of an early distress (or multi-annual financial re-balance), in which the rebalance procedure is still managed by the political bodies of the municipality. In this case, the municipality has to prepare a plan according to the following steps: a) a precise determination of the distress causes and evaluation of the municipality budget balance; b) a plan of action with deadlines to solve financial problems within 10 years; c) clear definition of resources to realize the plan (own revenues, debt). More recently (decree 16/2014) the terms for financial rebalance have been further extended, provided the rebalance is significantly conditioned by the reduction of public services' costs and the reorganization of municipalities' owned private companies that offer public services.

The upshot of these schizophrenic procedurals is that several small and large cities, especially in the South, are still on the verge of bankruptcy. It will have to be seen if this multi-annual financial rebalance will work or whether it will just be a way for a city to sit and wait for central government's support without having to declare a financial distress and pay the consequent costs.[38, 39]

4.5 Off-Budget Debts and Arrears

Another way to look at the financial health of Italian local governments is to consider off-budget debts and public arrears. In the Italian legal framework, off-budget debts are defined as debts originated by practices not in compliance with accounting rules. Thus, these debts are not recorded and undermine a budget's accuracy and transparency; in addition, part of these debts is not formally recognized. According to Corte dei Conti's estimates, this problem concerns about a quarter of Italian municipalities; and in the time period between 2010 and 2012, off-budget debts of municipalities increased to about 1.265 million euros (Table 9.12).

Concerning public arrears, these differ from off-budget debts because in this case debts are often generated by practices in compliance with accounting rules but with shortage of funds, but may also represent irresponsible contracting. There are no available official and reliable data about the exact amount of arrears. The Bank of Italy[40] in 2013 estimated them to be about 90 billion euros, half of them originating in the health care sector (arrears of Health Care Units). Notice that at least for municipalities some of these arrears were a result of the working of the Internal Fiscal Pact itself, which, since 2011, required municipalities to reach budget targets on both accrual and cash bases. Hence, a municipality might have had the money to pay private suppliers, but was unable to spend it as it had already met its cash limit.

In 2012 and 2013 the central government approved two decrees, in order to pay off a big chunk of these arrears[41] – 40 billion euros between 2013 and 2014 or about 2.5 percent of GDP. In particular, 23.5 billion euros of arrears were repaid by March 2014, 13.7 billion of which concerned arrears owed to suppliers of health care services (Table 9.13).

Table 9.12 Off-budget debts of municipalities, 2010–12 (euro millions)

Year	No. of municipalities	Recognized	To be recognized	Total
2010	2006	628,763	353,055	981,818
2011	1930	551,079	264,953	816,032
2012	1951	576,548	688,646	1,265,194

Source: Corte dei Conti, Sezione delle autonomie, *Relazione sulla gestione finanziaria degli enti locali, 2011–2012.*

Table 9.13 Arrears payments (euro billions, on 28 March)

	Resources assignment	Resources available	Payments
Total amount	27.2	24.9	23.5
Total amount as % of assignment		92	86
Central administration	3.0	3.0	3.0
Regions – autonomous provinces	15.8	13.8	13.7
Provinces and municipalities	8.4	8.2	7.0

Source: Ministry for the Economy and Finance, '*Sblocca debiti*', *stato di attuazione*, 2014.

To understand the rationale for these policies, one should note that payment of arrears for current expenditure increases the public debt, but not the public deficit of the general government, because the national institute of statistics (ISTAT), following European rules, computes such expenditures on an accruals basis. Therefore, they are already budgeted in the deficits of previous years. On the contrary, payments made in order to extinguish commercial debts for capital expenditure also increase the deficit because ISTAT calculates this expenditure on a cash basis.

Repayment of the commercial debts in 2013–14 represented perhaps the only counter-cyclical fiscal measure that Italy had been able to adopt since the beginning of the crisis while still complying with European rules.[42] It is hard to estimate the impact of these payments on growth. The Bank of Italy (2013) estimates fiscal multipliers which depend on how firms use the amounts they receive (close to unity in the case of investment in machinery and working capital, and close to zero for the amounts that firms hold for precautionary purposes); in particular the effect of the measures to unblock general government commercial debts (totaling €47 billion in the two-year period 2013–14) on GDP is estimated to be a little over half a percentage point in the three-year period 2013–15.

Repayment of commercial debts by local units was therefore probably a good policy to follow for the national government. Still, it has to be acknowledged that it worsened the soft budget constraint problem at local level that, as we discussed above, is still rampant in the Italian structure of governments. The necessary financial resources have been disbursed by the central government through cash advances to regions and municipalities; they should be reimbursed in the future, but of course it will have to be seen if this really happens.

5. THE ITALIAN VERSION OF THE FISCAL COMPACT AND THE NEW CONSTITUTION

5.1 The New Art. 81 and the 'Legge Rinforzata'

In 2014, the Italian version of the European treaty known as the Fiscal Compact entered in force, via a constitutional amendment (rewriting art. 81) and an implementing law (Legge Rinforzata; literally enhanced law) voted in with a super-majority. As well known, the new fiscal rule does not allow for debt to finance investment, but only to balance finances in the economic cycle. The 'Legge Rinforzata' further specifies this requirement by clarifying that the country will be assumed to be in budget equilibrium if it reaches its medium-term objective, as defined at the European level. For Italy, the medium-term objective is to have (starting in 2015) a balanced structural budget. The rule applies to general government. For the law to apply to central government requires an overall (structural) budget in equilibrium, including transfers to local governments and social security entities.

For the local governments, the law specifies something different. Overall budget equilibrium must be reached (each year) at the regional level for all local governments belonging to that region, including the regional government itself, but there are no specific constraints for each single local government. This means that, say, a single municipality can still use debt financing for an investment, provided that this new debt is matched by a corresponding surplus of another municipality located in the same region, or by a surplus at regional government level.[43] Thus, this constitutional provision replicates what is already implied by ordinary laws, through the vertical (the region pays) or the horizontal pact (the other municipalities pay), with the difference being that now the national horizontal pact seems to be excluded, as the overall budget equilibrium must be reached at the level of each region.

The problem with this provision is that, as we saw above, these pacts do not seem to be working. Only the vertical pact has worked so far, and only in those regions where the regional government had some extra money to spare, basically in the North. And it is not obvious why the horizontal pacts should work in the future. As discussed above, one of the reasons why they did not work is that in a situation of economic difficulty and uncertainty concerning both future grants and future regulations, municipalities with a surplus do not trust lending their money to other municipalities. To make it work, there should be a more explicit guarantee that this money will be returned, and also rules that are more flexible (mimicking a true market mechanism) and that would allow payment of interest on the loan.

One way to proceed would be to strengthen the role of regional governments with respect to their own municipalities, giving regions control of local finances, currently under the control of the national government; i.e., permitting grants and grant allocation to municipalities to be decided at the regional government level. The central government could simply transfer to each region the money it now uses to finance the municipalities of that region,[44] letting the region decide how to allocate this money. And the fact that regions control present and future transfers would allow them to guarantee that the money a municipality gives up today (letting others use its surplus) comes back tomorrow (with some interest). In other words, the regional government would then have the powers to guarantee that all local governments in the same region, including the regional government itself, would respect the overall balanced budget rule, even allowing for a breaking of that rule at single municipality level.

Unfortunately, although this enhanced role for regions versus their municipalities is perfectly compatible with the current constitution, it has never been applied.[45] Municipalities, which in Italy traditionally have had a stronger role than regions, in particular the big cities, resent regional 'centralism' and have always resisted such a move, preferring to maintain a direct financial link with the central government. Worse, as we discuss below, this enhanced role for regions is less compatible with the new proposed constitution that undoubtedly weakens the institutional and political role of regions.

The conclusion is that the new fiscal rules might turn out to be too strict to allow for debt financing of even economically meaningful public investments, forcing each local government to be continuously in a balanced-budget equilibrium. This can dampen growth in a country where: a) local investments are traditionally very important (approximately two-thirds of public investments are usually carried out at the local level); b) they are usually the only ones that work;[46] c) the amount of investment has already been dramatically reduced during the crisis, as we saw above.

5.2 Local Government in the New Proposed Constitution

The process leading to a constitutional reform has just started and will require time to be approved (if ever), as it needs two readings in both houses, with a minimum time span of two months between each reading, and possibly a confirmative referendum. But the new government is very determined to bring it to a conclusion and the amended text has the support of the main parties represented in the parliament. As already stated, the main aim of the constitutional reform is to eliminate the Italian perfect bicameralism, transforming the upper house into a Senate of local authorities, whose support is no longer needed for the central government to rule. But the constitution also implies profound changes in the structure of local governments. Provinces are definitely abolished; regions' functions are drastically reduced, in particular the category of shared functions is abolished; and a supremacy clause is introduced,[47] so that in case of a conflict, central government legislation is now much more likely to dominate than regional.[48]

Regions' exclusive legislative functions are still enumerated in the constitution,[49] but this is hardly protection for a region's autonomy, as the supremacy clause will presumably allow the central government to have an upper hand in these matters too. The role of regions also changes. They will gain a role in the Senate, as out of 100 senators, 74 will be representatives of regional councils (elected by the regional councilors, among themselves).[50] But they will share this role with the mayors of the main cities, as 21 senators (one for each region) are mayors.[51] The role of the new Senate is basically only advisory, except for constitutional changes, international treaties and the election of the President of the Republic, in which it has the same status as the lower chamber, as a potential guarantee against a too-powerful national government.

More specifically, the new Senate may ask to examine all legislation, but the lower chamber has no obligation to take into account the Senate's suggestions. More protection is offered in regard to laws referring to articles of the constitution that have a direct impact on local government functions, particularly the new article 117, in which the main regional functions are indicated. Here, an examination by the Senate of proposed legislature is compulsory. But the lower chamber is still the final decision maker, as it can always overrule Senate amendments by an absolute majority (50 percent + 1 of votes among all MPs),[52] and the legislative initiative is in the hands of the lower house. Even the remuneration of the regional president and the regional councilors will from now on be decided by central government, as is the case for municipalities, and it will be set at the same level as the remuneration of the mayor of the main municipalities.

Interestingly, while there is still a debate in parliament about the nature of senators (if directly or indirectly elected), no one has raised serious objections about the reduced role of regions, an indication of the low level of support that regions presently enjoy among citizens.

Article 119 on fiscal federalism (never really applied) remains basically unchanged, although it makes even less sense in the new structure. This is a problem, because as it is already in existence, in order to conciliate this article with reality, the legislator will have to introduce several unnecessary complications into local finance.[53] Furthermore, the number and identity of regions remain unchanged, although this would have been the right opportunity to at least merge the smaller ones.

Summing up, while the current constitution has, in the regional level of government, the fundamental agent for decentralization, in the future, if the new constitution is approved, many functions will be de facto or de jure re-centralized, and regions will basically have the same rank as municipalities. In the future, Italy will then only be composed of the central government and municipalities, quasi-municipalities (the regions), and unions of municipalities (these are also the new metropolitan cities). The question is whether this will work.

6. CONCLUDING REMARKS

The economic crisis that started in 2008 and deepened in 2011 profoundly affected fiscal relationships between levels of government in Italy. The crisis was not a direct result of mismanagement of local finances, although the poor quality of several institutions concerned with regional and local government played a role in explaining the dismal performance of the economy both before and during the crisis. As a consequence of the crisis, the Italian system of government clearly moved in the direction of a re-centralization of policies. More than likely, this new equilibrium will also find a new constitutional basis. It will have to be seen whether this new equilibrium will be able to offer a more efficient and responsive system of government. Some steps clearly point in this direction; others less so.

NOTES

1. Currently, the Italian Senate is directly elected by citizens, and its vote is necessary to approve all laws. Consequently, in order to rule, the executive needs to have a majority in both houses. According to the reform, in the future the Senate will not be elected but

composed of representatives of regional councils and mayors of the main Italian cities. Its role will be mostly advisory, except for constitutional legislation and the election of the President of the Republic.
2. International developments at the European level also played a role. The increasing functions devolved to the European Union and the launch of the unique market at the beginning of the 1990s supported the idea that the role of the national states was going to decline, with the EU taking the place of the old national states in the provision of fundamental public services, such as defense, security, basic infrastructures and the opening of markets. The continent could then safely evolve into a 'Europe of Regions'. The European Commission itself supported this view, organizing its main transfer system ('structural funds') on a regional basis. This in effect led many European countries to create or to reinforce their regional governments. Indeed, decentralization was quite common in Europe in the '90s, with important developments taking place in Spain, Belgium but also France and the UK. This view was halted by the French referendum in 2006, rejecting the federal constitution for Europe proposed by the Convention, and by the Lisbon treaty of 2011, that re-institutionalized the role of national countries in the European Council.
3. With the exception of an 18-month period, from 2006 to 2008, in which a composite Center-Left coalition was in power. In 2011, the then premier, Silvio Berlusconi, was forced to resign in the midst of the financial crisis.
4. The decentralization of the '90s mostly occurred on the revenue side. But some extra functions were given to regions and local governments (through the so-called Bassanini Decrees at the end of the '90s) and the level of autonomy in some previously allocated functions (such as health care for regions) was increased.
5. See Balduzzi (2014) for more details.
6. Bordignon et al. (2013a) argue that the different degree of autonomy also affected the selection of the local political class and the degree of efficiency in the provision of local public services.
7. The third is province, but it always mattered less in terms of functions and resources. Plus, as we discuss below, it has now been substituted for by a political union of municipalities.
8. In particular, the VAT tax share for regions that is needed to finance health care provision. Health care, the main function of regional governments, is, as a matter of fact, a jointly provided function, where the central government defines standard levels of provision of services and guarantees financing through the VAT share that is given, adding to the regional taxes earmarked for health financing. The regions organize the network, to offer services through the local health units, both territorial and hospitals. See note 12 for further details.
9. Problems of soft budget constraints have always been endemic in the Italian structure of governments, beginning with the massive bailout of cities' debts at the beginning of the '80s (the so-called 'Stammati decrees'). See Bordignon and Turati (2009) for a theoretical and empirical analysis of soft budget constraint problems at the regional level concerning health expenditure.
10. A comprehensive survey of the development of the Internal Stability Pact is in Ambrosanio and Balduzzi (forthcoming). See also Ambrosanio and Bordignon (2007b) for international comparisons.
11. Utilizing the heterogeneity of the municipal fiscal rules over time and for different population size of municipalities, several authors have investigated the effect of the fiscal rules on local government's behavior. See Balduzzi and Grembi (2011) and Grembi et al. (2014). Results are somewhat mixed.
12. Italy is somewhat peculiar in so far as the main function attributed to regions is the management of the National Health System; indeed, health expenditure covers more than 80 percent of total expenditure of the Italian Ordinary Regions (all of them, except the two islands and three small regions at the northern border of the country, which have Special Statutes, a different system of financing and more functions; see Ambrosanio

et al., 2010). Healthcare provision is however heavily regulated by the central government that fixes the basic services that have to be supplied and that directly (through transfers) or indirectly (through regional taxes as IRAP and the regional surcharge on IRPEF that de facto or de jure are earmarked for health expenditure) guarantees the funding of the services. This explains the difference of treatment of this type of expenditure in terms of the internal pacts. The overlapping of competences between the central and the regional governments in the health sector has reduced accountability and supported soft budget constraints problems; see again Bordignon and Turati (2009).

13. See for instance Bordignon et al. (2013c) on the new electoral rules for electing the mayor. The reform at the municipality level certainly worked in strengthening the political legitimacy of mayors; it is not a coincidence that mayors are the only component of the Italian political class that escaped the loss of support induced by scandals and the dire conditions of the country during the recent crisis. The present prime minister is an ex-mayor and many ex-mayors are currently part of the national government.

14. See Giarda (2001, 2004 and 2009) for a detailed discussion of the new Constitution and its implications for the Italian version of fiscal federalism. See also Bordignon (2005) and Ambrosanio et al. (2010) for further discussions of the new Constitution's financial implications.

15. The new Constitution also included a provision for 'asymmetric federalism', a detailed procedure according to which a single region could ask the national parliament to obtain exclusive competence on some policies whose competence was initially shared. However, this clause was never activated. It is hard to understand why Italian constitutional lawmakers never seriously considered the possibility of a two-speed federalism in a country so divided, not only on economic grounds, but also in terms of administrative ability of local and regional governments. A sort of two-speed federalism has been de facto introduced on public health care, as most of the Center–South regions have presently lost their full autonomy and are under control of central government officials (because they were not able to respect the 'Patto per la Salute' mentioned earlier, accumulating deficits that have been partially covered by the central government).

16. An important exception is the pay-as-you-go public pension system that remained under the control of the central legislator. Pension payments in Italy represent about 30 percent of total expenditure. Regions were able, however, to legislate on the second pillar of the pension system (integrative regional funds), and some did.

17. As discussed in Section 5, partly because of these problems and partly as a consequence of the financial crisis, Title V is currently under review in the parliament. A previous attempt to change the constitution, proposed by the Center-Right Government in 2005, was rejected by a national referendum in 2006. See Bordignon (2005) for details.

18. The tightening of the Internal Stability Pacts is interpreted in these computations as a reduction in expenditure. As a matter of fact, local governments met the harsher requirements by increasing taxation as well, so that the increase in taxes has been higher and the reduction in expenditure lower than these figures would lead one to believe.

19. The reform postponed retirement ages for most people and reduced the gap between benefits under the old, and more generous, system (reformed in 1995, but that still applies to most workers) and the new one.

20. It should be added that fiscal consolidation measures were heavier for Special Statute regions than for ordinary ones (see Bordignon, 2013). Special Statute regions have traditionally enjoyed a more generous financing system than ordinary ones and the central government took the opportunity of the crisis to somewhat rebalance the situation.

21. Which abolished ICI on the dwelling of main residence of the taxpayer, except for a handful of very expensive houses.

22. Regional vat shares are computed by the central government in order to finance health expenditure. They are akin to earmarked grants. See note 7.

23. Thus, the system mimics a 'market' for the right to raise debt in order to finance public investments, except of course that in a market prices are not defined ex ante but left to adjust to clear demand and supply.

24. This schizophrenic behavior is a result of the varying majority in government during the period. The percentage of Italians owning the house in which they live is 80 percent, and the abolition of property tax on the main residence has long been a political token for Center-Right parties.
25. In 2011, as a consequence of the 2009 Framework Law, the same government passed a decree to introduce, from 2014, a new local real estate tax called IMUP (principal municipal tax). This tax was intended to replace ICI entirely, but with some differences: it could not tax the main residence; the basic tax rate was fixed at 0.76 percent, but mayors could vary it in the interval 0.46–1.06 percent. Another important difference is that while with ICI, the presumed rents on property that was unrented were still subjected to personal taxation through IRPEF, this was no longer the case with IMU. As IRPEF is progressive and second-home owners are generally richer than the average, this implied a reduction in the overall tax burden for these taxpayers. Moreover, municipalities could introduce tax allowances for particular categories of buildings (e.g., whether they were rented or not). Nonetheless, this reform never took place.
26. In this case, the basic tax rate was fixed at 0.4 percent and mayors could vary it in the interval 0.2–0.6 percent (for other buildings, the 0.76 percent tax rate still applies). A fiscal deduction of 200 euros on the main residence tax was also introduced (plus an additional 50 euros for any cohabiting child younger than 26 years old).
27. See Ambrosanio and Balduzzi (2011).
28. All computations were carried forward by Sose, a Treasury fully owned private firm specializing in empirical analysis.
29. In principle, the process should be repeated every three years.
30. That is, the Internal Stability Pact imposes on each municipality in year $t-1$ in preparing the budget for year t an improvement on the mixed budget balance in some percentage of the average expenditure registered over a period of three years, two years ahead, from $t-2$ to $t-5$. The time distance is due to data availability.
31. Municipalities were divided into four classes considering financial autonomy, current balance, and revenue-collecting ability. The best local authorities then obtained the status of 'virtuous', gaining a 'discount' on the year's target. This discount had to be financed by non-virtuous authorities. Almost 150 Municipalities were selected in 2012.
32. One of the main reasons why large public works in Italy take so much time and cost so much is certainly due to this excessive fragmentation. It takes a lot of time to get the agreement of all these bodies, and at the end one needs to compensate all of them for any proposal to be accepted and implemented. The other reason is the excessive delay in administrative justice, which magnifies the veto power of each of these bodies.
33. As provinces are explicitly mentioned in the Constitution, they cannot be truly abolished without changing the latter.
34. As a matter of fact, central government tried several times to enforce merging among small towns, even by providing monetary incentives, but with very little success. Since 2014, only 57 municipalities decided to merge, and this process, carried out through consultative referenda, gave birth to 24 new and bigger municipalities.
35. For instance, Milan is a relatively small city, slightly more than one million inhabitants, with approximately 600,000 people commuting each day in and out the city. But around Milan live another five million people, all somewhat related economically to the main city.
36. Thus, the Provincia di Milano became the Città Metropolitana di Milano, and similarly for all the other nine metropolitan cities.
37. The most common practice is to play around with 'active residuals', sums that the municipality has not cashed in the past but that it declares to expect to cash in the next budget (for instance, due payments for fines or tariffs) so allowing it to 'close' this budget in equilibrium. When the future arrives, the game is played again. The abnormal size of these residuals is one of the indicators used by the Corte dei Conti to indicate the presence of a financial distress.
38. Despite the law, for instance, at the beginning of 2014 the central government

transferred 400 million euros to Rome in order to avoid the almost certain bankruptcy of the city.
39. This might be too harsh. One positive effect of the new rules, and in particular the implicit treatment by the Corte dei Conti, is that it forced several municipalities to clean up their budgets, reducing many bad accounting practices (see note 39). It should also be noted that as a consequence of the European rules a reform was also passed concerning the *harmonization of accounting rules and procedures for all public entities*. The accounting reform has only so far been applied experimentally to a sample of cities, but it should be applied universally starting with 2015. One important request of the new accounting procedural is the introduction of a *consolidated account* for local authorities, including all owned private companies. This will certainly improve accountability as the Internal Stability Pact stimulated municipalities to transfer debts and workforce to private societies they owned, as the latter are not subject to fiscal rules. The central government is currently trying to force municipalities to sell or shut down many of these companies (according to some estimates, Italian municipalities own completely, or have the majority shares in, almost 14,000 private companies).
40. Bank of Italy, *Economic Bulletin*, n. 68/2013 and n. 2/2014; the Bank of Italy makes a yearly estimate of commercial debts on the basis of sample surveys of firms and supervisory reports.
41. Payments concern debts that were assessed as 'certain, liquid and collectable' at the end of 2012; a debt is certain when its existence is not challenged (i.e., it is not the subject of disputes or contested in some other way); it is liquid when its amount has been determined or can easily be determined; and it is collectable when the deadline for payment has expired.
42. The European Commission took the view that they were not problematic as they referred to past behavior. Plus, as noted in the text, by and large, these payments did not affect the deficit rule but only public debt. And the European rule on debt reduction only applies from 2015 onward.
43. This pooling of municipalities' surpluses and deficits at the regional level, exploiting the lumpy nature of investment at local level, makes sense for large regions such as Lombardia, with 10 million inhabitants and more than 1,600 municipalities. It makes far less sense for smaller regions such as Calabria or Molise.
44. It should not necessarily be a transfer. For example, the central government could just raise the regional tax share on VAT or the regional surcharge tax on IRPEF, duly reducing its own tax rates.
45. Only the three small special regions in the North have full control of the financing of their municipalities.
46. See note 33 for a discussion of why large public works in Italy are difficult to decide on and to execute.
47. Central government can invoke reasons of 'national interest' to bypass regional legislature.
48. In case of a conflict, it is however always up to the Constitutional Court to decide.
49. The new constitution enumerates all exclusive functions of central government, where many of the previous shared functions are now allocated. For example, all previous shared functions on energy, infrastructure, banking systems, labor, trade, etc. return to the exclusive competence of the national government. All other functions are in theory exclusive functions of regions, subjected to the supremacy clause. But the new art. 117 is more specific on some of the functions that remain in regions. They mostly coincide with the main ones currently attributed to regions: health care provision, vocational training, local transport, and the environment.
50. Seats will be allocated to regions according to population, but as there is a minimum number of senators for each region and the number of regional senators is limited, representation will follow population only faintly.
51. The remaining five senators are directly appointed by the President of the Republic.
52. The constitutional lawmaker would hope that the fact that regions are already involved,

through their representatives in the Senate, in the definition of the legislature concerning their (reduced) functions, should reduce ex ante the reasons for conflict with the national government, while the supremacy clause should reduce it ex post, by making it less likely that a region will appeal to the Constitutional Court (being less likely that it can now win).
53. Recall that according to art. 119, transfers can only be redistributive and without strings attached. This has meant, in applying the 2009 Framework Law, having to 'invent' a lot of *fake tax shares* to be able to provide local governments with the same specific grants they received before.

REFERENCES

Ambrosanio, M.F. and Balduzzi, P. (forthcoming), 'Patti di Stabilità Interni: efficaci, verticali, orizzontali?', Secondo Rapporto sulla Finanza Pubblica, Fondazione Rosselli.

Ambrosanio, M.F. and Balduzzi, P. (2013), 'La finanza pubblica negli anni della crisi', *Osservatorio Monetario*, **2**, 64–84.

Ambrosanio, M.F. and Balduzzi, P. (2011), 'Federalismo fiscale: a che punto siamo?', *Osservatorio Monetario*, **2**, 66–84.

Ambrosanio, M.F. and Bordignon, M. (2007a), 'Il federalismo fiscale in Italia: fatti e problemi', ASSBB, Quaderni rossi, no. 234.

Ambrosanio, M.F. and Bordignon, M. (2007b), 'Internal stability pacts: the European experience', *EEGM Papers*, P-4, pp. 1–38.

Ambrosanio, M.F., Bordignon, M. and Cerniglia, F. (2010), 'Constitutional reforms, fiscal decentralization and regional fiscal flows in Italy', in N. Bosch, M. Espasa and A. Solé-Ollé (eds), *The Political Economy of Inter-Regional Fiscal Flows, Measurement, Determinants and Effects on Country Stability*, Cheltenham, UK and Northampton, MA, USA: Edward Elgar, pp. 75–107.

Balduzzi, P. (2014), 'La nuova finanza locale', in M. Savino and L. Fragolent (eds), *Città e politiche in tempo di crisi*, Milan: Franco Angeli, pp. 247–60.

Balduzzi, P. (2015), 'La spending review nel 2012', in M.F. Ambrosanio, M. Bordignon, U. Galmarini and L. Rizzo (eds), *Finanza pubblica, decentramento e riforme costituzionali. Scritti in onore di Piero Giarda*, Milan: Vita e Pensiero.

Balduzzi, P. and Grembi, V. (2011), 'Fiscal rules and window dressing: the case of Italian municipalities', *Giornale degli Economisti e Annali di Economia*, **70** (1), 97–122.

Bank of Italy (2013), *Economic Bulletin*, no. 68.

Bank of Italy (2014), *Economic Bulletin*, no. 2.

Baldersheim, H. and Rose, L.E. (2010), *Territorial Choice: The Politics of Boundaries and Borders*, London: Palgrave Macmillan.

Bordignon, M. (2005), 'Some theses on Italian fiscal federalism', *Review of Economic Conditions in Italy*, **2**, 207–35.

Bordignon, M. (2013), 'Economic crisis and recentralization of government: the Italian experience', in N. Bosch and A. Solé-Ollé (eds), *IEB's Report on Fiscal Federalism '12*, IE, Barcelona, 62–7.

Bordignon, M., Giannini, S. and Panteghini, P. (1999), 'Corporate tax in Italy: an analysis of the 1998 reform', *FinanzArchiv: Public Finance Analysis*, **56** (3/4), 335–62.

Bordignon, M., Gamalerio, M. and Turati, G. (2013a), 'Decentralization, vertical fiscal imbalance, and political selection', CESifo Working Paper Series No. 4459, available at SSRN: http://ssrn.com/abstract=2353334.

Bordignon, M., Grembi, V. and Piazza, S. (2013b), 'Who do you blame in local finance? An analysis of municipal financing in Italy', mimeo.

Bordignon, M., Nannicini, T. and Tabellini, G. (2013c), 'Moderating Political Extremism: Single Round vs Runoff Elections under Plurality Rule', IZA DP No. 7561.

Bordignon, M. and Turati, G. (2009), 'Bailing out expectations and public health expenditure', *Journal of Health Economics*, **28** (2), 305–21.

COPAFF (Technical Commission for Fiscal Federalism, 2014), 'Condivisione tra i livelli di governo dei dati sull'entità e la ripartizione delle misure di consolidamento della finanza pubblica', First Report.

Corte dei Conti, Sezione delle Autonomie (2013), 'Relazione sulla gestione finanziaria degli enti locali, 2011–2012', Rome.

Corte dei Conti (2014), 'Audizione sul D.D.L. "Disposizioni urgenti in materia di finanza locale, nonché misure volte a garantire la funzionalità dei servizi svolti nelle istituzioni scolastiche, A.C. 2162 21 marzo 2014"', Rome.

Giarda, P. (2001), 'Fiscal federalism in the Italian constitution: the aftermath of the October 7th referendum', in *Nations, Federalism and Democracy*, Editrice Compositori, Bologna 2001, pp. 105–18.

Giarda, P. (2004), 'Decentralization and Intergovernmental fiscal relations in Italy: a review of past and recent trends', *Rivista di diritto finanziario e scienza delle finanze*, **LXIII** (4), 527–61.

Giarda, P. (2009), 'Il sistema italiano di federalismo fiscale, XXI secolo – Il mondo e la storia', *Enciclopedia Treccani*, http://www.treccani.it/enciclopedia/il-sistema-italiano-di-federalismo-fiscale_(XXI-Secolo)/.

Grembi, V., Nannicini, T. and Troiano, U. (2014), 'Policy Responses to Fiscal Restraints: a Difference-in-Discontinuities Design', IGIER Working Paper no. 397, 2011 (updated February 2014).

Iommi, S. (2014), *Un approccio più scientifico per la riforma delle città metropolitane*, http://www.lavoce.info.

IRPET (2012), *Dimensioni dei governi locali, offerta di servizi pubblici e benessere dei cittadini*, IRPET.

ISTAT (2014), *100 statistiche per capire il Paese in cui viviamo*, Rome: ISTAT.

Moretti, E. (2012), *La nuova geografia del lavoro*, Milan: Mondadori.

Petretto, A. (2012), 'Costituzionalizzazione dell'equilibrio di bilancio, stabilità e crescita economica', paper presented at the conference 'Crisi economica e trasformazione della dimensione giuridica. La costituzionalizzazione del pareggio di bilancio tra internazionalizzazione economica, processo d'integrazione europea e sovranità nazionale', Fondazione CESIFIN, Florence.

PART IV

Cities, the Olympics and Growth

10. A tale of two cities: the Olympics in Barcelona and Turin

Giorgio Brosio, Stefano Piperno and Javier Suarez Pandiello

INTRODUCTION

This chapter analyzes the impact of the organization and considerable investment associated with the Olympic Games on the finances of two of its host cities, Barcelona and Turin. Two cities represent only a small portion of the aggregate revenues and expenditures of local governments in Italy and Spain respectively. Given that there are more than 8,000 municipalities in both Italy and in Spain, neither city can claim to be representative in either country. However, both cities have been submitted to the special level of stress associated with the Olympic Games.

The Olympics pose a big challenge for the soundness of municipal finances, as they represent a highly costly and financially risky event. Although the host cities usually receive an assured level of financial support from higher levels of government, and from sponsors, which in principle should cover the entirety of the costs, they are in the end held responsible for the success of the event, something that can imply financing unexpected and unplanned expenditures. The host cities can also be tempted by the exceptionality of the event to proceed to develop projects associated with urban transformation, and hence to incur broader expenditures. In this perspective, the survival of the finances of the organizing cities can be taken as an indicator of the capacity of the local system to withstand economic/financial stresses. This can be gauged by their ability to avoid excessive deficits and bailouts.

Obviously the comparison between Barcelona and Turin has limits. The cities are different, both in importance and characteristics. In particular, they hosted different games in different times; the Summer Games in 1992 in Barcelona and the Winter Games in Turin in 2006.

To give context to the concept of reaction to and survival of the stress of the Games, this chapter makes a loose reference to the displacement effect hypothesis. Peacock and Wiseman (1961) used this concept to explain the impact of epochal events, such as wars and big economic depressions, on the long-term evolution of public expenditure. Peacock and Wiseman showed that wars produce a sudden big upward movement in the expenditure that is maintained during the war. At the end of hostilities, expenditures fall to pre-war levels – although not entirely, because citizens have become accustomed to higher levels of taxation, permitting higher expenditures. The expenditures will therefore continue to grow at the pre-war rate, but starting from a higher level. Some authors (Bird 1972; Diamond 1977; Henrekson 1990) have presented contrary evidence showing expenditures returning entirely to pre-war levels. Applied to our two case studies, the displacement theory would imply mainly that the Games are epochal events as far as cities are concerned and that they displace the taxes, expenditures and other budget variables upward. This hypothesis should apply best to Barcelona – where the Games, their preparation and their aftermath took place in a period of economic and political growth – than to Turin, which immediately after the end of the Games has been immersed in the worst economic crisis of the post-World War II period.

The chapter is structured in two parts, with a common structure and with each of them devoted to one of the two cities. Each part starts with a presentation of the governance structure adopted for the organization of the Games. This ad hoc structure is imposed by the International Olympic Committee to allow better control of the organization of the Games. The governance structure also introduces a separation between the finances of the Games and the finances of the hosting city, which allows researchers to have a better appreciation of the financial impact of the Games. A very short illustration of the local fiscal institutions impacting on the organization of the Games follows. The readers of the volume will find more detailed presentations of the Italian and Spanish local finance systems in the two separate chapters dedicated to these two countries.[1] The third sub-section presents the core of the analysis: the evolution of the main aggregates of the city budget from the preparation of the Games to their aftermath and their interpretation.

The conclusions will relate to both cities, as examples of adaptation to epochal shocks.

1. TURIN

1.1 Turin as a Games Host City

The municipality of Turin – the central city of the metropolitan area – has a population of about 900,000. This number has been stable over the last 15 years, but represents a fall from a peak of 1,200,000, reached in the early 1970s. The city thereafter lost most of its industrial economic base and has been trying hard in recent decades to find a new economic mission. Recent evolution signals a gradual transformation to an economic system dominated by tertiary services, in particular those tied to leisure and cultural activities, even though Turin continues to be the most industrialized metropolitan area in Italy.

The application submitted in 1998 to host the Winter Games was a starting point in the growth strategy substantiated in the first Strategic Plan of the Turin Municipality (Torino Internazionale, 2000). The Strategic Plan aimed to revitalize an area that had been adversely impacted by the decline of the manufacturing industry and to diversify the economy through urban regeneration. It is worth noting that Turin largely benefited from Barcelona's experience in developing a process of strategic planning, and also from the direct advice of one of the Catalan city mayor's deputies[2] (Campbell, 2012). More precisely, Turin committed itself to a concerted effort to reinforce the city's ability to produce wealth and innovation by diversifying the local economy through the promotion of the not yet adequately developed sectors of culture and tourism and reinvigorating the international image of the city – a goal which culminated in the organization of the Turin Winter Olympics.

The choice of Turin as host city confirms the trend toward holding the Games in large (or at least medium-sized) cities, a tendency that, for the Winter Games, characterized the period between 1964 and 1988 (with the sole exception of Lake Placid in 1980), interrupted by Albertville in 1992 and Lillehammer in 1994 and continued after Turin with Vancouver in 2010, but partially discontinued in 2014 with Sochi (see Table 10.1).

A natural implication of the choice of a large city[3] for the winter sports is that Turin itself hosted only the indoor events (namely, skating and hockey). This meant that other venues had to be located outside the city, thus generating high costs for transportation, road construction, communication networks, and two Olympic Villages in the mountainous areas. This required the financial involvement of other levels of government and other public agencies to support the construction of the infrastructure and of the sporting venues.

Table 10.1 Some basic figures on hosting cities and the financing of the Olympic Winter Games

	Lake Placid 1980	Sarajevo 1984	Calgary 1988	Albertville 1992	Lillehammer 1994	Nagano 1998	Salt Lake City 2002	Turin 2006	Vancouver 2010	Sochi 2014
Population of the city/county	2,700	448,000	640,000	20,000	24,000	362,000	852,000	2,214,934	2,200,000	328,000
Athletes	1,072	1,278	1,445	1,808	1,737	2,305	2,399	2,508	2,566	2,781
Revenues	97.6	277.81	626	800	525	1050	1264	1300	1840	n.a*
Costs	115.36	72.93	590	859	868	1002	1317	1333	1840	n.a*
Profit or loss	17.76	204.87	36	−59	−343	48	−54	−33	0	n.a

Notes: * Total estimated costs equal to $51 billion. They include new infrastructure and security costs. Values for operating revenues and costs in $ million.

Source: Bondonio and Campaniello (2006), IOC and Wikipedia.

1.2 Peculiarities of Turin's Governance Model

The overall task of organizing the Olympic Games can be broken down to two distinct activities: (1) the construction of the venues for the sporting events and of other infrastructure and (2) the organization itself. To cope with the two mandates, the city of Turin 2006 followed the traditional International Olympic Committee (IOC) tenets.[4] The organization and management of the events were assigned to the local Organizing Committee for the Olympic Games (*TOROC*), which had the status of a private law foundation. The construction and financing of the infrastructure was assigned to the Agenzia Torino 2006, a public body with the dual function of acting as general contractor and as the bearer of responsibility for the timely completion of the planned works.

The Olympics are now so expensive that host cities cannot afford the cost alone. This applies also to very large cities, such as London and Beijing.[5] It is essential to have outside funding, be it private or public. Turin, like most of the contemporary host cities, chose a mixed model – with public financing for investments and private financing for recurrent spending and organizational expenses. The private funding was mainly generated by sales of tickets and TV rights and sponsoring.

1.3 Funding the Investment

Most of the funding of investments made by *Agenzia Torino* – more precisely 71 percent of the total as reported in Table 10.2 – came from the Italian central government. The City of Turin contributed, according to reporting by *Agenzia*, only a sum of 70 million dollars, representing 3.5 percent of the total. The new infrastructure built by *Agenzia Torino* was directly related to the sporting events and was also located mostly in the mountainous areas outside the city.

According to an internal document,[6] the City of Turin provided a total amount of financial support of US $261 million for investment, which is larger than the $70 million reported by *Agenzia Torino*, but is also unlikely to represent the entire capital expenditure cost of the Games, as we will see below.

1.4 Funding the Organization and the Running of the Games

TOROC's initial budget presented with Turin's first bid, in June 30, 1998, had projected a surplus of US $35 million. This surplus did not materialize, however, and at the end, TOROC incurred a deficit of about the same amount as the predicted surplus: US $38 million. According to

Table 10.2 Turin Winter Olympic Games of 2006: cost and financing of infrastructure sustained by Agenzia Torino (US dollars at constant 2000 prices)

	Total	In %
Transport	1023	46.34
Housing, offices	523	23.7
Sports facilities	654	29.61
Environmental infrastructure	8	1
Total	**2007**	**100.0**
Funded by central government	*1425*	*71.0*
Regional government	*40.14*	*2*
City of Turin	*70.245*	*3.5*
Other regional and local agencies	*471.615*	*23.5*
Private funds	*120.42*	*6*

Source: Authors' calculations based on Bondonio and Campaniello (2006).

the previously mentioned internal document, the City Council provided financial support of US $84 million to TOROC to fund the organization expenses.

1.5 European and Domestic Stability Pacts

The 2006 Winter Olympic Games were awarded to Turin in 1999. This was the terminal year of a process of rebuilding municipal taxes for local autonomy, whose pillars were – and still are – the property tax (introduced in 1994) and the surcharge on personal income tax (introduced in 1998). Hence, the municipality of Turin was appropriately equipped with the main instruments – a substantial tax autonomy – which the literature suggests would allow local governments to address stiff financial challenges through access to financial markets and avoid the need for central government bailouts.

In the very same year, however, the Italian government introduced the first Domestic Stability Pact aimed at involving sub-national governments in the national effort required to comply with the European Stability and Growth Pact. The content of the Domestic Stability Pact (DSP) has changed several times during the years (see Ambrosanio et al., Chapter 9 in this volume). The first Domestic Pacts – those from 1999 to 2005 – mainly required that the municipalities reduce their operating deficits, meaning the difference between expenditure and revenue. The constraints imposed on Turin, which was engaged during those years in the preparation of the

Games, were relatively mild, in the sense that the Pacts impacted only on the difference between current expenditures and own revenues. Thus, the city maintained the possibility of financing a surge of investment expenditures, provided that it increased its own revenue and respected the borrowing rules. However, a paradoxical policy that accompanied the Domestic Pact was the freezing of the personal income tax surcharge, making it a shared tax rather than an autonomous source of revenue. This forced the municipalities to act mainly on the expenditure side to respect the balanced budget rule. Starting from 2005, and continuing for the next two years, a ceiling on expenditure, including for the first time spending on capital, replaced the former rule, making it a much tighter-binding constraint. From 2008 onwards, the deficit constraint came again into the spotlight, and with more binding impact. However, since the Domestic Stability Pact's inception in 1999, the city has infringed it only once, in 2011 (and has been duly punished).

As we will see below, in recent years the most striking effect of the stricter limitations of the DSP, together with the reduction of state and regional transfers, has been the strong reduction of investments, a pattern that is common across Italy (Ambrosanio et al., Chapter 9 in this volume).

1.6 A Closer View of the Municipal Budget

Impact on expenditure. There is no doubt that the impact of the Games has been huge. An inverted U curve emerges for total expenditure[7] that is determined entirely by the capital expenditure component, with a peak in 2004, two years in advance of the opening of the Games.

Current expenditure stays remarkably stable, with a small fall in 2004 determined by the reassignment of local transport competencies from municipalities to a newly created Metropolitan Transport Authority, entitled to receive the regional specific grant for urban transport previously paid to Turin.

The final level of capital expenditure is much lower than the initial level, where for current expenditure there is no substantial difference between the extremes (see Figure 10.1). This would imply no evidence of a displacement effect *à la* Peacock and Wiseman. The impact of the national crisis has been profound, and the country embarked on a major fiscal consolidation effort toward the end of the period that is hardly compatible with even a minimal amount of displacement effect.

Role of own revenue in keeping the budget balanced. For much of the period between the submission of the application for the Games and the most recent years, the Olympics had no discernible impact on the municipality's deficit. For most of these years, more precisely from 1999

256   *Multi-level finance and the Euro crisis*

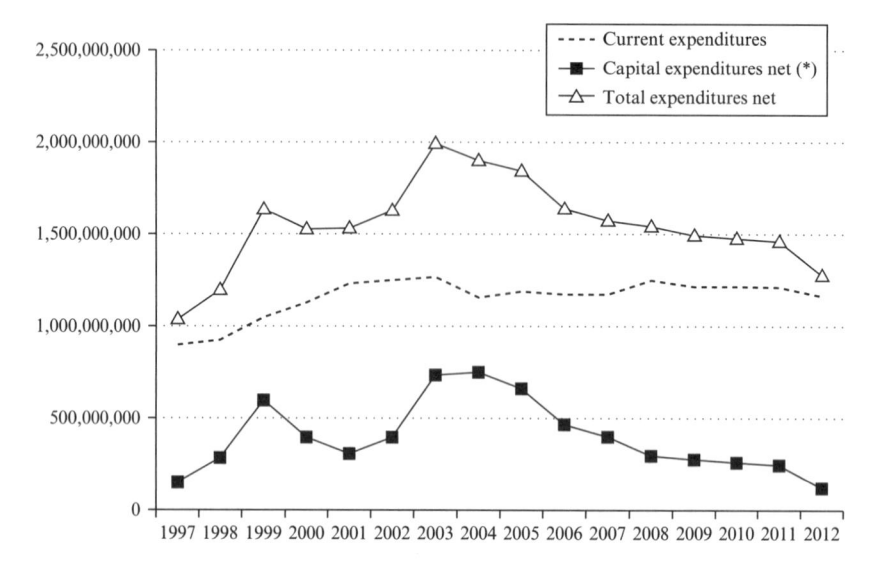

[Chart showing three lines from 1997-2012: Current expenditures (dashed), Capital expenditures net (*) (black squares), Total expenditures net (triangles). Y-axis ranges from 0 to 2,500,000,000.]

Note: (*) Excluded short- and medium-term loans.

Source: Authors' elaboration on data from the Ministry of Interior and the Municipality of Turin.

Figure 10.1   Turin: trends in current and (net) capital expenditure, 1997–2012 (euros)

to 2008, the city has been able to rely on expanding its own revenues (see Table 10.3). These revenues came especially from property tax, the surcharge on Personal Income Tax (PIT) – whose rate central government had frozen for several years – and the waste collection tax. The trend in property tax is not particularly dynamic: its collection totals remained stable until 2007 and declined from 2008 to 2011 due to the elimination, imposed by central government, of the tax from owner-occupied residences. They almost tripled from 2011 to 2012 when the tax was levied again on owner-occupied residences. Transfers compensated for the missing collections only up till 2009. From 2010 on, a distinct trend emerges: transfers are subjected to a huge drop – in 2012 they represented one-fourth of what they had been two years earlier – and are compensated for by a surge in own personal taxes, particularly in the surcharge on PIT.

Sales of assets allow financing the infrastructure for the Games. The municipality has been able to mobilize a considerable amount of resources through the sale of assets (reducing its stock of real estate property and through the partial privatization of municipal utilities). More precisely,

Table 10.3 Turin: trend in current revenues, 1997–2012 (millions of euros)

Years	Tax revenues	Of which: property tax	Grants from other levels of government	Non-tax revenues (User charges, fees, stamp duties, etc.)	Total current revenues
1997	290	247	352	137	779
1998	406	248	325	229	960
1999	412	244	420	201	1,032
2000	399	244	444	310	1,153
2001	378	245	588	281	1,246
2002	401	244	471	280	1,273
2003	415	246	404	333	1,322
2004	441	252	271	289	1,176
2005	452	250	260	301	1,186
2006	452	250	257	262	1,147
2007	491	252	362	303	1,179
2008	393	155	486	330	1,232
2009	408	152	471	328	1,232
2010	424	154	460	369	1,280
2011(*)	490	155	110	350	1,205
2012	834	445	107	267	1,260

Note: (*) In 2011 tax revenues are net of shared taxes but include VAT sharing attributed to Communes, which amounted to 52.9 million euros.

Source: As for Figure 10.1.

after taking into account the annual repayment of principal on debt, the city has been able to devote to investment expenditure a non-negligible surplus (as reported in Table 10.4).

Deferred recognition of a huge accumulation of debt. Here the good news practically ends. Debt accumulation has been deferred with reference to capital expenditure due to a technicality (Figure 10.2). More precisely, banks agreed to wait for the loans for infrastructure until the moment when construction work effectively starts and the municipality has to make the first payment. In any case, debt accumulation has been huge. In the span of seven years – from 2000 to 2007 – total debt almost doubled. The ratio of total stock of debt to current revenues also increased to close to 700 percent.

Debt accumulation took place without the infringement of the discipline of the DSP. Until 2004, the legal limit was a ceiling on interest payments on debt of 25 percent of current revenue. The ceiling has been hugely reduced – in compliance with the growing stringency of the DSP's

Table 10.4 Turin: determination of the surplus for investment, 1997–2012 (millions of euros)

Years	Current expenditures (1)	Current revenues (2)	Deficit (−)/surplus (+) (3 = 1 − 2)	Debt reimbursement (principal) (4)	Current economic balance (5 = 3 − 4)	Capital revenues (6)	Surplus for investment (7 = 5 + 6)
1997	899.3	778.9	−120.4	99.1	−219.5	53.9	−165.6
1998	920.7	959.6	38.9	141.4	−102.5	55.5	−47.0
1999	1052.6	1032.3	−20.3	85.6	−105.8	107.5	1.7
2000	1135.1	1152.9	17.8	201.0	−183.2	261.9	78.7
2001	1233.7	1245.9	12.2	67.7	−55.5	87.5	32.0
2002	1243.7	1272.5	28.8	90.8	−62.0	126.4	64.4
2003	1272.5	1322.0	49.5	126.4	−76.9	150.0	73.2
2004	1151.1	1176.3	25.2	172.4	−147.2	184.4	37.2
2005	1191.7	1186.4	−5.3	87.2	−92.5	158.5	65.9
2006	1170.8	1147.0	−23.8	114.5	−138.3	315.8	177.5
2007	1177.4	1179.1	1.8	96.5	−94.8	327.7	232.9
2008	1243.2	1232.3	−10.9	93.7	−104.7	242.6	137.9
2009	1214.4	1232.3	17.9	103.5	−85.5	196.3	110.7
2010	1216.7	1279.6	62.9	109.2	−46.4	140.4	94.0
2011	1214.9	1205.4	−9.5	106.9	−116.4	266.8	150.5
2012	1167.4	1259.9	92.6	122.0	−29.4	254.0	224.6

Source: As for Figure 10.1.

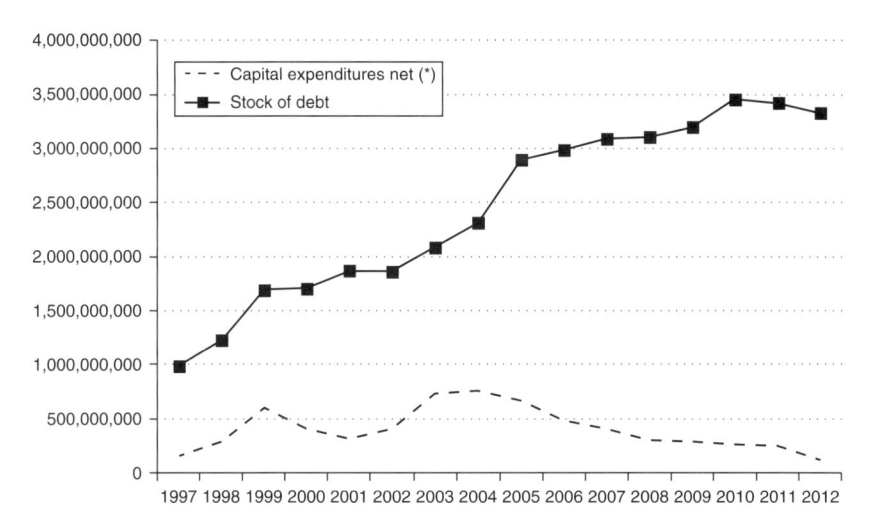

[Chart: Turin capital expenditures net and stock of debt, 1997–2012, values in euros from 0 to 4,000,000,000]

Note: Values in euros. (*) Excluded short- and medium-term loans. Stock of debt at the end of each year.

Source: As for Figure 10.1.

Figure 10.2 Turin: trends in capital expenditure and debt accumulation, 1997–2012

constraints and with the downward trend in interest rates – to 15, 12, and now to 8 percent (Table 10.5).

Only in 2012 were interest payments above the limit, amounting to 10.6 percent of current revenue against a limit of 8 percent.[8] Moreover, it must be recalled that Italian municipalities are subject to the golden rule and can borrow only to finance investment expenditure. Consequently, borrowing to finance current expenditure or to roll over pre-existing debt is banned.

A possible time bomb. The Municipality's *Accompanying Reports to the Budget* mention that the municipality signed a certain number of derivative contracts before 2008, when they were banned, to hedge against surges in interest rates. The magnitude of the resulting liabilities is not known and it is impossible to guess their possible future impact. Complete disclosure would help to dissipate fears and suspicions on the soundness of municipal finances.

Other future liabilities? The city has possibly avoided the problem of 'white elephants' draining resources for the maintenance of venues that do not yield adequate return. However, economically sustainable re-use of the athletes' and media Olympic villages built for the occasion is far from being accomplished, due to stagnation in the domestic housing market. The mountainous areas also have significant problems, having to deal

Table 10.5 Turin: debt accumulation and its parameters, 1997–2012 (millions of euros)

Year	Stock of debt	Interest on debt	Total current revenues	% of debt on current revenues	% interest on current revenues	Legal limits: % interest on current revenues
1997	986	81	779	1.27	10.40	25
1998	1,228	77	960	1.28	8.02	25
1999	1,689	70	1,032	1.64	6.80	25
2000	1,703	87	1,153	1.48	7.55	25
2001	1,870	91	1,246	1.50	7.31	25
2002	1,860	90	1,273	1.46	7.07	25
2003	2,084	87	1,322	1.58	6.57	25
2004	2,313	90	1,176	1.97	7.69	25
2005	2,897	94	1,186	2.44	7.90	12
2006	2,987	112	1,147	2.60	9.75	12
2007	3,150	138	1,179	2.67	11.69	15
2008	3,107	159	1,232	2.52	12.90	15
2009	3,200	144	1,232	2.60	12.22	15
2010	3,454	131	1,280	2.70	10.63	15
2011	3,423	139	1,205	2.84	11.29	12
2012	3,330	136	1,260	2.64	10.64	8

Source: As for Figure 10.1.

with decaying and idle infrastructure, especially, for example, the venues for bobsleigh, biathlon and ski jumping. Since 2007 a Foundation (TOP, Turin Olympic Park), composed of the three local governments (Region, Province and Commune) and the Italian Olympic Committee (CONI), is operating in order to manage and valorize all the Olympic facilities, promoting private involvement. In 2009 a concessional agreement through an international tender was set up with a private company, and management of all the Olympic facilities has been taken over by Parkolimpico, an enterprise owned by a multinational firm (70 percent) and by TOP (30 percent). The organization is now close to reaching a balanced operating budget.

2. BARCELONA

2.1 Barcelona as Olympic Summer Games Host

With 1.6 million inhabitants within its city borders, Barcelona is the second most populous city in Spain. Its metropolitan area has a population of around 4.5 million people, ranking it as the sixth most populous urban area in the European Union. It is also the largest metropolis on the Mediterranean shore. Barcelona is a world-leading tourist, economic, trade fair/exhibition, cultural and sports center. In 2012 Barcelona had a GDP of $170 billion, and was the most important urban hub in Spain, both in terms of employment and growth of GDP per capita. In 2009 the city was ranked Europe's fourth-best city for rapid improvement of business conditions. However, since then it has been in a full recession, with declining employment and GDP per capita. Only in 2014 are signs emerging of the beginning of an economic recovery.

Barcelona hosted the 1992 Summer Olympics. The application to host the 1992 Summer Games was submitted in 1981, after only two years of democratic existence for Spanish local councils. Emerging from a 40-year-long dictatorship, Spain had a level of public services similar to those of Third World countries and was emerging from a period of isolation.

Municipalities were considered to be the level of government best able to respond to the demands of their citizens. The officials, democratically elected for the first time in 1979, were trying hard to contribute to democratic renewal and also to make their cities more habitable. Unfortunately, the Spanish political transition to democracy coincided with the eruption of an economic crisis in the late 1970s, and this made the transition more difficult. As a major city and capital of a region with a concentration of industry and services, Barcelona suffered particularly in this situation. With decaying industries, between 1977 and 1984, unemployment skyrocketed, reaching 20 percent in the city, or in absolute terms about 150,000 people (Solé y Subirats, 1994).

Consequently, the choice of Barcelona as the site to host the Olympics in 1992 was seen as a unique opportunity to transform the city. All levels of government (central, regional and local) and private agents agreed to pool their efforts and resources in order to make the most of it.

2.2 Peculiarities of Barcelona's Governance Model

As in the Turin case, there were two distinct activities involved in the overall task of organizing the Games: the construction of infrastructure and the organization of the event itself. In the case of Barcelona a holding company named HOLSA (*Holding Olympic, Sociedad Anónima*) was created to coordinate the main enterprises linked to the Olympic Committee (COOB '92), which managed 40 percent of public investments.[9] The Spanish Central Government held 51 percent of the holding capital and the city of Barcelona the remaining 49 percent. Political reasons induced the Autonomous Government (*Generalitat*) to stay out of the joint venture in the initial period.

Once initiated, the magnitude of the project required close collaboration between all (public and private) institutions, and the city of Barcelona decided to take the leadership in exploiting the opportunity offered by the Games to build a city for the future.

Table 10.6 reports the revenues and investments made directly by the city or indirectly throughout HOLSA.[10]

Regarding HOLSA, loans raised by this holding reached 406.9 million euros in the autumn of 1989, with added interest of €269.7 million (making liabilities of €676.6 million, overall). Both stockholders agreed at that moment to pay €562.4 million to the holding company over ten years, with the proviso that the joint venture had to be closed in 1998. It was also agreed to cover the gap between expenditure and revenue throughout, by means of further underwriting of capital by the stockholders (€19.2 million, of which €9.4 million were underwritten by the municipality of Barcelona); the sale of the residences built for athletes, journalists and officials supervising the competitions (*Villa Olímpica*); and contributions from building companies involved in the Games.

However, the real financial needs were far bigger. Thus, central government and the municipality of Barcelona accepted responsibility for reimbursing all outstanding debt on Olympics work by 2009. Finally, all debts (banking debt and debts with constructors) were to be refunded by the public administration within 17 years. The final budget deviation from the original estimate was €231.4 million.

2.3 A Closer View of the Municipal Budget

2.3.1 Impact on expenditures

As to be expected, the city of Barcelona exploited the opportunity offered by the Games to improve public service delivery that otherwise would have taken much longer.

Until 1992 total expenditure shows a strong increase, with two-digit rates of growth, as a response by the democratic administration to the task of meeting the demands of their citizens (current expenditure) as well as the expenditures incurred in preparing the city for the Games.

Once the Games were over, the trend of growth in public expenditure slowed down. However, expenditures peaked between 2002 and 2004. Relevant events in those years were the Meeting of Heads of Government in the European Council (Barcelona, 2002) and the Universal Forum of the Cultures (Barcelona, 2004). The investments linked to this last event explain the higher capital expenditures in the preceding period.

Table 10.6 Barcelona: origin and destination of revenue for the 1992 Olympic Games

1986–1993	Total amount (millions of euros)	In %
A. ORIGIN OR FINANCING OF REVENUE (= B)	6,728.39	100.0
1. Commercial Revenue	4,017.09	59.7
Private national investment	1,230.25	18.3
Private foreign investment	651.02	9.7
Investment of state enterprises	783.82	11.6
HOLSA: self-generated revenue of the enterprises of the group	254.26	3.8
COOB '92		
• *TV Rights*	*325.53*	*4.8*
• *Contribution of sponsors of materials*	*604.62*	*9.0*
• *Lotteries*	*121.06*	*1.8*
• *Others*	*46.52*	*0.7*
2. Revenue from taxation	2,711.30	40.3
Investments in public budgets	1,956.81	29.0
• *City of Barcelona*	*136.96*	*2.0*
• *Generalitat Catalunya*	*857.80*	*12.7*
• *Central Government Spain*	*697.92*	*10.4*
• *European Union*	*48.68*	*0.7*
• *Other Public Administrations*	*215.45*	*3.2*
HOLSA: credit (contributions of the Ministry of Economy and Finance, and the City of Barcelona)	676.68	10.1
Transfer payments from the Central State to the COOB '92	77.81	1.2
B. APPLICATION OR USE OF RESOURCES	6,728.39	100.0
1. Resources applied to the organization	978.93	14.5
Programs of the COOB '92	978.93	14.5
2. Resources applied to construction projects	5,749.46	85.5
Investment of private enterprises	1,881.27	28.0
Investments of the City of Barcelona	13.70	2.0
Investments of HOLSA	930.94	13.8
Investments of the COOB '92	196.62	2.9
Investments of other public administrations (including Central Spanish Government)	2,726.94	38.8

Source: Brunet (1995).

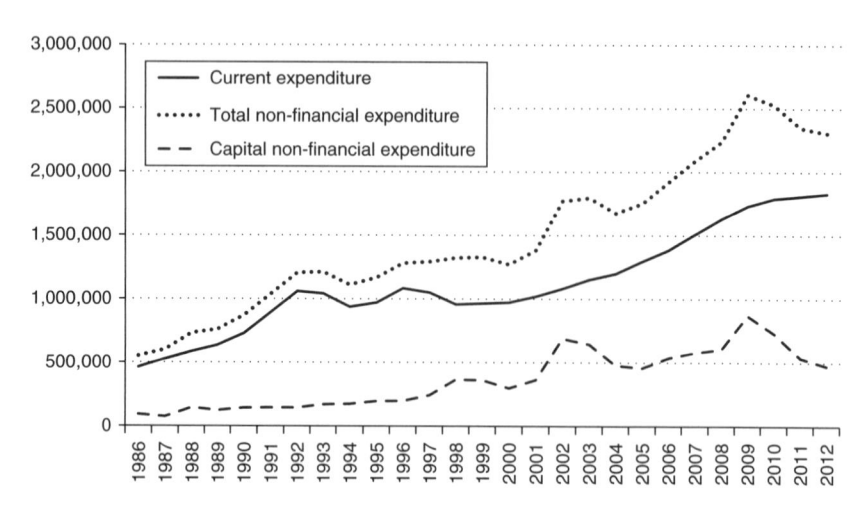

Figure 10.3   Barcelona: trends in expenditure (thousands of euros)

After 2004, Spain's rapid economic expansion was also reflected in renewed high rates of growth in current expenditure in Barcelona (8 percent on average between 2004 and 2009). However, from 2009, the economic crisis and the requirements of the European and Domestic Stability Pacts put an end to this 'era of joy' and the city radically cut spending levels, principally for investment.

Figure 10.4 shows the amount and the structure of capital expenditure incurred by the municipality over the years. It is worth noting the increasing role of capital transfers to public and private firms involved in public and private partnerships that were successfully developed for the financing of the Games.

2.3.2   The Games as an opportunity to expand local own revenues

In Spain, own-source local taxes, fees and user charges fund more than 50 percent of total municipal expenditures. From 1983, municipalities could set the rates of their own taxes freely, making the collection of business tax, vehicle tax and, especially, property tax critically dependent on local politicians' decisions. The system introduces greater visibility over the cost of public expenditures and allows an important degree of fiscal accountability for municipalities, in contrast with what happened to other levels of government (typically regional autonomous governments), which were for many years very largely funded through grants.

As expected, the Olympic Games were seen by the municipality as an extraordinary opportunity to markedly increase tax revenues without facing

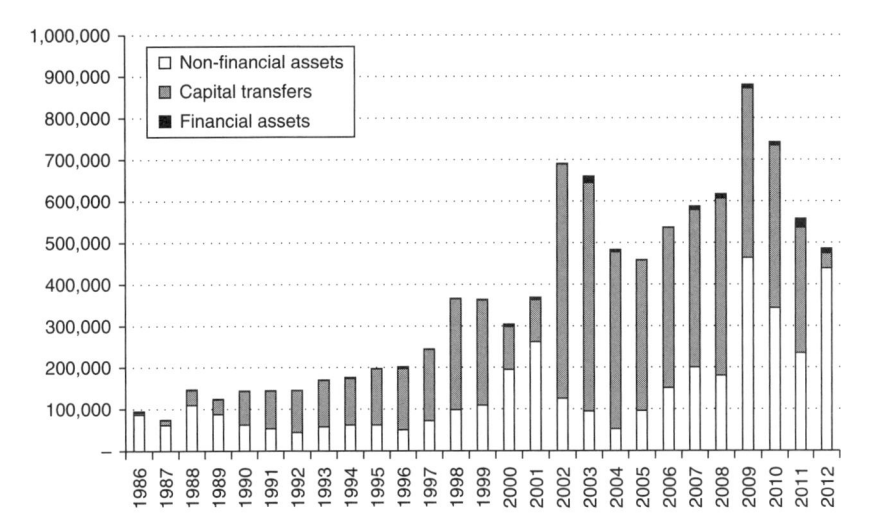

Figure 10.4   Barcelona: structure of capital expenditures, 1996–2012

the traditional cost of unpopularity for such a move. Given the collective excitement generated by Barcelona having won the bid for the Games over important competing cities, people were ready to accept a bigger tax burden as an inevitable price of progress, as emphasized by politicians.

As seen in Table 10.7, tax revenues increase dramatically until 1992.

Moreover, the formulae for the distribution of unconditional transfers have changed over time, but have always been particularly favorable for large cities, especially Madrid and Barcelona.[11] The formulae had no redistributive aim and gave huge weight to population. As a consequence, some alignment between the fiscal revenues and the unconditional grants can be observed.

However, once the Olympics were over, the rising trend of tax revenue became much more moderate, but it seems that people were unwilling to take the new tax pressure as normal, with a behavior reminiscent of Peacock and Wiseman's (1961) 'displacement effect'. The trend, similar to the above-mentioned for expenditures, may reinforce this a priori hypothesis of behavior. One has also to take into account that the Games generated a very large expansion of the tax base, particularly for the property tax. This occurred through the increased value of properties situated close to the new infrastructure, and/or located in the renovated areas of the city. Reassessment of the values of these properties did not take place on a large scale, as was also the experience of Turin, due also to the centralization of the cadaster.

Table 10.7 Barcelona: municipal revenues, 1986–2012 (thousands of euros)

Year	Fiscal Revenues	% change over the previous year	Current Grants	% change over the previous year	Capital Grants	% change over the previous year
1986	309,901		182,383		5,137	
1987	326,520	5.36	218,942	20.05	–	–
1988	375,624	15.04	258,153	17.91	–	–
1989	387,494	3.16	276,513	7.11	8,414	–
1990	444,203	14.63	291,894	5.56	4,508	(46.43)
1991	574,701	29.38	413,810	41.77	5,894	30.74
1992	705,198	22.71	535,727	29.46	7,279	23.52
1993	760,168	7.79	503,846	(5.95)	18,179	149.73
1994	775,809	2.06	429,386	(14.78)	7,878	(56.66)
1995	755,520	(2.62)	496,552	15.64	22,312	183.20
1996	800,327	5.93	599,866	20.81	14,807	(33.63)
1997	786,757	(1.70)	618,453	3.10	23,303	57.38
1998	835,084	6.14	517,476	(16.33)	30,776	32.07
1999	822,552	(1.50)	562,366	8.67	38,316	24.50
2000	725,212	(11.83)	567,002	0.82	13,523	(64.71)
2001	734,078	1.22	606,516	6.97	32,455	140.00
2002	903,466	23.07	689,231	13.64	61,079	88.20
2003	882,144	(2.36)	809,136	17.40	57,604	(5.69)
2004	905,606	2.66	854,523	5.61	14,966	(74.02)
2005	1,080,793	19.34	817,346	(4.35)	17,965	20.04
2006	1,142,795	5.74	876,043	7.18	41,438	130.66
2007	1,212,452	6.10	1,061,336	21.15	14,516	(64.97)
2008	1,195,448	(1.40)	1,084,354	2.17	24,937	71.80
2009	1,178,561	(1.41)	1,095,009	0.98	300,021	1.103.10
2010	1,256,839	6.64	947,583	(13.46)	182,465	(39.18)
2011	1,264,737	0.63	967,284	2.08	95,699	(47.55)
2012	1,284,634	1.57	1,011,324	4.55	34,786	(63.65)

Sources: Ministry of Finance and Public Administrations and Generalitat of Catalunya.

2.3.3 Impact on deficit and debt

Despite the buoyancy of revenues, the impact of the Games on the budget has been substantial. The city registered large deficits from 1986 to the eve of the Games (1992). There was also a huge surge in expenditure for interest payments. The conjunction of the end of the construction of the Olympic venues with a period of high interest rates in financial markets brought about a record payment of €227 million.

2.3.4 Consolidation of the municipal finances

The city undertook a Municipal Action Program (initially for the period between 1996 and 1999) based on the principle of 'managing with austerity'.[12] On one hand, it tried to maintain the level of investment and self-financing and thereby of saving. On the other, it undertook to streamline current spending and improve expenditure management control. Since the city had been in surplus since 1992, the result of the action program was a continued surplus in budget from 1992 until 2000 (see Table 10.8).

Regarding the control strategy concerning current expenditures, the city tried to focus on the reduction of financial expenses. Various financial management tools were used intensively – such as disintermediation, improved cash management and hedging transactions.

The diversification of funding sources, and an improved rating regarding financial solvency by international rating agencies, helped to gradually reduce spreads and alleviate financial burden. Diversification (something very rare in the Spanish municipalities) was reached by combining competitive loans from financial institutions with direct appeals to capital markets, both domestic and foreign. Consequently, with better terms on loans, Barcelona was able to align itself with the national goals of compliance with the European Plan of Stability and Growth.

In short, the aims of the city seem to have been satisfactorily achieved. This is evidenced by the record low interest bill paid on debt (€21 million) in 2010, despite the depth of the economic and financial crisis.

However, the effects of this crisis have been felt in recent years. Spain has been heavily hit by the disproportionate increases in the risk premium on public borrowing, which inevitably worsens the conditions for access to funding by all levels of government. Barcelona has not been an exception either, and hence has returned to show deficit budgets (fiscal years 2009, 2010 and 2011), and the pace of both the accumulation of debt and the financial burden of delivering its services has picked up.

In the final analysis, the legacy of the Olympics does not appear to have resulted in a permanently heavy burden on the finances of the city. The Olympics facilitated a revitalization of a declining city, with decaying industries and blighted neighborhoods. Barcelona could be an exception (along with London 2012, which looks to be a success story of urban rejuvenation), perhaps because of the particular circumstances of the time and place in which the events took place. For example, although we may only talk about it in the field of conjecture, Figure 10.5 shows a comparison between the evolution of debt in Barcelona and in Madrid. From this, it can be gauged how much weight Madrid places on the goal (so far not achieved) of hosting a future Olympics.

Table 10.8 Barcelona: key financial figures, 1996–2012 (thousands of euros and as %)

Year	Deficit (−) or Surplus (+)	Interest on Debt	Financial Charges as a % of Current Revenues (%)	Total Financial Debt Barcelona
1986	(39,408,85)	77,995	17.22	N.A.
1987	(37,400,53)	88,847	17.50	N.A.
1988	(70,220,28)	103,036	17.96	N.A.
1989	(62,437,08)	107,420	19.78	N.A.
1990	(90,152,08)	142,797	23.97	N.A.
1991	(15,544,03)	184,953	24.55	N.A.
1992	59,064,03	227,109	25.13	N.A.
1993	109,938,93	202,401	27.72	1,554,572
1994	123,848,19	187,014	46.74	1,706,959
1995	124,766,44	191,189	35.74	1,614,243
1996	147,549,84	173,194	20.23	1,564,761
1997	137,565,65	149,664	17.31	1,444,952
1998	78,366,03	133,299	16.54	1,386,868
1999	79,944,14	123,402	19.16	1,364,213
2000	43,770,50	111,098	15.75	1,239,268
2001	(13,709,09)	124,348	15.53	1,152,606
2002	(132,672,18)	77,801	6.40	1,259,474
2003	(43,125,93)	66,833	8.98	1,244,580
2004	139,554,50	59,818	14.29	1,206,618
2005	171,972,24	42,120	10.41	1,148,430
2006	146,441,25	35,352	5.98	1,061,315
2007	250,268,68	35,516	7.30	927,999
2008	97,551,19	28,522	8.03	770,102
2009	(276,015,97)	26,227	5.92	753,337
2010	(269,964,75)	21,064	5.43	1,201,543
2011	(33,769,10)	33,895	6.29	1,090,104
2012	33,082,22	32,439	5.29	1,177,836

Note: N.A.: not available.

Sources: Ministry of Finance and Public Administrations and Generalitat of Catalunya.

CONCLUSIONS

Barcelona and Turin are two large European cities with a significant impact on the economies of their countries. Hosting the Games impacted on the finances, the stock of infrastructure and service delivery in both cities.

It is well known that the final impact on a city of hosting the Olympics

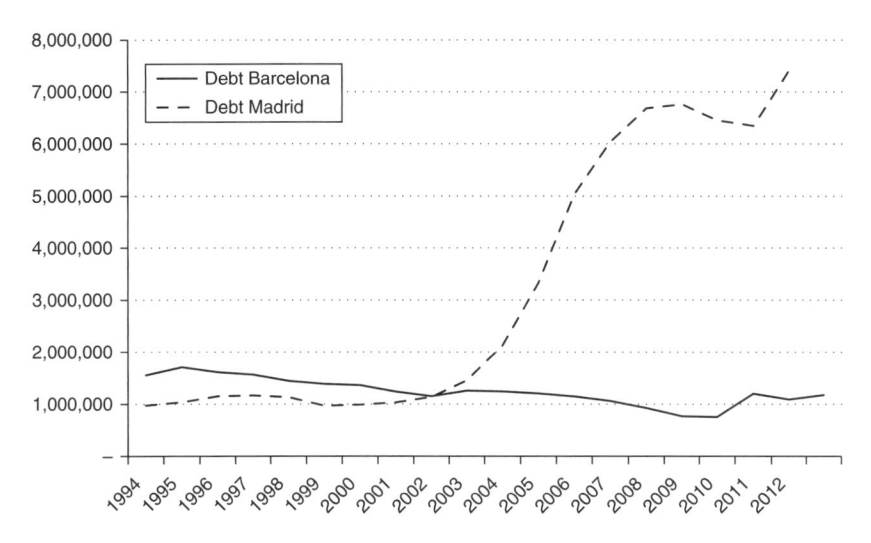

Figure 10.5 Barcelona vs Madrid: debt trends (thousands of euros)

is controversial. Often, supporters point to the positive impact on the growth of economic activities. Thus, the necessary investments would generate new employment in the building sector in the years preceding the Games (especially in the run-down and blighted areas), and the tourist sector would be greatly expanded. Also, the Olympic Games, particularly the Summer Games because of their larger size, might generate positive effects in the long run for the country hosting them, in terms of openness of markets and international visibility, and in terms of new and sustainable activities.

However, the empirical literature about sport economics is not so positive (Llobet, 2013). For instance, Miller (2002) did not find any evidence that levels of employment in the construction industry were higher during the construction of sporting venues. Porter (1999) found that there is no measurable impact on activity levels in the cities for spending associated with big events such as the Super Bowl in the United States.

Relating concretely to the Olympics, Baade et al. (2010) provide an empirical examination of the 2002 Winter Olympic Games in Salt Lake City, Utah. Their analysis shows that some sectors, such as hotels and restaurants, prospered, while other sectors, such as general merchandisers and department stores, suffered. Overall, the gains in the hospitality industry are lower than the losses experienced by other sectors in the economy. Baade and Matheson's (2002) estimations for Atlanta 1996 show that the city of Atlanta and the state of Georgia spent about 1.6 billion dollars in creating up to 25,000 permanent jobs. That is, each job cost over $64,000 to create. Furthermore, Giesecke and Madden (2007), in their study on the Sydney Olympics, conclude that 'in terms of purely measurable economic variables, the Sydney Olympics had a negative effect on New South Wales and Australia as a whole. New South Wales GDP is positively affected, but not real private and public consumption, as it is that state which covers the construction costs of the Games'.

Referring to the long-term effects, Rose and Spiegel (2011) conclude that hosting the Olympics had a positive impact on national exports. This effect is statistically robust, permanent, and large; trade is around 30 percent higher for countries that have hosted the Olympics. Interestingly, however, they also find that unsuccessful bids to host the Olympics have a similar positive impact on exports. So, they conclude that the Olympic effect on trade is attributable to the signal a country sends when bidding to host the Games, rather than the act of actually holding such mega-event.

Probably, this could be the cause of the relative success of the Barcelona Olympics in 1992. However, in both Barcelona and Turin the Olympics radically changed the cities because there was a general consensus to exploit the event in order to build the planned infrastructure that had been deferred for decades, and also to transform an event lasting only two weeks into a unique opportunity for the development of the city and region through a strategic plan approach. The transformation was possibly more profound in Barcelona than in Turin.

Of particular importance is the more diverse infrastructure required for the Winter Games, which is also spatially very dispersed because alpine disciplines need to be located in mountainous areas, whereas the Summer Games can be concentrated in urban ones, with more focused attention in rebuilding areas affected by declining activities.

Both cities are, however, considered as examples of reasonably good use of the Games.

Similar governance institutions were used in the two cities for building the infrastructure and for the organization of the Games. This facilitates comparison, although it is weakened by the different circumstances in which the Games took place and especially by the very different aftermaths of the Games.

Support from the central and the regional governments granted a flow of new investments and coordination between the various levels was effective.

To respond successfully to an extraordinary financial challenge, sub-national governments need – in addition to help from outside – wide room for maneuver in their finances, more specifically use of their own revenue bases. For Barcelona, this room came mostly from own taxes, and anchored access to private financing. For Turin, it came mostly from the sale of assets and from exploiting the possibility of asking for contributions (building and/or development fees) from developers and building firms. The central government decision to freeze the surcharge on income tax did not help.

Barcelona seems to have thrived up until the recent crisis and, in any case, the Games were a huge opportunity not only with reference to its sporting events, but particularly as an opportunity for developing the city during the transition from dictatorship to democracy. People accepted the need to pay important increases in local taxes, and central government was able to provide help to the city beyond what the requirements of inter-territorial equity would have allowed in other circumstances.

However, after the Olympics, fiscal pressure in Barcelona was not reduced, and has remained among the highest in the country, an evolution that is compatible with Peacock and Wiseman's displacement effect, while this was not the case for Turin.

With the coming of the 2008 crisis, a tough adjustment plan became necessary in Barcelona in order to consolidate municipal finances. It was marked by the strong control of current expenditure and the intensive use of innovative financial management tools. However, finally, Barcelona was able to align itself with national goals of compliance with the European Plan of Stability and Growth.

Turin is facing at the moment both the impact of the crisis and the legacy of the Games. The present stress on Turin's finances is quite high: huge debt-service liabilities, and the practical stalling of new investment. This leads part of public opinion to advance the view that a more cautious approach to the Games, avoiding the 'Games frenzy', would have been better. The city administration – the political coalition governing the city remains basically the same – retorts that the current fiscal stress is due mainly to the international and domestic crisis and the national public finance consolidation efforts that have hugely impacted sub-national finances.

It is worth noting that one of the main targets of Turin's above-mentioned strategic plan – to enable the city to become a new touristic destination, removing its label of 'old and decaying industrial city' – has been partially attained. As a matter of fact, the number of visitors in the Piedmont region increased from 3.3 million in 2006 to 4.3 million in 2012, and in the same period the city has also been able to attract a growing number of major events. A number of old and decaying industrial areas have been renovated, although many still await transformation and, above all, the development of new economic activities that could fill the empty spaces and contribute to the resurgence of growth in the city.

From a financial point of view the budget of Turin seems to have sustained 'fiscal stress', following the increase in investments and debt, in abiding (sufficiently although not completely) by the fiscal rules imposed by the Pacts.

The large tax autonomy that the municipality is presently enjoying, after the cuts in transfers, should give it more capacity to face financial emergencies, coming most of all from the likely future rise in the interest rate.

NOTES

1. See Ambrosanio et al., Chapter 9 in this volume and Lago-Peñas and Solé-Ollé, Chapter 8 in this volume.
2. Turin was the first Italian city to adopt a strategic plan.
3. The same constraint would not apply equally to the Summer Sports.
4. Most of the information on the governance model is derived from Bondonio and Campaniello (2006).
5. The cost of the London Games is estimated at more than $10 billion, while Beijing spent $44 billion. The contribution of private funding is also frequently overestimated, because private investors benefit from substantial tax breaks.
6. 'Olympic expenses of the Municipality of Torino', unpublished document by P. Lubbia, Communications Coordinator, Olympics and City Promotion, Turin City Council, personal interview, May 26, 2006, quoted by Bondonio and Campaniello.
7. The information used in this chapter derives from the so-called 'Final Budget Statement' sent to the Ministry of Interior and to the General Auditor (Corte dei Conti). It refers to budgeted revenues and expenditures. Some information, particularly that referring to the initial years, is not considered as completely reliable by the ministry. This has induced the Authors to undertake a number of checks using the *Final Budget Statement Accompanying Report* drafted by the Municipality. In case of discordance, we have relied on the information provided in the *Accompanying Reports*, understanding that the information sent to the Ministry is more timely, but less reliable. This – a Ministry knowing that information sent is not reliable, but not acting effectively to correct the problem – is a rather odd finding that is explained (not justified) by the consideration that the Ministry of Interior has no involvement and responsibility whatsoever in the municipal finances and acts mostly as their advocate.
8. However, we cannot exclude that the rule has been respected due to the reimbursement of a share of interests by the state.
9. *Anella Olímpica de Montjuíc, AOMSA, Vila Olímpica*, VOSA and Institut Municipal de Promoció Urbanística, IMPUSA.
10. In spite of having a relatively broad literature available in trying to quantify the final effects of the Olympics for the city and the whole country – see for example Moragas and Botella (1995), Clusa (1999), and Brunet (2012) – here we are only considering the relevant information for public finance in the city of Barcelona.
11. See Pedraja and Suárez Pandiello (2002) and Suárez Pandiello (2008) for details.
12. See Ayuntamiento de Barcelona (1999).

REFERENCES

Ayuntamiento de Barcelona (1999), *Barcelona: Gobierno y Gestión de la Ciudad*, Madrid: Ed. Díaz de Santos SA.

Baade, R.A., Baumann, R. and Matheson, V.A. (2010), 'Slippery slope? Assessing the economic impact of the 2002 Winter Olympic Games in Salt Lake City, Utah', *Region et Developpement*, **31**: 81–92.

Baade, R.A. and Matheson, V.A. (2002), 'Bidding for the Olympics: fool's gold?', in C. Pestana Barros, C., Ibrahimo, M. and Szymanski, S. (eds), *Transatlantic Sport: The Comparative Economics of North American and European Sports*, Cheltenham, UK and Northampton, MA, USA: Edward Elgar, pp. 127–51.

Bird, R.M. (1972), 'The displacement effect: a critical note', *Finanzarchiv*, **30**: 454–63.

Bondonio Piervincenzo and Nadia Campaniello (2006), 'Torino 2006: an organizational and economic overview', Omero Working Paper no. 1, Turin.

Brunet, F. (1995), 'An economic analysis of the Barcelona '92 Olympic Games: resources, financing and impacts', in Moragas, M. and Botella, M (eds), *The Keys to Success: The Social, Sporting, Economic and Communications Impact of Barcelona '92*, Barcelona: Servei de Publicacions de la UAB, pp. 203–37.

Brunet, F. (2012), *Análisis del impacto económico de los Juegos Olímpicos, Mosaico Olímpico. Investigación multidisciplinar y difusión de los estudios olímpicos*. CEO-UAB, 20 años, Barcelona: Ajuntament de Barcelona.

Campbell, T. (2012), *Beyond Smart Cities: How Cities Network, Learn and Innovate*, London: Routledge.

Clusa, J. (1999), 'La experiencia Olímpica de Barcelona 1986–92 y las expectativas del Forum 2004', *Ciudades*, **5**: 85–102.

Diamond, J. (1977), 'Econometric testing of the displacement effect: a reconsideration', *Finanzarchiv*, **35**: 387–404.

Giesecke, J. and Madden, J.R. (2007), 'The Sydney Olympics, seven years on: an ex-post dynamic CGE assessment', Center of Policy Studies (COPS). Monash University. General Paper, No. G-168.

Henrekson, M. (1990), 'The Peacock and Wiseman displacement effect: a reappraisal and a new test', *European Journal of Political Economy*, **6**: 245–26.

Llobet, G. (2013), 'Los dudosos beneficios de albergar unos Juegos Olímpicos', http://www.fedeablogs.net/economia/?p=29366.

Miller, P.A. (2002), 'The economic impact of sports stadium construction: the case of the construction industry in St. Louis, MO', *Journal of Urban Affairs*, **24** (2): 159–73.

Moragas, M. and Botella, M. (eds) (1995), *Las Claves del éxito: impactos sociales, deportivos, económicos y comunicativos de Barcelona '92*. Bellaterra: Centre d'Estudis Olímpics, Universitat Autònoma de Barcelona.

Peacock, A.T. and Wiseman, J. (1961), *The Growth of Public Expenditure in the United Kingdom*. Princeton, NJ: Princeton University Press.

Pedraja, F. and Suárez Pandiello, J. (2002), 'Subvenciones generales a los municipios: Valoración y propuestas de reforma', *Papeles de Economía Española*, **92**: 120–29.

Porter, P.K. (1999), 'Mega-sports events as municipal investments: a critique of impact analysis', in Fizel, J., Gustafson, E. and Hadley, L. (eds), *Sport Economics: Current Research*, Westport, CT: Praeger, pp. 61–73.

Rose, A.K. and Spiegel, M.M. (2011), 'The Olympic effect', *The Economic Journal*, **121** (553): 652–77.

Solé Tura, J. and Subirats, J. (1994), *La organización de los Juegos límpicos de Barcelona '92: un ejemplo de economía mixta o de sociedad pública-privada*

(artículo en línea). Barcelona: Centre d'Estudis Olímpics, http://ceo.uab.cat/2010/docs/wp028_spa.pdf.
Suárez Pandiello, J. (ed.) (2008), *La Financiación Local en España: Radiografía del Presente y Propuesta de Futuro*, Madrid: FEMP.
Torino Internazionale (2000), *Il Piano strategico della città*, Turin: Torino Internazionale, http://www.torinostrategica.it/pubblicazioni/primo-piano-strategico/.

PART V

Accession States

11. The impact of the global crisis on Macedonian local governments
Marjan Nikolov

1. INTRODUCTION

Although Macedonia is only an EU candidate country, and the relative lack of financial integration has shielded it from many (but not all) of the adverse effects of the economic crisis, fissures in intergovernmental fiscal relations, and lack of clarity as to who spends what, create disincentives that resemble, e.g., those in Greece. Consequently, the chapter focuses on the key elements that need to be addressed as a prelude to EU entry, in order for Macedonia to be better prepared for an environment in which the disincentives are not so easily addressed.

In Macedonia the central government still finances a large share of local expenditure through earmarked grants to the main sectors of expenditure. These grants are also disaggregated by economic categories, dictating how much has to be spent, e.g., for salaries and for acquisition of goods and services. Consequently, many functions carried out at the local level appear on the central budget, contributing to an obfuscation of responsibilities for spending. The 2008 and 2011 crises impacted severely on the Macedonian real economy that is relatively open to trade. The impact on the financial sector has been much more moderated, given the insulation of the Macedonian financial institutions. The recovery has been quick, especially after 2008. Macedonia, engaged in the accession process to the EU, which has many obligations to reform its legal and economic institutions, had no specific constraints on balancing its public sector budget apart from the general obligation to put it in order.

Without the EU constraints, the central government was able to engage in a countercyclical fiscal effort whose effectiveness was curtailed only by its inability to spend quickly on capital projects. The central government financing of local governments eased the impact of the crisis on local governments. Own taxes were, however, raised to counterbalance the decrease of central transfers for recurrent purposes, while local governments quickly spent grants for capital projects.

The Macedonian denar is pegged to the euro. There has been discussion about abandoning the peg, but this has not happened. Financial stability is considered more important than reaping temporary gains in competitiveness through a devaluation of the local currency vis-à-vis the euro.

Macedonia entered the global crisis with its public finances in better shape than those in many countries in the Euro area. At the same time, its government was free of the constraints, such as the European fiscal rules, that have impacted severely on the capacity of some economies of the Euro area to react to the crisis.

2. THE GLOBAL CRISIS IMPACT ON MACEDONIA

The Macedonian economy has not remained immune to the spillover effects from the deepest post-war world economic recession. Due to the limited capital account openness, the Macedonian economy was shielded from the first wave of the global economic turmoil.[1]

The deepening global downturn was transmitted to Macedonia through the fall in exports. Initially exports fell by 20 per cent (yoy) in November 2008 after five years of almost uninterrupted growth. Then, the fall in external demand for textiles, shoes and ores led to the slump in exports by 43 per cent in the first quarter of 2009 as illustrated in Figure 11.1.

As a result, industrial production declined by 8 per cent in the last quarter of 2008 and by 10 per cent in the first quarter of 2009. This led to a GDP decline in 2009 since industrial production accounts for 22 per cent of GDP (Figure 11.2).

As a response to the shock, the government embarked on a counter-cyclical fiscal policy. After the extraordinary high fiscal spending in the last quarter of 2008 that created a budget deficit of 3.6 per cent (Q4), the government continued with its high spending in Q1 of 2009, thus creating a fiscal deficit of 0.5 per cent (there was a surplus of 1.1 per cent in 2008).[2]

Despite expectations that the government would boost capital expenditure, it declined by 1 per cent, while current expenditure increased by 17 per cent in Q1 (yoy). Capital expenditures were expected to grow by 46 per cent in 2009 to compensate for the expected fall in private investments and lower external demand. However, weak implementation turned out to be the main obstacle for timely execution of publicly funded projects. On the other hand, current expenditures are dominated by non-discretionary spending (wages, pensions, social assistance, agricultural subsidies), which were substantially increased in 2007–08.

The credit boom of the years preceding 2008 came to a sudden stop in

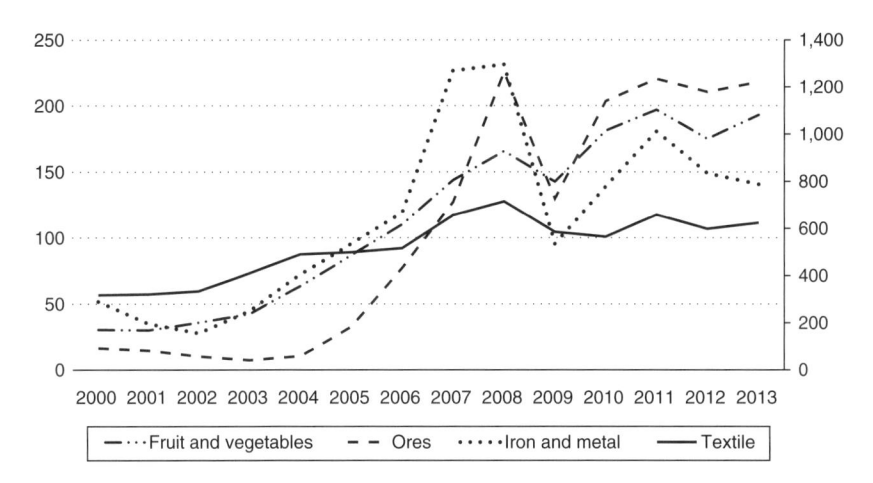

Figure 11.1 Exports of iron and metal (right axis), ores, food and textiles 2000–2013 (in $US million)

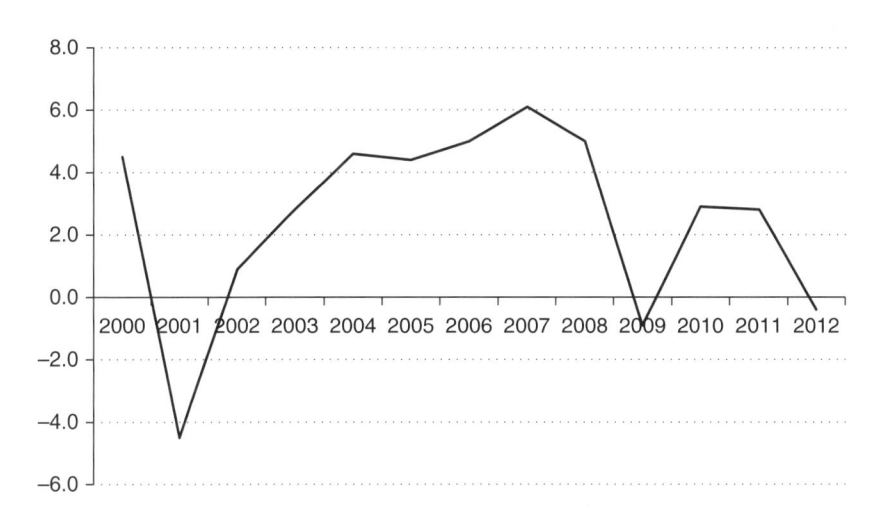

Figure 11.2 Real GDP growth in Macedonia in 2000–2012

November 2008 as a direct consequence of the escalation of the financial crisis (Figure 11.4). Nevertheless, this was more a precautionary reaction of domestic banks rather than a response to serious liquidity problems. The credit expansion in the Macedonian banking sector started in 2006, lagging behind the other Central and Eastern European economies. As a result, the loan portfolio was predominantly financed by domestic

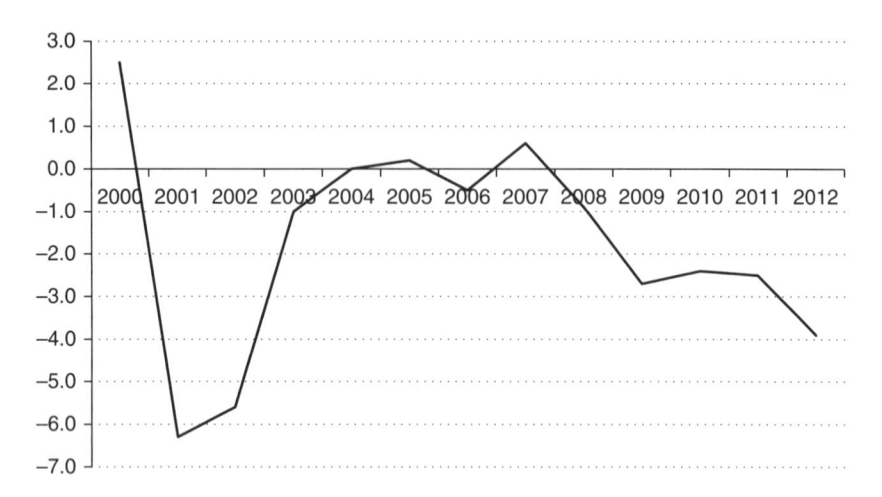

Figure 11.3 Budget balance in Macedonia as a percentage of GDP in 2000–2012

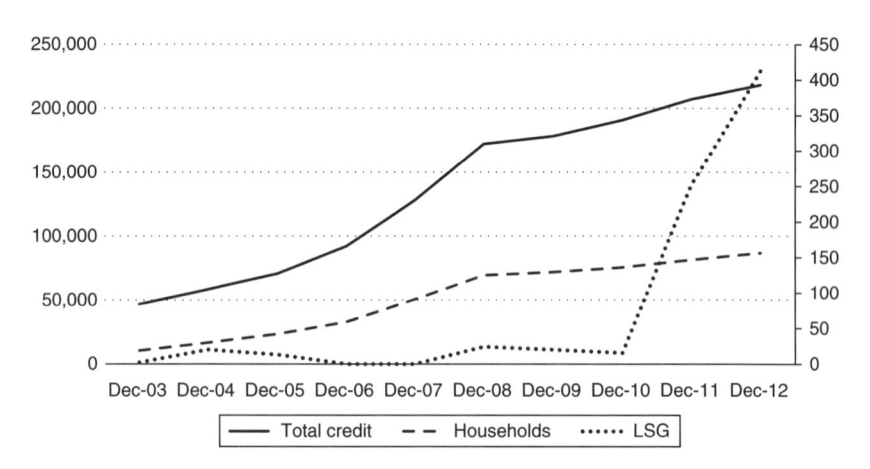

Figure 11.4 Total credit and credit to households and local government credits (right axis) in 2003–12 (in million denars (1 euro = 62 denars))

deposits, as indicated by the loans-to-deposits ratio of 93 per cent at the end of 2008.

Initial autonomous credit tightening by the banks was then strengthened by the reaction of monetary policy and later by crowding out effects of expansionary fiscal policy. Fiscal policy in the first four months of 2009

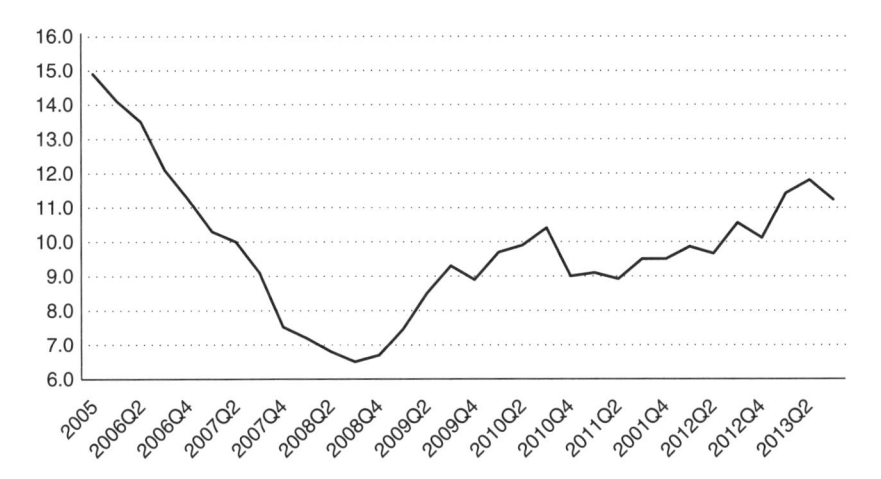

Figure 11.5   Non-performing loans in Macedonia

generated a deficit of 0.8 per cent of GDP that was financed with borrowing on the domestic market, thus competing with the private sector for already scarce funds. Eventually, at the beginning of April 2009, the National Bank of Macedonia increased its policy rate from 7 per cent to 9 per cent, indicating further tightening. As a consequence, the private sector credit growth rate (yoy) was almost halved from 40 per cent in October 2008 to 21 per cent in April 2009. The deceleration of credit growth was followed by increasing non-performing loans (NPLs) from 6.5 per cent in Q3 2008 to 11.8 per cent in Q2 2013 (Figure 11.5).

The global crisis impacted on local government in 2009 by lowering own and other revenues. However, local revenues recovered quickly because the non-elastic property tax provided stability to local revenues, while the higher local fiscal effort in 2010 and 2011 also provided more local revenues, as we will see later.

Legislative changes were aimed at widening the tax base, obliging businesses to pay property taxes. These policy changes were not connected directly to the global crisis, but the increased tax effort was. Thus, local governments proved more flexible than the central government in coping with the impact of the global crisis by using its tax potential.

At the same time, there were no efforts by the central government to compensate local government for the possible revenue shortfall due to the global crisis. Instead, VAT transfers were reduced, despite legal requirements, thus causing time-inconsistency problems for local governments.

3. LOCAL GOVERNMENT IN MACEDONIA: BACKGROUND

In Macedonia, 43.87 per cent of the population lives in 67 municipalities (out of 84) that have fewer than 40,000 inhabitants. Almost 38 per cent of the Macedonian population lives in 13 other municipalities, which vary in size between 40,000 and 80,000 inhabitants. The City of Skopje comprises 25 per cent of the Macedonian population and encompasses 10 municipalities with populations of between 22,000 and 73,000 inhabitants.

There are 43 urban and 41 rural municipalities. Urban municipalities comprise 1,625,098 inhabitants (80 per cent) and the rural municipalities comprise 397,449 inhabitants (20 per cent).

The average 2002 GDP at PPP for Macedonia was US$6,850 per capita (expert estimated data). But the variation of GDP across municipalities ranged from a minimum of US$734 per capita up to a maximum of US$53,466 per capita. The average unemployment rate in Macedonia was 38.1 per cent in 2002, with a municipal minimum of 11.0 per cent and a municipal maximum of 79.4 per cent.

In August 2001, the Ohrid Framework Agreement (OFA) was signed, ending the clashes between Macedonians and Albanians.[3] It resulted in a change of the constitution that extended the rights of the minorities in Macedonia. The OFA rejects ethnic territorial solutions, i.e., changes of boundaries. The OFA states that the multi-ethnic character of Macedonia's society must be preserved and reflected in public life. The development of local government through decentralization is essential in encouraging the participation of citizens in democratic life, and in promoting respect for the identity of communities. The speed of decentralization reforms in Macedonia greatly accelerated during 2004, as the Ministry of Local Government moved forward with a number of initiatives. In April 2005, administrative decentralization was planned in terms of transfer of institutions, assets, employees and documentation. Under that plan, the de-concentrated units of line ministries were transferred to the local level as well.

4. DEGREE OF DECENTRALIZATION

As in countries such as Greece, the recorded numbers on spending do not fully reflect responsibilities for functions. The recorded share of local government expenditure in GDP is less than 6 per cent, one of the lowest in Europe. There is, however, a large sector of local utilities and local companies owned by the local governments, which provide basic services, such as

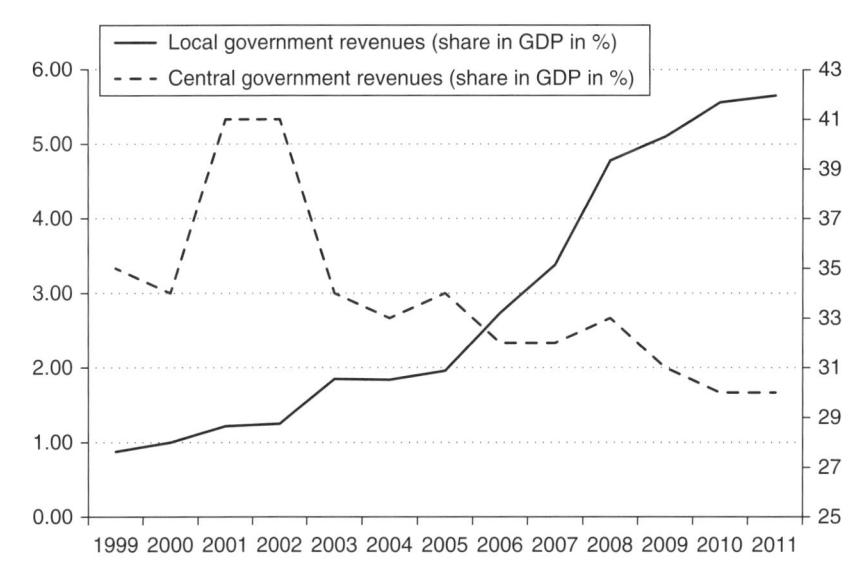

Figure 11.6 Central (right axis) and local government revenues as percentages of GDP

water and waste collection and disposal. Consolidation of this sector with municipalities would significantly increase the size of the local government.

Figure 11.6 shows the contrasting trends in terms of revenue. The importance of central government revenues declined after the introduction of the flat tax[4] and the impact of the global crisis (Table 11.1), while that of the local government increased.

Taking a longer-term view, from 1999 to 2011 total revenues of local government in Macedonia grew quite rapidly with the share of total local revenues in the GDP increasing, from a mere 0.88 percent in 1999 to 5.65 per cent in 2011. This share is still lower than in most countries that became EU members between 2004 and 2007.

5. COMPETENCIES AND THE DECENTRALIZATION PROCESS

At the same time, there were no efforts by the central government to compensate local government for the possible revenue shortfall due to the global crisis. Instead, VAT transfers were reduced, despite legal requirements, thus causing time-inconsistency problems for local governments.

Education dominates local expenditures in Macedonia, followed by

Table 11.1 Local and central government revenues and expenditures in Macedonia for the period 2008–11 (% GDP)

	Total revenues % of GDP	Total expenditures % of GDP	Total revenues % of GDP	Total expenditures % of GDP
	Local government total (own)		Central government	
2008	4.8 (2.1)	4.5 (2.0)	33.0	33.9
2009	5.1 (2.0)	5.1 (2.1)	31.3	33.9
2010	5.6 (2.4)	5.4 (2.3)	30.4	32.9
2011	5.7 (2.5)	5.6 (2.5)	29.6	32.1

Source: Author's calculation based on Ministry of Finance (MoF) data.

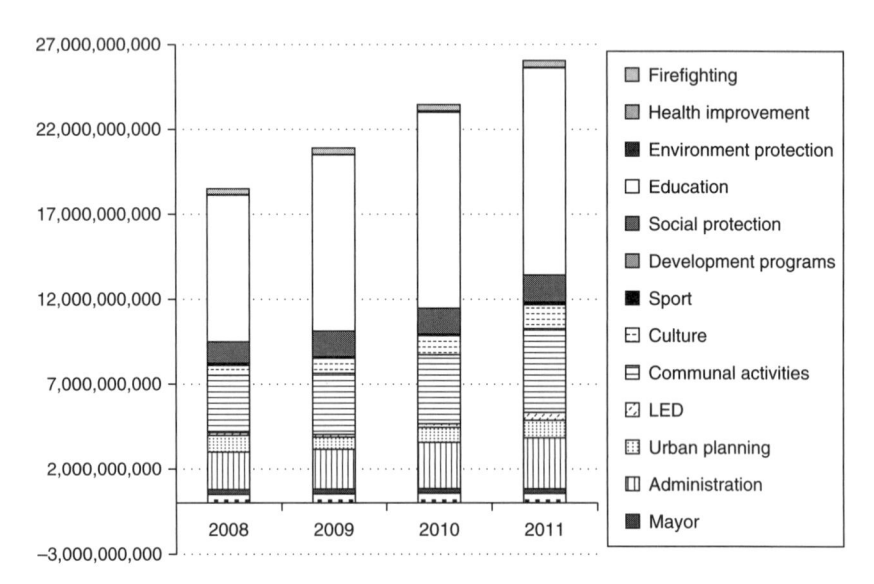

Figure 11.7 Local government expenditures by functions for the period 2008–12 (Macedonian denars)

typical urban services and administration. Figure 11.7 shows the structure of expenditures by sector from 2008 to 2011.

Since 2005, most of the competencies have been funded with earmarked grants, covering payment of salaries; reconstruction, maintenance and operation of premises for education, social services and culture; also utilities: heating, communication and transport, materials and tools, repairs, current maintenance, and contractual services. Table 11.2 illustrates the

Table 11.2 Total budget of Macedonian municipalities in 2010 by type of expenditures and source of financing in euros

Budget item/source of expenditures	Own budget	Donations	Borrowing	Self-financing activities	Transfers from central government	Total
Wages and salaries	27,490,872	2,419	0	539,779	160,906,870	188,939,941
Reserves	662,256	0	0	726	484	663,466
Goods and services	47,680,322	461,091	0	12,819,211	36,852,124	97,812,747
Interest payment	23,079	0	0	0	0	23,079
Subsidies and transfers	11,654,009	45,314	0	272,366	131,266	12,102,955
Social transfers	353,668	0	0	0	0	353,668
Capital expenditures	71,785,405	2,451,415	575,491	923,136	2,301,488	78,036,935
Principal payment	64,385	0	0	0	32,258	96,643
Total	**159,713,997**	**2,960,239**	**575,491**	**14,555,217**	**200,224,491**	**378,029,434**

Source: Ministry of Finance Republic of Macedonia, 2012.

economic type of expenditures and source of financing in euros. These assignments are far from encouraging local responsibilities even for the clearly local functions. The issue of locally owned companies to carry out local services further obfuscates responsibilities, and distorts the true extent of local operations in the economy.

6. LOCAL REVENUES

A mix of own taxes, shared taxes and transfers finance local governments. The devolution of the administration of the local property taxes (property and property transaction tax, inheritance and gift tax) and also of communal and business fees resulted in an increase of own revenue collections in the period 2008–11 from 92 million euros to 108 million euros. In the same period, the share of personal income tax (PIT) transferred to local governments increased 44 per cent from 3 million euros in 2008 to 4 million euros in 2010, but then decreased to 3.4 million euros due to the crisis. The large increase of business fees in 2009 is due to a policy change, whereby producers of energy from fossil fuels have been forced to pay compensation for pollution to local governments (Table 11.3). Note that only three local governments benefit from this fee.

In 2009 the property tax was also levied on businesses. Local governments could set tax rates and adjust the base on business properties. The resulting higher fiscal effort changed the structure of revenues, helping to create a more resilient tax base and buoyant total revenues.

7. REDUCED GRANT DEPENDENCY

In principle, the process of decentralization was based on the gradual devolution of responsibilities given the increasing capacity of local governments

Table 11.3 Structure of the local government own revenues and transfers from central budget as a share of total local revenues in Macedonia for the period 2008–11

Revenues	2008	2009	2010	2011
Own revenues	37.02	31.84	38.56	39.42
Transfers	62.96	68.15	61.41	60.57
Total	100.00	100.00	100.00	100.00

Source: Author's calculation on MoF data.

to manage affairs, and on the provision of equitable and adequate transfers from the central government aimed at fostering efficient execution of the transferred competencies.

Local governments benefit from the following shared revenues and transfers from the central government:

1. Value added tax (VAT) revenue sharing. This is unconditional and at least 50 per cent is distributed according to population. The remaining share is allocated according to criteria defined by the government in agreement with the commission responsible for monitoring the development of the financing system. Since 2009 a gradual increase of the VAT transfer took place, reaching 4.5 per cent of GDP in 2013.
2. Personal income tax (PIT) revenue sharing is unconditional and distributed on an origin basis. The total pool is calculated as 3 per cent of the PIT from salaries paid to the local governments where the employee resides and 100 per cent PIT collected from artisan activities.
3. Earmarked transfers are allocated for operational costs in the areas of education, culture and social policy. The ministries and agencies concerned monitor the use of these earmarked funds. Earmarked transfers will be phased out once all local governments enter the second phase of decentralization.
4. Capital transfers are distributed in accordance with programs specified by the government.
5. Block transfers are earmarked and also include funding for wages and salaries. The concerned ministries and agencies are responsible for defining the methodology and criteria to be used in this transfer formula. For example, the Ministry of Education defines the criteria for distribution for primary and secondary education.

Table 11.4 illustrates the grant dependency on central government. Own revenues as a share of total local government revenues dropped in 2009 compared to 2008, but since then have been increasing as a share in total revenues. Overall transfers from the central budget to local governments have declined since 2009 from 68 per cent to almost 61 per cent of total local government revenues due to higher own-source revenues since 2009.

There is also some obfuscation, particularly for the VAT, concerning the total amount of shared revenue to be disbursed. The VAT share seems to follow the legally prescribed amounts for the period 2008–10, but not for the year 2011. In 2011 the VAT share should have been 22 million euros but instead 18.8 million euros were distributed, in contravention of the law. No

Table 11.4 Stability of revenues at local government level in Macedonia for the period 2008–11 in euros

	2008	2009	2010	2011
PIT share	2,905,527	3,072,684	4,173,211	3,487,972
Own revenues	113,057,465	102,586,740	141,295,083	152,417,617
VAT share (actual)	15,951,613	18,616,910	19,288,097	18,776,882
PIT + Own + VAT	131,914,605	124,276,334	164,756,391	174,682,470
Proper share of VAT*	15,949,355	17,503,065	19,288,419	22,494,806

Note: * In 2009 there are amendments to the law on financing local government gradually increasing the VAT transfer share: 3.4 per cent of GDP in 2010; 3.7 per cent of GDP in 2011; 4 per cent of GDP in 2012 and 4.5 per cent of GDP in 2013.

Source: Author's calculation on MoF data.

explanation has been provided for this, either by the Ministry of Finance or by the Association of Local Governments. The lack of transparent fiscal operations explanation comes as no surprise because, in general, the fiscal transparency in Macedonia is declining, as measured by the international budget partnership's open budget survey.[5]

8. INEQUALITY AMONG LOCAL GOVERNMENTS

Inequality pervades the local government sector. In 2008 (Table 11.5) the richest 20 per cent of local government units in Macedonia had own revenues 23.7 times higher than the poorest 20 per cent. The richest 17 local governments also generate more than 50 per cent of the total from own revenues. In comparison, the poorest 17 local governments generate only 9–12 per cent of the total from own revenues. The global crisis led to an increase in inequality among local governments in Macedonia, despite the implicit assumption for equalization of the existing VAT unconditional grant scheme. An effective equalization mechanism is absent.

9. CAPITAL EXPENDITURES BY LOCAL GOVERNMENTS

The central government capital expenditure in 2009 decreased as a result of the global crisis, but has increased since then, reaching 3.8 per cent of GDP in 2011 (Table 11.6). In the same period, the local government capital expenditure increased continuously (from 0.95 per cent of GDP in 2008 to

Table 11.5   Inequality of own revenues across local governments in Macedonia for the period 2008–11

	2008	2009	2010	2011
Share of top 20% to the bottom 20%	23.7	19.2	21.1	24.2
Share of top 20% in total own revenues	52.6	50.9	50.9	53.2
Share of bottom 50%	8.9	11.6	10.2	9.0

Source: Author's calculation on MoF data.

Table 11.6   Central and local government capital expenditures in Macedonia for the period 2008–11

	Central government capital expenditures		Local government capital expenditures	
	% of GDP	% of total central government expenditures	% of GDP	% of total local government expenditures
2008	4.9	14.3	0.95	21.17
2009	3.3	9.6	0.99	19.54
2010	3.5	10.7	1.17	20.65
2011	3.8	11.9	1.55	24.62

Source: Author's calculation on MoF data.

1.55 per cent of GDP in 2011). At the same time, the share of local government capital expenditure in total local government expenditure declined until 2009, recovered thereafter and reached almost 25 per cent of the total local government expenditures in 2011.

Involvement by international agencies and the central government was significant in the reconstruction of local roads and streets, as well as the construction of new kindergartens and schools. The local governments' involvement in infrastructure provision is minimal.

10.   FINANCIAL MANAGEMENT AMONG LEVELS OF GOVERNMENT

The local government financial management system was designed along with the new wave of decentralization in Macedonia that began in 2005, and there have been no policy changes in it as a result of the global crisis. Anyway, the structure of the local government financial management in Macedonia enabled local governments to overcome the impact of the global crisis by greater reliance on an expanded property tax.

10.1 Budgeting

The law on financing local government operating since 2005 separated capital and recurrent budgets. It requires that the budget should be balanced, on a cash basis. This provides plenty of scope for game-play with liabilities, including the operations of locally owned companies.

10.2 Accounting

Local governments use cash accounting for its simplicity, but with all its limitations, such as not adequately recording liabilities, future services, and arrears – recognition of services and goods received which are not yet paid. Actually, there is neither a recent study nor data available on arrears and/or contingent liabilities either at the central or the local government level in Macedonia. Consequently, the story on Macedonia having handled the crisis effectively may be somewhat biased.

As a consequence of the crisis, increasing challenges may arise from new arrears by local governments and from increasing subsidies to communal enterprises. These will be difficult to assess, as the budget is cash based and because the communal enterprises are not consolidated with the local government finances. For example, just to gain an insight into the possible scale of the challenge, subsidies to public enterprises from local government declined in 2009 compared to 2008 by 30 per cent, but increased by 30 per cent in 2011 compared to 2008.

10.3 Treasury Management

There is a Treasury Single Account (TSA) in Macedonia, so that, in principle, the government knows the aggregate amount of resources available in the Treasury at all times. However, unless sub-national operations are clearly delineated – e.g., with correspondent accounts within the TSA, or with zero-balance arrangements, permitting unfettered local operations, the TSA can become a stranglehold on local operations (see Ahmad, Chapter 2 in this volume). As with the assignments, and the budget and accounting framework, there is considerable work to be done regarding Treasury management for full local operations in Macedonia.

10.4 Reporting

Local governments in Macedonia prepare internal financial reports on a monthly basis and provide quarterly reports to the Ministry of Finance. The Ministry has prepared guidelines for the local government on how to report, including arrears, borrowing, financial planning, etc. This is hard to achieve if the recording bases are incomplete.

10.5 Overall Assessment

Despite improvements in budget preparation and in some parts of the budget planning and reporting process, there are objective reasons (given the scale of the reforms) for concern at the sub-national level in effectively tracking spending and liabilities.

There may be a significant capacity constraint, as staff need to be trained, but also the appropriate standards need to be put in place. There are also 'ethnic' issues, as some local governments are requesting tax returns in two languages. But tackling these issues will require additional money, more staff and time for development, and can have a negative impact on the economic efficiency of public service delivery at local government level in Macedonia (Nikolov and Hrovatin, 2013).

In Macedonia, there is neither a law nor a separate regulation on insolvency, but financial instability is defined in the law on financing local governments. Financial instability in a municipality occurs if the state auditor determines that there have been major irregularities in financial undertakings. Financial instability also occurs if the municipality account has been blocked for 30 consecutive days or if there have been 45 days with interruptions occurring in a period of 60 days. Finally financial instability occurs in cases where the municipality fails to pay its debt within 90 days of its due date or if its approved loans limits are exceeded. In these circumstances, a special committee must be established to prepare a plan of action to set measures for overcoming the financial instability. So far, financial instability has not occurred, even in the event of the global crisis.

The legal framework for the rights and obligations of participants involved in a process of public procurement is set in the law on public procurement. A local government is obliged to provide all bidders with an equal and non-discriminatory position in public procurement processes, with fair competition, transparency and exposure to public scrutiny.

Table 11.7   Borrowing at local government level in Macedonia for the period 2008–11 in euros

	Short-term domestic loans		Other domestic loans	
	In euros	% of total revenues	In euros	% of total revenues
2008	0	0.00	486,259	0.15
2009	−96,774	−0.002	775,759	0.13
2010	209,677	0.05	1,676,781	0.43
2011	0	0.00	7,682,088	1.82

Source: Author's calculation on MoF data.

11. LOCAL GOVERNMENT BORROWING

Borrowing is almost non-existent, representing less than 2 per cent of local revenues. This does not include arrears (see Table 11.7).

Macedonian local government can only borrow after obtaining consent from the Ministry of Finance. Public enterprises established by the local governments can also borrow, but first a guarantee should be issued upon the decision being adopted by the local government's council. The mayor then reports to the Ministry of Finance about the guarantees issued.

There can be short-term and long-term local borrowing. Short-term non-interest bearing borrowing is one form of borrowing from the central budget to overcome liquidity problems during the fiscal year. There can be also long-term non-interest bearing borrowing from the central budget. Macedonian local governments can also issue securities (muni-bonds) but cannot mortgage property that is used for public interest.

Local governments can generate long-term borrowing to finance capital projects and investments, but also to refinance debts, to cover for guarantees issued, and in cases of natural or environmental incidents. The local government council approves long-term borrowing after a public hearing has been conducted. Local government can borrow long term. The service (principal, interest and other costs) of the long-term debt cannot be higher than 30 per cent of the total revenues of the current operational budget from the previous fiscal year. The debt due (including guarantees issued) cannot be higher than the total revenues of the current operational budget from the previous fiscal year.

12. THE EU AGENDA

It is important to note that in Macedonia, as a candidate country for EU accession, the set of rules that ensures sound public finances and coordination of fiscal policies with those of EU, as per the Stability and Growth Pact, is not binding. The only requirement Macedonia has as a candidate country for EU accession is to prepare and implement the national program for economic reforms following the Stabilization and Association Agreement that was signed in April 2001.

No significant material experiences are noted in this period from the EU IPA in Macedonia at local level except the change in budget presentation format in order to separately account for IPA funds in the capital part of the budget presentation. In terms of improved project preparation and management there are no serious developments, except for the urban planning project of the World Bank Institute. Macedonian local government in that regard should increase administrative capacity and improve networking and partnering with civil society especially. In that way the use of IPA funds can be increased.

13. CONCLUSIONS

The global crisis has impacted on local and central government in Macedonia on different economic grounds. The global crisis impacted on local government in 2009 by lowering own and other revenues. However, local revenues recovered quickly, helped by the stability of collections from the property tax and because of the higher local fiscal effort in 2010 and 2011.

In Macedonia there were no efforts made by central government to compensate local government for the revenue shortfall due to the global crisis. Instead, VAT transfers were reduced, even against the ones enacted by legislation, thus causing time-inconsistency problems for local governments.

The vulnerability of local revenues in Macedonia depended on the revenues structure. Property taxes collection proved to be stable, but there were also legislation changes aimed at widening the tax base by including business property, as well as a higher tax effort from local government during the period under observation. This policy change for widening the tax base was not connected to the global crisis, but the increased tax effort was. Another dimension within this context is that heterogeneity of local government might increase inequalities and dispersion among local governments in Macedonia, since local governments have different tax bases and/or skills to collect own sources. In this regard lessons learned from the global crisis are that levels of inequality and variation are rising among local governments in Macedonia, despite the implicit engagement towards equalization built into the existing VAT unconditional grant scheme. In a symmetric decentralization, as exists in Macedonia, where all local governments assume the same responsibilities regardless of the size and tax potential, the benefits of local autonomy go arm in arm with greater levels of inequality among them, thus the central government should consider introducing a more explicit grant scheme for horizontal equalization in that regard.

Possible problems may arise from building arrears from local government and increasing subsidies to communal enterprises. These will be difficult to assess as the budget is cash based and not accrual based and because the communal enterprises are not consolidated with local government finances.

Less debated in Macedonia is the experience related to increased efficiency, cost control, benchmarking, performance measurement, value for money and improved accountability. In that regard, local government did move towards energy efficiency projects with PPP instruments in street lighting and alteration of windows in schools and kindergartens. However, in the absence of a proper framework for recording and provisioning for liabilities, it is not clear that the problems faced elsewhere in the EU during the crisis have been avoided in Macedonia. Learning from the experiences of those EU countries in crisis will have important dividends for countries like Macedonia as they seek membership of the EU.

NOTES

1. The banking sector of Macedonia is recognized as being solid and well capitalized (the average capital adequacy ratio was 15 per cent in September 2008). The Macedonian banks are not relying on foreign credit and therefore are not exposed to the foreign financial markets. In fact, in 2008 only 2.8 per cent of the total liabilities were based on borrowings from foreign banks. The main sources of financing for Macedonian banks are household and company deposits.
2. Note that the budget deficit of 2001 is connected to the ethnic clashes from that period in Macedonia, as illustrated in Figure 11.3. This resulted in the Ohrid Framework Agreement peace treaty and the start of the new wave of decentralization.
3. The OFA is a peace treaty that brought to a halt the ethnic clashes in Macedonia. The OFA was 'written in Ohrid' and signed in Skopje on August 13, 2001, after a seven-month 'war'. The negotiators were the leaders of four political parties, two Macedonian and two Albanian, in the spirit of consensus democracy. Negotiations went on under the 'patronage' of Macedonia's president and in the presence of two 'witnesses', one from the USA and one from the EU. The witnesses held the role of 'whips' in disciplining the negotiators and they were the key actors in creating solutions. The 'procedure' was neither transparent nor democratic (Siljanovska-Davkova, 2007).
4. The main pillars of the tax system reform in Macedonia initiated in 2006 are the

elimination of the progressive personal income tax, the reduction and unification of the statutory rates for the personal income and corporate taxes, and the introduction of zero tax rate on reinvested profits. The so-called flat tax refers to personal income and corporate profits being taxed at a single rate (12 per cent in 2007 and 10 per cent in 2008 onwards).
5. See more at: http://www.mkbudget.org/docs/OBI2012-MacedoniaCS-English.pdf.

REFERENCES

Center for Economic Analyses – CEA (2006). 'The future of local public finances'. Retrieved September 8, 2014, http://www.cea.org.mk/documents/studii/CR_ANG_WEB.pdf.

EPI (2013). 'IPA: why and for what'. Retrieved September 8, 2014, http://epi.org.mk/docs/analiza_za_iskoristuvanjeto_na_sredstvata_od_ipa.pdf.

IBP (2012). 'Open budget survey'. Retrieved September 8, 2014, http://internationalbudget.org/wp-content/uploads/OBI2012-Report-English.pdf.

International Monetary Fund (2009). 'Macedonia: selected issues. Country Report No. 09/61'. Retrieved September 8 2014, 2009, http://www.imf.org/external/pubs/cat/longres.aspx?sk=22717.0.

International Monetary Fund. (2013). 'Article IV consultation and first post-program monitoring discussions. Country Report No. 13/178'. Retrieved September 8 2014, from http://www.imf.org/external/pubs/ft/scr/2013/cr13178.pdf.

Nikolov M. and Hrovatin N. (2013). *Cost Efficiency of Municipalities in Service Delivery: Does Ethnic Fragmentation Matter?* Maribor, Slovenia: Lex Localis, ISBN-13: 978-961-6842-16-7.

SchlumbergerSema (2004). 'Municipality debt assessment in Macedonia'. TA to the Ministry of Finance on Fiscal Decentralization under EAR contract.

Siljanovska-Davkova, G. (2007). 'Globalisation, democracy and constitutional engineering as mechanism for resolving ethnic conflict', paper presented at the VIIth World Congress of Constitutional Law, Athens.

PART VI

Some General Lessons

12. Clientelistic politics and multi-level finance: some implications for regional inequality and growth

Alex Mourmouras and Peter Rangazas[1]

1. INTRODUCTION

The persistence of backward regions in generally fast-growing middle- and high-income countries in Europe and elsewhere has been a longstanding policy concern during the last half-century. Regional incomes diverged, or certainly have not converged, since the 1970s (Arcalean et al., 2012; Sacchi and Salotti, 2011). Concerns over persistent regional differences in levels of economic development led to increased regional transfers over time.

The acceleration of regional economic and financial integration in the 1980s and 1990s helped raise the level of transfers to backward regions. As countries became more integrated, access to global capital markets improved dramatically, and borrowing costs came down to record lows, helping raise domestic transfers to backward regions. Countries with backward regions received additional 'structural' or 'cohesion' funding from supranational entities to help them develop poor areas as a quid pro quo for agreeing to reduce barriers to trade, investment and capital flows.

But while financial constraints were quickly relaxed in countries with backward regions, improvement in economic institutions, including those in their poor areas, came at a much slower pace. This affected the ability of recipient countries to monitor growing government spending in general and of transfers and investment to their backward regions in particular. Supranational fiscal rules notwithstanding, the combination of easier financing, weak monitoring from the supranational authorities and weak domestic institutions in the recipients led, in effect, to soft budget constraints in recipient countries.

Government budget constraints have become much harder everywhere following the 2008–09 global economic and financial crisis. This is especially the case in countries where access to capital markets has been lost and sovereigns must endure sharp, multiyear macroeconomic and fiscal adjustments. As elaborated elsewhere in this volume, the crisis helped expose previously unseen fiscal skeletons, including large-scale quasi-fiscal activities at the national and regional levels, by governments, state-owned enterprises and banks. Such off-budget spending contributed mightily to the buildup of unsustainable debts in many countries. And we have now come full circle: fiscal adjustment requires crisis-affected countries to reconsider, recalibrate and in some cases reconstitute their federal fiscal relations.

This chapter provides a political economy perspective on fiscal relations between different levels of government, focusing on the causes and consequences of clientelistic politics. Political economy approaches to the analysis of fiscal relations among different levels of governments have proved extremely useful (see, for instance, treatments by Lockwood, 2006; Shah, 2007; and Bordignon et al., 2008). Here we follow this general approach but focus on clientelistic politics, defined as the pursuit by decision makers at different levels of government of mutually beneficial political trades, focusing on the delivery of votes from local officials to politicians at the center in exchange for higher allocations of public investment for the region.

Clientelistic politics is a special case of transactions costs politics (see Dixit, 1996) and is made possible by information asymmetries and the operation of special interest groups, including in our case ones organized along regional lines. Politicians at the national and regional levels take advantage of their political power and superior information to make decisions affecting different regions to serve narrow political objectives. These political trades distort regional government spending decisions and create soft budget constraint between different levels of government, with deleterious consequences for growth and inequality.

In addition to helping politicians meet narrow but legal objectives (such as getting re-elected), clientelistic politics also features corruption, defined as the diversion of public funds (say intended for regional investment) for personal use. Tanzi (2000) has argued that institutional changes and balances are stronger at the central government level and that corruption is more prominent at the regional/local level. While this idea remains controversial, it is important, especially in light of the fiscal crisis, to understand the incentives and effects of fiscal transfers when corruption is a concern.

Our line of inquiry has a long tradition. Grossman and Helpman (1994) and Grossman et al. (1997) formalized the idea that special interest groups can exert political pressure via financial contributions to electoral campaigns that results in equilibria in which general public welfare is reduced relative to the first best optimum of public finance. Bordignon et al. (2008)

considered lobbying in models with federal fiscal structures, although they are concerned with the endogeneity of decentralization decisions.

Here we take the allocation of tax bases and instruments across national and local governments as given. We focus on the allocation of public investment across regions in the presence of clientelistic politics. Following Phillip Grossman (1994), we assume that local officials 'deliver' voters from their region to the national government in exchange for center policies that favor their region. To deliver these votes, regional officials must use their time campaigning on behalf of the central official's re-election.

We establish that clientelistic politics can lead to underfunding of investment in poor regions and potentially high returns to investment. This suggests that there may not be a trade-off between the goals of increasing equality and economic growth. However, the limitations associated with local investment disincentives and local corruption make a trade-off between equality and aggregate growth more likely.

Incentive mechanisms at the national and supranational levels can help reduce the effect of clientelistic politics and raise investment in backward regions. For example, co-financing arrangements for transfers can help reduce leakages. Other fiscal rules can be used to fortify budgetary constraints. For example, we show that relaxation of financing constraints, which enables national governments to access private market borrowing, can raise regional inequalities. A debt rule limiting borrowing by national governments may therefore help reduce regional inequalities. But fiscal rules must be incentive compatible, respecting participation and incentive constraints arising from agency problems. Analyzing fiscal rules, regional transfers and fiscal federal relations from the point of view of political-economic models grounded in information economics and the theory of second best is a promising line of analysis.

The rest of the chapter is organized as follows. Section 2 considers an illustrative model that helps to clarify the impact of corruption on the level and effectiveness of fiscal transfers to a poor region. We proceed in steps, first considering perfect information and then examining the effects of information asymmetries. The models in Section 2 are useful pedagogical devices. They generate useful insights regarding the impact of corruption on the size and effectiveness of transfers to backward regions, but the models are not easy to quantify. Section 3 analyzes a prototype quantitative macroeconomic model calibrated in the computable general equilibrium tradition. It is an initial attempt to quantify the effect of political mechanisms in generating and sustaining regional inequalities. The main insight is that regional clientelistic politics influences the effectiveness of foreign attempts to reduce regional inequality. The impact of foreign funds on a region's investment and growth is not only undermined by household preferences for consumption and by local corruption, but also by a withdrawal of central government funds that are built on clientelistic links. In addition, we examine how debt issued by the central government has important interactions with politics and with corruption, including the related issues of debt overhang and debt relief. Possible ways to blend clientelistic politics into richer settings, including the role of regional migration, debt rules and deeper institutional changes, are discussed in Section 4.

2. CORRUPTION AND REGIONAL TRANSFERS: A MODEL INSPIRED BY TANZI

To fix ideas and notation, let us follow Tanzi (2000) and consider first fiscal transfers in the presence of regional corruption.

2.1 Transfers with Corruption in the Poor Region

We consider a country with two regions – one rich, the other backward. The national government, denoted N, uses revenue from an income tax to fund investment projects in the poor region, denoted L. N is not corrupt. It cares about national income, denoted by Y_R, a proxy of general welfare outside of the poor region, which in our case coincides with the welfare of citizens in the rich region, and the income of the poor region, Y_L. Here, links between the center and the poor region are based on altruism. In Section 3, we introduce links based purely on politics. Parameter α $(1 - \alpha)$ denotes the strength of national officials for the welfare of the rich (poor) region.

Regional income depends on resource endowments and on transfers from the national budget to the region, denoted G. In the absence of corruption, a transfer from the center (G) would raise income in the poor region according to $Y_L(G) \geq 0$, $Y'_L(G) > 0$, $Y''_L(G) < 0$. However, an exogenously given fraction of the transfer is diverted for the private use of officials in L. N makes the transfer in full knowledge that L will divert for private purposes a fraction f of every dollar transferred, leading to the following payoffs for the two officials:

$$u_N = \alpha(Y_R - G) + (1 - \alpha) Y_L((1 - f)G) \qquad (12.1a)$$

$$u_L = \lambda Y_L((1 - f)G) + (1 - \lambda)(1 - f)G, \qquad (12.1b)$$

where λ denotes the local official's concern for the backward region's population.

We can calculate the equilibrium transfer once we make an assumption about the bargaining powers of the two officials. Assuming for now that N has full bargaining power, the transfer is implicitly given by

$$Y_L((1-f)G) = \frac{\alpha}{(1-\alpha)(1-f)} > 0. \qquad (12.2)$$

The transfer is higher the more the national government cares about the population of the backward region (G declines with α). The transfer is also higher the more honest local governments are: G rises with $(1-f)$, the fraction of each dollar of budgeted investment funds reaching the backward region. The transfer is higher the more it helps raise local output, which depends on the levels of complementary private factors (capital and labor) in the backward region. Note that with N possessing full bargaining power, the transfer does not depend on regional politics: the degree of L's representativeness does not affect G.

2.2 Transfers with Corruption at the Central and Local Levels

Corruption can be endemic of course. Let us consider how transfers are affected when N and L are both corrupt. Assume that N diverts fraction ρ of every dollar transferred; L diverts a fraction ϕ of every dollar received. Assume $\alpha > \rho$ and $\rho + \phi < 1$. The payoffs of the two players are now:

$$u_N = \alpha(Y_R - G) + \rho G + (1-\alpha)Y_L((1-\rho-\phi)G) \qquad (12.3a)$$

$$u_L = \lambda Y_L((1-\rho-\phi)G) + (1-\lambda)\phi G \qquad (12.3b)$$

With full bargaining power vested with the center, the transfer is now:

$$Y'_L = \frac{\alpha - \rho}{(1-\alpha)(1-\rho-\phi)} > 0. \qquad (12.4)$$

The main insight now is that corruption at the center *raises* gross transfers: An increase in ρ (while still $\alpha > \rho$) results in a higher transfer and higher private income for the two officials. Public welfare in the rich region falls with ρ and welfare in the poor region rises since some of the transfer is invested. This result provides an apt illustration of the incentives for more transfers which relaxed (soft) budget constraints provide.

Things can actually get worse. The foregoing assumed that N had a minimum level of concern toward the general public. That is, we limited kleptocratic incentives by maintaining $\alpha > \rho$. In effect the private gain to an official of a dollar diverted from public investment is less than the political support (through higher national income) she could obtain indirectly, by raising investment by a dollar. If, on the other hand, $\rho > \alpha$, then we are at a corner solution: a dollar of private income to central government officials is worth privately more than a dollar of income.

2.3 Foreign Transfers

When a country is a member of a supranational entity, such as the European Union, it benefits from transfers to its poor regions intended to reduce inequalities within the entity. Foreign transfers change the incentives of officials at the central and regional governments. Consider an unconditional foreign transfer T from a supranational entity to the central government N.

$$u_N = \alpha(Y_R + (1-\rho)T - G) + \rho(G+T) + (1-\alpha)Y_L((1-\rho-\phi)G) \tag{12.5a}$$

$$u_L = \lambda Y_L((1-\rho-\phi)G) + (1-\lambda)\phi G \tag{12.5b}$$

The transfer G is unchanged from (12.4). We conclude that unconditional, untargeted foreign transfers raise regional income inequality in the recipient country. They also raise income differentials between government officials at the national and local levels and make local officials and residents envious of national officials and residents.

Foreign transfers could be more effective if they target poor regions in recipient countries. Assume that F is Stackelberg leader and selects $T = T_N + T_L$ taking into account the efficiency of the recipient's center and local governments, (ρ, ϕ), as well as the center's reaction to the foreign transfer $(G' = dG/dT_N)$. The problem of the supra-national entity is to select transfers in order to maximize the recipient's welfare, defined as a weighted sum of welfare in the recipient's center and local jurisdiction, net of sums siphoned off by officials:

$$\alpha(Y_R + (1-\rho)T_N - G) + (1-\alpha)Y_L((1-\rho-\phi)G + (1-\phi)T_L) \tag{12.6}$$

The transfer to the center, T_N, satisfies

$$Y'_L = \frac{\alpha(1-\rho) - G'}{(1-\alpha)(1-\phi) - (1-\rho-\phi)G'} \tag{12.7}$$

If there were no reaction of N and $G' = 0$, this would lead to

$$Y'_L = \frac{\alpha}{1-\alpha}\frac{1-\rho}{1-\phi} \qquad (12.8)$$

We conclude that, as expected, F would adjust aid to N and L in proportion to their respective efficiency in utilizing resources.

2.4 Corruption, Transfers and Asymmetric Information

This section considers the effect of asymmetric information on national transfers to regions. There are two officials, N and L. N, who is altruistic, makes a transfer T to L. L governs a poor region and is selfish, diverting a fraction of the transfer to private consumption. The type of official L is unknown: with probability π, L diverts fraction ϕ_1 of the transfer T, while with the probability $1-\pi$ she diverts ϕ_2, with $\phi_1 < \phi_2$. We think of type 1 as being the relatively honest type and type 2 as the relatively corrupt type. From the perspective of N, let ϕ denote the random variable that can take the values ϕ_1 and ϕ_2.

N will select the amount of the transfer G taking into account the uncertainty about the type of the receiving official. N's payoff is

$$u_N = \alpha[Y_R - G] + (1-\alpha)E[Y_L] \qquad (12.9)$$

where

$$E[Y_L] = \pi Y_L((1-\phi_1)G) + (1-\pi)Y_L((1-\phi_2)G) \qquad (12.10)$$

The optimal transfer is given by

$$E[(1-\phi)Y'_L((1-\phi)G)] = \frac{\alpha}{1-\alpha}. \qquad (12.11)$$

Assuming that the effect of transfer G on local incomes is a power function, $Y_L(G) = A_L G^\theta$, we have $Y'_L(G) = \theta A_L G^{\theta-1} = \frac{\theta Y_L(G)}{G}$ and $Y'_L((1-\phi)G) = \theta A_L(1-\phi)^{\theta-1}G^{\theta-1} = \frac{\theta Y_L((1-\phi)G)}{(1-\phi)G}$

The FOC reduces to $\frac{\alpha}{1-\alpha} = \frac{\theta}{G}E[Y_L]$, where $E[Y_L] = \pi A_L(1-\phi_1)^\theta G^\theta + (1-\pi)A_L(1-\phi_2)^\theta G^\theta$.

The reduced form for the transfer G is seen to be

$$G^{II} = \left[\frac{1-\alpha}{\alpha}\theta A_L E[(1-\phi)^\theta]\right]^{\frac{1}{1-\theta}}. \qquad (12.12)$$

Several observations follow. Even without informational asymmetries, the ability of local officials to divert funds reduces the transfer relative to the first best of no diversion.

When there is full information, $\phi_1 = \phi_2 = \phi$, this reduces to

$$G^{FI} = \left[\frac{1-\alpha}{\alpha} \theta A_L (1-\phi)^\theta\right]^{\frac{1}{1-\theta}}. \tag{12.12'}$$

As expected, the transfer is increasing in θ, A_L, and decreasing in α and ϕ.

More importantly, incomplete information about the type of local officials reduces the center's incentive to transfer resources to the regions. To see this, compare the transfer under full information to the transfer that would prevail under incomplete information when the two outcomes, ϕ_1 and ϕ_2, represent a mean-preserving spread in ϕ. From Jensen's inequality it follows that $G^{FI} > G^{II}$. Incomplete information reduces the transfer by lowering its expected benefit.

3. CLIENTELISTIC POLITICS: A QUANTITATIVE MODEL

In the rest of this chapter we present a simple model that highlights the role of clientelistic regional politics in generating and sustaining regional inequalities. It shares some of the features from the analysis in Section 2 with two main differences. First, the preferences and behavior of all agents are made more explicit. Second, the links between the center and the poor region are based purely on a political exchange.

Like Section 2, we consider a country with a rich and a backward region. But now clientelistic politics is introduced: L enters into a political trade with N, exchanging votes from the backward region's voting population for more transfers to the backward region. L delivers these votes by using his time to campaign on behalf of N's re-election.[2]

In our model, the national government levies an income tax and uses the revenue to fund investment projects in the two regions. To illustrate the effects of clientelistic politics, we assume that the national government exhibits no altruism toward the poor region. In the absence of altruism, politics alone determines the distribution of public investment across regions. For the poor region to receive any funds from the center, L will have to deliver political support to N.

The first step in solving for the political equilibrium is to find the central official's preferred policy in the absence of political support from the poor region. One can also view this policy as the one that would prevail if the poor region had no political influence on the central government. In this sense, it can be thought of as an equilibrium that can be compared to ones where there is effective political influence from the poor region.

3.1 Equilibrium in the Absence of Regional Political Influence

Households in the rich region are identical. They care about their own current consumption and the future wages of their children when they become adults. The future wages of the children in the rich region are given by

$$w_R^* = A_R(N_R I_R)^\theta, \tag{12.13}$$

where A_R is a productivity index of exogenous region-specific factors that affect wages (e.g. parents' human capital and the production technologies used in the region), I_R are current government investment expenditures per household in productive public capital (roads, public education, public health), N_R is the number of households in the rich region, and θ is a parameter that determines return on investment. We assume that the investments are in productive public goods with no crowding. Thus, total investment creates public capital that raises each household's wages. We discuss impure public goods and publically provided private goods in our extension section.

The public capital investments can be funded locally (g_R) or from the central government (G_R), so that $I_R = g_R + G_R$. Households are in perfect agreement about their preferred local investment contributions and we model the local investment level as being chosen directly by the households.

Household preferences are given by the following utility function

$$u_R = \ln[(1-\tau)w_R - g_R] + \beta \ln w_R^* \tag{12.14}$$

where τ is the national income tax rate, w_R is the exogenous current wage of rich region households, and β is the preference weight on future wages relative to current consumption. Local households take the central government's contribution to local public capital investments as given and then choose their local contributions. This yields the local investment function

$$g_R = \frac{\beta\theta}{1+\beta\theta}(1-\tau)w_R - \frac{G_R}{1+\beta\theta}. \tag{12.15}$$

National investment in local public capital creates a decline in local investment contributions, however total investment still rises. As long as g_R is positive, national investment expenditures are equivalent to cash transfers. An increase in income will be partly consumed (this is why g_R falls) and partly invested (this why g_R falls less than one-for-one).

The funding for central government public investment comes from the national income tax,

$$\tau W \equiv \tau(N_R w_R + N_P w_P) = N_R G_R + N_P G_P, \qquad (12.16)$$

where W is aggregate income. Central officials are aligned with rich region households. They have the same preferences and current wage, and reside in the rich region. They differ from the rich households in that they have political ambitions and want to be re-elected to office. For this reason, central officials would consider altering national policy in favor of the poor region if they thought it would garner enough political support. The political support is generated by local officials that campaign on the central official's behalf in the poor region. The poor region's official will then have to deliver compensating levels of political support to move the central official away from their preferred policy.

The time the local official spends campaigning is denoted by c_P. The political gain to the central official from the campaigning of the local official in the poor region is given by $\psi n \ln(1 + c_P)$. The parameter ψ measures the effectiveness of L's campaigning and $n \equiv N_p/N_R$ is the relative population size. For now, we think of n as exogenous; endogenous regional migration is discussed later. The log form simply captures diminishing returns to campaigning and the presence of the constant '1' means that receiving campaign support from the poor region is not essential.

If ψ is zero, the poor region is of no political consequence to re-election, the central official can simply ignore all political offers from the poor region and set national policies to make the rich region happy. The central official will use all tax revenue to finance public investment in the rich region, $\tau(w_R + n w_P) = G_R$. Using (12.15), we can write

$$g_R + G_R = \frac{\beta\theta}{1 + \beta\theta}(w_R + \tau n w_P). \qquad (12.17)$$

The rich region's income is effectively their before-tax income plus a subsidy from the tax revenue collected from the poor region via the national income tax. The rich households invest the optimal share of their effective income in local public capital.

For purposes of illustration, we develop a numerical example that will be used throughout the chapter. The income or wage elasticity of public investments, θ, is generally estimated to be between 0.20 and 0.40.[3] We set θ to 0.30. We further assume that the fraction of income devoted to public investments in the rich region, which we view to be infrastructure and public health and education, is 0.15. This target gives us $\beta = 0.5882$.

With no political influence, the poor region is left on its own to finance public investment. The preferences of poor-region households take the same form as in the rich region

$$u_P = \ln[(1-\tau)w_P - g_P] + \beta \ln w_P^* \qquad (12.18)$$

where $w_P^* = A_P(N_P(1-f))I_P)^\theta$. The variable f is the fraction of investment funding in the poor region that is diverted for private use by local officials. We refer to f as the 'corruption tax'. A major concern in funding the poor region is that it may lag behind the rich region in terms of its institutional development, in particular the institutions needed to identify and check corruption (accounting and legal systems). In line with Tanzi (2000), local officials in the poor region may have a greater ability to divert outside funds from their intended purpose than do central government or rich-region officials.

With no assistance from N, local investment in the public capital of the poor region is

$$(1-f)g_P = (1-f)\frac{\beta\theta}{1+\beta\theta}(1-\tau)w_P, \qquad (12.19)$$

Investment is a smaller amount than in the rich community because of lower local income, because national policy taxes the poor region to subsidize the rich region, and because investment funds are diverted by local officials.

The return on investment may differ across regions, indicating productive inefficiency in the allocation of investment. The ratio of the return to investment across the two regions is

$$\frac{dw_R^*/dI_R}{dw_P^*/dI_P} = \frac{A_R}{A_P}\frac{(1-f)(1-\tau)w_P}{w_R + \tau n w_P}. \qquad (12.20)$$

The rich region has superior complementary inputs and technologies ($A_R > A_P$), but if the investment level in the poor region is sufficiently below that of the rich region, the rate of return on investment could be higher in the poor region.

To get a feel for the likelihood that the ratio in (12.20) is less than one, let's look at some reasonable numbers. We are considering budgets for government investment only, so we set the associated tax rate used to cover these expenses at 10 percent, $\tau = 0.10$. Higher tax rates would only further increase the subsidy to the rich region and further reduce the ratio in (12.22). We assume that there is a two-fold, before tax, wage-gap across regions with $w_P = 1$ and $w_R = 2$.[4] We arbitrarily assume equal populations in the two regions, so $n = 1$.

Finally, we need to set the corruption tax. Evidence from Tanzi and Davoodi (1997) suggests diverted cost overruns of over 50 percent on public investment projects in Italy. In developing countries corruption associated with investment spending is even worse. Reinikka and Svensson (2004) document that about 85 percent of funds allocated for public school projects were diverted for private use in Uganda. More comprehensively, Pritchett (1996, 2000) provides evidence indicating that less than half of public investment budgets are actually invested in developing countries. In our running numerical example, we assume the corruption tax is 50 percent. In this case,

$$\frac{dw_R^*/dI_R}{dw_P^*/dI_P} = \frac{A_R}{A_P} \times 0.215. \qquad (12.20')$$

So, it is only when $A_R / A_P > 4.65$ that the return on investment is higher in the rich region. Given that investment levels differ across regions to favor the rich, and that a wage gap of 2 is likely an upper bound, it is unlikely that A_R / A_P would be greater than 2. Parente and Prescott (2000), for example, view a TFP gap of 3 to be a reasonable estimate, across the richest and poorest *countries* in the world. Thus, it seems likely that the rate of return to capital investment in the poor region is higher than in the rich region. This suggests that there may not be a trade-off between equity and growth, as funds are redistributed from the rich to the poor regions.

We now develop a theory of the local official's behavior that makes corruption endogenous. The objective function of the local official takes the form

$$\ln(f(g_P + G_p + T_p)) - \varepsilon \ln(1 + c_p) + \gamma V_P. \qquad (12.21)$$

The local official values funds that are diverted from investment projects, whether the funds are from local households, the central government (G_p) or outside the country (T_p). The fraction of funds, f, that are diverted for personal use is a choice variable.

The second portion of the objective function does not enter the analysis until we consider the equilibrium where the poor region has some political influence nationally. It reflects the lost time and utility associated with campaigning for the central official's re-election. With $\psi = 0$, campaigning is not productive so $c_P = G_p = 0$ and this term vanishes.

The last term in the objective function is the satisfaction the local official receives from the utility of the local households, which includes the local officials themselves. This term captures the utility from income generated by legal means. Thus, we are assuming that the local officials do not value legal and illegal income equally; the two sources of income are not perfect substitutes because of guilt or risk associated with illegal income flows and because of possible altruism toward local households other than themselves. The utility function of local households is of the same form as that in the rich region, given by (12.18). The relative value of household utility generated from legal income is governed by the preference parameter, $\gamma \geq 0$.

The utility of the local households is related to policy variables by computing the household's value function defined as

$$V_P = \max_{g_P} \{\ln((1-\tau)w_P - g_P) + \beta \ln[A_P((1-f)(g_P + T_P))^\theta]\}. \quad (12.22)$$

The local official maximizes (12.21) subject to (12.22). The resulting optimal choices of f and total investment in the poor region is given by

$$f = \frac{1}{1 + \gamma\beta\theta} \quad (12.23a)$$

$$(1-f)(g_P + T_P) = \frac{\beta\theta}{1 + \beta\theta} \frac{\gamma\beta\theta}{1 + \gamma\beta\theta}[(1-\tau)w_P + T_P]. \quad (12.23b)$$

Investment is a fraction of the resources that are available to the local regions. The marginal rate of investment out of total resources is lower in the poor region because of the corruption tax, $f = 1/(1 + \gamma\beta\theta)$. The investment fraction is increasing in the relative weight placed on the utility of poor-region households. If γ is low, much of the funds available to the poor region will be diverted as illegal income for private consumption by the local officials and the effect on investment will be weak. In our running numerical example, we targeted a corruption tax of 50 percent. This implies that $\gamma = 5.6657$.

The investment rate in the poor region is then just half that in the rich region. Despite the possibly high returns on investment in the poor region, the portion of any aid funds that are invested is low. Surprisingly, we shall see that the marginal investment rate becomes even lower when the poor region has political influence.

3.2 Equilibrium with Regional Political Influence

Now suppose that ψ is positive, the poor region's official has the ability to influence voting and the votes are important for the re-election of the central official. We assume that the poor region's official offers policy proposals that keep the central official indifferent about moving away from their preferred policy by compensating the central official with political support. The compensating political support can be determined by equating the utility of the central official under their preferred policy, with no political support from the poor region, to the utility of the central official under any arbitrary policy chosen by the poor region's official. The required political campaigning from the poor region is

$$c_p = \left(\frac{(1-\tau)w_R + G_R^0}{(1-\tau)w_R + G_R}\right)^{\frac{1+\beta\theta}{\psi n}} - 1, \qquad (12.24)$$

where G_R^0 denotes the preferred policy choice of the central official. Policies that are proposed with smaller investments made in the rich region require increased campaigning to deliver added political support from the poor region that adequately compensates the central official. The more effective the campaigning and the greater the relative population of the poor region (ψn), the less campaigning is needed to derive the required votes.

Before calculating the political equilibrium, let's adjust the government budget constraint to allow for outside funds that are either provided as unconditional budget support to the central government (T) or are conditionally provided as funds to be delivered to the poor region for investments in local productive public goods (T_P). The central government's budget constraint becomes

$$\tau W + T(N_R + N_P) + T_p N_p = N_R G_R + N_P G_P \qquad (12.25)$$

The poor region official now selects both G_P and f to maximize (12.21) subject to (12.22), (12.24) and (12.25). The resulting political equilibrium is given by

$$f = \frac{1}{1+\gamma\beta\theta} \qquad (12.26a)$$

$$(1-\tau)w_P + G_P + T_P = \frac{1+\gamma(1+\beta\theta)}{1+\gamma(1+\beta\theta) + \frac{\varepsilon(1+\beta\theta)}{\psi n}} R_P \qquad (12.26b)$$

$$I_P \equiv (1-f)(g_P + G_P + T_P) = \frac{\beta\theta}{1+\beta\theta}\frac{\gamma\beta\theta}{1+\gamma\beta\theta}[(1-\tau)w_P + G_P + T_P]$$

$$= \frac{\beta\theta}{1+\beta\theta} \frac{\gamma\beta\theta}{1+\gamma\beta\theta} \frac{\gamma(1+\beta\theta)}{1+\gamma(1+\beta\theta) + \dfrac{\varepsilon(1+\beta\theta)}{\psi n}} R_P, \quad (12.26c)$$

where $R_P \equiv w_P + \frac{w_R}{n} + T_P + (1 + \frac{1}{n})T$ is the aggregate resources of the economy per household in the poor region. The corruption tax in (12.26a) is the same as in the no-political influence equilibrium. The total resources available to the poor region (12.26b) and the total investment in the poor region (12.26c) are functions of aggregate resources, including the unconditional and conditional outside funds.

From (12.26) we see that the targets of the outside funds do not matter. Outside funds of equal value will generate the same domestic outcome regardless of their intended use. This happens because domestic funding is linked through the central and local budgets, as a result of the endogenous political connection between the poor region and the center. Domestic funding flows will adjust so that rich households, local officials, and poor households share in the economy's total resources.

The cost of political influence ($\varepsilon / \psi n$) and the aversion of the local official toward illegal income (γ) determine the shares of resources flowing to the poor region and the portion that reaches poor households. A lower cost of political influence raises the poor region's share. As before, the share to poor households naturally increases with the aversion of the local official toward illegal income. As in the rich region, the investment share of the poor region's resources is increasing in $\beta\theta$. A greater weight placed on future generations and greater productivity of investment raise investment.

Most importantly, the endogenous transfers from the central government resources to the poor region lower the marginal investment rate relative to the no-political influence equilibrium. Even a conditional foreign transfer to the poor region is shared by the entire economy because there will be an endogenous reduction in domestic transfers to the poor region.

Continuing with our numerical example, let's look at the purely domestic political equilibrium with $G_P > 0$, $T = T_P = 0$. Under our assumptions, when there is no political influence, the poor region commands only 30 percent of the economy's resources. If we assume sufficient political influence to increase the share to 40 percent in (12.26b), then ε / ψ 9.7735. The political effort to receive funds from the central government raises the total resources available for investment but lowers the *marginal* rate of investment from within the poor region from 0.075 to 0.03.

Table 12.1 contrasts the no-political influence equilibrium to the political-influence equilibrium across several dimensions. Political influence causes resources to be redistributed toward the poor region. Despite

Table 12.1 Equilibrium comparison

	I_P	I_R	$w_R^* + w_P^*$	w_R^*/w_P^*
No political influence	0.068	0.315	3.012	2.381
Political influence	0.090	0.270	2.997	2.086

the lower marginal investment rate in the poor region, investment is higher there because of the increased resources available. As investment increases in the poor region and decreases in the rich region, the net effect on aggregate per capita wages is negative but very small. However, there is a significant reduction in future wage inequality. The trade-off between growth and equality is not severe.

3.2.1 Decentralization

Let's now think about what it means for the government to be centralized or decentralized in this setting. The extent to which the government is centralized in our model is measured by the national tax rate, τ. The higher the value of τ, the greater the national government expenditures and the lower the local government expenditures. The composition of expenditures by level of government is a common measure of the degree of government centralization. However, the equilibrium is not sensitive to the value of τ. Instead, the equilibrium is determined by aggregate resources, political influence, and altruism.

To make this point concrete, we can write net national expenditures sent to the poor region as

$$n(G_P - \tau w_P) = \frac{[1 + \gamma(1 + \beta\theta)]w_R - \frac{\varepsilon(1 + \beta\theta)}{\psi} w_P}{1 + \gamma(1 + \beta\theta) + \frac{\varepsilon(1 + \beta\theta)}{\psi}}$$

The net transfer is independent of the 'size' of the central government and is instead determined by the difference in *before-tax* wage income and the cost of providing political support to the central government. Suppose that τ falls, perhaps associated with a 'trend toward decentralization'. The fall in the national tax implies a decline in expenditures, but the net expenditure remains the same. While total national tax revenue is lower, the net transfer is constant. Thus, the central government has become more progressive. So, the central government is smaller but is more progressive and nothing changes.

This 'irrelevance result' seems inconsistent with the recent co-trends of decentralization and greater regional inequality. How does this irrelevance result hold up against the econometric evidence that attempts to estimate the conditional correlations between the decentralization and regional inequality, holding other things constant? For richer countries, the econometric estimates suggest either no relationship or a negative relationship between decentralization and regional inequality (e.g. Rodriguez-Pose and Ezcurra, 2010 and Sacchi and Salotti, 2011). It is only for lower- and middle-income countries that decentralization has a positive conditional correlation with regional inequality.

One way of explaining the positive correlation in developing countries is through migration from the poor region to the rich region. Development is typically associated with urbanization, as the economy goes through the structural transformation away from traditional agriculture and toward industry. While our model does not explicitly incorporate migration, one can see that it might play an important role. Urbanization would cause n, the relative size of the poor region, to fall. Other things being constant, this would weaken the political influence of the poor region. Weaker political influence lowers the poor region's share of aggregate resources and lowers total investment there (see (12.28c)). Lower investment in the poor region would lead to increased regional inequality. Thus, it may be weakened political power, and not decentralization per se, that is linked to the increase in regional inequality. For this reason, the correlation between decentralization and inequality in developing countries may be spurious.

3.2.2 Debt overhang I

We don't yet have government borrowing explicitly in the model (see section 3.4), but we can think about the consequence of repayment obligations from debt issued in the past for current policy. Repayment obligations would reduce the funds from outside sources net of debt service outflows. This means that T would be lower, and possibly even negative. A reduction in T causes a reduction in R_P. This reduces consumption and investment throughout the economy, but predominately consumption, especially in the poor region where the investment rate is particularly low. Debt overhang should not have a significant negative effect on investment in the poor region.

3.3 Conditional and Unconditional Supranational Transfers

From (12.26c), we see that a one unit increase in T_p and R_p gives rise to much less than a one unit increase in I_p. An increase in T_p is partly transferred to rich households, as G_p is reduced, partly 'taxed' by local corruption, and partly converted to local household consumption, as g_P is reduced. This makes one wonder whether stricter conditions could realistically be imposed that would raise the portion of outside funds that are invested. It would be relatively difficult to monitor and control the local behavior, but perhaps it may be possible to do so at the central level.

The outside donors could require that G_p remain fixed as a condition for increasing T_p. This condition would keep central officials indifferent about the inflow of funds and clearly make local officials and local households better off, so the added condition would be accepted if not welcomed. Holding G_p fixed, causes the fraction of the outside funds that are invested to increase. This can be seen explicitly by comparing the first equality in (12.28c) to the second equality. With G_p fixed, the first equality remains valid and the investment share of an increase in T_p is $\frac{\gamma(1+\beta\theta)}{1+\gamma(1+\beta\theta)}$. The second equality only holds when G_p is allowed to vary optimally. In this case the investment is only $\frac{\gamma(1+\beta\theta)}{1+\gamma(1+\beta\theta)+\frac{\varepsilon(1+\beta\theta)}{\psi n}}$. The difference is large when the poor region is politically weak and the cost of generating votes is high. In this case, the central government is able to transfer more resources to the favored rich region. In our example, the condition imposed on the central government would cause the investment rate to more than double, from 0.03 to 0.075.

The Structural Funds provided by the EU actually impose an even stronger condition. Structural Funds require a co-financing condition where the central government *increases* funding to the poor region. For a given inflow of funds to the poor region, T_p, the outside authority pays xT_p and the central government pays $(1-x)T_p$, where x is a fraction. In political equilibrium, the cost imposed on the central government must be compensated for by increased political support from the poor region. Thus, the cost of the co-financing condition is actually borne by the local official of the poor region. It is not clear if the policy will make the local official better off, and thus it is not clear if the country would be anxious to receive the outside aid under these terms.

We can examine the effect of a small increase in T_p on the welfare of the local official under the co-financing condition. The portion of the local official's value function that may vary with the introduction of the policy is

$$\ln \bar{f}(\bar{g}_P + \overline{G}_P + T_P) + \frac{\varepsilon(1+\beta\theta)}{\psi n} \ln[w_R + \tau n w_P - n(\overline{G}_P + T_P) + nxT_P] + \gamma V_P(\bar{g}_P, (1-f)(\overline{G}_P + T_P))$$

where $\bar{f}, \bar{g}_p$, and $\overline{G}_p$ are the optimal choices in the case where $T_p = 0$. Now we can increase T_p, keeping $\overline{G}_p$ constant and allowing $\bar{f}$ and $\bar{g}_p$ to optimally respond, and then compute the change on welfare. Note that a change in T_p has an impact on behavior and welfare that is equivalent to a change in $\overline{G}_p$, if $x = 0$.

Differentiating with respect to T_p, evaluating at $T_p = 0$ and using the envelope theorem (i.e., the first order conditions satisfied for $\bar{f}, \bar{g}_p$, and $\bar{G}_p$), the change in welfare is

$$x \frac{\varepsilon(1 + \beta\theta)}{\psi n} \frac{1}{(1-\tau)w_R + \bar{G}_R} > 0.$$

The change in welfare is positive, for $x > 0$, because on the margin it is less costly to compensate the central government for their portion of the co-financing than it is to compensate for a full unit of central government investment in the political equilibrium. Thus, under the co-financing condition, there exists some positive inflow of funds from outside the country that will keep the central government indifferent and make the local official better off.

From the first equality in (12.26c), we see that the co-financing condition will generate the same increase in local investment as under the weaker condition that G_p is required to remain constant. However, the outside authority is able to achieve this outcome at a lower financial cost because the recipient country's central government will absorb part of the cost (in exchange for compensating increase in political support from the poor region). Of course, this all comes at the expense of rich households, who receive less central government investment under the stronger condition.

3.4 Central Government Borrowing

In the previous section, we examined the effect of outside aid on the political equilibrium. In this section we examine the consequences of allowing the central government to borrow internationally at the interest rate r. The government can borrow as much as it would like, subject to the repayment condition that future taxes are sufficient to cover the principle and interest,

$$(1 + r)BN = \tau W^* + T^*, \qquad (12.27)$$

where B is borrowing per household, N is the total population size of the country, W^* is future aggregate wage income, and T^* is future net income transfers into the country. Future aggregate wages depend on the public investment in the two regions, $W^* = N_P A_P I_P^\theta + N_R A_R I_R^\theta$.

Borrowing expands the opportunity for government spending in the current period,

$$N_P G_P + N_R G_R = \tau\left(W + \frac{W^*}{1+r}\right) + T + \frac{T^*}{1+r}. \qquad (12.28)$$

Borrowing also gives the central government a selfish reason to invest in the poor region. There is an investment level in the poor region that maximizes net revenue available to spend on G_R. Rewriting the government budget constraint gives us

$$G_R = \Pi + \frac{1}{N_R}\left\{\tau\left(W + \frac{w^*_R}{1+r}\right) + T + \frac{T^*}{1+r}\right\}, \quad (12.29)$$

where the net revenue from the poor region is $\Pi \equiv \frac{\tau n}{1+r} A_p I_p^\theta - n G_p$.

In the absence of political influence from the poor region, the central government will now choose the positive value of G_P that maximizes Π. As before, the central government takes into account the local behavior, local investment and corruption, in choosing the revenue-maximizing value of G_P. There is a unique solution for G_P and Π that solves this problem.

Plugging the maximum Π back into (12.29) generates the implicit maximum value for G_R under borrowing, $G_R = G(\Pi)$. We have a no-political influence equilibrium as before, except that now $G_P > 0$. Using this equilibrium to establish the level of utility that the poor official must maintain in their negotiations with the center generates a campaign function of the same form as (12.24), with $G_R^0 = G(\Pi)$. Thus, as in the case with political influence, the poor region's local official has an objective function that has the same form as before

$$\ln f + \ln G_P + \frac{\varepsilon(1+\beta\theta)}{\psi n}\ln((1-\tau)w_R + G(\Pi)) \quad (12.32)$$

$$+ \gamma(1+\beta\theta)\ln((1-\tau)w_P + G_P) + \gamma\beta\theta\ln(1-f)$$

As before, the official chooses f and G_P to maximize (12.30). The choice of f is unaffected by the new features of the problem associated with borrowing. This implies that the form of the I_P function that we assumed above in the no-political influence setting remains valid. In choosing G_P there are positive effects on the local region that are completely ignored by the central official in the no-political influence equilibrium. This means that to satisfy the local official's first order condition for the choice of G_P, $d\Pi/dG_p$ must be negative. The positive benefits to the local region cause G_P to be set above its revenue maximizing level, causing G_R to fall. However, the fall in G_R is smaller than without borrowing because there is always some future revenue generated when G_P increases. We have then the following inequalities, $0 > d\Pi/dG_P$ (with borrowing) $> -n$ (without borrowing). This means that the marginal cost of choosing G_P is lower with borrowing than without it, causing the political equilibrium level of G_P to be higher.

Thus, borrowing expands investment in the poor region in both the no-political influence and the political influence equilibria.

3.4.1 Debt overhang II

For borrowing to be a possibility, it must be the case that the maximum value of W^*, $\overline{W}^*$, is sufficiently high so that $\tau \overline{W}^* + T^* > 0$. If T^* is sufficiently negative, because of outflows associated with debt repayment obligations, then borrowing is not possible and both consumption and investment in the country suffer. However, the extent to which investment in the poor region suffers depends on the fundamentals captured by the cost of political influence ($\varepsilon/\psi n$) and the aversion of the local official toward illegal income (γ). If $\varepsilon/\psi n$ is high and γ is low, then the negative impact of a borrowing constraint on investment in the poor region is small.

3.5 Summary

The model of clientelistic politics presented in this section generates some stark predictions.

- First, a backward region's share of national transfers is based on its relative political influence. The costlier it is for this region's officials to deliver votes (buy political influence) to the central government, the lower the region's share of national resources. This causes the fraction of any outside funds coming into the country, regardless of how they are earmarked, that are invested in the poor region to be low. In part, this is due to an inverse relationship between central funding and outside funding of investment in the backward region. The capture of outside funds by reduced domestic financing is only possible in the political-influence equilibrium that causes *all* resources available to the economy to be shared.
- Second, given the extent of political influence of a backward region, a smaller central government will be more progressive, giving the same net transfer to the region with a lower level of central revenues. The size of the net transfer is determined by the difference in before-tax incomes across regions and the cost of providing political support to the center only; the size of the central government is irrelevant.
- Third, tough conditions are needed to prevent central government offsets to outside investment funding targeted to the poor region. This provides a justification for the co-financing conditions associated with EU Structural Funds. In our model, co-financing conditions improve the welfare of households in the backward region,

have a neutral effect on central government officials, and lower the welfare of local officials in the poor region and households in the rich region.
- Fourth, the trade-off between equality and growth is not severe: political influence that raises investment in the backward region and reduces it in the rich region does not impose a significant cost in terms of aggregate economic growth in the country. It is possible to reduce regional income inequality significantly without hurting growth much.
- Fifth, debt relief will not provide much benefit to households in backward regions or reduce regional inequalities. Debt relief does not address the root causes of low rates of public investment in backward regions. As is the case with official international assistance, debt relief should carry tough conditions that the freed funds to the central government are used in the poor regions with no central government funding offsets. Of course, it remains an open question whether tough conditions associated with aid and debt relief can be effectively enforced.

4. EXTENSIONS

In this section we elaborate on the implications of this analysis and discuss possible extensions. Our intent is to indicate possible directions of future research integrating regional political considerations into a more complete macroeconomic model.

4.1 Soft Regional Budgets, National Corruption and Debt

As emphasized by Ter-Minassian (Chapter 1 in this volume), some countries affected by the euro area crisis lacked effective mechanisms to monitor their sub-national public finances, including state enterprises under local government control, leading to soft budget constraints that drove local clientelistic politics and corruption. In the models presented in this chapter, soft budget constraints take the form of diversion by local officials of public resources budgeted for investment projects in their regions. Our formal analysis started with the case, emphasized by Tanzi, that corruption is more of an issue at the *regional* government level. But we also considered the case – quite relevant in some of the countries affected by the crisis – that soft budget constraints and weak institutional checks and balances are also a critical weakness at the *central* government level.

Relaxing the assumption that central government officials are incorruptible has important consequences. One of the main differences in the authority of central officials relative to local officials is the ability to borrow. By facilitating the growth of government budgets, central government borrowing enlarges the size of the political pie and the incentives of officials to engage in corruption. Soft budget constraints thus grease the wheels of clientelistic politics and can help drive public debt and adverse debt dynamics. Hence, soft budget constraints were, indirectly, at the heart of the crises, contributing to higher borrowing costs, and adverse public debt dynamics to fears about sovereign insolvency and to country runs.

The interaction between central government corruption and borrowing is important and complex. For example, as stressed in Ivanyna et al. (2015), in the presence of clientelistic politics and corruption, the ability to issue debt can lead to the buildup of government debt even when fundamentals would suggest that optimal public debt should be zero. The connection between corruption and debt can lead to endogenous periodic equilibria, where the level of government debt cycles between high and low values.

These debt cycles offer a possible explanation for the observation that countries tend to accumulate debt for extended periods of time, only to abruptly carry out fiscal reforms designed to reduce government borrowing. The mechanism is as follows: corruption initially rises as the size of the budget available for public investment increases and the benefit of increasing the size of the corruption tax grows. Simply put, large budgets for public investment create greater opportunities for corruption in countries with weak institutional checks and balances. In later years, following the increase in debt-financed public investment and higher corruption, the need to service debt tends to tighten public investment budgets, which reduces the marginal benefit of corruption. Higher spending obligations also raise the cost of maintaining a development budget of a given size (it now requires more borrowing). Thus, debt overhang puts the breaks on corruption and growth in public debt. Enforceable debt limits for countries with high central government corruption would help stabilize the cycles, lower the average level of debt, and increase economic growth.

Debt rules have limits, however. They can be circumvented by putting investment spending off budget and, in more extreme cases, by falsifying data on budget deficits. Empirically, cycles of increased government borrowing and rising public debt in countries with clientelistic regional politics tend to stop with crises – when markets wake up to the realization that debt levels have become unsustainable and countries are cut off from market financing. Clientelistic officials are affected only partially by such debt crises: fresh rents from their clientelistic activities decline in the general malaise that occurs amid a crisis. Public investment, on which officials depend for these rents, tends to decline sharply in a crisis, and a share of wealth accumulated via clientelistic and corrupt activities is taxed away in the fiscal adjustment effort that the crisis precipitates. But these adjustments are partial, officials get to keep *some* of the proceeds from corrupt activities made possible by the soft budget constraints, and they continue to obtain rents so long as the clientelistic equilibrium remains unchanged.

Deeper institutional changes would be needed to permanently change clientelistic attitudes and reduce corruption at the national and regional levels. But permanent changes in *formal* institutional checks and balances, spearheaded by a reform of the judiciary and judicial review of assets (known in Greek as ποθεν εσχες), take years to realize. They also require wholesale changes in societal attitudes and norms, or in the informal institutions that underpin and are incentive compatible with the formal ones. Economics has not yet come up with a good quantitative model of how structural change affects the macroeconomy, including the causal mechanisms and time frame and lags involved.

4.2 Migration

An important factor influencing the degree and persistence of regional inequality, and of the ability of clientelistic politicians to enjoy 'monopoly rents' in the region, is the extent to which households in poor regions can migrate to rich ones. If production technologies and public goods provision were superior in rich regions and if regional migration was not too costly, then households from poor regions would move there. Clustering in rich regions to take advantage of higher wages there would be a natural response to differentials in wages and public services. These flows would tend to increase in crisis periods, when rich regions with better social safety nets would be more attractive.

Now we do observe long-term migration flows from poor to rich regions. But migration tends to be slow: it takes decades for rural–urban migration accompanying structural transformation in developing economies to be completed, even in the absence of explicit government migration policies that restrict migration. This suggests that migration is quite costly, owing to incomplete markets for labor and housing and other barriers having to do with language and incomplete social security and social safety net arrangements (see Das et al., 2015).

There may also be structural differences across regions that offset wage advantages of rich areas. One might be congestion costs, in the form of living expenses, or a compromised health environment, for which wage gaps provide compensation in equilibrium. However, changes in fiscal policy that affect the wage gap will also impact the migration flow across the region. This should make it easier for the poor region to negotiate a larger portion of the central budget because rich region households would benefit from reduced congestion costs.

A different type of congestion cost occurs when the government provides impure public goods or private goods. In this situation, crowding of the services provided by the government occurs when the population of a region increases. In Mourmouras and Rangazas (2013), we find that crowding creates an incentive for a central government that completely favors the rich region to nevertheless provide government goods to the poor region in an effort to slow migration flows. Thus, even when the poor region has no political influence, there will be some portion of the central government budget allocated to the poor region. Overall, the inclusion of some type of congestion costs associated with migration would narrow the predicted inequalities in good government provision across regions.

Now as an empirical matter, we do tend to observe a picking up of migration flows from crisis-affected countries. This was true during the long transition of formerly planned economies in the 1990s and 2000s, and is also the case with the European periphery countries in the most recent global financial crisis. But the barriers mentioned above seem to be substantial, and migration flows from crisis-affected countries are relatively small. An examination of the factors inhibiting greater migration in Europe, relative to the easy labor mobility prevailing in the United States, would be a worthwhile research topic.

4.3 Common Agency Approach

A more detailed analysis of the effect of politics on regional fiscal policy gaps would assume that *both* regions are actively influencing the central officials' choices. Instead of assuming that one region is completely aligned with the central government, one could assume that the central government is neutral. The two regions then must compete with each other to influence the central government allocations. This approach can be patterned after the common agency approach taken by Grossman and Helpman (1994), in which multiple interest groups compete with each other to influence government policy. The approach is much more difficult analytically but may generate a more nuanced understanding of the effect of political influence. For example, the competition for political influence is more likely to offset across regions, reducing the ultimate effect of politics on redistributive policy.

NOTES

1. An earlier version was presented at the seminar on Multi-level Finance, Moncalieri, Turin, 3–4 July 2014. For useful comments on earlier drafts we wish to thank Satoshi Fukuda, Teresa Ter-Minassian, the editors and seminar participants. The points of view are those of the authors and do not reflect IMF official views.
2. The model follows Phillip Grossman (1994). In his empirical study of the US Grossman argues that 'the federal politician uses grants to purchase political capital – the influence of politically powerful state politicians and interest groups – to influence the voting decisions of state residents'. He finds that common party affiliation with the House majority, size of the majority party in the state, size of the state bureaucracy, and union membership, all raise per capita grants to the state.
3. See Arcalean et al. (2010) and Mourmouras and Rangazas (2007) for surveys of the estimates of this parameter.
4. The numerical choices can be motivated by the data used in Arcalean et al. (2012). They conduct an analysis of regional inequalities in Portugal. In Portugal the tax rate is 35 percent and the combined national budget share for public capital and public education is 29 percent. So, the tax rate used to fund national public investment is 10 percent. They also report that the per capita output of the rich region relative to that of the poor region is 1.64.

REFERENCES

Arcalean, C., Glomm, G., Schiopu, I. and Suedekum, J., 2010, 'Public Budget Composition, Fiscal (De)Centralization and Welfare', *Canadian Journal of Economics*, **43**, 832–59.

Arcalean, C., Glomm, G. and Schiopu, I., 2012, 'Growth Effects of Spatial Distribution Policies', *Journal of Economic Dynamics and Control*, **36**, 988–1008.

Bordignon, M., Colombo, L. and Galmarini, U., 2008, 'Fiscal Federalism and Lobbying', *Journal of Public Economics*, **92**, 2288–301.

Das, S., Mourmouras, A. and Rangazas, P., 2015, *Economic Growth and Development: A Dual Economy Approach*, New York: Springer.

Dixit, A., 1996, *The Making of Economic Policy: A Transactions Cost Politics Perspective*, Cambridge, MA: MIT Press.

Dixit, A., Grossman, G. and Helpman, E., 1997, 'Common Agency and Coordination: Theory and Applications to Government Policy Making', *Journal of Political Economy*, **105**, 752–69.

Grossman, P., 1994, 'A Political Theory of Intergovernment Grants', *Public Choice*, **78**, 295–303.

Grossman, G. and Helpman, E, 1994, 'Protection for Sale', *American Economic Review*, **84**, 833–50.

Ivanyna, M., Mourmouras, A. and Rangazas, P., 2015, 'Corruption, Public Debt, and Economic Growth', mimeo.

Lockwood, B., 2006, 'The Political Economy of Decentralization', in E. Ahmed and G. Brosio (eds), *Handbook of Fiscal Federalism*, Cheltenham, UK and Northampton, MA, USA: Edward Elgar, pp. 33–60.

Mourmouras, A. and Rangazas, P., 2007, 'Foreign Aid Policies and Sources of Poverty: A Quantitative Framework', *IMF Staff Papers*, **54**, 59–90.

Mourmouras, A. and Rangazas, P., 2013, 'Efficient Urban Bias', *Journal of Economic Geography*, **13**(3), 451–71.

Parente, S. and Prescott, E.C., 2000, *Barriers to Riches*, Cambridge, MA: MIT Press.

Pritchett, L., 2000, 'The Tyranny of Concepts: CUDIE (Cumulated, Depreciated Investment Effort) is *Not* Capital', *Journal of Economic Growth*, **5**, 361–84.

Pritchett, L., 1996, 'Mind Your Ps and Qs: The Cost of Public Investment is *Not* the Value of Public Capital', World Bank Policy Research Working Paper No. 1660.

Reinikka, R. and Svensson, J., 2004, 'Local Capture: Evidence from a Central Government Transfer Program in Uganda', *Quarterly Journal of Economics*, **119**, 679–709.

Rodriguez-Pose, A. and Ezcurra, R., 2010, 'Does Decentralization Matter for Regional Disparities?', *Journal of Economic Geography*, **10**, 619–44.

Sacchi, A. and Salotti, S., 2011, 'Income Inequality Regional Disparities and Fiscal Decentralization in Industrialized Countries', Department of Economics Working Paper 142, University Roma Tre.

Shah, A., 2007, 'A Framework for Evaluating Alternative Institutional Arrangements for Fiscal Equalization Transfers', in J. Martinez-Vazquez, J. and B. Searle (eds), *Fiscal Equalization: Challenges in the Design of Intergovernmental Transfers*, New York: Springer, pp. 141–62.

Tanzi, V., 2000, 'Some Politically Incorrect Remarks on Decentralization and Public Finance', in J.-J. Dethier (ed.), *Governance, Decentralization and Reform in China, India, and Russia*, Boston, MA, Dordrecht and London: Kluwer Academic Publishers, pp. 47–63.

Tanzi, V. and Davoodi, H., 1997, 'Corruption, Public Investment, and Growth', IMF Working Paper No. 139.

13. Incentives facing local governments in the absence of credible enforcement

Leo Fulvio Minervini and Annalisa Vinella

> The soft budget constraint literature may give the impression that hardness is 'good' and softness 'bad'. But if this were literally true, it is hard to imagine that the soft budget constraint syndrome would be so widespread or recurrent. (Kornai et al., 2003, p. 1132)

1. INTRODUCTION

Very often, financial crises precede sovereign debt crises. As crises occur, they require restructuring or, at least, containing government debt, which in turn challenges the sustainability of public finances.[1] Following the 2008 and 2009 financial crises, the sustainability of public finances has been called into question in heavily indebted countries within the Euro zone, as well as others, some of which, such as Ireland and Spain, were well within Maastricht limits in 2007. Furthermore, as central and sub-central governments are mutually dependent, concerns have arisen – and do persist – about the effects of the former's conduct and performance spilling over onto the latter, and vice versa. However, it is essential to disentangle financial crises caused by adverse macroeconomic shocks, which are beyond the governments' control, from those caused by strategic behaviour, which depend on the decisions made by economic agents (von Hagen and Dahlberg, 2002). Sub-central governments (henceforth, SCGs) are little motivated to manage public resources efficiently if they expect the centre (CG) to provide financial aid and, perhaps, to bail them out, as the need arises. Essentially, the CG suffers from a *lack of dynamic commitment*. This commitment problem has long been known as one of *soft budget constraint* (SBC).

The SBC concept was originally introduced by Kornai (1979, 1980) in his studies on socialist and transition economies under stress. In this context, bailouts of state enterprises in financial distress were so frequent that managers could count on being rescued, which led Kornai to refer to an SBC syndrome. This concept has been extended to similar situations in market economies. A major cause of the recent Euro crisis lies in the fiscally irresponsible policies that some countries and sub-national levels of government have long followed, expecting to be bailed out either by European institutions or by other member states (or higher levels of government within countries) interested in limiting negative spillovers.[2] In practice, a neat distinction between macro-led and micro-led crises is often difficult to make. On the one hand, the two causes coexist and exacerbate each other. On the other, the SBC syndrome is not only a cause but also an effect of a crisis. As emphasized by Kornai (2009, pp. 1–2), precisely because it is perpetuated through an iterated practice, 'the SBC syndrome breeds irresponsibility and disdain of risk', going well beyond the standard moral-hazard problem familiar to insurance theory. The way is paved for excessive spending and borrowing, which in turn makes 'financial troubles more frequent and rescue demands more strident'. In substance, 'the SBC syndrome becomes a self-inducing, self-reinforcing process.'

When macro- and micro-causes mutually reinforce each other, there are dramatic and potentially extreme consequences for a crisis. With persistent socioeconomic difficulties, due to macroeconomic shocks, together with perverse economic behaviour by SCGs, due in part to a lack of commitment of the CG, the sustainability of federations (more generally, decentralized economies with a central authority) may be in question. The literature has argued that, under some circumstances, joining a federation may be beneficial to a region if the CG uses its economy-wide taxation power to smooth distortionary taxes across regions (Cooper et al., 2008). A CG that commits to a sound fiscal policy could provide financial aid to SCGs running deficits, in such a way that all gains from tax smoothing are reaped. By contrast, when the CG is unable to commit, tax smoothing is less beneficial. In the latter case, joining the federation is beneficial only if tax-smoothing gains exceed bailout costs, more likely when spending shocks are only weakly correlated across regions. Transposed in the EU context, this suggests that, while a fiscal federalism scheme is desirable to smooth taxes across member states, it requires a strong commitment.

Economic crises reveal and crystallize problems challenging multi-level fiscal governance in decentralized political systems. Essentially, as fewer resources are available, pressure on budgets increases, both at central and sub-central levels. Furthermore, intergovernmental transfers are affected as well, thus exacerbating the pressure on sub-central budgets. As budget deficits worsen, due to difficult economic conditions, the risk of default becomes more serious. If this leads governments to adopt more rigorous fiscal policies, then an economic crisis may be at the root of budget restructuring efforts, which may have been delayed for too long before the crisis erupted. However, opportunistic governments might be tempted to play with budget rules, rather than forcing substantial budget restructuring. Although this might happen at any government level, opportunism is more likely to show up at the sub-central level, given the probability of being rescued by the CG, notwithstanding the negative effects of the crisis on general government finances. Besides, budget restructuring and rigorous use of public policy instruments require a degree of expertise, which SCGs often lack. Thus, while SCGs are best placed to identify relevant patterns for local development (knowing the characteristics and preferences of their constituencies), they may face greater difficulties in using sophisticated policy instruments and addressing complex policy issues, especially those triggered by financial crises.

The use of public–private partnerships (PPPs) in infrastructure projects, especially at sub-national levels, displays all the difficulties mentioned above. Under PPPs, the construction of infrastructure is bundled with operation and maintenance activities, in order to incentivize contractors to engage in reducing future operation and maintenance costs. When undertaking PPPs, governments need to assess carefully these advantages over a sufficiently long term, compared to traditional procurement and private-sector provision. PPPs at the sub-national level entail more risks for governments than traditional projects. In fact, in many instances, PPPs have been dogged by unrealistic expectations, and waste. SCGs are often tempted to use PPPs to finance infrastructure while the payments become the responsibility of subsequent administrations. This 'kicking the can down the road' also leads to lack of care and severe incompetence in tackling contract design complexities, which have actually led to excessive costs for taxpayers in many cases.

Commitment problems in multi-level regimes affect public finances, at central and sub-central levels, especially when the economy faces negative shocks with persistent effects; in particular, they affect the incentives faced by SCGs to generate budget deficits. In this regard we focus on (ab)use of PPPs. However, under some conditions soft budget approaches may ultimately result in better policies. By and large, the incompleteness of information about the relevant circumstances plays a crucial role in the choice and implementation of public policies.

The remainder of the chapter is organized as follows. In Section 2, we review the literature on the SBC syndrome. After considering the extreme case of complete information (decentralized leadership), we discuss the role of informational asymmetries. In Section 3, we comment upon alternative ways to foster fiscal discipline at sub-central levels. Section 4 is devoted to PPPs. After describing them in light of the theoretical literature and providing some data on their use in the European Union (EU), we explain how they can be exploited to circumvent fiscal rules and suggest some possible remedies. In Section 5, we present the 'public capitalism' phenomenon, i.e., the reliance on publicly owned enterprises to provide services, as another instrument to circumvent fiscal constraints. In Section 6, we discuss some situations where the standard recommendations have been challenged, due to specific environmental circumstances or economic consequences. Section 7 concludes.

2. LACK OF COMMITMENT IN DECENTRALIZED SYSTEMS: THE GOOD, THE BAD, AND THE UGLY

It is useful to put the assessment of SBCs in the context of decentralized systems based on fiscal and political incentives, especially those facing subnational officials. Public officials may have goals other than maximizing citizen welfare, possibly driven by institutional structures (Weingast, 2009).

2.1 The SBC Syndrome in Decentralized Systems

The SBC framework is similar to lending by private financiers, in that a decentralized financial market with capital-constrained banks is less likely to incur an SBC than a centralized market with a well-capitalized single bank (Dewatripont and Maskin, 1995). The key to this result is that a bank that faces some rationing constraint may not refinance a project for which it provided funds at an earlier stage. Consequently, other banks must provide financing at later stages. As they are less informed than the first bank regarding the quality of the project, they will offer credit at a premium. The higher cost of late credit motivates the borrowers to undertake good projects, those which will not require refinancing. This argument supports the idea that joint control between the state and local authorities, or full decentralization to SCGs with harder budget constraints, may be beneficial.

However, there is a problem with this idea. In decentralized financial markets, small capital-constrained banks have no supporting organizations which can help them in the event of financial distress. By contrast, lower-level governments are in a hierarchical relationship with higher-level governments; they can thus expect a rescuing intervention by the latter. Therefore, their budget constraints do not need to be harder. In practice, indeed, although centralized regimes have been regarded as vulnerable to the SBC syndrome, decentralized regimes have proved far from immune.[3] Thus, the fundamental problem of the syndrome, which appears in government-firm relationships, is replicated within multi-level governmental systems. 'The government cannot commit not to extend further credit to a loss-making organization after providing initial financing, which creates bad incentives for managers when choosing projects. In the same way, the central government's inability to commit not to bail out local governments affects their incentives' (Rodden, 2005, p. 5).

Under the assumption that the CG aims to maximize social welfare in the federation, a benevolent CG cannot credibly preclude bailing out an SCG. Moreover, the commitment problem holds even if the CG is concerned with its political power and maximizes its (re)election probability. An important potential explanation for the SBC syndrome is the inability of the supporting organization (a government) to make dynamic commitments (Kornai et al., 2003). However, the ex ante and ex post perspectives of the supporting organization are radically different. Ex ante, the supporting organization might wish to refrain from rescuing firms or lower-level governments, in order to keep the risk of financial distress low. But, once a financial crisis has occurred, the supporting organization has strong reasons to bail them out. There are two important categories of costs that a CG might bear from failing to bail out an SCG in deficit distress. 'The first, called the financial costs of no bailout (. . .) occurs because the local default creates financial spillovers onto the rest of the economy (. . .). The second, called the distributional costs of no bailout (. . .) represents the differential costs to the central government of having the debt burden of local government borne directly by local taxpayers or by its bondholders rather than by national tax-payers' (Inman, 2003, p. 46). As a consequence, the CG falls prey to a dynamic commitment problem.

Expectations play a crucial role in the SBC syndrome. SCGs may anticipate these bailout imperatives, resulting in a moral-hazard problem. Therefore, the effect of decentralization on fiscal discipline depends on whether the institutional setting provides expectations by SCGs that they will be bailed out.

An extreme situation occurs when local leaders take decisions, certain of a bailout. This is usually referred to as *decentralized leadership*.[4] Breuillé et al. (2010, p. 205) note that 'empirical evidence suggests that the SBC phenomenon induces selective (and usually rare) bailouts from the federal government (. . .) which contrasts with generalized (and systematic) ex post equalizing transfers with decentralized leadership.' Hence, in those circumstances SCGs can accumulate non-sustainable debt levels (Foremny, 2014). Especially when SCGs are responsible for providing a key public service (such as health care), it is difficult for the CG not to bail them out. Likewise, absence of sub-national fiscal autonomy, particularly own-source revenues at the margin, affects the credibility of local debt contracts (Ambrosanio et al., Chapter 9 in this volume) and likelihood of bailout (Sorribas-Navarro, 2011).

2.2 Decentralized Leadership

Under decentralized leadership, the relationship between CG and SCGs can be represented as a complete-information Stackelberg game. The CG's lack of commitment is captured by the order of moves. SCGs move first, certain that their actions will force CG responses.

Qian and Roland (1998) model a three-level federation, with CG, a number of independent SCGs in the middle, and a number of state and non-state enterprises at the bottom. They show that the devolution of fiscal authority to SCGs ('federalism', in their terminology) contributes to hardening their budget constraints. Financial discipline is induced because SCGs compete among themselves to develop infrastructures that will attract capital to their non-state enterprises. By doing so, each region does not take into account the negative externality it imposes on the other regions as it lures capital away from their enterprises. Because the social marginal benefit to infrastructure investment is higher than the private marginal benefit, the opportunity cost of bailing out failing state enterprises is larger in a federation (as compared to a decentralized regime), thus leading to a hard budget constraint (henceforth, HBC) at the local level. While this work contributes to providing theoretical foundation to decentralization, its results are questioned in other studies, which highlight that competition among regions does not necessarily result in harder budget constraints.

Breuillé and Vigneault (2010) also consider a three-level hierarchy, with CG at the top and regional governments (henceforth, RGs) at the intermediate level. However, the bottom level is now comprised of a number of municipalities administered by local governments (henceforth, LGs), rather than enterprises. Moreover, regions compete through taxation of capital, rather than through investment in infrastructure. Decentralized leadership is two-tiered: regional jurisdictions act as leaders vis-à-vis the CG; LGs act as leaders vis-à-vis both their RGs and the CG. Unlike in Qian and Roland (1998), competition among regions to attract capital fails to induce fiscal discipline. This follows from two factors. The first is related to the characteristics of the capital market. While in Qian and Roland (1998) capital comes entirely from outside sources, in Breuillé and Vigneault (2010) citizens own capital, in addition to using it. Therefore, distortive effects, through the net return to capital, compensate each other.

The second factor is related to how governmental transfers are granted, i.e., according to overlapping equalization schemes. Each region allocates transfers to the municipalities located in its territory so as to equalize marginal utilities from local public good provision. Then, the CG redistributes public funds across regions, in order to equalize marginal utilities from regional public good provision. Transfers across regions are such that the latter perfectly internalize the externalities they impose on each other when competing on capital taxation. Therefore, in this context, the beneficial effect of competition among regions vanishes. This is not all, though. The overlapping equalization scheme structure induces higher-level governments to be more generous, ex post, with lower-level governments, thus hindering the latter's incentives to manage resources efficiently. That is, regions are more generous towards the municipalities in their territories than is the CG towards the regions themselves; consequently, local jurisdictions are even less disciplined than regional ones. A 'snowball effect' is triggered. The softer the regional budget constraint, the softer the local budget constraint, the worse the SBC problem in the country.

The bottom line is that the multi-level institutional architecture with decentralized leadership, together with the overlapping structure of top-to-bottom transfers, exacerbates the SBC problem within the hierarchy. Challenging the wisdom that decentralization helps lessen budgetary problems, this result rather suggests that a smaller number of government layers may be desirable, as this prevents cumulative budget burdening, in frameworks where governments are unable to commit at each such layer. This result, however, is questioned in studies that have been conducted in other analytical environments.

2.3 Is Lack of Commitment Always Bad?

A few studies show that lack of commitment is not always bad. Under some circumstances, the inability to pre-commit does not lead to negative economic consequences, and it might even be exploited to promote efficiency. From this perspective, two studies on expenditures on public goods provide relevant insights, as they consider circumstances where public goods can be optimally provided, notwithstanding limited commitment. The idea that a lower-level government might make efficient borrowing decisions – even if the higher-level government is unable to commit – is sketched in Goodspeed (2002) and formalized in Akai and Sato (2008), where two-tier government hierarchies are considered.

Goodspeed (2002) proposes a decentralized leadership model where RGs can spend money on a public good, which the CG would like to be produced in some optimal amount, because this would maximize the

CG's re-election chances. Technically speaking, RGs choose how much to borrow in the first period, anticipating the decision that the CG will make about grants in the second period. Further, RGs choose a tax rate in the second period. Thus, in this Stackelberg game, there is the additional twist that RGs make decisions in both periods and the second-period choice is simultaneous to that of the CG, which is taken as given. In the model, the RG knows that the CG will bail it out if it is unable to raise enough taxes to finance the optimal amount of public good. The RG will face two opposite incentive effects: on the one hand, its opportunity cost of borrowing is lowered by support from the CG, which will pay extra grants for the desired public good; on the other hand, its tax cost increases, as for other RGs, because they will share the cost of grants paid out to balance local budgets. As long as the first incentive is more powerful than the second, RGs will over-borrow to provide the public good (Inman, 2003). Furthermore, RGs are more likely to be bailed out if they are not natural allies of the incumbent political party. This is because the CG's payment of grants may cause a steep rise in the marginal probability of voting for the incumbent party (thus increasing re-election chances).

Nevertheless, an efficient outcome might plausibly occur. The CG might wish to punish inefficient borrowing by increasing grants, not only to regions which over-borrow, but to every region under its jurisdiction. Under these circumstances, the two incentives discussed above will counter-balance, and efficient borrowing is realized. However, while Goodspeed (2002) does not provide a formal model for the case of efficient borrowing under limited commitment, the CG's ability to commit to increasing grants to every region seems to be at odds with its inability to prevent excessive regional borrowing in the first place.

Akai and Sato (2008) provide a formal analysis and show that a pure public good can be provided efficiently under decentralized leadership. They consider that, due to commitment problems, the CG will bail out RGs ex post, thus leading to ex ante adverse incentive consequences. In their study, a critical question concerns what decision is made ex ante by the RGs, which may initially decide, either over public expenditure, or over tax collection – with the remaining policy instrument residually adjusted by ex post transfers. They find that lack of commitment of the CG to its own transfer policy leads to inefficiency. The direction of the ex ante distortion depends on the ex ante choice of the policy instrument at the local level. Therefore, the RG may be too large, i.e., it overspends and/or over-borrows (because of cost sharing incentives), or it may be too small, i.e., it raises less of its own revenues from taxes (because of revenue sharing incentives). Furthermore, in this model, smaller regions gain at the expense of larger ones. However, if local over-borrowing occurs to finance a pure public good (with positive spillovers for all the other jurisdictions), an ex post bailout will not cause inefficiencies: the cost of the additional grant, which the CG pays to the indebted RG providing a pure public good, will be shared among other RGs, which also benefit from the same public good.

Although information is complete in Akai and Sato (2008), the authors mention issues of incomplete information. They argue that while uncertainty – concerning local public projects as well as the CG's commitment ability – is not accounted for in their model, it could be incorporated. In particular, with project cost uncertainty, interregional transfers, on the one hand, would provide insurance; on the other hand, they would introduce moral hazard by creating excessive risk at the regional level.

Köthenbürger (2008) considers that federal and state governments often differ in their capacity to pre-commit to expenditure and tax policies; he investigates whether the sequence of public decisions has any efficiency implications. He starts from a framework where federal and state governments make decisions simultaneously. He then contrasts the improvements that can be attained by moving to a situation of centralized leadership, where the federal government pre-commits vis-à-vis state governments, with those that can be attained by moving to a situation of decentralized leadership, where state governments pre-commit instead. He finds that *centralized* leadership enhances welfare. This result is very much in line with previous studies of higher-level government's commitment ability, which enables efficient outcomes, as generally achieved under HBCs. However, efficiency is not attained over all public decision options. Under decentralized leadership, the welfare implications are more ambiguous. With high capital mobility, if a state government raises taxes on capital, its capital tax revenues may fall; at the same time, capital tax revenues rise in neighbouring jurisdictions. If capital taxes rise overall, then the federal government can rely less on distortionary labour taxes. Furthermore, federal government transfers are re-shuffled to the tax-raising state, thus creating a positive transfer effect, which may counteract the tax competition effect of an increase in capital taxation. Thus, importantly, decentralized leadership also enhances welfare, when the tax-price effect of the federal transfers counteracts the states' incentives to engage in a 'race to the bottom' as a result of fiscal competition.

2.4 Expectations of Fiscal (In-)Discipline

Under incomplete information, expectations play a crucial role in determining economic consequences in environments with lack of commitment.

A bailout requires, under SBC, some discretion by the CG in the allocation of resources. At the time when the SCGs decide their expenditure and taxation policies, they face uncertainty about the decisions to be made by the CG. That is, the SCGs are not sure whether the CG will provide financial aid. This grants an informational advantage to the CG.

In some cases, information incompleteness about the 'type' of the CG may provide incentives to the lower-level governments to implement more effective fiscal measures. This uncertainty would force SCGs to observe financial discipline, even if the CG is ready in reality to provide support.

In other contexts, uncertainty about the type of the CG may be detrimental. This is the case when local initiatives, which are desirable from the viewpoint of the CG, are not undertaken, for fear of incurring future financial difficulties, unless the CG is credibly committed to actually support such initiatives. Softening the budget constraint represents a tool to dissipate any uncertainty on the supportive attitude of the CG.[5]

2.5 What Is Your Type? Private Information 'at the Top'

Bordignon and Turati (2009) test a model of SBC which closely resembles the intergovernmental relationships in the Italian public health care sector. To represent the strategic interactions between levels of government, they design a dynamic game of incomplete information, in which the informational gap concerns the type of CG. Two types are possible, namely tough and weak. Regardless of the type, the best for the CG would be if the SCG were financially disciplined. A tough CG is opposed to granting any supplementary financial aid to the SCG, whereas a weak CG is amenable to pressure to help the SCG if it incurs financial difficulties. The CG knows its type, the SCG does not. Nonetheless, the SCG knows that there are two possible types, and their respective probabilities. Accordingly, after learning which level of health expenditure the CG will finance, the SCG sets its own expenditure level. If this is high and the SCG runs a deficit, then either the CG refuses to accommodate and lets the SCG take care of the deficit, or it finances the ensuing SCG deficit. Of course, in equilibrium, a tough CG imposes financial discipline and local expenditures are set low. Importantly, this outcome may also be achieved by a weak CG if it is able to camouflage itself as being tough.

Although the SCG anticipates that a tough CG may actually be quite weak, it still chooses a low expenditure level, with some probability, provided that the threat of not being bailed out is credible enough. The expectations of the SCG are crucial. The more likely that it will have to face a tough CG, the more credible an actually weak CG will be at pretending to be tough. As a result, the behaviour of the SCG is likely to be responsible. The authors' empirical analysis detects a stronger link between the ex ante financing at the central level and regional health expenditure, when the regional expectations of future bailouts were presumably lower.

Incomplete information on the CG type also plays a crucial role in Rodden (2005). He considers a dynamic game where the information structure is the same as in Bordignon and Turati (2009), with only a terminological difference, i.e., the CG is now either 'resolute' (tough) or 'irresolute' (weak). The game is, however, adapted to account for a negative shock with lasting effects, leading to a recession. This is interesting, in that the ensuing theoretical findings shed some light on aspects related to the recent Euro crisis. In a nutshell, bailout expectations induce SCGs to delay or avoid financial adjustments that are needed when SCGs face negative revenue shocks. To tackle their financial needs, they resort to additional borrowing. This behaviour results in debt accumulation, which further exacerbates the financial distress. The bottom line is that an economic crisis creates conditions for SBC, and the crisis is, in turn, deepened by SBC.

Let us now provide details. To represent the recession, it is assumed that the SCG faces an adverse fiscal shock with lasting effects. To allow for debt accumulation, as things get worse, it is further assumed that the SCG has two options. Either it becomes more parsimonious and adjusts immediately to the shock (early adjustment), or it resorts to debt. As borrowing involves future distress, this choice is made only if the SCG has a sufficiently solid expectation to receive help by the CG. Indeed, when the SCG borrows, the CG has two options, in turn. Either it provides financial aid to solve the problem (early bailout), or it does not intervene. In this latter case, the crisis is exacerbated. Yet, the SCG will still avoid adjusting to the crisis (late adjustment) if it has an expectation of rescue by the CG. Default follows if the CG does not provide a late bailout.

The main insight on the information advantage enjoyed by the CG reflects that derived by Bordignon and Turati (2009). An irresolute CG may be able to impose discipline on the SCG by mimicking a resolute CG in a sufficiently credible manner. If an irresolute CG can persuade the SCG that it is resolute by not providing aid at the onset of financial distress, it can induce the SCG to a late adjustment, thus eliminating the need for an ultimate, more costly, rescue (and avoiding default).

As mentioned above, the more novel (and interesting) prediction of the Rodden model is that SCGs are less likely to adjust to negative shocks when they expect bailouts. As they keep on borrowing, expecting intervention by the centre, a debt accumulation makes financial difficulties progressively more serious. The empirical analysis, developed in Rodden's paper using data on the German Länder, provides support for these theoretical predictions. SCGs with rational bailout expectations are found to be less responsive to negative shocks than those without such expectations, and this seems to cause long-term differences in debt burdens.

The analysis in Saljanin (2011) is also built around incomplete information regarding the type of CG. However, the perspective is now different. In Bordignon and Turati (2009) and in Rodden (2005), a weak CG would like to disguise itself as being tough, in order to induce a virtuous behaviour at the local level. When camouflage is not credible, an SBC problem arises. In Saljanin (2011), instead, a 'competent' or 'supportive' government may want to reveal itself as being such, rather than being perceived differently. The reason is that some projects, which are desirable from the perspective of the government, will not be undertaken in the absence of its unequivocal support, and that support is essential for project profitability. This is highly plausible for large and long-term investments, such as infrastructure projects, especially if there are significant political and social implications. Under these circumstances, disguising information about its 'type' is no longer an advantage for the government. To dissipate any uncertainty, the CG engages in a signalling game, in which it deliberately indicates support, possibly inducing SBC, as a credible signal of its attitude.[6] Thus, SBC does not necessarily reflect a commitment problem.

The kind of uncertainty that Saljanin (2011) represents is a recurrent phenomenon in countries where governments are unable to act in transparent and predictable ways. The deeper the lack of transparency, the lower the confidence that projects will succeed, and the more likely that a supportive CG will subsidize its priority projects.

An important point is that uncertainty, lack of transparency and absence of confidence are all problems that economies typically experience during periods of acute crisis. Thus, Saljanin's theoretical result allows for a better understanding of the decision to waive balanced-budget rules at the sub-national level. Central governments in several European countries were already doing this when it became clear that the consequences of the crisis would be persistent, while consolidation needs required severe reductions in national grants to SCGs.[7] Noticeably, inducing an SBC to dissipate uncertainty and restore confidence may have both good and bad consequences. The pool of projects abandoned in the absence of explicit CG support may include both projects that are socially desirable (the 'good' ones) and projects that are not (the 'bad' ones). As far as good projects are concerned, uncertainty about the attitude of the government is detrimental. It may thus be reasonable to induce some resource waste to dissipate the uncertainty to protect the projects. The same cannot be said with regard to bad projects. SBC is never desirable when it finances dubious projects.

The literature surveyed so far suggests that fiscal discipline may be hard to achieve under limited commitment, especially when this is coupled with incomplete information, leading to SBC. However, there may be circumstances where, under limited commitment, private information about the type of the CG can be exploited to induce more rigour with regard to SCG budgets, as shown by Bordignon and Turati (2009) and Rodden (2005). Nonetheless, incentive structures based on this may prove insufficiently effective. Therefore, other instruments may have to be considered, and relied upon, by CGs to counter excessive deficits and over-borrowing by lower-level governments. We touch on this issue below.

3. ARE THERE BETTER WAYS TO COUNTER FISCAL INDISCIPLINE?

The discussion above suggests that limited commitment usually implies fiscal indiscipline and that an SBC syndrome can negatively affect financial decisions at decentralized levels, resulting in excessive spending and economic inefficiencies. Moreover, those issues have been discussed taking into consideration the incentive structure that governments face in various circumstances, but use of direct instruments to constrain fiscal behaviour (such as fiscal rules) has been neglected so far.

Noticeably, to promote fiscal discipline, two different approaches are identified in the literature, namely *rules-based HBCs* and *market discipline HBCs*. Generally, with rules-based HBCs, CGs place legal restrictions on borrowing by SCGs. With market discipline HBCs, no restrictions are placed on SCGs ex ante, but CGs can pre-commit not to bail out an SCG if it cannot repay its loans (Rodden et al., 2003; Ahmad et al., 2006; Besfamille and Lockwood, 2008). Indeed, imposition of fiscal constraints on governments within a federation, typically in the form of debt limits, is one way to substitute for the inability of CGs to commit to no bailout policies vis-à-vis lower-tier governments (Cooper et al., 2008).[8] A major example, though at a supra-national level, is the Stability and Growth Pact (SGP), adopted by the EU to ensure that member states, once admitted in the Euro area, would adopt sound fiscal policies, together with the national internal stability pacts (see Ter-Minassian, Chapter 1 in this volume, and Milbradt, Chapter 3 in this volume).

Fiscal rules can take the form of caps on spending and/or borrowing to finance public investments. For instance, reliance on such caps has been recently advocated in the economics literature to discourage pork-barrel politics, typical in the presence of informational asymmetries. In particular, Maskin and Tirole (2008) propose the introduction of spending (or borrowing) caps as a way to prevent public officials from selecting infrastructure projects, which they know will involve high costs, in order to please specific interest groups, taking advantage of the fact that the public at large will learn the relevant characteristics (the costs, in their model) of the realized projects only at a later stage.

In a framework of decentralized leadership with complete information, Breuillé et al. (2006) offer results suggesting that CGs should settle for a threshold of regional debt, in order to favour regional fiscal responsibility. This is implied by their finding that, when regions are not deeply in debt, tax interactions harden the regional budget constraint. In their study, the authors analyse circumstances in which the SBC syndrome may occur, as the benevolent CG is always inclined to increase grants in response to borrowing by SCGs. Specifically, the CG takes inter-temporal regional budgetary decisions and allocates grants in order to equalize marginal utilities of second-period local public good consumption across the federation. While the CG's grant behaviour creates an SBC, both vertical and horizontal tax competition act as a deterrent to regional borrowing.[9]

However, fiscal constraints have an obvious cost. They limit the SCG's ability to smooth fiscal policy over time according to economic circumstances. Moreover, especially in times of economic crisis or slow-down (i.e., when fiscal constraints tend to become tighter), general limits on public deficit and spending may be inadequate, at least as long as a common ceiling is imposed on both productive and unproductive spending. This issue affecting the European Stability and Growth Pact is considered by Krogstrup and Wyplosz (2010). The authors take into account that deficits are used to finance unproductive transfers to interest groups as well as productive spending, which increases tax revenues in the future (contrary to unproductive spending). Their two-country two-period model shows that a deficit bias is created by two debt externalities: a domestic common pool problem (because of interest groups' disagreement on transfers) and an international externality. They find that 'an externally set ceiling cannot fully eliminate the deficit bias in the presence of productive spending. The reason is that the ceiling constrains total borrowing, but not its breakdown into what finances productive spending and what finances unproductive net transfers' (Krogstrup and Wyplosz, 2010, p. 276). Nevertheless, an externally set ceiling fares better than national arrangements. Furthermore, to reach social optimum, the external deficit restraint should be complemented by a national institutional arrangement. As the authors argue, 'the specific institutional arrangement of allowing for pre-commitment to productive spending before unproductive transfers are determined will deliver social optimum in the presence of an optimally set external debt restraint' (Krogstrup and Wyplosz, 2010, p. 277).[10]

The arguments presented above suggest that remedies based on fiscal rules may be ineffective, for various reasons. First, just as with the denial of rescue grants, fiscal constraints require commitment and credibility. When, in 2003, the European Commission did not initiate the excess deficit procedure against France and Germany, although they breached the Stability and Growth Pact, other member states perceived inaction as a signal that the Pact was not destined to be enforced in a serious and systematic manner. Consequently, many of them felt entitled to undertake less than prudent fiscal policies. Using a dataset that covers 26 OECD countries, over the 1975–2009 period, and applying a methodology based on difference-in-difference regressions, Baskaran and Hessami (2013) find that the failure to censure Germany and France contributed to SBCs being implemented in countries with traditionally high deficits. They conclude that this failure was, thus, partially to blame for the European sovereign debt crisis.

Second, even if lower-tier governments seemingly comply with the fiscal constraints they are faced with, strategies might be found to circumvent those constraints. Particularly, in the absence of adequate accounting rules, ways to avoid deficit targets and rules are offered by public–private partnerships in infrastructure projects, as well as by utilities and companies belonging to SCGs.

4. PUBLIC–PRIVATE PARTNERSHIPS

In this section, we describe how public–private partnerships have been used, in practice, to circumvent fiscal constraints. We first explain what PPPs are and why reliance on such arrangements can be useful to attain efficient outcomes in the realization of infrastructure projects. We then complete the analysis with a discussion on how to limit the abusive and inappropriate use of PPPs.

4.1 From Theory . . .

A PPP consists of a long-term development-and-service contract between a (central or sub-central) government and a private firm or consortium. In exchange for a mix of government payments and user fees,[11] the private partner engages in developing, operating and servicing the project. The private partner may also bear substantial risk and raise private finance. The very novelty, with respect to traditional procurement, is that the responsibility for the initial capital investment is bundled with that for future operation and maintenance activities. The benefit is that it alleviates moral-hazard problems, which are core to infrastructure projects where synergies are present between the construction phase and the operation phase. Indeed, bundling motivates the private partner to account for, and hence to minimize, *the lifecycle costs of the project*, when the initial investment is made.[12] At the same time, this kind of arrangement leads to more complexity in tendering and contractual design, and calls for higher skills and expertise in implementation and monitoring. Availability of sophisticated legal and regulatory structures is, thus, a fundamental prerequisite.[13]

4.2   . . . To Practice

In recent decades, PPPs have gained much momentum as a promising solution for efficient public procurement, which represents a sizeable share of economic activity in most countries. In Europe, between 1990 and 2005/6, PPPs experienced a six-fold increase, on an annual basis, in defence, government buildings, hospitals, municipal services, schools, tourism, water and, above all, transportation.[14] Many such initiatives display local dimensions, as in many countries municipalities are responsible for infrastructure provision (Allain-Dupré, 2011). More generally, CGs coordinate national PPP programmes and provide guidelines for tenders and contracts, while delegating implementation and monitoring of local projects to local authorities, in order to ensure that contracts do reflect relevant local information (Iossa and Martimort, 2014).

During the crisis, PPPs have increased in the EU. Their use has been widely promoted at the sub-national level. For instance, France introduced a guarantee scheme to facilitate reliance on PPPs, notably at the sub-national level. However, strategies of this kind may not be prudent, especially in the crisis context. The reason is twofold. First, setting up and managing PPP projects and contracts is more challenging at the sub-national level, as it is unlikely that the public sector staff is skilled enough to handle the complexities involved. Second, the growing number of PPPs contributes to exacerbating the fiscal risks precisely for those government tiers that are more vulnerable to those risks (Allain-Dupré, 2011). Third, while decentralization is meant to ensure that relevant local information is taken into account, it exposes contract and project performance to the risk of local corruption (Iossa and Martimort, 2014).

4.3   Budgetary Gymnastics

The pronounced increase recorded in PPP arrangements is not always attributed to their innate qualities, namely incentives for better management and enhanced efficiency. More often, the rapid increase in PPPs is attributed to the possibility, which they offer to governments, of evading fiscal constraints. This is done by taking the associated liabilities[15] off the balance sheet, which backs the claim that PPPs relax budget constraints and replace public resources with cheap private financing, while, in fact, the reported public debt figures fail to mirror all future commitments and liabilities.[16] Looking at the UK, where PPPs account for nearly one-third of total infrastructure investments, Engel et al. (2011) argue that *the original motivation for their introduction was precisely that PPPs represented a source of off-budget public investment*.[17] Provided the UK experienced no rationing in the credit market, PPPs were a way to raise additional funds for public investment, without breaching the debt limits imposed by the European rules. Similar accounting tricks have been used in other countries. Maskin and Tirole (2008) mention the case of Italy, where in 2002 an off-budget agency (ISpa) was created with the objective of settling PPPs, to a great extent in public utilities projects, and raising private capital by issuing state-guaranteed bonds. As in the UK, the ultimate goal was to finance new infrastructure investments, without breaching the European Stability and Growth Pact.

In general, the justification put forward for not recording PPPs in balance sheets is that the private sector finances projects. Two benefits are asserted to follow. First, more public resources can be devoted to implement other socially desirable policies, which are unprofitable, hence could not be delegated to the private sector. This possibility looks especially appealing during a crisis and in its aftermath, when public resources become dramatically scarce compared to social needs. Second, it is not necessary to raise taxes to have new infrastructure built and operated. Engel et al. (2010–11) are sceptical about the validity of these arguments. The reason they provide is that, as compared to any public investment, a PPP affects the timing of government revenues and disbursements, together with the financial structure of the project. However, it does not change the inter-temporal budget constraint. In self-liquidating projects, in which user fees are the main or the only source of revenue, the future revenue ceded by the government to the private sector offsets the investment savings made by the government early on. Similarly, when government payments are the main or the only source of revenue, future payments to the private sector replace repayments of standard public debt. This suggests that PPPs should be accounted for in government budgets, in the same fashion as any other government investments, with respect to which debt or spending limits are actually more effective.[18] The new international standards (IPSAS 32) for recognition of the liabilities associated with PPPs have been largely ignored in the EU (see Ahmad, Chapter 2 in this volume).

The inter-temporal budgetary equivalence between PPPs and public investments does admit some exception, though. Governments may be prevented from borrowing by higher-tier authorities, particularly when they already have huge debt burdens that require severe restructuring. An extreme case is represented by the experience of Greece during the recent sovereign debt crisis.[19] For governments facing temporary borrowing constraints, public investments are unfeasible, while PPPs are still viable, provided that loans are available on the market.[20] Then, PPPs represent the unique option to finance and undertake projects within the necessary time horizon. Engel et al. (2011) point out that if a PPP is launched under such circumstances, it is then crucial to separate the revenue flows of the project from the rest of the public budget. Nonetheless, they emphasize, this may be very difficult for governments, which are not in a position to borrow.

Importantly, shortcomings may arise even if PPP projects are properly recorded, at least in formal terms, at the time when contracts are signed. Unlike public investments performed under separate contracts, precisely because of bundling, PPPs allow for hidden inter-temporal transfers. Maskin and Tirole (2008) elaborate on this point. The PPP contract can be designed to enable the private party to pocket, in the future, a rent which is not yet visible early on in the relationship. To fix ideas, rents of this kind may result from deliberate omissions in contractual specifications, which pave the way for later renegotiations. Those omissions are easy to make, given the pervasiveness of uncertainty and informational asymmetries in PPP arrangements. In substance, contractual incompleteness may be used strategically. This favours both private contractors and public officials. On the one hand, projects are more easily awarded to contractors who agree on payments smaller than total costs, anticipating that they will recoup shortfalls in the future. On the other, by back-loading private rents, public officials can mask the true PPP liabilities and gain social consensus.[21] As a result, even if PPP investments are recorded on the balance sheet, official figures may fail to reflect the true ensuing liabilities if a part remains hidden until after renegotiation takes place. To mitigate this problem, regulations limiting renegotiations have sometimes been enforced, say, in the form of caps on the percentage of the contract value that can be renegotiated.

4.4 Limitations to Renegotiations

Iossa and Martimort (2014) argue in favour of remedies with regard to decentralized systems, in which higher-tier governments delegate supervision on contractors to local public officials. Their argument rests on the findings of a model in which the contractor, in charge of building and operating an infrastructure, privately observes the unverifiable shocks that affect the revenues from the activity, say, due to fluctuations in legal standards or macroeconomic conditions. In turn, the public official learns privately of the costs incurred as it comes to process and interpret the messages sent by the contractor about these contingencies. When the supervisor is biased towards the contractor, he is eager to exaggerate these contracting costs vis-à-vis the government, anticipating that the latter will then find it attractive to induce contractual rigidities, in the place of state-contingent clauses, even though this will raise agency costs. Consequently, excessive contractual incompleteness will result, thus making renegotiation limits desirable in the fight against corruption at the local level. In consideration of the rapid decentralization of PPP projects during and in the aftermath of the crisis, recipes of this kind look appealing for European countries.

Besides, implicit guarantees that a contract will be renegotiated (or, in the same vein, that the government will bail out a troubled private contractor) prevent filtering out wasteful projects (Engel et al., 2011). Maskin and Tirole (2008) suggest that, in addition to imposing appropriate spending or borrowing caps, and to treating PPP investments adequately in the accounting system, contracts should be reviewed by independent authorities in charge of detecting back-loading of hidden rents. Establishing such authorities is expensive and adds to budgetary pressures. This all seems to mirror the principle that if wasteful practices are to be discouraged, then frictions must be created and transaction costs must be raised.

4.5 The Creation of Conflicts as a 'Money-Burning' Strategy

If renegotiation is to be made unattractive, then the stake from it must be eliminated or, at least, reduced. According to Tirole (1994) it might be necessary to rely on rigid decision rules, rather than on the information held by government officials who deal directly with private contractors. Martimort et al. (2005) further assess that, since enacting new rules takes time and is costly, it is useful to establish rules over discretion in order to dissipate renegotiation benefits.

An alternative is to create multiple regulatory institutions and assign them conflicting missions and objectives. Martimort (1999) derives this lesson from a model, in which a firm holds private information on the production technology and acts as a common agent vis-à-vis two different regulators, who hold different positions in the institutional hierarchy and behave non-cooperatively. To fix ideas, a federal regulator may disagree with a local regulator on the size of a project undertaken in a certain jurisdiction if that project generates externalities in other jurisdictions. The very fact that missions and goals differ across authorities creates, for the parties involved, the necessity to bargain in the attempt to reach an agreement. This process is complex due to the informational asymmetries, which generate frictions that are difficult to redress. Anticipating that renegotiation would be money-burning, the firm is not prone to argue for milder regulatory conditions. Therefore, separation of powers and attribution of biases and limited objectives to different authorities serve to enhance commitment ex ante.[22]

In terms of governmental organization, this all seems to confirm that decentralizing control to SCGs, as advocated on the basis of the arguments in Dewatripont and Maskin (1995), does not suffice to eliminate SBC problems associated with limited commitment.[23] It is also necessary to induce conflicts among authorities. This argument is in line with the result that decentralization helps the CG induce financial discipline to the sub-central level, because SCGs engage in competition among themselves to attract outside capital (Qian and Roland, 1998).[24]

Creation of authorities with conflicting interests is not free from shortcomings, though. Martimort (1999) shows that together with the firm's informational rent, allocative efficiency is also hindered, as compared to the case of integration of powers in a unique authority. Another possible issue is that, in the attempt to generate conflicts, which are useful ex post, undesirable conflicts are induced at the decision stage, thus making the decision process cumbersome. According to Olsen and Torsvick (1991), the number of public authorities with conflicting missions to be created in order to boost commitment should trade off the benefits of ex post conflicts against the costs of ex ante conflicts, and should not grow too large. This recommendation looks especially important with regard to periods of acute crisis, during which strong socioeconomic considerations challenge effective decision making deeply.

5. 'PUBLIC CAPITALISM' – GOVERNMENT-OWNED ENTERPRISES AT SUB-NATIONAL LEVELS

We previously mentioned that another way out of fiscal constraints imposed on SCGs is offered by the enterprises they hold to provide goods or services to their constituencies. We shall now elaborate on this issue, drawing on the political economy literature.

The pervasive presence of government-owned enterprises (GOEs) at the local level mirrors a 'public capitalism' phenomenon, often resulting from the decision to convert budget-burdening bureaus and functions of the local administration into separate corporations or firms, with the ultimate aim of placing their losses off the balance sheet. To the extent that those losses remain non-visible in sub-central budgets, redundant workers can be hired and unnecessary managerial positions can be created so as to build clientelistic networks, which will provide support in future electoral competitions, without explicitly violating budgetary and fiscal constraints. This was a problem in Greece (see Garello, Chapter 5 in this volume). Italy also represents a good example of widespread municipal capitalism, with a plethora of municipal enterprises experiencing serious financial distress, a problem that has come to the forefront of public attention today.[25]

Robinson and Torvik (2009) develop a political economy model to highlight the political appeal of GOEs. They represent politicians as being unable to commit to policies which are not optimal ex post and, in particular, to not refinance poor projects. These have some value – at least for some social categories – but cannot be completed without the injection of additional funds. While this time-inconsistency problem affects politicians, it does enable them to commit to redistribute income in favour of specific categories of citizens, who will then be motivated to vote for them in the future. There are three core ingredients to the story. First, as aforementioned, there is a standard dynamic commitment problem. Politicians do not commit to ex post sub-optimal actions. Second, any uncertainty is ruled out: politicians can identify the quality of the projects at the time when they are selected and launched.[26] Third, poor projects promoted by a certain group of citizens would be refinanced by one political party but not by its opponents (say, because that would be prohibitively costly for them). Hence, they are not brought to completion unless that political party is confirmed in power at the subsequent election round. Under these circumstances, rather than rejecting a given project, which is known to be poor, the incumbent politician can select it deliberately, being aware that she will need to refinance it at a later stage, and anticipating that this will be rational for her, whereas it would not be for any other politician. In this way, the inability to commit to actions which are sub-optimal ex post, together with knowledge of the project quality, is what really allows the politician to commit to redistribute in favour of those who would profit from the project, and to be the only one who is able to do so. To avoid a future shutdown of the project, its promoters vote for the incumbent politician.[27]

In this environment with complete information, the SBC does not follow from the combination of the dynamic commitment problem with agency problems related to informational asymmetries, and it becomes an effective tool to make re-election more likely (Robinson and Torvik, 2009). This ultimately provides us with an important conclusion concerning the GOE phenomena. If publicly owned (particularly, municipal) enterprises are so difficult to eradicate, this is because of the political attractiveness of SBC. With these enterprises, clientelistic purposes can be pursued, circumventing any budgetary constraints. This is all the more appealing for politicians during and in the aftermath of a crisis, when cuts and redeployment of resources toward anti-crisis measures are put in place in an austere fiscal environment, and additional revenues at sub-central levels can no longer be mobilized.

6. ONE SIZE DOES NOT FIT ALL: REMARKS ON SELECTED CASES

Inefficient and excessive public expenditure, in the realization of projects and provision of services at the local level, as well as opportunistic renegotiation of contracts that discipline those activities, follow from the inability of governments to manage budgets, or from the possibility of circumventing fiscal constraints. Furthermore, in most cases, non-commitment hinders fiscal discipline. However, there are situations where things are more subtle than that. First, overspending may result from the deliberate attempt of a fully committing government to prevent local authorities and contractors from taking advantage of their knowledge of local preferences and technological conditions to extract more from the government. Moreover, SBC may result from the decision of a fully committing government to prevent local authorities from under-investing in socially valuable projects and exerting excessive effort in project development. Lastly, renegotiation of contracts to generate ex post efficiency gains may be promoted by local authorities, in compliance with HBCs, through a reduction in contractors' profits. These situations are all rooted in the presence of informational asymmetries among the parties involved (governments, lower-tier authorities and firms) and in the incentives they display. We discuss them in turn below.

6.1 Private Information 'at the Bottom' and the Optimality of 'Upward' Distortions

Governments may deliberately incur wasteful expenditure in order to solve the incentive problems they face in their relationship with local authorities. As far as local projects are concerned, information problems are likely to arise at the bottom, rather than at the top, as argued by Rodden (2005) and Bordignon and Turati (2009). Actually, local authorities hold private information about relevant conditions at the jurisdictional level, such as preferences for the projects considered. In addition, provided local authorities deal directly with delegated firms, they are likely to acquire information about technological conditions. Of course, local authorities may attempt to take advantage of their information to extract more from the CG. To address this problem, the CG must provide proper incentives to local authorities. This may involve inducing distortions away from efficiency. That is, the government may decide to fund projects/activities which are inefficient and/or too costly for society.

Besfamille (2003) considers an institutional context where infrastructure decentralization coexists with the provision of federal grants. He shows that a local authority may be tempted to exaggerate the jurisdictional preferences for some local project and, possibly, the efficiency of the firm implementing the project, in order to induce the CG, which is uninformed in both dimensions, to fund the project. In this world of two-dimensional asymmetric information, it might be optimal for the CG to direct funds to the realization of projects that are not beneficial to society in order to eliminate the incentives of the local authority to camouflage information. The bottom line is that, while the government perfectly commits to its decisions, it deliberately induces spending distortions at the local level in order to overcome the incentive issues, which arise on the side of local authorities, under asymmetric information about local preferences and technological conditions. This conclusion is all the more true, and even exacerbated, in situations where the local authority can collude with the delegated firm to extract more from the uninformed CG. Focusing on a (more standard) one-dimensional information problem, Besfamille (2004) further shows that not only can the government deliberately fund socially inefficient projects, in order to prevent the local authority from misrepresenting private information, but it can also optimally let such projects be undertaken at a high cost, in order to make it unattractive for the local authority to collude with the firm.[28]

6.2 Moral Hazard and the Optimality of 'Less' Effort

Turning from adverse selection to moral hazard, further considerations are possible. One of the main consequences of SBC is that it creates a standard moral-hazard problem. The organization facing SBC is induced to exert too little effort in its activities and to over-invest, launching projects which are actually not worth undertaking. However, HBC may cause a reverse, equally undesirable, kind of problem. The organization facing HBC may be motivated to exert too much effort in its activities and to under-invest in projects of a good quality. In environments in which this is likely to occur, a CG may prefer to not impose HBC on SCGs so as to avoid the associated inefficiencies. This might entail that a soft budget policy may well follow from a deliberate choice of the government, rather than from its inability to commit.[29]

Besfamille and Lockwood (2008) reach this finding in a model in which moral-hazard concerns arise in the relationship between a CG and a multiplicity of RGs, which finance and develop local projects (or provide local public goods). At the time when a project is financed and launched, the RG does not know how successful it will be. However, the RG is aware that if it exerts some effort when developing the project, then this will certainly generate a benefit, and without requiring any further financing. If no effort is exerted, instead, there is a positive probability that the project will generate no benefit unless an additional investment is made. RGs do not have enough resources to refinance poor projects. Only the CG can fund their continuation. Unless the CG decides to commit to an HBC before the projects are financed at the regional level, poor projects will actually be refinanced, because the benefits to the regions, once they are initiated, are greater than the additional costs, which are then borne by the CG. If faced with an HBC, RGs may be over-incentivized to provide effort. This is due to the fact that if the project is terminated, the region loses any benefit. Therefore, it might be the case that too much effort is exerted and that, more worrisome, some projects will not be launched at all, even when that would be efficient. In a nutshell, an HBC may result in the under-provision of local public goods.

The lesson to be drawn is twofold. First, a CG, although perfectly able to commit to an HBC, may deliberately choose to induce an SBC, with the aim of incentivizing SCGs to behave virtuously, in the presence of information problems. Second, just as with too little effort, too much effort exerted on poor projects at the sub-central level is the root of inefficiencies and thus must be discouraged.

One last point is worth making about Besfamille and Lockwood (2008). In their model, the probability of projects requiring refinancing, which is exogenous and alike across RGs, captures the general environmental conditions under which projects are developed. A high probability of failure, in the absence of effort, may thus mirror difficult environmental conditions and, in the worst cases, even an economic crisis. Because the distortions associated with an HBC are greater the higher the probability of failure, this suggests that an HBC may lead to very inefficient outcomes, in particular exacerbating investment shortages in difficult economic periods when investments are especially needed to revamp growth.

6.3 Renegotiation and Local Public Budgets

As discussed above, the renegotiation of contracts that discipline infrastructure service provision at the local level reflects an SBC problem and has perverse consequences on local public budgets. However, this is not necessarily the case. LGs may well be faced with an HBC and, yet, they may return to the contracting table with the delegated firm, after some time, in order to appropriate ex post benefits. These benefits become available because information on the operating conditions is revealed over time and can be embodied in a new contractual agreement to enhance efficiency of the activity. This ultimately leads to a reduction in the surplus available to contractors, but does not need to worsen the public budget. Gagnepain et al. (2013) model the presence of an HBC by assuming that the LG is risk-averse. Moreover, they capture the information problem by assuming that the unit cost of the service, which the LG observes, blends together an adverse selection component, measuring the inner efficiency of the service, and a cost-reducing effort, generating a cost for the firm's manager which the LG is unable to disentangle. Information is revealed by the specific contractual choice that the firm makes at the early stage of the relationship. As it comes to re-auction the contract, the local authority embodies the acquired information in a new deal with the same operator. This enables the authority to incentivize the operator to achieve a better performance. In particular, if the operator is only mildly efficient, then he is assigned higher subsidies so that he is now motivated to engage in cost-reducing activities, whereas this was not the case under the initial agreement. Provided that the social value of the cost-cutting effort is large enough, relative to the extra information rents to be conceded to foster that effort, renegotiation enhances social welfare and is, thus, attractive. Of course, these benefits arise ex post, but social welfare is hindered ex ante. Using a set of contracts for urban transport services, signed in 49 French urban transport networks over the period 1987–2001, the authors estimate that social welfare would be significantly higher should LGs stick to the initial contracts. However, the important point is that the net losers of renegotiation are the operators, who experience an overall reduction in their profits. Consumers and taxpayers instead benefit. This suggests that there is no (direct) negative impact of the renegotiation on local public budgets.

7. CONCLUSIONS

Policies of fiscal decentralization have been promoted in many European countries over the last decades. Those policies have been aimed at reassigning spending and revenue collection responsibilities from the CG to SCGs in order to enhance governance and budgetary efficiency. In fact, both the spending and the revenue share have increased at the sub-national level in the EU, although the increase in the revenue share has been lower (Escolano et al., 2012).

The economic case for decentralization was based on efficiency gains relating essentially to information, competition and accountability. However, there were also drawbacks. Indeed, SCGs may not fully internalize the costs of local expenditures when the latter are financed through a common pool of transfers from the CG. A moral-hazard problem may arise with SCGs overspending and economizing on their tax effort. This effect is exacerbated if SCGs anticipate that the CG will step in to rescue them in case of financial distress. Thus, SCGs fall prey to a dynamic commitment problem, with bailout expectations softening their budget constraints.

Timely financial adjustments are needed when SCGs face negative revenue shocks, as happened in the aftermath of the 2008–09 global financial and economic crisis. In fact, the state of the public finances worsened substantially in many economies, and borrowing by SCGs further aggravated the financial distress.

In this chapter, we investigated the idea that decentralized systems of government may pose special difficulties, particularly relating to the SBCs, for countries experiencing a financial crisis of the kind that occurred in Europe in recent years. The ensuing lessons are somewhat mixed and depend crucially on a number of factors, such as the governance structure and the policy instruments at hand. Yet, they all suggest that the extent and allocation of information among economic agents play an essential role in determining outcomes.

A multi-level institutional architecture, together with the overlapping structure of top-to-bottom transfers, exacerbates the SBC if SCGs know that the CG will bail them out in case of financial distress. Thus, a limited number of government layers reduces the risk of cumulative budget deficits. However, the CG's inability to pre-commit is not necessarily bad, as it may serve to promote efficiency on other grounds. In particular, welfare is enhanced if top-to-bottom transfers induce a tax-price effect that counteracts the SCGs' incentives to engage in a race to the bottom under fiscal competition.

In situations of incomplete information, instead, SCGs cannot be sure that the CG is ready to provide financial support. To some extent, the CG can take advantage of this uncertainty as a way to avoid rescuing SCGs, even though it might be inclined to do so. This may incentivize SCGs to implement effective fiscal measures. Importantly, under incomplete information, an SBC is not always an undesirable consequence of limited commitment. In some cases, the CG might strategically use an SBC to signal its commitment to support specific projects, which would not receive investment financing otherwise. Thus, if such projects are socially desirable, the SBC may enhance efficiency.

In situations in which an SBC has undesirable consequences, institutional arrangements should be fine-tuned to boost coordination between levels of government and reinforce fiscal discipline at the lower levels by correcting incentives, anchoring agents' expectations, and fostering accountability. Specifically, SCGs could be endowed with sufficiently large fiscal autonomy to be able to cover most of their expenditures at the margin with their own resources, rather than depending heavily on top-to-bottom transfers. The CG could then more easily resist bailout pressures. This view is supported by the results of an econometric analysis of the fiscal impact of decentralization in the EU27 Member States in the period 1995–2010 (European Commission, 2012). Those results also support the notion that, under fiscal autonomy, sub-national policy makers are more accountable to their voters, and this exerts, in turn, a disciplining effect on SCGs' fiscal behaviour.[30]

A closer look at specific countries reveals that, in some, fiscal decentralization has had positive repercussions on accountability at the sub-national level. In other countries, fiscal responsibility has not ensued, and reliance on transfers tended to prevail over the use of own taxes to finance additional spending by SCGs. In this context, while SCGs may be subject to fiscal rules, such as borrowing and spending ceilings, with possibly tighter central control on sub-national policies, SBC results when the fiscal rules are circumvented.

The adoption of PPPs in infrastructure projects can lead to instances of SBC. While representing a potentially efficient solution for public procurement and management of projects, PPPs can also be used to evade limits on spending and borrowing by taking the associated liabilities off the balance sheet, with the justification that investments are to be financed by the private sector. In fact, PPPs only affect the timing of government disbursements, and the liabilities will materialize for future governments. The burden on future governments is even bigger if the liabilities include rents, which the private partners will pocket at a later stage, through contractual renegotiations that are not yet visible early on in the relationship. The opportunistic use of PPPs contributes to exacerbating the fiscal risks to which SCGs are particularly vulnerable. It should also be considered that, at the sub-national level, managing the complexity of PPPs goes well beyond the usual competences of the public officials, and can lead to local corruption and opacity. This suggests that entrusting SCGs with the full responsibility for the development of PPP projects should be recommended with caution. At a time of increasing demands for efficient spending of public monies under fiscal decentralization, the creation of local conditions of sound financial management for the delivery of works and services should not distract from the establishment of transparent rules and criteria[31] as well as the availability of technical expertise and monitoring capabilities.

A final point could be made for the EU in contrast to the US. In the latter, a long tradition of HBC at the state level has been in place. The US federal model differs from the emerging model in the EU, in that enforcement of rules, autonomously adopted at the state level, makes spending and borrowing limits more effective than under constraints imposed by the centre, particularly under credible no-bailout norms (Henning and Kessler, 2012). In the EU, instead, especially in the aftermath of the recent crisis, the prevailing model suggests removing tax and spending autonomy from irresponsible junior levels of government, leading to limited accountability (Ziblatt, 2014). The fiscal power of national governments is constrained with the EU exercising authority to monitor and review national budgets that violate debt and deficit ceilings. This is an attempt to harden national budget constraints by means of fiscal rules to promote responsible behaviour at the national (and sub-national) levels. However, when an important member state violates the rules mandated by the supra-national institution, the general applicability of the rules starts to lack credibility. Furthermore, while the US federal debt is supported by the full system of federal powers (including the power to levy taxes), in the EU the design of debt brakes at the national level may conflict with the creation of a common instrument of significant size at the supra-national level to counter economic and fiscal shocks, and may not even be effective in individual countries (see Milbradt, Chapter 3 in this volume).

Our study suggests that there are several pitfalls of the EU model that need to be fixed.

NOTES

1. The alternative scenario is outright default.
2. Fink and Stratmann (2011) report that, in an early analysis of the potential consequences of the European Monetary Union, Horstmann and Schneider (1994) expressed the concern that the Union might induce countries to adopt perverse fiscal policies, expecting to receive European rescuing interventions.
3. See, for instance, Maskin and Xu (2001) for examples in the US.
4. This may explain why the boundary between the literature on decentralized leadership and that on SBC is not always clear-cut.
5. To be rigorous, uncertainty is detrimental as long as the CG is benevolent and does aim at achieving the highest attainable social welfare. It is intuitive that different considerations are in order if the CG is not benevolent and pursues other objectives. See later in the text on this point.
6. In a *pooling* equilibrium, no type of government has an advantage in refinancing projects and SBC does not arise.
7. In Austria, the Internal Stability Pact was revised to allow for higher sub-national

deficits. In Italy, it was temporarily modified to allow for higher sub-national spending in investments (Allain-Dupré, 2011). In Western sub-national governments, gross borrowing was allowed to increase by nearly 40 per cent between 2007 and 2010 (Charbit, 2011). Fiscal rules are considered below in Section 3.

8. However, those fiscal constraints may limit the ability of RGs to smooth distortionary taxes over time and, more generally, to implement more flexible fiscal policies, as we will discuss below.
9. Two tax externalities are at work. First, a *horizontal* externality results from horizontal tax competition among regions to attract mobile capital. Second, a *vertical* externality arises from the co-occupation of the same tax base by CG and SCGs.
10. In this model, the ceiling is optimally chosen, rather than being set at an arbitrary level through a fixed rule. However, the authors also discuss a few of the limitations of their model.
11. Compensation arrangements in public–private contracts are many. They range from those, very close to the conventional forms of infrastructure provision, in which the government pays for the activity and the firm earns no money from consumers, to those in which the firm only relies on market revenues. In particular, in the EU, Build-Operate-Transfer concession holders are required to obtain revenues only from market sales. This is meant to ensure that they bear the operation risks and the demand risks entirely (see, for instance, Auriol and Picard, 2013, who provide the example of the Channel Tunnel project).
12. Hart (2003), Bennett and Iossa (2006), Martimort and Pouyet (2008), Danau and Vinella (2014), Iossa and Martimort (2014) justify the reliance on PPPs in infrastructure projects by the very presence of synergies between construction and operation, which are internalized if a single firm is made responsible for both activities.
13. See, for instance, Asian Development Bank (2008).
14. In the US, instead, they became very popular a bit later, in the immediate aftermath of the recession (Engel et al., 2011).
15. The liabilities induced by PPP contracts are different in nature and timing, and often complex to classify. They include both *direct* liabilities, i.e., payment commitments independent of the occurrence of uncertain future events, and *contingent* liabilities, i.e., payment commitments whose occurrence, timing and magnitude do depend on some uncertain future event outside the control of the government (World Bank, 2012).
16. According to the 2004 Eurostat recommendations, the project is to be recorded off the balance sheet if at least 50 per cent of the revenues come from user fees. Otherwise, PPP assets are to be considered as governmental and, hence, recorded on the balance sheet, unless the private partner bears the construction risk, together with either the availability or the demand risk. See Ahmad, Chapter 2 in this volume, for further details on the generation and diffusion of relevant information in PPP projects.
17. Up to April 2009, only 23 per cent of capital costs of 599 projects were on the balance sheet.
18. Also Hart (2003) disagrees with the thinking that the private sector is a cheaper source of financing compared to the public sector. In his view, it is difficult to imagine an agent more able to borrow than the government. He identifies contracting costs as being the central issue to explain reliance on the private sector. Danau and Vinella (2015) show that private investment in PPP projects is an important tool to motivate the partners to comply with the contract under limited commitment.
19. De facto, Greece was excluded from international financial markets by the end of April 2010, to be readmitted only four years later.
20. In economically difficult periods, even governments that are not 'institutionally' constrained may be unable to raise funds on the market at affordable conditions. Allain-Dupré (2011) reports that, during the crisis, SCGs sometimes experienced this difficulty, in spite of CGs lifting their borrowing constraints or facilitating sub-central borrowing through the provision of guarantees (as loans were not readily available on the market, due to the financial crisis).

21. Discussing evidence from renegotiations in Chile, Engel et al. (2010) argue that Chilean governments had incentives to renegotiate PPP contracts and evade spending limits in order to raise their probability of being re-elected.
22. This is related to the 'money burning' concept, which expresses the possibility that some party to a contractual relationship takes actions, leading to a reduction in the value of the assets or to the dissipation of the surplus therein generated. One such possibility appears when additional agents are introduced into a pre-existing relationship (see Fuchs, 2007).
23. See Section 2.
24. Recall from Section 2 that the authors draw this result in a three-tier federation model of complete information.
25. In Italy, in 2008, a law was passed, imposing consolidation of the losses incurred by publicly owned enterprises on the balance sheet. However, the Court of Appeal declared the law unconstitutional and no consolidation has yet occurred.
26. In other SBC models, such as Dewatripont and Maskin (1995), the quality of long-term projects is privately known to their proponents, when public financing is required. It will become apparent to politicians only at a later stage, when additional financing becomes necessary to bring poor projects to completion.
27. In autocratic (rather than democratic) regimes, this 'static' effect is supplemented by two 'dynamic' effects, related to how many poor projects are launched by the incumbent politicians. We do not touch on them as our interest resides in how the study can help us interpret political and economic phenomena in democratic environments.
28. This leads to the so-called 'white elephants'.
29. Recall, from Section 2, that the idea that SBC may be a deliberate choice of the government is in line with Saljanin (2011).
30. Outside Europe, the Canadian case seems to be in line with this view as well (see Simeon et al., 2014).
31. The establishment of a clear European legislative framework for an efficient delivery of works and services is the purpose of the Directive 2014/23/EU on the award of concession contracts.

REFERENCES

Ahmad, E., M. Albino-War and R. Singh (2006), 'Subnational public financial management: institutions and macroeconomic considerations', in E. Ahmad and G. Brosio (eds), *Handbook of Fiscal Federalism*, Cheltenham, UK and Northampton, MA, USA: Edward Elgar, pp. 405–28.

Akai, N. and M. Sato (2008), 'Too big or too small? A synthetic view of the commitment problem of interregional transfers', *Journal of Urban Economics*, **64**, 551–59.

Allain-Dupré, D. (2011), 'Multi-level governance of public investment: lessons from the crisis', OECD Regional Development Working Papers, 2011/05, OECD Publishing.

Asian Development Bank (2008), *Public–Private Partnership Handbook*, Manila, Philippines: ADB.

Auriol, E. and P.M. Picard (2013), 'A theory of BOT concession contracts', *Journal of Economic Behaviour and Organization*, **89**, 187–209.

Baskaran, T. and Z. Hessami (2013), 'Monetary integration, soft budget constraints, and the EMU sovereign debt crisis', Working Paper Series No. 2013-03, Department of Economics, University of Konstanz.

Bennett, J. and E. Iossa (2006), 'Building and managing facilities for public services', *Journal of Public Economics*, **90**, 2143–60.

Besfamille, M. (2003), 'Local public works and intergovernmental transfers under asymmetric information', *Journal of Public Economics*, **88**, 353–75.
Besfamille, M. (2004), 'Collusion in local public works', *International Economic Review*, **45**(4), 1193–219.
Besfamille, M. and B. Lockwood (2008), 'Bailouts in federations: is a hard budget constraint always best?', *International Economic Review*, **49**(2), 577–93.
Bordignon, M. and G. Turati (2009), 'Bailing out expectations and public health expenditure', *Journal of Health Economics*, **28**, 305–21.
Breuillé, M.L, T. Madiès and E. Taugourdeau (2006), 'Does tax competition soften regional budget constraint?', *Economics Letters*, **90**, 230–36.
Breuillé, M.L., T. Madiès and E. Taugourdeau (2010), 'Gross versus net equalization scheme in a federation with decentralized leadership', *Journal of Urban Economics*, **68**, 205–14.
Breuillé, M.L. and M. Vigneault (2010), 'Overlapping soft budget constraints', *Journal of Urban Economics*, **67**, 259–69.
Charbit, C. (2011), 'Governance of public policies in decentralised contexts: the multi-level approach', OECD Regional Development Working Papers, 2011/04, OECD Publishing.
Cooper, R., H. Kempf and D. Peled (2008), 'Is it is or is it ain't my obligation? Regional debt in a fiscal federation', *International Economic Review*, **49**(4), 1469–504.
Danau, D. and A. Vinella (2015), 'Public–private contracting under limited commitment', *Journal of Public Economic Theory*, **17**(1), 78–110.
Desai, R.M. and A. Olofsgard (2006), 'The political advantage of soft budget constraints', *European Journal of Political Economy*, **22**, 370–87.
Dewatripont, M. and E. Maskin (1995), 'Credit and efficiency in centralized and decentralized economies', *Review of Economic Studies*, **62**(4), 541–55.
Engel, E., R. Fischer and A. Galetovic (2010), 'The economics of infrastructure finance. Public–private partnerships versus public provision', Documentos de trabajo, Serie Economia No. 276.
Engel, E., R. Fischer and A. Galetovic (2011), 'Public–private partnerships to revamp US infrastructures', Discussion Paper 2011-02.
Escolano, J., L. Eyraud, M. Moreno Badia, J. Sarnes and A. Tuladhar (2012), 'Fiscal performance, institutional design and decentralization in European Union countries', IMF Working Papers No. 12/45.
European Commission (2012), 'Report on Public finances in EMU', European Economy 4/2012.
Eurostat (2004), 'Treatment of public–private partnerships', Decision 18/2004, 11 February.
Fink, A. and T. Stratmann (2011), 'Institutionalized bailouts and fiscal policy: consequences of soft budget constraints', *Kyklos*, **64**(3), 366–95.
Foremny, D. (2014), 'Sub-national deficits in European countries: the impact of fiscal rules and tax autonomy', *European Journal of Political Economy*, **34**, 86–110.
Fuchs, W. (2007), 'Contracting with repeated moral hazard and private evaluations', *American Economic Review*, **97**(4), 1432–48.
Gagnepain, P., M. Ivaldi and D. Martimort (2013), 'The cost of contract renegotiation: evidence from the local public sector', *American Economic Review*, **103**(6), 2352–83.
Goodspeed, T.J. (2002), 'Bailouts in a federation', *International Tax and Public Finance*, **9**, 409–21.

Hart, O. (2003), 'Incomplete contracts and public ownership: remarks, and an application to public–private partnerships', *The Economic Journal*, **113**(486), C69–C76.
Henning, C.R. and M. Kessler (2012), 'Fiscal federalism: US history for architects of Europe's fiscal union', Peterson Institute for International Economics, WP 12-1.
Horstmann, W. and T. Schneider (1994), 'Deficits, bailout and free riders: fiscal elements of a European Constitution', *Kyklos*, **47**(3), 355–83.
Inman, R.P. (2003), 'Transfers and bailouts: enforcing local fiscal discipline with lessons from U.S. federalism', in J.A. Rodden, G.S. Eskeland and J. Litvak (eds), *Fiscal Decentralization and the Challenge of Hard Budget Constraints*, Cambridge, MA: MIT Press, pp. 35–83.
Iossa, E. and D. Martimort (2014), 'Corruption in PPPs, incentives and contract incompleteness', CEIS Research Paper Series, Vol. 12, Issue 6, No. 317.
Iossa, E. and D. Martimort (2015), 'The simple microeconomics of public–private partnerships', *Journal of Public Economic Theory*, **17**(1), 4–48.
Köthenbürger, M. (2008), 'Federal tax-transfer policy and intergovernmental pre-commitment', *Regional Science and Urban Economics*, **38**, 16–31.
Kornai, J. (1979), 'Resource-constrained vs demand-constrained systems', *Econometrica*, **47**, 801–19.
Kornai, J. (1980), *Economics of Shortage*, Amsterdam: North Holland.
Kornai, J. (2009), 'The soft budget constraint syndrome and the global financial crisis. Some warnings from an East European economist', unpublished manuscript.
Kornai, J., E. Maskin and G. Roland (2003), 'Understanding the soft budget constraint', *Journal of Economic Literature*, **XLI**, 1095–136.
Krogstrup, S. and C. Wyplosz (2010), 'A common pool theory of supranational deficit ceilings', *European Economic Review*, **54**, 269–78.
Martimort, D. (1999), 'Renegotiation design with multiple regulators', *Journal of Economic Theory*, **88**, 261–93.
Martimort, D. (2006), 'An agency perspective on the costs and benefits of privatization', *Journal of Regulatory Economics*, **30**, 5–44.
Martimort, D., P. De Donder and E. Billette de Villemeur (2005), 'An incomplete contract perspective on public good provision', *Journal of Economic Surveys*, **19**(2), 149–80.
Martimort, D. and J. Pouyet (2008), 'To build or not to build: normative and positive theories of public-private partnerships', *International Journal of Industrial Organization*, **26**(2), 393–411.
Maskin, E. and J. Tirole (2008), 'Private–public partnerships and government spending limits', *International Journal of Industrial Organization*, **26**, 412–20.
Maskin, E. and C. Xu (2001), 'Soft budget constraint theories: from centralization to the market', *Economics of Transition*, **9**(1), 1–27.
Olsen, T. and G. Torsvick (1991), 'The ratchet effect in common agency: implications for regulation and privatization', *Journal of Law, Economics and Organization*, **91**, 136–58.
Qian, Y. and G. Roland (1998), 'Federalism and the soft budget constraint', *American Economic Review*, **88**(5), 1143–62.
Robinson, J.A. and R. Torvik (2009), 'A political economy theory of the soft budget constraint', *European Economic Review*, **53**, 786–98.
Rodden, J.A. (2005), '"And the last shall be first": federalism and soft budget constraints in Germany', unpublished manuscript.

Rodden, J.A., G.S. Eskeland and J. Litvak (eds) (2003), *Fiscal Decentralization and the Challenge of Hard Budget Constraints*, Cambridge, MA: MIT Press.

Saljanin, S. (2011), 'A signalling approach to soft budgets', *Economics Letters*, **111**, 272–74.

Simeon, R., J. Pearce and A. Nugent (2014), 'The resilience of Canadian federalism', in P.E. Peterson and D. Nadler (eds), *The Global Debt Crisis: Haunting U.S. and European Federalism*, Washington, DC, The Brookings Institution, pp. 201–22.

Sorribas-Navarro, P. (2011), 'Bailouts in a fiscal federal system: evidence from Spain', *European Journal of Political Economy*, **27**, 154–70.

Tirole, J. (1994), 'The Internal Organization of Government', *Oxford Economic Papers*, **46**(1), 1–29.

von Hagen, J. and M. Dahlberg (2002), 'Swedish local government: is there a bailout problem?', prepared for the Project on Fiscal Federalism in Sweden, Center for Business and Policy Studies.

Weingast, B.R. (2009), 'Second generation fiscal federalism: the implications of fiscal incentives', *Journal of Urban Economics*, **65**, 279–93.

World Bank (2012), *PPP Reference Guidance – Version 1.0*, Washington, DC: World Bank.

Ziblatt, D. (2014), 'Between centralization and federalism in the European Union', in P.E. Peterson and D. Nadler (eds), *The Global Debt Crisis: Haunting U.S. and European Federalism*, Washington, DC: The Brookings Institution, pp. 113–33.

Index

accounting, local government, Macedonia 290
accounting standards 55–6, 58–61
   France 125
Agence France locale 122
Ahmad, E. 54
Akai, N. 332, 333–4
Allain-Dupré, D. 354
Alogoskoufis, G. 142
Ambrosanio, M.F. 242
Argentina, accounting standards 60–61
arrears, Italy 235–7
asymmetric information
   and soft budget constraints 15
   and transfers to regions 305–6
Australia, accounting standards 60
Austria, Internal Stability Pacts 34
Autonomous Communities, Spain 187–9
Autonomous Liquidity Fund, Spain 199
Azores 148, 160–67
   budget deficits 151–2
   debt refinancing 170
   VAT 162

Baade, R.A. 269
backward regions 299
bailout failure costs 330
bailouts 52–3
   and fiscal indiscipline 334–5, 336–7
   Spain 187–8, 199
Baldersheim, H. 232
Baleiras, R. 53, 164
bank lending, France 122
bankruptcy procedures, Italy 233–5
Barcelona, impact of Olympic Games 249, 260–67, 270–71
Baskaran, T. 340
Belgium, internal stability pacts 34–5
Bennett, J. 354

Besfamille, M. 348, 349
Bilhim, J. 153, 155
Blöchliger, H. 33, 44
Bordignon, M. 53, 241, 242, 300–301, 335, 336, 337, 338, 347
borrowing
   and bailout expectations 336
   central governments 317–19
   and corruption 321
   local governments, France 121–3
   local governments, Macedonia 292
borrowing caps 338–9
borrowing limits 32
   circumventing 61–3
   Germany 67, 71
   see also debt brake
Brazil
   Fiscal Responsibility Legislation 59, 62
   and IMF GFSM 56, 62
   standardized generation of information 58–9
Breuillé, M.L. 330, 331, 339
budget consolidation, Germany 86
budget deficits, *see* deficits
budget framework law, Portugal 169–70
budgetary institutions reform, Spain 205–6
Budgetary Stability Acts, Spain 35–6
budgets, local government
   France 109–11, 117–20
   Macedonia 290
   see also revenues; spending
Buiter, W.H. 158
business taxes, France 114

Campos, B. 155
Canada, accounting standards 60
capital expenditures, Macedonia 288–9

capital investment financing,
    municipalities, Italy 216
Carvalho, J. 158
Catalunya, secessionism movement
    204–5
central governments
    borrowing and regional inequalities
        317–19
    corruption and debt 321
    tough and weak 335–8
CGCT (General Code for Territorial
    Communities), France 119
China, accounting standards 60
Chortareas, G. 142
Christodoulakis, N. 142
circumventing borrowing limits 61–3
    Germany 7, 71–2
Città metropolitane 232–3
clientelistic politics 300–323
    Greece 142–4
co-financing condition, Structural
    Funds 316
Coelho, C. 144
COFOG (UN functional classification)
    55
Committee for Local Finances, France
    128
common agency approach, regional
    inequalities 323
common pool problem 52
competencies and decentralization,
    Macedonia 283–6
conditional supranational transfers
    315–17
conflicts, and public–private
    partnerships 344–5
congestion costs, and migration 322–3
*Conseil de normalisation des comptes
    publics* 125
constitutional reform 16
    Germany 16, 71–2, 72–3
    Italy 16, 220, 239–40
constitutions
    France, local government finance
        111–12
    Germany, fiscal and monetary
        stability 66–7
corruption 300
    and debt 321
    and regional inequalities 310–11
    and regional transfers 302–6
    Spain 201–2
Cunha, J.C. da 156

Da Cunha, J.C. 156
Dahlberg, M. 144
Danau, D. 354
Davoodi, H. 310
debt
    and Barcelona Olympics 266
    and central government corruption
        321
    Euro area 21
    France 108–9
    and German constitution 67
    Italy 221
    and Turin Olympics 257–9
debt brake
    Germany 3, 7, 62–3, 72–7, 86, 92–5
    Switzerland 72
debt controls
    Madeira 161–2
    Portugal 156–7, 164–5
debt overhang 315, 319
decentralization 350–51
    France 103, 104–6
    Italy 214–15
    and lack of commitment 329–38
    Macedonia 282–3
    Portugal 153–9, 160–67
    public opinion, Spain 203
    and regional inequalities 314–15
    and soft budget constraints 329–31,
        351–2
    Spain 194–201
decentralized leadership 330–32
deficit limit, West Germany 68
deficits
    Barcelona, impact of Olympic
        Games 266
    effect of fiscal decentralization
        170–71
    Euro area 21
    France 106–8
    Portugal 150, 166, 168
    sustainability, Azores and Madeira
        166–7
Dewatripoint, M. 345, 355
Dexia 122, 123
displacement effect 249–50, 265

distributional costs of no bailout 330
Domestic Stability Pacts, Italy 35
   and Turin Olympics 254–5

economic activities, impact of Olympic Games 269–70
economic classification of public activities 55–7
economic crises, *see* financial crises
EDP (Excessive Deficit Procedure) 96–7
efficiency, and decentralized leadership 333–4
elections, implications for local government finances 142–3
electoral process, local government, Greece 134–5
employment, public sector
   Greece 138–40, 142–4
   Italy 228
   Spain 186–7
enforcement mechanisms, fiscal rules 17–18, 33, 41–2
Engel, E. 342, 343, 355
enterprises, local
   Greece 141–2
   Portugal 157
EPCI (*Etablissements publics de coopération intercommunale*) 104–5, 126
EPP (Euro-Plus Pact) 97
Erhard, Ludwig 66
Escolano, J. 33, 50, 51
Etablissements publics de coopération intercommunale (EPCI) 104–5, 126
Euro area, sub-national fiscal policies 21–43
Euro crisis
   and Germany economy 83–6
   and local government sector 90–92
   and multilayer fiscal policy 87–90
Euro-Plus Pact (EPP) 97
European currency union, and Germany 70–71
European Fiscal Compact, *see* Fiscal Compact
European Union
   accession, Macedonia 293
   compared with US 353
   fiscal framework 46–7

fiscal framework reforms 36–7, 37–42
   impact of financial crisis 1–2
Excessive Deficit Procedure (EDP) 96–7
expectations of fiscal (in)discipline 334–5
expenditure, *see* spending
exports, Germany, impact of Euro crisis 83

Fedelino, A. 44
Federalism Reform, Germany 72–3
federations, benefits for regions 327
financial consolidation, Barcelona 267
financial costs of no bailout 330
financial crises
   impact on Europe 1–2
   impact on Greece 133–4, 144–6
   impact on Macedonia 278–81
   impact on sub-national finances 23–7
   Portugal 150–53
financial distress, municipalities, Italy 233–5
financial management system, Macedonia 289–91
financing rules, Portugal 155
Fink, A. 353
fiscal adjustments
   Greece 133–4
   Italy 222–8
   Spain 186–92
fiscal autonomy, Italy, impact of fiscal adjustment 224–5
Fiscal Compact 47, 97–9
   Belgium 34
   Italy 212–13, 237–8
fiscal consolidation, *see* fiscal adjustments
fiscal decentralization, effect on deficits 170–71
fiscal discipline 338–40
   expectations of fiscal indiscipline 334–5
   Germany 96–9
   Spain 199–201
fiscal federalism, Italy 214–21, 221–8, 229–37
fiscal imbalances, Spain 206–7
fiscal policy, Germany 87–90

Fiscal Responsibility Legislation, Brazil 59, 62
fiscal rules 18, 32–3, 338–40
  enforcement 17–18
  enforcement mechanisms 33
  see also Fiscal Compact
fiscal rules evasion
  Madeira 53–4
  see also game-play
fixed capital formation, local government, Germany 92
flexible pacts, Italy 226–8
foreign transfers 304–5, 315–17
Foremny, D. 44, 170
Fortuna, M. 158, 159, 166, 167, 170
France 8–9, 103–26
  administrative organization 104–6
  local government budgetary policies 111–25
  public finances 106–11
funding, Olympic Games
  Barcelona 261–2
  Turin 253–4

Gagnepain, P. 350
game-play 3–4, 17, 51–4
Gekas, R. 141
General Code for Territorial Communities (CGCT), France 119
general government deficit, Euro area 21
Germany 3, 6–7, 8, 66–79, 83–100
  accounting and reporting standards 59–60
  budget controls 92–6
  debt brake rule 3, 62–3, 72–7, 92–5
  fiscal discipline 96–9
  fiscal policy during crisis 87–90
  impact of financial crisis 83–6
  local finance reforms 90–92
GFMIS, Brazil 62
GFSM 2014 55–7, 61, 62
Giarda, P. 242
Giesecke, J. 270
global financial crisis, impact on Macedonia 278–81
GOEs (government-owned enterprises) 345–7
Goodspeed, T.J. 332–3

governance crisis, Spain 201–2
government financial information management systems (GFMIS), Brazil 62
government-owned enterprises (GOEs) 345–7
government quality, and overspending, Spain 184–6
government support programs, Germany 84–6
government transfers, *see* transfers from central government
governments, number of 16–17
  Italy 214, 231–3
  municipalities, Greece 135–6
grant revenues, *see* transfers from central government
Great Public Finance Reform, West Germany 68
Greece 9–10, 133–46
  electoral process and employment 142–4
  local institutions 134–42
Grossman, G. 300, 323
Grossman, P. 300, 301
guided distress, municipalities, Italy 234

hard budget constraint (HBC) 331, 338
Harden, I. 51
Hart, O. 354
Helpman, E. 300, 323
Hessami, Z. 340
High Finance Council, Belgium 34
HOLSA (*Holding Olympic, Sociedad Anónima*) 261, 262
horizontal distribution of EU targets and limits 39–40
horizontal pacts, Italy 228
Horstmann, W. 353
housing boom, Spain 177

Ianchovichina, E. 158
IMF GFSM 2014 55–7, 61, 62
incentives to evade fiscal rules 301, 326–53
  limiting 54–61
income tax
  Italy 216
  Macedonia 287

inequalities
  local government, Macedonia 288
  regional, and clientelistic politics 306–20
information problems
  and wasteful public expenditure 347–8
  see also asymmetric information
inheritance tax revenues, Spain 177–8
Inman, R.P. 330
Instrument for Pre-Accession Assistance (IPA), Macedonia 293
intergovernmental relationships
  and financial crisis 2–4
  Portugal 167–73
internal stability pacts 33–6
  Italy 218, 219, 231
International Accounting Standards Board, guidelines on PPPs 58
international standards for economic classification of public activities 55–7
investment
  France 119–20
  Germany 69, 92
  Italy 226
  regional inequalities and clientelistic politics 301–23
  spending/borrowing caps 338–9
investment financing
  debt financing, Italy 237
  debt financing, Portugal 154
  tax funding, Italy 216
investment program, Germany 84
Iossa, E. 343, 354
IPA (Instrument for Pre-Accession Assistance), Macedonia 293
IPSAS 32 58
Italy 12, 212–40
  constitutional reform 239–40
  Domestic Stability Pacts 35
  economic impact of crisis 221–8
  Fiscal Compact 237–8
  fiscal federalism pre-crisis 214–21
  institutional and political impacts of crisis 229–37
  municipal capitalism 346

public–private partnerships (PPPs) 342
Turin Olympics 249, 251–60, 270–72
Ivanyna, M. 321

Kornai, J. 326–7
Köthenbürger, M. 334
Krogstrup, S. 339

'Legge Rinforzata' 237
Liu, L. 158
loans, see bailouts; borrowing
Local Finance Law, Portugal 153–7
local government, see municipalities; regions
local government, France 106, 109–25
  balancing budgets 119–20
  borrowing 121–3
  budgetary rules and policies 111–25
  responsibilities 106
  revenues 112–17
  spending 109–10, 117–18
local government, Germany 90–92
local government, Italy, and constitutional reform 239–40
local government, Macedonia 282
  impact of global crisis 281
local government, Spain
  financial control 198–9
  fiscal adjustment 191–2
local political reforms, Italy 218–21
local public enterprises
  Greece 141–2
  Portugal 157
Lockwood, B. 349

Macedonia 13–14, 277–94
  borrowing 292
  competencies and decentralization 283–6
  decentralization 282–3
  EU accession requirements 293
  expenditures 288–9
  financial management 289–91
  impact of global crisis 278–81
  local government 282
  revenues 286–8
Macroeconomic Imbalance Procedure (MIP) 97, 98
Madden, J.R. 270

Madeira 148, 160–67, 171
  budget deficits 151–2
  debt 161–2
  debt refinancing 170
  evading fiscal rules 53–4
  support from central government 165, 168
  VAT 162
market discipline HBCs 338
Martimort, D. 343, 344, 345, 354
Maskin, E. 338–9, 342, 343, 344, 345, 355
Matheson, V.A. 269
Medium Term Objective (MTO) 36
Memorandum of Understanding
  Greece 135–6
  Portugal 169
Metronet 57
métropoles 105, 127
Mexico
  accounting standards 60–61
  and IMF GFSM 56
migration, and regional inequalities 322–3
Milas, K.C. 142
Miller, P.A. 269
MIP (Macroeconomic Imbalance Procedure) 97, 98
Mitsou, K. 141
monitoring sub-national fiscal rules 32–3, 41–2
moral hazard, and wasteful public expenditure 348–9
Mörk, E. 144
Mourmouras, A. 323
municipal capitalism 345–7
municipal enterprises
  Greece 141–2
  Portugal 157
municipal grants, *see* transfers from central government
Municipal Support Fund Law, Portugal 172–3
municipalities, *see* local government
municipalities, France 106
municipalities, Germany, and social security system 78
municipalities, Greece
  employment 138–40
  finances 137–8
  number of 135–6
  responsibilities 136
municipalities, Italy
  impact of fiscal adjustment 224–6
  tax revenues 216
municipalities, Portugal, budget deficits 151–2
municipalities, Spain, tax revenues 179–80

National Council for Standardization of Public Accounting, France 125
Neyapti, B. 170
number of governments 16–17
  Italy 214, 231–3
  municipalities, Greece 135–6

OFA (Ohrid Framework Agreement) 282
off-budget debts, Italy 235–7
Ohrid Framework Agreement (OFA) 282
Oliva, E. 126
Olsen, T. 345
Olympic Games 13, 249–72
Open Method of Coordination (OMC) 97
Ordoliberalism 66
overspending during boom, Spain 181–6
own-source revenues 17
  and Barcelona Olympics 264–5
  local government, France 113–15
  see also tax revenues

Paixão, M. 53, 164
Parente, S. 310
Peacock, A.T. 250, 265
personal income tax
  Italy 216
  Macedonia 287
Persson, T. 53
Philippopoulos, A. 142
Political Budget Cycles 142–3
political economy 14–15
  of information generation and liability management 49–51
political environment, Greece 134–5
political equilibrium, and regional inequalities 307–11

political influence, and regional inequalities 312–15
political reforms, Italy 218–21
Porter, P.K. 269
Portugal 10–11, 148–73
  decentralization to local governments 153–9
  decentralization to regional governments 160–67
  impact of crises 150–53
  intergovernmental relations 167–73
  see also Azores; Madeira
Poterba, J. 51
Potrafke, N. 151, 170
Pouyet, J. 354
PPPs, see public–private partnerships
Prescott, E.C. 310
Pritchett, L. 310
professional tax, France 114
property taxes
  Italy 216
  Spain 177, 179–80, 181–3
public arrears, Italy 235–7
public capitalism 345–7
public debt, see debt
public deficits, see deficits
public enterprises
  Greece 141–2
  Portugal 157
public finances during crisis, France 106–11
public–private partnerships (PPPs) 57–8, 328, 340–45, 352–3
  France 124
public sector employment
  Greece 138–40, 142–4
  Italy 228
  Spain 186–7
public spending, see spending

Qian, Y. 331, 345
quality of government, and overspending, Spain 184–6

Rangazas, P. 323
real estate market bubbles, Spain 4
recentralization, Spain 203–4
recession, West Germany 67–8
regional inequalities, and clientelistic politics 306–20

regions, Italy
  impact of fiscal adjustment 223–4
  tax revenues 216–17, 226
regions, Portugal 160–67
regions, Spain
  financing system 195
  spending 181–6
  tax revenues 177–8
Reinikka, R. 310
Reischmann, M. 151, 170
renegotiation of contracts 343–4, 349–50
reporting requirements
  Macedonia 291
  Portugal 172
reunification, Germany 70–71
revenue sharing, Portugal 154–5, 157
revenues
  Barcelona, impact of Olympic Games 264–5
  Germany 87–8
  local government, France 112–17
  local government, Macedonia 283, 286
  municipalities, Greece 137
  municipalities, Italy 224
  municipalities, Portugal 154–5
  property taxes, Spain 181–3
  regional governments, Portugal 160–61
  see also tax revenues; transfers from central government
Robinson, J.A. 346
Rodden, J.A. 330, 336, 337, 338, 347
Roland, G. 331, 345
Rose, A.K. 270
Rose, L.E. 232
rule enforcement 17–18, 33, 41–2
rules-based HBCs 338

Saljanin, S. 337
sanctions 41–2, 46, 61–3
  Italy 219
  Madeira 163
Santos, T. 175
Sato, M. 332, 333–4
SBB (structural budget balance) 36–7, 40
Schneider, T. 353
Schuldenbremse, see debt brake

secession, Catalunya 204–5
SGP, *see* Stability and Growth Pact
short-term borrowing, local government, Germany 91–2
Silva, P. 156
Six-Pack 46–7, 97
Skouras, S. 142
social security system, and German debt brake 78
soft budget constraints 52, 320–22, 326
  decentralized systems 329–31, 351–2
  Spain 197–8
soft regional budgets 320–22
Solé-Ollé, A. 175, 184
Spain 11–12, 175–207
  Barcelona Olympics 249, 260–67, 270–71
  Budgetary Stability Acts 35–6
  fiscal boom and crisis 176–80
  fiscal decentralization 194–201
  fiscal discipline 199–201
  governance crisis 201–2
  impacts of boom and crisis 181–92
  reform proposals 205–7
  territorial crisis 202–5
spending
  Barcelona, impact of Olympic Games 262–4
  local government, France 109–11, 117–18
  local government, Macedonia 283–6
  Spain 181–6
  Turin, impact of Olympic Games 255–60
spending caps 338–9
spending cuts, public sector, Spain 189
spending responsibilities 54–61
Spiegel, M.M. 270
Stability and Growth Pact 96, 97, 339
  and Portugal 168–9
Stability Council, Germany 95–6
standards for economic classification of public activities 55–7
Stratmann, T. 353
structural budget balance (SBB) 36–7, 40
Structural Funds 316
structural imbalances, Germany 90–92
sub-national deficits, Portugal 150–52
sub-national finances
  impact of crises 23–7
  impact of EU fiscal framework reforms 37–42
sub-national fiscal discipline 28–36, 41–2
sub-national fiscal policies 21–43
sub-national pro-cyclicality risk mitigation 40–41
supranational transfers 304–5, 315–17
sustainability of budget deficits
  Azores 166
  Madeira 166–7
sustainability of local public finances, Portugal 158–9
Svensson, J. 310
Switzerland, debt brake 72

Tabellini, G. 53
Tanzi, V. 300, 302, 310
tax autonomy, Italy 213–14, 215
tax decentralization, Spain 194–6
tax reforms, Italy 229–30
tax revenues 17
  and Barcelona Olympics 264–5
  Italy 216–17, 226
  local government, France 112–13, 114
  Macedonia 286
  Spain 177–8, 179–80, 197
  see also VAT revenues
tax-sharing revenues, Spain 197
taxe professionelle, France 114
Tepe, M. 144
Ter-Minassian, T. 44
territorial crisis, Spain 202–5
Territorial Economic Contribution, France 114
Tesoreria Unica 231
Tirole, J. 338–9, 342, 343, 344
Torsvick, G. 345
Torvik, R. 346
tough central governments 335–8
Tournemire, G. 44
toxic loans, local government, France 123
transfers, supranational 304–5, 315–17
transfers from central government
  Azores 165
  and corruption 302–6
  France 115–17

Germany 88
Italy 225–6, 230–31
Macedonia 286–8
Madeira 161–2, 165
Portugal 155–6, 158, 160–61, 161–2, 165
Spain 183
transparency, lack of, Spain 198
Transport for London 57
treasury management, Macedonia 290
Treasury Single Account (TSA)
Italy 231
Macedonia 290
Treaty on Stability, Coordination and Governance (TSCG) 47
Turati, G. 241, 335, 336, 337, 338, 347
Turin, impact of Olympic Games 249, 251–60, 270–72
Two-Pack legislation 47

UK, public–private partnerships 57–8, 342
UN functional classification (COFOG) 55
unconditional supranational transfers 315–17

US
accounting standards 60
hard budget constraint 353

Vanhuysse, P. 144
VAT revenues
Azores and Madeira 162
Macedonia 287–8
Spain 178, 196–7
vertical apportionment of EU targets and limits 39
vertical imbalances, Spain 197, 206–7
vertical pacts, Italy 228
Vigneault, M. 331
Viladecans-Marsal, E. 175, 184
Vinella, A. 354
von Hagen, J. 44, 51

weak central governments 335–8
Weingast, B. 63
Wiseman, J. 250, 265
Wolman, H. 44
Wyplosz, C. 339

Zbyszewski, J.P. 153, 155, 156
zero base budget, Portugal 172